Harrisburg

Wheeling

Grafton

D0618237

For a...
see back
endpaper 2

Kelly's
Ford
Chancellorsville
Fredericksburg
13 DEC 62

Cincinnati

Charleston

Staunton

Richmond

Frankfort

Lexington

Lynchburg

Norfolk

Bardstown

Lebanon

Pikeville

Danville

Weldon

London

Barbourville

Abingdon

MORGAN
RAID:
LEFT 2 JULY 63;
CAPTURED 26 JULY,
E. LIVERPOOL, OHIO.

Cumberland
Gap

Greensboro

Goldsboro
12-18 DEC 62

LONGSTREET
RAIL ROUTE TO
NORTH GEORGIA

Raleigh

Knoxville
SIEGE: 17 NOV
4 DEC 63

New
Bern

"Monitor"
sinks
30 DEC 62

BRAGG

Asheville

Charlotte

Fayetteville

hattanooga

Missionary Ridge
25 NOV 63

Spartanburg

Cheraw

Chickamauga
19-20 SEP 63

Greenville

Florence

Wilmington

Rome

Columbia

Cape Fear

Atlanta

Athens

Augusta

Atlantic
Ocean

Milledgeville

Millen

Macon

Charleston
GUNBOAT REPULSE:
7 APR 63
SIEGE: 10 JULY-
6 SEP 63

Columbus

"Hunley" vs.
"Housatonic"
17 FEB 64

Ft.
Gaines

Albany

Savannah

Waycross

Brunswick

Thomasville

Theater
of War
1862~1864

Tallahassee

Olustee
20 FEB 64

Jacksonville

St.
Augustine

The Civil War
A Narrative

ALL THESE WERE HONOURED IN THEIR GENERATIONS

AND WERE THE GLORY OF THEIR TIMES

THERE BE OF THEM

THAT HAVE LEFT A NAME BEHIND THEM

THAT THEIR PRAISES MIGHT BE REPORTED

AND SOME THERE BE WHICH HAVE NO MEMORIAL

WHO ARE PERISHED AS THOUGH THEY HAD NEVER BEEN

AND ARE BECOME AS THOUGH THEY HAD NEVER BEEN BORN

AND THEIR CHILDREN AFTER THEM

BUT THESE WERE MERCIFUL MEN

WHOSE RIGHTEOUSNESS HATH NOT BEEN FORGOTTEN

WITH THEIR SEED SHALL CONTINUALLY REMAIN

A GOOD INHERITANCE

AND THEIR CHILDREN ARE WITHIN THE COVENANT

THEIR SEED STANDETH FAST

AND THEIR CHILDREN FOR THEIR SAKES

THEIR SEED SHALL REMAIN FOR EVER

AND THEIR GLORY SHALL NOT BE BLOTTED OUT

THEIR BODIES ARE BURIED IN PEACE

BUT THEIR NAME LIVETH FOR EVERMORE

Ecclesiasticus xliv

THE
Civil War
A Narrative

★ ★

GETTYSBURG
to VICKSBURG

★ ★

Unvexed to the Sea

By SHELBY FOOTE

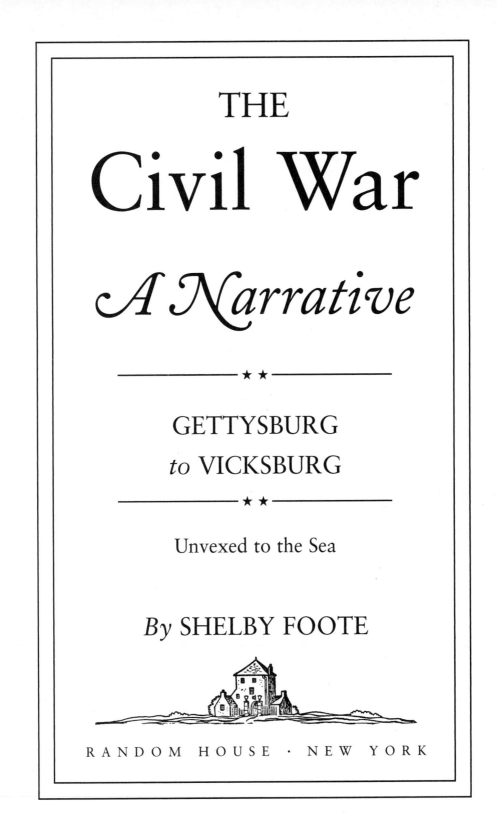

RANDOM HOUSE · NEW YORK

CONTENTS

★ ✠ ☆

☆

Gettysburg
to
Vicksburg

☆

SITUATION
LATE SPRING, 1863
Major commands
— ★ —

HOOKER 115,000
LEE 76,000
Richmond
PECK 20,000
FRENCH 17,000 — Norfolk
HILL 10,000
FOSTER 16,000
WHITING 5,000
BEAUREGARD 16,000
HUNTER 14,000
BUCKNER 15,000
BURNSIDE 33,000
ROSECRANS 84,000
BRAGG 45,000
RUGGLES 5,000
HURLBUT 56,000
MAURY 14,000
PEMBERTON 35,000
SCHOFIELD 25,000
HOLMES 15,000
GRANT 47,000
GARDNER 15,000
TAYLOR 4,000
BANKS 35,000

Gettysburg
Baltimore
Washington
Winchester
Lynchburg Petersburg
Greensboro
Raleigh
Goldsboro
Charleston
Wilmington
Charleston
Savannah
Jacksonville
St. Augustine
Columbus
Cincinnati
Charleston
Indianapolis
Louisville
Lexington
Bowling Green
Nashville
Knoxville
Chattanooga
Rome
Atlanta
Macon
Columbia
Montgomery
Pensacola
Mobile
Tallahassee
Terre Haute
Springfield
St. Louis
Cairo
Ivonton
Jefferson City
Rolla
Little Rock
Fort Smith
Memphis
Helena
Corinth
Decatur
Grenada
Jackson Meridian
Vicksburg
Monroe
Alexandria
Shreveport
Baton Rouge
New Orleans
Port Hudson
Beaumont
Houston

0 Miles 100

The Beleaguered City

★ ✗ ☆

WHILE HOOKER WAS CROSSING THE RAPPA-hannock, unaware as yet that he would come to grief within a week, Grant, having caught what he believed was a gleam of victory through the haze of cigar smoke in the former ladies' cabin of the *Magnolia*, was putting the final improvisatorial touches to a plan of campaign that would open, two days later, with a crossing of the greatest river of them all. He too might come to grief, as two of his three chief lieutenants feared and even predicted, but he was willing to risk it for the sake of the prize, which had grown in value with every sore frustration. As spring advanced and the roads emerged from the drowned lands adjacent to the Mississippi — although so far they were little more than trails of slime through the surrounding ooze, not quite firm enough for wagons nor quite wet enough for boats — the Illinois general, with seven failures behind him in the course of the three months he had spent attempting to take or bypass Vicksburg, reverted in early April to what he had told Halleck in mid-January, before he left Memphis to assume command in person of the expedition four hundred miles downriver: "[I] think our troops must get below the city to be used effectively."

His plan, in essence, was to march his army down the Louisiana bank to a position well south of the fortified bluff, then cross the river and establish a bridgehead from which to assail the Confederate bastion from the rear. The Duckport canal, designed to give his transports access to Walnut and Roundaway bayous, and thus allow them to avoid exposure to the plunging fire of the batteries at Vicksburg and Warrenton, had failed; only one small steamer had got through before the water level fell too low for navigation; but exploration of the route had shown that, by bridging those slews that could not be avoided by following the crests of levees flanking the horseshoe curves of the several bayous, it might be practicable to march dry-shod all the way from Milliken's Bend to New Carthage, a west-bank hamlet about midway between Warrenton and Grand Gulf, third of the rebel east-bank strong-holds. In late March, by way of preparation, Grant had assigned Mc-Clernand the task of putting this route into shape for a march by his own corps as well as the two others, which would follow. This, if it worked, would get the army well south of its objective. Getting the troops across the river was quite another matter, however, depending as it did on the co-operation of the navy, which, as Grant said, "was absolutely essential to the success (even to the contemplation) of such an enterprise." For the navy to get below, in position to ferry the men across and cover the east-bank landing, it would have to run the batteries, and this had been shown in the past to be an expensive proposition even for armored vessels, let alone the brittle-skinned transports which would be required for the ferrying operation. Moreover, Porter was no more under Grant's command than Grant was under Porter's. The most Grant could do was "request" that the run be made. But that was enough, as it turned

out. The admiral — who had returned only the week before from the near-disastrous Steele Bayou expedition, considerably the worse for wear and with his boats still being hammered back into shape — expressed an instant willingness to give the thing a try, though not without first warning of what the consequences would be, not only in the event of initial failure but also in the event of initial success, so far at least as the navy was concerned. He could make a downstream run, he said, and in fact had proved it twice already with the ill-fated *Queen*

of the West and the equally ill-fated *Indianola,* but his underpowered vessels could never attempt a slow-motion return trip, against the four-knot current, until Vicksburg had been reduced. "You must recollect that when these gunboats once go below we give up all hopes of ever getting them up again," he replied, wanting it understood from the start that this would be an all-or-nothing venture. Moreover: "If I do send vessels below, it will be the best vessels I have, and there will be nothing left to attack Haines Bluff, in case it should be deemed necessary to try it." Grant replied on April 2 that McClernand's men were already at work on the circuitous thirty-mile road down to New Carthage; he had no intention of turning back, even if that had been possible; and in any case Haines Bluff had cost the army blood enough by now. "I would,

Admiral, therefore renew my request to prepare for running the block-ade at as early a day as possible."

Two days later he wrote Halleck: "My expectation is for a por-tion of the naval fleet to run the batteries of Vicksburg, whilst the army moves through by this new route [to New Carthage]. Once there, I will move either to Warrenton or Grand Gulf; most probably the latter. From either of these points there are good roads to Vicksburg, and from Grand Gulf there is a good road to Jackson and the Black River Bridge without crossing the Black River." Much could be said for mak-ing the landing at either place. Warrenton, for example, was some fifteen air-line miles closer to his objective. But he knew well enough that a straight line was not always the surest connection between two military points. A Grand Gulf landing, in addition to giving him access to Vicks-burg's main artery of supply, would also afford him a chance to supple-ment his own. By holding the newly established bridgehead with part of his army and sending the balance downstream to assist in the reduc-tion of Port Hudson by Banks, who presumably was working his way upstream at the same time, he then would have an unbroken, all-weather connection with New Orleans and would no longer be exclusively and precariously dependent on what could be brought down from Memphis, first by steamboat, then by wagon over the new road skirting the west-bank complex of bayous across from the fortified bluff, and then again by steamboat in order to get the supplies over the river and into the east-bank bridgehead. Grant pondered the alternatives, and by April 11, a week after the dispatch giving Halleck a brief statement of the problem, he had made his choice: "Grand Gulf is the point at which I expect to strike, and send an army corps to Port Hudson to co-operate with Gen-eral Banks."

He did not know how Old Brains, whose timidity had been dem-onstrated in situations far less risky than this one, would react to a plan of campaign that involved 1) exposing the irreplaceable Union fleet to instantaneous destruction by batteries that had been sited on command-ing and impregnable heights with just that end in mind, 2) crossing a mile-wide river in order to throw his troops into the immediate rear of a rebel force of unknown strength which, holding as it did the interior lines, presumably could be reinforced more quickly than his own, and 3) remaining dependent all the while, or at least until the problematical capture of Port Hudson, on a supply line that was not only tenuous to the point of inadequacy, but was also subject to being cut by enemy in-tervention or obliterated by some accident of nature, by no means un-usual at this season, such as a week of unrelenting rain, a sudden rise of the river, and a resultant overflow that would re-drown the west-bank lowlands and the improvised road that wound its way around and across the curving bayous and treacherous morasses into which a wagon or a gun could disappear completely, leaving no more trace than a man or a mule whose bones had been picked clean by gars and crawfish. Whether Halleck would approve the taking of all these risks, Grant did not know; but he was left in no such doubt as to the reaction closer at hand. So far, of his three corps commanders, only his archrival McClernand had indicated anything resembling enthusiasm for the plan. Hard at work constructing makeshift bridges from materials found along the designated route to New Carthage, which he reached before mid-April, the former Illinois politician was in high spirits and predicted great results, for both the country and himself, because his corps had been assigned to lead the way. By contrast, though perhaps for the same reason — that is, because the nonprofessional McClernand had the lead — Sherman and McPherson, along with Dana and practically every member of Grant's own staff, considered the proposed operation not only overrisky and unwise, but also downright unmilitary. Sherman in fact was so alarmed at the prospect that he sat down and wrote Grant a long letter, insisting that the proper course would be for the army to return at once to Memphis and resume from there the overland advance along the Mississippi Central, abandoned in December. When his friend and chief replied that he had no intention of canceling his plans, Sherman had no choice except to go along with them, although he still did not approve. "I confess I don't like this roundabout project," he told one of his division commanders, "but we must support Grant in whatever he undertakes." He was loyal and he would remain so, but he also remained glum, writing home even as he ordered his men out of their camps at Milliken's Bend to join the movement: "I feel in its success less confidence than in any similar undertaking of the war."

Porter too had doubts as to the over-all wisdom of Grant's plan, as well as fears in regard to the specific risk the plan required the navy to assume, but he took no counsel of them aside from the more or less normal precautions the prospect of such exposure always prompted, as in the case of a farmer sending eggs to market in a springless wagon over a bumpy road. Unlike Sherman, he wrote no Cassandran letters and made no protest after his initial warning that once the fleet had gone below it could not come back up again until the batteries had been silenced in its rear. Instead, he kept busy preparing his crews and vessels for the passage of bluffs that bristled with 40-odd pieces of artillery, light and heavy, manned by cannoneers whose skill had improved with every chance to show it. By April 16 he was ready. Seven armored gunboats, mounting a total of 79 guns, were assigned to make the run, accompanied by three army transports, loaded with commissary stores instead of troops, and a steam ram captured the year before at Memphis when the Confederate flotilla was abolished in a brief half-morning's fight. At 9.30, two hours after dusk gave way to a starry but moonless night, the column cleared the mouth of the Yazoo, Porter leading aboard the flagship *Benton*.

The "run," so called, was in fact more creep than sprint, however, at least in its early stages; stealth was the watchword up and down the line of eleven boats steaming southward in single file on the dark chocolate surface of what one observer called "the great calm river, more like a long winding lake than a stream." Furnaces had been banked in advance, so as to show a minimum of smoke. All ports were covered and all deck lights doused, except for hooded lanterns visible only from dead astern for guidance. It was hoped that such precautions would hide the column from prying eyes. To reduce the likelihood of noise, which also might give the movement away, low speed was prescribed and exhaust pipes were diverted from the stacks to the paddle boxes, where the hiss of steam would be muffled. Pets and poultry were put ashore, moreover, lest a sudden mewing or cackling alert the rebel sentries. The admiral was leaving as little as possible to chance; but in the event of discovery he was prepared to shift at once from stealth to boldness. Coal-laden barges were lashed to the starboard flanks of the warships, leaving their port-side weapons free to take up any challenge from the high-sited batteries on the Mississippi shore, and water-soaked bales of hay were stacked around the otherwise unprotected boilers and pilot-houses of the transports. Instructed to maintain a fifty-yard interval, each helmsman was also told to steer a little to one side of the boat he followed, so as not to have to slow engines or change course to avoid a collision in case of a breakdown up ahead. Thus, though he wanted no trouble he could avoid, Porter was prepared to give as well as receive it in the event that his carefully woven veil of secrecy was ripped away. Passing Young's Point at about 10.30, the dark and silent column swung north as it approached the mouth of Sherman's abandoned canal, then rounded the final turn at 11 sharp, altering course again from north to south, and headed down the straightaway eastern shank of the hairpin bend that led past Vicksburg's dark and silent bluff. Ten minutes later all hell broke loose.

Grant was there to see the show, and he had his two families with him, one military and the other personal, the former consisting of his staff, the latter of his wife and their two sons, who had come down-river from Illinois to afford him a sort of furlough-in-reverse. Both were gathered tonight on the upper deck of the *Magnolia*, which was anchored three miles below Young's Point, just beyond range of the heaviest enemy guns, so that they watched as if from a box in a darkened theater, awaiting the raising of the curtain. The general and Mrs Grant occupied deck chairs near the starboard rail — front row center, as it were — with twelve-year-old Fred beside them; Ulysses Junior, who was ten, sat nearby in young Colonel Wilson's lap. Behind and on both sides of them stood twenty-odd men in uniform, staff officers and two high-ranking observers. One was Dana, who had been sent by Stanton to watch Grant, and the other was no less a personage than Adjutant General Lorenzo Thomas, who had arrived five days ago, five days after Dana, to watch them both. Or so it was said at any rate, so deep was the supposed mistrust the War Department felt. Just now though, whatever truth there was to the rumored assignment, there was a good deal more to watch than the unimpressive-looking department commander. First there was the passage of the hooded and muffled warships, disappearing northward in the direction of the bend that swung them south toward the rebel batteries; then a long wait in the blackness; then, eastward — across the narrow tongue of land called Vicksburg Point, beyond which the dark loom of bluff reared up to blot out the low-hanging stars — a sudden burgeoning incandescence, exposed as if by a rapid lifting of the awaited curtain. The show was on. It began, so to speak, in mid-crescendo as the guns came alive on the bluff and were replied to by those down on the brightly lighted river, growling full-throated, jarring the earth and water for miles around, and adding their muzzle flashes to the vivid illumination of the scene. "Magnificent, but terrible," Grant later called the sight. For the present, however, aside from ordering the younger boy to bed when he heard him whimper and saw him press his face against Wilson's chest in terror at the holocaust of flame and thunder, he said nothing. He merely smoked and watched the fireworks, holding all the while to his wife's hand. After ninety minutes of uproar, during which Dana tallied 525 shots fired by the Confederates, the bluff was once more dark and silent except for the reflection of fires still burning fitfully on the lower level where the boats had been. How much damage had been done and suffered, no one aboard the *Magnolia* could tell, although presently it was clear that some at least of the vessels had got past, for the Warrenton batteries came alive downstream, reproducing in miniature the earlier performance. Finally these too fell silent; which told the watchers exactly nothing, save that the final curtain had come down. Near and far, the fires burned out and the former blackness returned to the bluff and the river.

Unable to wait for word from below — news, perhaps, that the indispensable fleet had gone out of existence — Grant went ashore, got on his horse, and rode south under the paling stars, galloping along the crude and pot-holed road McClernand's corps had spent the past three weeks constructing. This was quite unlike the old Grant, who had never seemed in a hurry about anything at all. Something had come over him, here lately. "None who had known him the previous years could recognize him as being the same man," one officer observed. He had never seen the general ride at even a fast trot, let alone a gallop; but now, he said, "[Grant's] energies seemed to burst forth with new life," with the result that he rode at top speed practically all the time and "seemed wrought up to the last pitch of determination and energy." Shiloh and the long hot unproductive summer of 1862, the ill-wind fiasco near Iuka and the fruitless victory at Corinth, the period of indecision in

Memphis and the recent seven failures above Vicksburg, all were behind him now; he was launched at last on an all-or-nothing effort, a go-for-broke campaign, of which the passage of the batteries by the fleet was the first stage. If this failed, all failed; he would never get his troops across the mile-wide Mississippi. It was no wonder he rode fast.

Near New Carthage about midday he drew rein and breathed a sigh of relief at the sight of the fleet riding at anchor, apparently intact. Closer inspection showed that the boats had been knocked about considerably, however. All were damaged to various degrees, some in their hulls and others in their machinery. One was missing altogether: a transport, as it turned out, set afire by repeated hits and sunk to the accompaniment of cheers from the rebel batteries. But all the rest were seaworthy, or soon would be, after the completion of repairs already under way by bluejackets swarming over their ripped-up decks and pounded bulwarks. Porter and his captains were in excellent spirits, though they were frank to admit that last night's experience had been little short of horrendous. For one thing, all their precautions involving stealth and secrecy had availed them nothing. As they proceeded, dark and silent, down the straightaway eastern shank of the hairpin bend, Confederate sentries posted in skiffs on the river spotted them quickly; whereupon some rowed eastward to give the alarm to the Vicksburg cannoneers, while others, risking capture, crossed to the opposite bank, where they set fire to prepared stacks of pitch-soaked wood, as well as to the abandoned De Soto railroad station midway up the point. Quick-leaping flames floodlighted the approaching Yankee gunboats and the alerted rebel gunners promptly took these well-defined targets under fire. Another difficulty was that the prescribed low speed left the vessels to the mercy of the eddying current, which caught them alternately on the bow and quarter, swinging them broadside to the stream and in some cases even spinning them halfway around, so that they were obliged to come full circle under the plunging fire, as if responding to cruel encores that held them on the brightly lighted stage for further pelting by an irate audience. Clear at last, they played a brief epilogue at Warrenton, then swept on south to anchor above New Carthage in the predawn darkness. Assessing damages, Porter was grateful to discover that, despite a total of 68 hits received, the transport *Henry Clay* was the flotilla's only loss. Not a man had been killed, even aboard the missing boat, and only 13 — in this case a decidedly lucky number — had been wounded. Give him a couple of days in which to complete repairs, he said, and he would be quite ready to co-operate with the army.

Grant returned to Milliken's Bend, much pleased with the outcome, and prepared for another run within the week, this time by transports alone, in order to provide more ferries for the crossing. "If I do not underestimate the enemy," he wrote Halleck on April 21, "my force is abundant, with a foothold once obtained, to do the work." Next night six river steamers, loaded with rations, forage, and medical supplies, attempted the second run under instructions "to drop noiselessly down with the current . . . and not show steam until the enemy's batteries began firing, when the boats were to use all their legs." This was an all-army show, the steamers being army-owned and manned by army volunteers, since the civilian crews had balked at exposing their persons to what they had watched six nights ago from a safe distance. Now as then, Grant was there to see the show; an Illinois private later told how he "saw standing on the upper deck of his headquarters boat a man of iron, his wife by his side. He seemed to me the most immovable figure I ever saw." Then came the fireworks across the way, the sudden illumination and the uproar of the guns on the fuming bluff. Grant took it calmly, the soldier recalled; "No word escaped his lips, no muscle of his earnest face moved." Presently the batteries fell silent and word arrived from below that, now as before, only a single vessel had failed to survive the run — the steamer *Tigress*, McClernand's former headquarters boat, which Grant had ridden to Shiloh a year ago. Loaded with medicines and surgical equipment, she was hulled a dozen times or more and broke in two and sank, her skeleton crew floating downstream to safety on bits of wreckage. Once more not a man had been killed and the wounded were only a handful. Half the steamers had their engines permanently smashed, but that was no real drawback, since they would hold as many troops as ever and could be pushed or towed across the river as barges. As Grant saw it, this second run had been quite as successful as the first, and he was twice as pleased.

Belittling the loss of the *Tigress* and her cargo, which he said amounted to nothing more than "little extras for the men," he set off southward again on horseback to join Porter for a naval reconnaissance of Grand Gulf, designated as the point where the army would obtain a foothold once the navy had blasted its batteries out of existence. Porter was experiencing misgivings, and Grant, looking the place over from just beyond range of its guns on the 24th, saw that he had indeed given the navy a tough nut to crack. Its batteries were sited high, as at Donelson and Vicksburg, and what was more they seemed altogether ready for whatever came their way. "I foresee great difficulties in our present position," he informed Sherman on his return from the exploratory boat ride, "but it will not do to let these retard any movements." In this connection it seemed to him there might be a chance for an assault to succeed at last up the Yazoo, despite the previous fiasco. "It may possibly happen," he wrote Sherman, "that the enemy may so weaken his forces about Vicksburg and Haines Bluff as to make the latter vulnerable, particularly with a fall of water to give you an extended landing." However: "I leave the management of affairs at your end of the line to you," he added by way of making it clear that he was not definitely ordering an assault.

Monday, April 27, was Grant's forty-first birthday. It also marked the completion of his first-stage preparations for getting his troops across the river in order to come to grips with the rebels on dry ground, which was what he had been after from the start. By now all four divisions of McClernand's corps, having extended their march southward around Bayou Vidal and Lake Saint Joseph, were at Hard Times, Louisiana, the designated point of embarkation for the landing at Grand Gulf, five miles downstream. One of McPherson's divisions was also there and the other two were closing fast, while Sherman's three remained at Young's Point, on call to follow but held in place for the present so as to confuse the lookouts on the Vicksburg bluff. Seven warships and seven transports were available below, and though Porter was still troubled by misgivings — he thought his gunboats could suppress the Grand Gulf batteries, all right, but he warned that they might get so knocked about in the process that they would not be able to provide adequate cover for the crossing that would follow — Grant himself, as usual, expressed no doubt as to the outcome. He foresaw "great difficulties," but he did not admit that they were any occasion for delay. All he asked of the navy was that the rebel guns be silenced, after which there would be no need for cover. Before the anniversary was over, he sent McClernand word to go ahead: "Commence immediately the embarkation of your corps, or so much of it as there is transportation for."

The showdown was unquestionably at hand; but Grant was disclosing nothing he could avoid disclosing until the final moment. He had, in fact, devised three separate feints or demonstrations, two of them designed to mislead the enemy as to his chosen point of attack, well downstream, and a third whereby he hoped not only to distract his opponent by diverting his attention from front to rear, but also to add to his confusion, throughout this critical period, by disrupting the lines of supply and communication leading back into the interior of the state whose welfare and defense were the southern commander's assigned concern.

Sherman was organically involved in two of these, one of which had already been accomplished during the first ten days of April. Lest Pemberton call in the troops disposed to guard against a penetration of the Delta, and thereby strengthen the Vicksburg garrison in time for the showdown fight now imminent, Fred Steele's division was sent a hundred miles up the Mississippi to Greenville, where the men went ashore and thrashed about for a week in the interior, giving the impression that they were merely the advance contingent for another major drive on the Gibraltar of the West. Having done so — to the extreme alarm of the local planters, who bemoaned the attendant loss of cotton, cattle, and Negroes, and the home-guard commanders, who called loudly for reinforcements — they got back aboard their transports and rejoined Sherman at Young's Point for a share in the second and more important feint, this time against Haines Bluff. Grant had suggested it in his letter of the 24th, after a look at the Grand Gulf defenses, but now on his birthday he returned to the matter in more persuasive terms. "The effect of a heavy demonstration in that direction would be good so far as the enemy are concerned," he wrote Sherman from Hard Times, where McClernand's men were preparing to embark, "but I am loth to order it, because it would be hard to make our own troops understand that only a demonstration was intended and our people at home would characterize it as a repulse. I therefore leave it to you whether to make such a demonstration."

In referring thus to the probable adverse reaction by "our people at home," who of course would get their information from the papers, many of which were hostile — particularly toward Sherman, who returned the hostility in full measure — Grant may or may not have intended to use psychology on his journalist-hating friend. But at any rate it worked. "Does General Grant think I care what the newspapers say?" Sherman exclaimed as soon as he read the letter. And despite his growing antipathy for the strategy his superior had evolved ("I tremble for the result," he wrote his wife that week; "I look upon the whole thing as one of the most hazardous and desperate moves of this or any other war") he replied at once with a pledge of full co-operation. "We will make as strong a demonstration as possible," he declared. "The troops will all understand the purpose and not be hurt by the repulse. The people of the country must find out the truth as best they can; it is none of their business. You are engaged in a hazardous enterprise, and for good reason wish to divert attention; that is sufficient for me, and it shall be done." Warming as he wrote, the red-haired general bristled with contempt for public opinion. "The men have sense, and will trust us. As to the reports in newspapers, we must scorn them, else they will ruin us and our country. They are as much enemies to good government as the secesh, and between the two I like the secesh best, because they are a brave, open enemy and not a set of sneaking, croaking scoundrels."

Accordingly, he spent the next two days in preparation, and on the final day of April — previously designated by Lincoln, at the request of Congress, "as a day of national humiliation, fasting, and prayer" because, in the words of the proclamation, the people had "forgotten God" and become "too proud to pray" — set off up the Yazoo with ten regiments from Frank Blair's division, escorted by the flotilla remnant Porter had left behind, three gunboats, four tinclads, and three mortars, under Lieutenant Commander K. R. Breese. Intent on making the greatest possible show of strength, Sherman spread his troops over the transport decks with orders for "every man [to] look as numerous as possible." Short of Haines Bluff and near the scene of their December repulse, the bluecoats went ashore; marching and countermarching, banners flying and bands playing for all they were worth in the boggy woodland, they demonstrated in sight of the fortified line of hills, while the gunboats closed to within point-blank range of the bluff itself. For three hours the naval attack was pressed, as if in preparation for an infantry assault. However, the defenders clearly had their backs up; nor was there anything wrong with their marksmanship. The overaged *Tyler*, a veteran of all the fights since Henry, retired early with a shot below the water line, and the other two hauled off at 2 p.m. roughly handled, one having taken a total of forty-six hits. Sherman might have let it go at that, but he was determined to play out the game to full advantage. May Day morning he wrote Grant: "At 3 p.m. we will open another cannonade to prolong the diversion, and keep it up till after dark, when we shall drop down to Chickasaw and go on back to camp." The other two divisions, waiting at Young's Point under Steele and Brigadier General James M. Tuttle, were alerted for the long march to Hard Times, while Blair was told to keep up the pretense of attack until darkness afforded cover for withdrawal, at which time he would "let out for home," meaning Milliken's Bend, where he was to shield the rear of the two divisions moving southward to join Grant. Meanwhile, Sherman told him, "I will hammer away this p.m. because Major Rowley, [a staff observer] now here, says that our diversion has had perfect success, great activity being seen in Vicksburg, and troops pushing up this way. By prolonging the effort, we give Grant more chance." The infantry continued to mass as if for attack, and the gunboats moved again within range of Haines Bluff, keeping up the action until 8 o'clock that evening. Then Blair's men got back aboard their transports and withdrew, returning to the west bank of the Mississippi, followed by the somewhat battered but undaunted ten-boat flotilla, which dropped anchor off the mouth of the Yazoo. Steele and Tuttle took up the march for Hard Times at first light next morning, accompanied by Sherman himself, who sent a courier ahead with a full account of the two-day affair. Casualties had been negligible, he reported, afloat and ashore. Whether matters had gone as well for Grant, far downriver at Grand Gulf, he did not know; but he was satisfied that the feint from above had held a considerable portion of the Vicksburg garrison in position north of the city, away from the simultaneous main effort to the south. "We will be there as soon as possible," he assured his friend and superior.

Such were the first two of the three diversions intended to confuse and distract the Confederate defenders in the course of this highly critical span of time during which Grant was preparing to launch, and indeed was launching, his main effort a good forty miles downriver from the bluff that was his goal. Though both appeared to have exceeded strategic expectations, the third, while altogether different in scope and composition, was even more successful, and in fact was referred to afterwards by Sherman, who had no direct connection with the venture, as nothing less than "the most brilliant expedition of the war." Grant was as usual more restrained in judgment, qualifying his praise by calling the exploit "one of the most brilliant," but he added that it would "be handed down in history as an example to be imitated."

In point of fact, it was itself an imitation. For two years now, in the West as in the East, the Federal cavalry had suffered from a well-founded inferiority complex; Stuart and Morgan and Forrest had quite literally ridden rings around the awkward blue squadrons and the armies in their charge. Now, perhaps, the time had come for them to emulate the example set by the exuberant gray riders. Hooker thought so, in Virginia, and so did Grant in Mississippi. Back in February he had suggested to Hurlbut, commanding in Memphis, that a cavalry force, "with about 500 picked men, might succeed in making [its] way south and cut the railroad east of Jackson, Miss. The undertaking would be a hazardous one," he added, "but would pay well if carried out. I do not direct that this shall be done, but leave it for a volunteer enterprise." A month later, in mid-March, his instructions were more specific. The conception had been enlarged, tripling the strength of the force to be employed, and the volunteer provision had been removed. Hurlbut was to have all "the available cavalry put in as good condition as possible in the next few weeks for heavy service. . . . The date when the expedition should start will depend upon movements here. You will be informed of the exact time for them to start." In early April the date was set and a leader chosen: Colonel Benjamin H. Grierson, of Grant's home state of Illinois. Hurlbut saw to it that the raiders got away on schedule, April 17, riding south out of La Grange, forty miles east of Memphis, into the dawn that saw Porter's battered gunboats drop anchor near New Carthage after their fiery run past the Vicksburg bluff. "God speed him," Hurlbut said of Grierson, who led the 1700-man column in the direction of the Mississippi line, "for he has started gallantly on a long and perilous ride. I shall anxiously await intelligence of the result."

The wait would necessarily be a long one. Before the raid was over, the blue riders would have covered more than six hundred miles of road and swamp, through hostile territory. At the outset, however, none of the troopers in the three regiments, two from Illinois and one from Iowa, nor of the cannoneers in the attached six-gun battery of 2-pounders, suspected that the warning order, "Oats in the nosebag and five days rations in haversacks, the rations to last ten days," was prelude to so deep a penetration. "We are going on a big scout to Columbus, Mississippi, and play smash with the railroads," one predicted. Only Grierson himself, riding at the head of the column, knew that the true objective was Pemberton's main supply line, the Southern Railroad east of Jackson, connecting Vicksburg with Meridian and thence with Mobile and the arsenals in Georgia and the East. Pennsylvania-born and just short of thirty-seven years of age, with a spade beard and an acquired mistrust of horses dating back to a kick received from a pony in childhood, which smashed one of his cheekbones, split his forehead, and left him scarred for life — he had protested his assignment to the cavalry in the first place, though to no avail; Halleck, who made the appointment, insisted that he looked "active and wiry enough to make a good cavalryman" — Grierson eighteen months ago had been a music teacher and bandmaster at Jacksonville, Illinois, but all that was left to remind him or anyone else of that now was a jew's-harp he carried inside his blouse, along with a pocket compass and a small-scale map of the region he and his men would be traversing in the course of their strike at the railroad some two hundred air-line miles away. Riding where no bluecoat had ever been before, he could expect to be surrounded en route by small bodies of home guardsmen, who would outnumber him badly if they were consolidated, as well as by sizable detachments of regulars, horse and foot, which Pemberton would certainly send to oppose him, front and rear, once his presence and intention became known. Even if he succeeded in his mission — that is, reached and wrecked an appreciable stretch of the railroad between Jackson and Meridian, temporarily severing the one connection by which reinforcements could reach Vicksburg swiftly from outside Mississippi — he would then be deep in the heart of a land where every man's hand would be raised against him. One suggestion, included in his orders, was that he return to Tennessee by swinging east, then north through Alabama; another was that he plunge on south and west for a hookup with Grant in the vicinity of Grand Gulf, anticipating a successful crossing by McClernand and McPherson at that point, or else take sanctuary within Banks's outpost lines at Baton Rouge, which would give him about as far to go from the railroad south as he would have come already in order to reach it. In any case, whatever escape plan he adopted as a result of the unfolding course of events, the tactical requisites were vigilance, speed, boldness, and deception. Without any one of these four, he and his troopers, in the cavalry slang of the time, would be "gone up."

Across the Mississippi line by sunup, they made thirty miles the first day — a good average march for cavalry, though Grant himself covered nearly as great a distance before noon, galloping south from Milliken's Bend to check on the condition of Porter's gunboats at New Carthage — and called a halt that night just short of Ripley, which they passed through next morning, brushing aside the few startled gray militia they encountered, to camp beyond New Albany at sundown. On the third day, April 19, they continued due south through Pontotoc. Eighty miles from base, with rebel detachments no doubt alerted in his front and rear, Grierson began his fourth day with an inspection, culled out 175 victims of dysentery, chills and fever, and saddle galls — "the Quinine Brigade," the rejected troopers promptly dubbed themselves — and sent them back, under a staff major, with one of the 2-pounders and instructions to "pass through Pontotoc in the night, marching by fours, obliterating our tracks, and producing the impression that we have all returned." He himself continued south with the main body, to Houston and beyond. Deciding to throw a still larger tub to the Confederate whale, he detached Colonel Edward Hatch's regiment of Iowans next morning, along with another of the guns, and gave its commander orders to strike eastward for the Mobile & Ohio, inflicting what damage he could to that vital supply line before heading north in the wake of the Quinine Brigade, thus spreading the scare and increasing the impression that all the raiders were returning. Hatch, a transplanted New Englander hungry for fame and advancement — tomorrow would be his thirty-second birthday — now began a five-day adventure on his own. Though he did not succeed in breaking the well-guarded railroad to the east, he fought two severe skirmishes — one at the outset, a delaying action which allowed Grierson to get away southward, the other near the finish, which allowed his own getaway northward — burned several cotton-stocked warehouses in Okolona, and succeeded handsomely in his primary mission of drawing most of the North Mississippi home guardsmen pell-mell after him and away from Grierson. At a cost of ten men lost en route, he reported that he had inflicted ten times as many casualties on the enemy and "accumulated 600 head of horses and mules, with about 200 able-bodied negroes to lead them." Returning to La Grange on Sunday morning, April 26, he brought Hurlbut the first substantial news of the raiders' progress since their departure, nine days back.

The unavailable news was a good deal better; Grierson by then had not only reached his objective, he was already forty hours beyond it, having formulated and put into execution his tactics for escape. Relieved of the threat to his rear on the 21st by Hatch's decoy action south of Houston, he and his 1000 troopers — all Illinoisans now, including the fifty cannoneers with the four remaining guns — rode on past Starkville, where he detached one company for a strike at Macon, twenty-odd miles southeast on the M&O, then took up the march at dawn and cleared Louisville by sundown. Beyond Philadelphia on the 23d he called a halt at nightfall, and made an early start next morning in order to reach the Southern Railroad before noon. Preceded by scouts who seized the telegraph office and thus kept the alarm from being spread — "Butternut Guerillas," these outriders called themselves, for they wore Confederate uniforms, risking hanging for the advantage gained — the raiders burst into Newton Station, a trackside hamlet twenty-five miles west of Meridian and about twice as far east of Jackson, where they at once got down to the work for which they had ridden all this way. Two locomotives were captured and wrecked, along with three dozen freight cars loaded with ordnance and commissary supplies, including artillery ammunition on consignment for Vicksburg, which afforded a rackety fire-

works display when set aflame. Meantime other details were ripping up
miles of track and crossties, burning trestles and bridges, tearing down
telegraph wires all the way to the Chunky River, and setting fire to a
government building stocked with 500 small arms and a quantity of
new gray uniforms. By 2 o'clock the destruction was complete;
Griersen had his bugler sound
the rally to assemble the smoke-
grimed raiders, some of whom
were showing the effects of
rebel whiskey they had "res-
cued" from the flames, then
took his accustomed post at the
head of the column and led
them away from the charred
and smoldering evidence of their
efficiency as wreckers. Now as
before, the march was south.
They did not bivouac till near
midnight, having covered a
good fifty miles of road despite
the arduous delay at Newton
Station. Next day, April 25, was
the easiest of the raid, however,
since the blue raiders spent most
of it on a plantation in the
piny highlands just short of the
Leaf River valley, resting their
mounts, gorging themselves on
smokehouse ham, and presumably nursing their hangovers.
Sunday followed, and while

Hatch was riding into La Grange at the end of his five-day excursion
through North Mississippi, the raiders turned west. In time, according to
Griersen's calculations, this would bring them either to Grand Gulf, in
case Grant had effected a crossing as planned, or to Natchez, which had
been under intermittent Federal occupation for nearly a year.

Either place would afford refuge for his saddle-weary troopers
if all went as he hoped and planned, but he knew well enough that the
most dangerous part of the long ride lay before him. By now, doubtless,
every grayback in the state would have learned of the presence of his
two regiments at Newton Station two days ago, with the result that a
considerable number of them must be hot on his trail or lying in wait
for him in all directions. However, this had its compensations as well as
its drawbacks. Scarcely less important than the temporary severing of
Vicksburg's main supply line was the disruption of its defenses, prevent-

ing the hasty concentration of its outlying forces against Grant in the early stages of his river crossing. In point of fact, Grierson was more successful in this regard than he had any way of knowing. Orders flew thick and fast from Pemberton's headquarters in the Mississippi capital, directing all units within possible reach to concentrate on the capture of the ubiquitous blue column. An infantry brigade, en route from Alabama to reinforce Vicksburg, was halted at Meridian to protect that vital intersection of the Southern Railroad and the Mobile & Ohio, while another moved east from Jackson in the direction of the break at Newton Station. Forces at Panola and Canton, under James Chalmers and Lloyd Tilghman, were shifted to Okolona and Carthage to block the northern escape route. All of these troops, amounting to no less than a full division, not counting the various home-guard units caught up in the swirl, were thus effectively taken out of the play and removed from possible use at this critical time against either Grant or Grierson, who were off in the opposite corner of the map. Not that Pemberton was neglecting matters in that direction, at least so far as Grierson was concerned. Detachments of fast-riding cavalry were ordered eastward from Port Hudson and Port Gibson — the latter a scant half dozen miles from Grant's intended point of landing at Grand Gulf — in case the marauders tried for a getaway to the south or the southwest. In short, Pemberton's reaction to the widespread confusion in his rear and along his lines of supply and communication, while altogether commendable from a limited point of view, amounted to full co-operation with the raiders in the accomplishment of their secondary mission, which was to divert his attention, as well as his reserves, away from the point at which Grant was preparing to hurl two thirds of the blue army.

Grierson wasted no time. Monday, April 27 — Grant's birthday; Sherman prepared for his feint up the Yazoo, and McClernand was told to get his troops aboard the transports at Hard Times — the blue riders pushed westward across Pearl River, aided considerably by the capture of a ferryboat by scouts who masqueraded as Confederates. While the crossing was in progress the company detached five days ago near Starkville rejoined the main body, reporting that in addition to throwing a scare into the defenders of Macon, as instructed, it had also made a feint at Enterprise, twelve miles below Meridian, thus adding to the difficulties of the rebel high command's attempt to pinpoint the location of the invaders. Safely across the Pearl, the reunited 1000-man column pressed on west to Hazlehurst, where a string of boxcars was set afire on a siding of the New Orleans, Jackson & Great Northern Railroad. Flames spreading to a nearby block of buildings, the erstwhile incendiaries turned firemen and worked side by side with the citizens in preventing the loss of the whole town. At dusk, in a driving rain which had helped to contain the fire, the colonel ordered his troopers to remount. The march was west; Grand Gulf was only forty miles away and he hoped to make it there tomorrow, in case Grant had crossed the Mississippi. However, morning brought no indication that any part of the Army of the Tennessee was on this side of the river, so Grierson veered a bit to the south for Natchez, his alternate sanctuary, which was only twenty miles farther away than Grand Gulf. But that too was not to be. Beyond Union Church that afternoon, the raiders were enjoying a rest halt when they were charged by what one of them called "a crowd of graylooking horsemen galloping and shooting in a cloud of dust and smoke." The result at first was panic and the beginning of a rout, but presently they stiffened and repulsed the attackers, who turned out to be nothing more than a couple of understrength companies on the prowl. The colonel prepared to push on next day to Natchez, but was warned that night by one of the Butternut Guerillas, who had ridden ahead and struck up a conversation with a rebel outpost group, that seven companies of cavalry from Grand Gulf were planning to ambush him when he moved westward in the morning. So Grierson once more changed his plans, abandoning Natchez as his destination. Determined now to press on down to Baton Rouge, though this added another hundred miles to the distance his weary men would have to ride, he turned back east at dawn of April 29, avoiding the ambush laid so carefully in what was now his rear.

By early afternoon they were in Brookhaven, twenty-five miles east, astride the railroad they had crossed two days ago, twenty miles to the north, when the march was west. "There was much running and yelling" on the part of the startled citizens, Grierson later reported, "but it soon quieted into almost a welcome." Here, as at Hazlehurst on Monday, sparks from the burning railroad station and another string of boxcars set a section of the town ablaze, and the troopers once more turned firemen to help the natives keep the flames from spreading. Meantime, however, a wrecking crew kept busy tearing up track and burning crossties, thus abolishing the possibility of a locomotive pursuit by troops from Jackson. Back in the saddle, the raiders moved south along the railroad and made camp that night, eight miles below Brookhaven and just over a hundred miles from Baton Rouge. At Summit before sundown of the last day of April, the colonel spared the depot lest his men have to turn firefighters again to save the town, but there was another unfortunate — or fortunate, depending on the point of view — encounter with rebel spirits when the troopers uncovered a cache of rum in fifty-gallon barrels. Grierson broke up the binge, got the revelers mounted at last, drunk or sober, and pressed on south another half dozen miles before stopping for the night. Dawn of May Day completed two full weeks the men had spent in the saddle, with only a half day's rest aside from the minimal halts for sleep and food. Once more the march was west. "A straight line for Baton Rouge, and let speed be our safety," Grierson told his officers as the column was put in motion.

Speed there was — the raiders covered no less than seventy-five miles of road in the following twenty-eight hours — but there was fighting, too, the first and only serious opposition the main body encountered in the course of the long raid. Even so, it was not much. At Wall's Bridge, which spanned the Tickfaw River just north of the Louisiana line, three companies of Confederates from Port Hudson laid a noonday ambush that cost the leading Union company eight casualties. Grierson promptly brought his artillery to the front, shelled the opposite bank, and ordered a charge that not only cleared the bridge but threw the rebels into headlong flight. Riding south all night, with no time out for rest or food, the blue column reached and crossed the Amite River, the last unfordable stream this side of Baton Rouge, before the aroused graybacks could bar the way. Six miles short of the Louisiana capital next morning, his troopers reeling in their saddles from lack of sleep, Grierson called a halt at last. The men tumbled from their mounts and slept where they fell, along the roadside, but the colonel himself, as befitted a former music teacher with an ingrained mistrust of horses, was refreshing himself by playing the piano in the parlor of a nearby plantation house when a picket burst in with news that they were about to be overwhelmed and captured. A rebel force was approaching from the west, he said, with skirmishers out! Grierson, knowing better, rode out to meet the reported enemy, who turned out to be members of the garrison at Baton Rouge, sent to investigate an improbable-sounding rumor "that a brigade of cavalry from General Grant's army had cut their way through the heart of the rebel country, and were then only five miles outside the city." Somewhat restored by their naps, the men remounted and rode into the capital that afternoon. Cheered by spectators, civilians as well as soldiers, the two-mile-long procession of road-worn men and animals, so weathered and dust-caked that they could scarcely be distinguished from the prisoners and Negroes they had gathered along the way, wound slowly around the public square, then south out of town to a grove of magnolias two miles south, where they dismounted, unsaddled, and fell so soundly asleep that they could not be aroused to accept hot coffee.

They had cause for weariness, having covered more than six hundred miles in less than sixteen days, and for thankfulness as well: thankfulness that Pemberton had lost Van Dorn to Bragg three months before, along with nearly all his cavalry, and that it was Abel Streight and not themselves who had been made the prime concern of Bedford Forrest. Streight had left Fort Henry on the day they left La Grange, and was surrendering in East Alabama while Grierson's men, having caught up on their sleep at last, were enjoying their first midday meal in the magnolia grove just south of the Louisiana capital. Different circumstances might well have led to different results, including perhaps a reversal of their current roles as prisoners on the one hand and heroes on the other, but the fact remained that the Illinois troopers had dealt with conditions as they found them. And having done so, they had cause for pride. At a total cost of barely two dozen casualties — "3 killed, 7 wounded, 5 left on the route sick . . . and 9 men missing, supposed to have straggled" — they had "killed and wounded about one hundred of the enemy, captured and paroled over 500 prisoners, many of them officers, destroyed between fifty and sixty miles of railroad and telegraph, captured and destroyed over 3000 stand of arms, and other army stores and government property to an immense amount." So Grierson later reported, adding as if by afterthought, despite his continued mistrust of all equine creatures: "We also captured 1000 horses and mules."

Within three days the colonel was on a steamboat for New Orleans, where he was feted and presented with a horse by the admiring citizenry. "My dear Alice," he wrote his wife that night, "I like Byron have had to wake up one morning and find myself famous. Since I have been here it has been one continuous ovation." In early June, with his picture on the covers of both *Harper's Weekly* and *Leslie's Illustrated*, he was promoted to brigadier general. But perhaps the finest tribute of all came from a man by no means given to using superlatives, on or off the record. Assessing the value of the raid in its relation to the over-all campaign for the taking of Vicksburg, of which it was very much a part, Grant said flatly: "It was Grierson who first set the example of what might be done in the interior of the enemy's country without any base from which to draw supplies."

For the present, however, Grant at Hard Times had no more knowledge of Grierson's progress, across the way, than Grierson had had of Grant's while riding west from Hazlehurst. All the cavalryman learned for certain as he pressed on toward the river was that the army had not crossed as planned, which meant that something must have gone awry. Something had indeed. When the raiders turned back east from Union Church at dawn of April 29, avoiding the ambush laid in what had been their front, they missed hearing the guns of the attackers and defenders at Grand Gulf, less than thirty air-line miles away. It was just as well, for otherwise they might have been lured into what would have been a trap. Except for the rather negative advantage of proving that this was no place to attempt an east-bank landing, the attack was an utter failure, and an expensive one at that.

Porter's doubts had been increasing all week, ever since his April 22 reconnaissance of the stronghold on the bluff across the way. Though he had kept up a show of confidence in his talks with Grant, privately he was airing his misgivings in dispatches to his Washington superiors, not only by way of preparing them for bad news, but also by way of divesting himself in advance of any responsibility for the failure he saw looming. "I am quite depressed with this adventure," he wrote Fox, "which as you know never met with my approval." This last was something less than strictly true, though when he signaled the flotilla captains to move against Grand Gulf at 8 o'clock next morning, April 29, his forebodings soon turned out to have been well founded. The navy's task was to silence the rebel batteries, then cover the crossing by the transports bringing the army over to take the place by storm; but when four of the seven ironclads closed to within pistol shot of the 75-foot bluff — so at least it seemed to Grant, who watched the contest from aboard a tug — they were severely mauled. The flagship *Benton* took 70 hits, the *Tuscumbia* 81; the *Lafayette* took 45, the *Pittsburg* 35. The other three boats, *Carondelet, Mound City,* and *Louisville,* all veterans of the river war from its beginning, did their fighting at long range, lobbing shells into the blufftop works, and consequently suffered little damage. Even so, when Porter hoisted the pennant for the flotilla to drop back out of action at 12.30 — all but the *Tuscumbia,* which had been struck in her machinery and swept powerless downstream until she fetched up short against the Louisiana bank — a total of 75 casualties, including 18 dead, had been subtracted from its crews. By contrast, although time would disclose that they had lost 3 killed and 15 wounded, the defenders seemed unhurt behind their earthwork fortifications. Grand Gulf was as much a failure for the Union navy as Fort Donelson had been, just over a year ago. Porter frankly admitted as much. A crossing might be managed elsewhere, he told Grant, but not here, under the muzzles of those guns across the way.

Grant had not expected a repulse, but he was prepared for what he considered the outside chance of one. Now that a repulse had been encountered, an alternate plan was put into execution without delay. McClernand's men would debark at Hard Times, march south across the point of land to De Shroon's, a plantation landing some four miles downstream, and be ready before dawn to get back aboard the transports, which were to steal past Grand Gulf under cover of darkness, hugging the western bank while the gunboats re-engaged the batteries. All this went as planned, afloat and ashore. The navy lost only one man in its renewal of the duel with the blufftop cannoneers, and the army made its night march unobserved, to find the transports waiting unscathed in the predawn darkness at De Shroon's. "By the time it was light," Grant later wrote, "the enemy saw our whole fleet, ironclads, gunboats, river steamers, and barges, quietly moving down the river three miles below them, black, or rather blue, with National troops."

Accomplishing this he showed the flexibility that would characterize his planning throughout the various stages of the campaign which now was under way in earnest. Other characteristics he also showed. An officer was to remember seeing the general sitting his horse beside the road at a point where a narrow bridge had been thrown across a bog. "Push right along, men," he told the marchers, speaking in almost a conversational tone. "Close up fast and hurry over." The soldiers recognized him and were obviously pleased to see their commander sharing their exertions, but the officer noted that their only reply was to do as he directed. They did not cheer him; they just "hurried over." It was as if, in the course of the long winter of repeated failures, they had caught his quality of quiet confidence. Charles Dana, for one, had begun to think so. He had come down here three weeks ago to report on Grant's alleged bad habits. So far, though, he not only had detected none of these; he had never even heard him curse or seen him lose his temper. Dana was puzzled. "His equanimity was becoming a curious spectacle to me," the former journalist later recalled. Tonight, for example, riding beside the general along the dark road from Hard Times to De Shroon's, he saw Grant's horse stumble. "Now he will swear," he thought, half expecting to see the rider go tumbling over the animal's head; "For an instant his moral status was on trial." But Grant lost neither his balance nor his temper. "Pulling up his horse, he rode on, and, to my utter amazement, without a word or sign of impatience."

Nor did the night march across the point of land, from Hard Times to De Shroon's, put an end to the need for sudden improvisation. Having bypassed Grand Gulf — which he could not allow to remain alive for long, so close in his rear — Grant still was faced with the problem of where to effect a landing on the Mississippi bank, in order to return for a strike at the fortified bluff from its vulnerable landward flank. A look at the map suggested Rodney, another twelve miles downstream. But that would not only give the troops a considerable distance to march, and the defenders time to improve their position and call in reinforcements, it would also place the bluecoats on the far side of Bayou Pierre, which would have to be crossed when they turned back north. Yet to make a landing short of the point where the bayou flowed westward into the river, five miles below, might be to founder the army in some unmapped and unsuspected swamp. What was needed was a guide, a sympathetic native of the region, and Grant sent a detachment of soldiers across the river in a skiff, with instructions to bring back what he wanted. They returned before midnight with an east-bank slave who filled the bill. At first he had been unwilling to come, and in fact had had to be taken by force, but now that he found himself in the lamp-lighted headquarters tent, facing the Union commander across an unrolled chart, he turned co-operative. "Look here," Grant said. "Tell me where this road leads to — starting where you see my finger here on the map and running down that way." The Negro studied the problem, then shook his head. "That road fetches up at Bayou Pierre," he said. "But you can't go that way, 'cause it's plum full of backwater." The thing to do, he replied to further questions, was to go ashore at Bruinsburg, six miles below De Shroon's. This would still be south of Bayou Pierre, but at least it was only half as far as Rodney. Moreover, there was a good road leading from there to Grand Gulf by way of Port Gibson, which lay ten miles inland, well back from the trackless swamps and canebrakes of the river bottoms. At Bruinsburg, the captive slave explained, "you can leave the boats and the men can walk on high ground all the way. The best houses and plantations in all the country are there, sir, all along that road."

So Bruinsburg it was. By midmorning of this last day of April — while Sherman was launching his demonstration against Haines Bluff, fifty air-line miles to the north, and Grierson was pressing southward along the railroad below Brookhaven, the same distance to the east — all four of McClernand's divisions and one of McPherson's, some 23,000 men in all, had completed their debarkation and were slogging inland toward Port Gibson. "When this was effected," Grant declared years later, "I felt a degree of relief scarcely ever equaled since." Then he told why. "I was now in the enemy's country, with a vast river and the stronghold of Vicksburg between me and my base of supplies. But I was on dry ground on the same side of the river with the enemy. All the campaigns, labors, hardships, and exposures from the month of December previous to this time that had been made and endured were for the accomplishment of this one object."

For all his northern birth and starchy manner, which some continued to find personally distasteful, Pemberton by now had either sustained or won the confidence not only of his military superiors but also of the people of Mississippi, who came within his charge. His four-month sequence of successes in the face of threats from all points of the compass far outweighed their original prejudice against him. On May Day, for example — unaware that Sherman was knocking at Vicksburg's upper gate or that Grant, with half his army over the river, already was marching inland from below — an editor in the capital, where the department commander had his headquarters, was taking a sanguine view of the situation. "It would be idle to say that our state and country was not in a position of great peril," he declared. "Yet, strange as it may seem to our readers, we have never felt more secure since the fall of Donelson. The enemy will never reach Jackson; we are satisfied of that.... General Pemberton, assisted by vigilant and accomplished officers, is watching the movements of the enemy, and at the proper time will pounce upon him. Let us give the authorities all the assistance we can, and trust their superior and more experienced judgment as to the management of the armies. We know we have a force sufficient, if properly handled, not only to defeat but to rout and annihilate Grant if he ventures far from his river base." As for doubts as to the proper handling of this sufficient

force: "Let any man who questions the ability of General Pemberton only think for a moment of the condition the department was in when he was first sent here. No general has evinced a more sleepless vigilance in the discharge of his duty, or accomplished more solid and gratifying results." Nor was this merely the opinion of one uninformed civilian. With reservations, Joe Johnston shared his view. Despite the gloom into which his inspection of the Vicksburg defenses had thrown him, back in December, the Virginian since had warmed to the Pennsylvanian as a result of his apparent skill in fending off the combinations designed for his destruction. In mid-March, reviewing the situation from three hundred miles away in Tennessee, he congratulated him handsomely. "Your activity and vigor in the defense of Mississippi must have secured for you the confidence of the people of Mississippi," he wrote, and added: "I have no apprehension for Port Hudson from Banks. The only fear is that the canal may enable Grant to unite their forces. I believe your arrangements at Vicksburg make it perfectly safe, unless that union should be effected."

Applause was one thing, assistance quite another: as Pemberton soon found out. Despite the denial of help from the vast department across the river, and despite the January transfer of three quarters of his cavalry to Middle Tennessee, he was so encouraged by the flooding of Grant's canal in March that he mistook the subsequent withdrawal of the diggers to Milliken's Bend for an abandonment by the Federals of their entire campaign. On April 11 he notified Johnston that the canal was no longer a danger, that Grant appeared to be pulling back to Memphis, and that he was therefore sending, as requested, a brigade to reinforce Bragg at Tullahoma. Five days later, however, with the blue army still in evidence on the opposite bank and Porter's gunboats preparing for their run past the batteries that night, he recalled the detached brigade, which by then was in northern Mississippi. "[Grant's] movement up the river was a ruse," he wired Johnston. "Certainly no more troops should leave this department." In fact, he said, it was he who stood in gravest need of help. Nothing came of that. Then on April 20, with Porter's ironclads riding at anchor near New Carthage, McClernand moving farther down the Louisiana bank, and Grierson on the rampage east of Grenada — "part and parcel of the formidable invasion preparing before my eyes" — Pemberton stepped up his plea for reinforcements: especially for the return of his 6000 troopers under Van Dorn, the loss of whom had left him three-fourths blind. "Heavy raids are making from Tennessee deep into this state," he warned. "Cavalry is indispensable to meet these expeditions. The little I have is . . . totally inadequate. Could you not make a demonstration with a cavalry force on their rear?" He protested that he had "literally no cavalry from Grand Gulf to Yazoo City, while the enemy is threatening to [cross] the river between Vicksburg and Grand Gulf, having now twelve vessels below the former place." Johnston, obliged as he presently was to send Forrest to Alabama after Streight, not only would not agree to make a demonstration against West Tennessee; he also declined to lessen the strength of Bragg's mounted arm, which included Wheeler and Morgan as well as Forrest and Van Dorn, despite the fact that Van Dorn was nominally on loan from Pemberton. It turned out, moreover, that the Pennsylvanian's previous successes worked against him now. Matters had seemed as dark several times before, in the course of the past four months, and he had managed to survive without assistance; apparently Johnston believed he would do as well again. At any rate he was still of his former opinion: "Van Dorn's cavalry is absolutely necessary to enable General Bragg to hold the best part of the country from which he draws supplies."

In effect this amounted to signing Van Dorn's death warrant, since it kept him within range of the Tennessee doctor's wife and her husband's pistol. Pemberton was inclined to think that in the end it might amount to much the same thing for Vicksburg, which Jefferson Davis referred to as "the nailhead that held the South's two halves together." For suddenly now the news grew more alarming. Two nights later, April 22, five unarmored steamboats ran the batteries, obviously to provide the means for a crossing, somewhere below, by the bluecoats slogging down the western bank. Throughout the week that followed, Pemberton sent what little cavalry he had in pursuit of Grierson, whose raiders were disrupting the interior of the state and playing havoc with his lines of supply and communication. Then on April 29 word came from Brigadier General John S. Bowen, commanding at Grand Gulf, that the place was under heavy attack by gunboats attempting to soften him up for an assault by infantry waiting in transports across the river at Hard Times. Scarcely had the news arrived next morning that the ironclads had retired, severely battered, than Pemberton was notified that Haines Bluff was under similar pressure to the north. By the time he learned that this too had been beaten off, a follow-up message from Bowen informed him that the Union fleet had slipped past Grand Gulf in the darkness, transports and all, and was unloading soldiers in large numbers at Bruinsburg, ten miles below. Then came word that the Federals had resumed their pounding of Haines Bluff. Deciding that the downriver threat was the graver of the two, Pemberton resolved to reinforce Bowen, whom he instructed to contest the blue advance on Port Gibson.

On May Day, with the issue still in doubt below — so he thought, though it could scarcely be in doubt for long; the enemy strength was reported at 20,000 men, while Bowen had considerably less than half that many — he appealed once more to Johnston for assistance, bolstering his plea with a wire directly to the President. Davis replied that, in addition to urging Johnston to send help from Tennessee, he was doing all he could to forward troops from southern Alabama. Secretary Seddon, alerted to the danger, informed Pemberton that "heavy reinforcements" would start at once by rail from Beauregard in Charleston. Both messages were gratifying, communicating assurance of assistance from above. But all the harassed Vicksburg commander got from Johnston was advice. "If Grant's army lands on this side of the river," the Virginian replied from Tullahoma, "the safety of Mississippi depends on beating it. For that object you should unite your whole force."

A Georgia-born West Pointer, Bowen had left the old army after a single hitch as a lieutenant and had prospered as a St Louis architect before he was thirty, at which age he offered his sword to the newly formed Confederacy. Promoted to brigadier within ten months, he now was thirty-two and eager for further advancement, having spent more than a year in grade because of a long convalescence from a wound taken at Shiloh, where he led his brigade of Missourians with distinction. On the afternoon of April 30, marching his 5500 soldiers out of Grand Gulf and across Bayou Pierre to meet Grant's 23,000 moving inland from Bruinsburg after their downriver creep past his blufftop guns in the darkness, he carried proudly in his pocket a dispatch received last night from Pemberton, congratulating him on the repulse of Porter's ironclads: "In the name of the army, I desire to thank you and your troops for your gallant conduct today. Keep up the good work.... Yesterday I warmly recommended you for a major-generalcy. I shall renew it." Bowen had it very much in mind to keep up the good work. Despite the looming four-to-one odds and the changed nature of his task now that he and the blue invaders were on the same bank of the river, he welcomed this opportunity to deal with them ashore today as he had dealt with them afloat the day before. Four miles west of Port Gibson before nightfall, he put his men in a good defensive position astride a wooded ridge just short of a fork in the road leading east from Bruinsburg. Presently the Federals came up and his pickets took them under fire in the moonlight. Artillery deepened the tone of the argument, North and South, but soon after midnight, as if by mutual consent, both sides quieted down to wait for daylight.

McClernand opened the May Day fight soon after sunrise, advancing all four of his divisions under Brigadier Generals Peter Osterhaus, A. J. Smith, Alvin Hovey, and Eugene Carr. The road fork just ahead placed him in something of a quandary, lacking as he did an adequate map, but this was soon resolved by a local Negro who informed him that the two roads came together again on the near side of Port Gibson, his objective. He sent Osterhaus to the left as a diversion in favor of the other three commanders, who were charged with launching the main effort on the right. Grant came up at midmorning to find the battle in full swing and McClernand in some confusion, his heavily engaged columns being out of touch with each other because the two roads that wound along parallel ridges — "This part of Mississippi stands on edge" was how Grant put it — were divided by a timber-choked ravine that made lateral communication impossible. The result was that McClernand's right hand quite literally did not know what his left was doing, though the fact was neither was doing well at all. In his perplexity he called for help from McPherson, who supplied it by sending one brigade of Major General John A. Logan's division to the left and another to the right. "Push right along. Close up fast," the men heard Grant say as they went past the dust-covered general sitting a dust-covered horse beside the road fork. They did as he said, and arrived on the left in time to stall a rebel counterattack that had already thrown Osterhaus off balance, while on the right they added the weight needed for a resumption of the advance. Outflanked and heavily outnumbered on the road to the south, Bowen at last had to pull back to the outskirts of Port Gibson, where he rallied his men along a hastily improvised line and held off the blue attackers until nightfall ended the fighting.

Casualties were about equal on both sides; 832 Confederates and 875 Federals had fallen or were missing. Bowen had done well and he knew it, considering the disparity of numbers, but he also knew that to fight here tomorrow, against lengthened odds and without the advantage of this morning's densely wooded terrain, would be to invite disaster. At sundown he notified Pemberton that he would "have to retire under cover of night to the other side of Bayou Pierre and await reinforcements." Pemberton, who had arrived in Vicksburg from Jackson by now, had already sent word that he was "hurrying reinforcements; also ammunition. Endeavor to hold your own until they arrive, though it may be some time, as the distance is great." At 7.30, having received Bowen's sundown message, he rather wistfully inquired: "Is it not probable that the enemy will himself retire tonight? It is very important, as you know, to retain your present position, if possible.... You must. however, of course, be guided by your own judgment. You and your men have done nobly." But Bowen by then had followed up his first dispatch with a second: "I am pulling back across Bayou Pierre. I will endeavor to hold that position until reinforcements arrive." He withdrew skillfully by moonlight, unpursued and unobserved, destroying the three bridges over the bayou and its south fork, northwest and northeast of Port Gibson, and took up a strong position on the opposite bank, covering the wrecked crossing of the railroad to Grand Gulf, which he believed would be Grant's next objective.

But Grant did not come that way, at least not yet. Finding Port Gibson empty at dawn, he pressed on through and gave James Wilson a brigade-sized detail with which to construct a bridge across the south fork of Bayou Pierre, just beyond the town. Wilson was experienced in such work, having built no less than seven such spans in the course of the march from Milliken's Bend, and besides he had plenty of materials at hand, in the form of nearby houses which he tore down and cannibalized. By midafternoon the job was finished, "a continuous raft 166 feet long, 12 feet wide, with three rows of large mill-beams lying across the current, and the intervals between them closely filled with buoyant timber; the whole firmly tied together by a cross-floor or deck of 2-inch stuff." So Wilson later described it, not without pride, adding that he had also provided side rails, corduroy approaches over quicksand, and abutments "formed by building a slight crib-work, and filling in with rails covered by sand." Grant was impressed, but he did not linger to admire the young staff colonel's handiwork. The second of McPherson's three divisions having arrived that morning, he was given the lead today, with orders to march eight miles northeast to Grindstone Ford, which he reached soon after dark. He was prevented from crossing at once because the fine suspension bridge had been destroyed at that point, but Wilson was again at hand and had it repaired by daylight of May 3, when McPherson pressed on over. Near Willow Springs, two miles beyond the stream, he encountered and dislodged a small hostile force which retreated toward Hankinson's Ferry, six miles north, where the main road to Vicksburg crossed the Big Black River. Instructing McPherson to keep up the march northward in pursuit, Grant detached a single brigade to accompany him westward in the direction of Grand Gulf.

McClernand, coming along behind McPherson, whom he was ordered to follow north, was alarmed to learn what Grant had done, striking off on his own like that, and sent a courier galloping after him with a warning: "Had you not better be careful lest you may personally fall in with the enemy on your way to Grand Gulf?" But Grant was not only anxious to reach that place as soon as possible, and thus reestablish contact with the navy and with Sherman, who was on the march down the Louisiana bank; he also believed that Bowen, chastened by yesterday's encounter, would fall back beyond the Big Black as soon as he discovered that his position on Bayou Pierre had been turned upstream. And in this the northern commander was quite right. Reinforcements had reached Bowen from Jackson and Vicksburg by now, but they only increased his force to about 9000, whereas he reckoned the present enemy strength at 30,000, augmented as it was by a full division put ashore at Bruinsburg the night before. When he learned, moreover, that this host had bridged both forks of Bayou Pierre to the east of Port Gibson and was headed for the crossings of the Big Black, deep in his rear, he lost no time in reaching the decision Grant expected. At midnight, finding that his staff advisers "concurred in my belief that I was compelled to abandon the post at Grand Gulf," he "then ordered the evacuation, the time for each command to move being so fixed as to avoid any delay or confusion." The retrograde movement went smoothly despite the need for haste. Bringing off all their baggage — which Pemberton, when informed of their predicament, had authorized them to abandon lest it slow their march, but which Bowen declared he was "determined to and did save" — the weary veterans and the newly arrived reinforcements set off northward, leaving the blufftop intrenchments, which they had defended so ably against the ironclad assault four days ago, yawning empty behind them in the early morning sunlight.

Soon after they disappeared over the northern horizon Porter arrived with four gunboats, intending to launch a new attack. He approached with caution, remembering his previous woes and fearing a rebel trick, but when he found the Grand Gulf works abandoned he did not let that diminish his claim for credit for their reduction. "We had a hard fight for these forts," he wrote Secretary Welles, "and it is with great pleasure that I report that the Navy holds the door to Vicksburg." He announced that his fire had torn the place to pieces, leaving it so covered with earth and debris that no one could tell at a glance what had been there before the bombardment. "Had the enemy succeeded in finishing these fortifications no fleet could have taken them," he declared, quite as if he had subdued the batteries in the nick of time, and added: "I hear nothing of our army as yet; was expecting to hear their guns as we advanced on the forts."

He heard from "our army" presently with the arrival of its commander, who had got word of the evacuation while en route from Grindstone Ford and had ridden ahead of the infantry with an escort of twenty troopers. Grant was glad to see the admiral, but most of all — after seven days on a borrowed horse, with "no change of underclothing, no meal except such as I could pick up sometimes at other headquarters, and no tent to cover me" — he was glad to avail himself of the admiral's facilities. After a hot bath, a change of underwear borrowed from one of the naval officers, and a square meal aboard the flagship, he got off a full report to Halleck on the events of the past four days. "Our victory has been most complete, and the enemy thoroughly demoralized," he wrote. Bowen's defense of Port Gibson had been "a very bold one and well carried out. My force, however, was too heavy for his, and composed of well-disciplined and hardy men who know no defeat and are not willing to learn what it is." After this unaccustomed flourish he got down to the matter at hand. "This army is in the finest health and spirits," he declared. "Since leaving Milliken's Bend they have marched as much by night as by day, through mud and rain, without tents or much other baggage, and on irregular rations, without a complaint and with less straggling than I have ever before witnessed.... I shall not bring my troops into this place, but immediately follow the enemy, and, if all promises as favorable hereafter as it does now, not stop until Vicksburg is in our possession."

He was on his own, however, in a way he had neither intended nor foreseen. His plan had been to use Grand Gulf as a base, accumulating a reserve of supplies and marking time with Sherman and McPherson, so to speak, while McClernand took his corps downriver to cooperate with Banks in the reduction of Port Hudson, after which the two would join him for a combined assault on Vicksburg. But he found waiting for him today at Grand Gulf a three-week-old letter from Banks, dated April 10 and headed Brashear City — 75 miles west of New Orleans and equally far south of Port Hudson — informing him of a change in procedure made necessary, according to the Massachusetts general, by unexpected developments in western Louisiana which would threaten his flank and rear, including New Orleans itself, if he moved due north from the Crescent City as originally planned. Instead, he intended to abolish this danger with an advance up the Teche and the Atchafalaya, clearing out the rebels around Opelousas before returning east to Baton Rouge for the operation against Port Hudson with 15,000 men. He hoped to open this new phase of the campaign next day, he wrote, and if all went as planned he would return to the Mississippi within a month — that is, by May 10 — at which time he would be ready to co-operate with Grant in their double venture. . . . Reading the letter, Grant experienced a considerable shock. He had expected Banks to have twice as many troops already in position for a quick slash at Port Hudson, to be followed by an equally rapid boat ride north to assist in giving Vicksburg the same treatment. Now all that went glimmering. Some 30,000 men poorer than he had counted on being, he was on his own: which on second thought had its advantages, since the Massachusetts general outranked him and by virtue of his seniority would get the credit, from the public as well as the government, for the reduction of both Confederate strongholds and the resultant clearing of the Mississippi all the way to the Gulf. Grant absorbed the shock and quickly made up his mind that he was better off without him. Banks having left him on his own, he would do the same for Banks. "To wait for his co-operation would have detained me at least a month," he subsequently wrote in explanation of his decision. "The reinforcements would not have reached 10,000 men after deducting casualties and necessary river guards at all high points close to the river for over 300 miles. The enemy would have strengthened his position and been reinforced by more men than Banks could have brought. I therefore determined to move independently of Banks, cut loose from my base, destroy the rebel force in rear of Vicksburg, and invest or capture the city."

So much he intended, though he had not yet decided exactly how he would go about it. One thing he knew, however, was that the change of plans called for an immediate speed-up of the accumulation of supplies, preliminary to launching his all-out drive on the rebel citadel two dozen air-line miles to the north. A look at the Central Mississippi interior, with its lush fields, its many grazing cattle, and its well-stocked plantation houses — "of a character equal to some of the finest villas on the Hudson," a provincial New York journalist called these last — had convinced him that the problem was less acute than he had formerly supposed. "This country will supply all the forage required for anything like an active campaign, and the necessary fresh beef," he informed Halleck. "Other supplies will have to be drawn from Milliken's Bend. This is a long and precarious route, but I have every confidence in succeeding in doing it." Accordingly, he ordered this supply line shortened, as soon as the river had fallen a bit, by the construction of a new road from Young's Point to a west-bank landing just below Warrenton. "Everything depends upon the promptitude with which our supplies are forwarded," he warned. He had already directed that two towboats make a third run past the Vicksburg guns with heavy-laden barges. "Do this with all expedition," he told the quartermaster at Milliken's Bend, "in 48 hours from receipt of orders if possible. Time is of immense importance." Hurlbut was ordered to forward substantial reinforcements from Memphis without delay, as well as to lay in a sixty-day surplus of rations, to be kept on hand for shipment downriver at short notice. To Sherman, hurrying south across the way, went instructions to collect 120 wagons en route, load them with 100,000 pounds of bacon, then pile on all the coffee, sugar, salt, and crackers they would hold. "It is unnecessary for me to remind you of the overwhelming importance of celerity in your movements," Grant told him, outlining the situation as he saw it now on this side of the river: "The enemy is badly beaten, greatly demoralized, and exhausted of ammunition. The road to Vicksburg is open. All we want now are men, ammunition, and hard bread. We can subsist our horses on the country, and obtain considerable supplies for our troops."

With all this paper work behind him, he left Grand Gulf at midnight and rode eastward under a full moon to rejoin McPherson, who had reached Hankinson's Ferry that afternoon and had already dispatched cavalry details to probe the opposite bank of the Big Black River. From his new headquarters Grant kept stressing the need for haste. "Every day's delay is worth 2000 men to the enemy," he warned a supply officer, and kept goading him with questions that called for specific answers: "How many teams have been loaded with rations and sent forward? I want to know as near as possible how we stand in every particular for supplies. How many wagons have you ferried over the river? How many are still to bring over? What teams have gone back for rations?" His impatience was such that he had no time for head-shaking or regrets. Learning on May 5 that one of the two towboats and all the barges had been lost the night before in attempting the moonlight run he had ordered, he dismissed the loss with the remark: "We will risk no more rations to run the Vicksburg batteries," and turned his attention elsewhere. This touch of bad luck was more than offset the following day by news that Sherman had reached Hard Times, freeing McPherson's third division from guard duty along the supply route, and was already in the process of crossing the river to Grand Gulf. The red-haired general was in excellent spirits, having learned that four newspaper reporters had been aboard the towboat that was lost. "They were so deeply laden with weighty matter that they must have sunk," he remarked happily, and added: "In our affliction we can console ourselves with the pious reflection that there are plenty more of the same sort."

One thing Grant did find time for, though, amid all his exertions at Hankinson's Ferry. On the 7th he issued a general order congratulating his soldiers for their May Day victory near Port Gibson, which he said extended "the long list of those previously won by your valor and endurance." He was proud of what they had accomplished so far in the campaign, he assured them, and proudest of all that they had endured their necessary privations without complaint. Then he closed on a note of exhortation. "A few days' continuance of the same zeal and constancy will secure to this army the crowning victory over the rebellion. More difficulties and privations are before us. Let us endure them manfully. Other battles are to be fought. Let us fight them bravely. A grateful country will rejoice at our success, and history will record it with immortal honor."

Pemberton at this stage was by no means "badly beaten." Neither was he "greatly demoralized," any more than Vicksburg's defenders were "exhausted of ammunition." Nor was the road to the city "open," despite Grant's suppositions in his May 3 note urging Sherman to hurry down to get in on the kill. It was true, on the other hand, that the southern commander had been acutely distressed by the news that the blue invaders were landing in force on the east bank of the river below Grand Gulf, for he saw only too clearly the dangers this involved. "Enemy movement threatens Jackson, and, if successful, cuts off Vicksburg and Port Hudson from the east," he wired Davis on May Day, before he knew the outcome of the battle for Port Gibson, and he followed this up next morning, when he learned that Bowen had withdrawn across Bayou Pierre, with advice to Governor Pettus that the state archives be removed from the capital for safekeeping; Grant most likely would be coming this way soon. Another appeal to Johnston for "large reinforcements" to meet the "completely changed character of defense," now that the Federals were established in strength on this side of the river, brought a repetition of yesterday's advice: "If Grant crosses, unite all your troops to beat him. Success will give back what was abandoned to win it."

If this proposed abandonment included Vicksburg, and presumably it did, Pemberton was not in agreement. He already had ordered all movable ordnance and ammunition sent to that place from all parts of the state, in preparation for a last-ditch fight if necessary, and he arrived in person the following day, about the same time Grant rode into Grand Gulf with a twenty-trooper escort. For all his original alarm, Pemberton felt considerably better now. Davis and Seddon had promised reinforcements from Alabama and South Carolina — 5000 were coming from Charleston by rail at once, the Secretary wired, with another 4000 to follow — and Sherman had withdrawn from in front of Haines Bluff, reducing by half the problem of the city's peripheral defense. Johnston moreover had agreed at last, now that Streight had been disposed of, to send some cavalry under Forrest to guard against future raids across the Tennessee line. Much encouraged, Pemberton telegraphed Davis: "With reinforcements and cavalry promised in North Mississippi, think we will be all right."

His new confidence was based on a reappraisal of the situation confronting him now that Bowen, with his approval, had fallen back across the Big Black River, which curved across his entire right front and center. Not only did this withdrawal make a larger number of troops available for the protection of a much smaller area; it also afforded him the interior lines, so that a direct attack from beyond the arc could be met with maximum strength by defenders fighting from prepared positions. Presumably Grant would avoid that, but Pemberton saw an even greater advantage proceeding from the concentration behind the curved shield of the Big Black. It greatly facilitated what he later called "my great object," which was "to prevent Grant from establishing a base on the Mississippi River, above Vicksburg." Until the invaders accomplished this they would be dependent for supplies on what could be run directly past the gun-bristled bluff, a risky business at best, or freighted down the opposite bank, along a single jerry-built road that was subject to all the ravages of nature. As Pemberton saw it, his opponent's logical course would be to extend his march up the left bank of the Big Black, avoiding the bloodshed that would be involved in attempting a crossing until he was well upstream, in position for an advance on Haines Bluff from the rear and the establishment there of a new base of supplies, assisted and protected by Porter's upper flotilla, which would have returned up the Yazoo to meet him. But the southern commander did not intend to stand idly by, particularly while the latter stages of the movement were in progress. "The farther north [Grant] advanced, toward my left, from his then base below, the weaker he became; the more exposed became his rear and flanks; the more difficult it became to subsist his army and obtain reinforcements." At the moment of greatest Union extension and exposure, the defenders — reinforced by then, their commander hoped, from all quarters of the Confederacy — would strike with all their strength at the enemy's flanks and rear, administering a sudden and stunning defeat to a foe for whom, given the time and place, defeat would mean disaster, perhaps annihilation. Such was the plan. And though there were obvious drawbacks — the region beyond the Big

Black, for example, would be exposed to unhindered depredations; critics would doubtless object, moreover, that Grant might adopt a different method of accomplishing his goal — Pemberton considered the possible consummation of his design well worth the risk. Having weighed the odds and assessed his opponent's probable intentions from his actions in the past, he was content to let the outcome test the validity of his insight into the mind of his adversary. "I am a northern man; I know my people," he was to say. Besides, he believed that the Federals, obliged to hold onto one base to the south while reaching out for another to the north, had little choice except to act as he predicted. It was true that in the interim they "might destroy Jackson and ravage the country," he admitted, "but that was a comparatively small matter. To take Vicksburg, to control the valley of the Mississippi, to sever the Confederacy, to ruin our cause, a base upon the eastern bank immediately above was absolutely necessary."

Whatever else was desirable in the conflict now about to be resumed, he knew he would need all the soldiers he could get for the close-up defense of the line on the Big Black. In this connection, at the same time he informed Richmond of the pending evacuation of Grand Gulf he requested permission to bring the so-far unthreatened garrison of Port Hudson north for a share in the coming struggle. "I think Port Hudson and Grand Gulf should be evacuated," he wired Davis on May 2, "and the whole force concentrated for defense of Vicksburg and Jackson." Accordingly, in conformity with Johnston's advice to "unite all your troops," ordered Major General Franklin Gardner, commanding the lower fortress, to strip the garrison to an absolute minimum and move with all the rest of the men to Jackson; those remaining behind would follow as soon as Richmond confirmed his request for total evacuation. On May 7, however, Davis replied that he approved of the withdrawal from Grand Gulf, but that "to hold both Vicksburg and Port Hudson is necessary to a connection with the Trans-Mississippi." So Pemberton countermanded the order to Gardner. He was to return at once to Port Hudson "and hold it to the last. President says both places must be held."

Such discouragement as this occasioned had been offset in advance, at least in part, by the defeat three nights ago of Grant's third attempt to run supplies downriver past the Vicksburg batteries. The sunken towboat and the flaming barges — not to mention the four Yankee journalists, who had not drowned, as Sherman had so fervently hoped, but had been fished out of the muddy water as prisoners of war — were evidence of improvement in the marksmanship of the gunners on the bluff, although it had to be conceded that the brilliant moonlight gave them an advantage they had lacked before. Another encouragement came soon afterwards from Johnston, who replied on May 8 to a report in which Pemberton explained his preparations for defense: "Disposition of troops, as far as understood, judicious; can be readily concentrated against Grant's army." If this was guarded, it was also approving, which was something altogether new from that direction. Then next day came the best news of all: Johnston himself would be coming soon to Vicksburg to inspirit the men and lend the weight of his genius to the defense of the Gibraltar of the West. Acting under instructions from Davis, Seddon ordered the general to proceed from Tullahoma "at once to Mississippi and take chief command of the forces, giving to those in the field, as far as practicable, the encouragement and benefit of your personal direction." Johnston was suffering at the time from a flare-up of his Seven Pines wound, but he replied without apparent hesitation: "I shall go immediately, although unfit for service." He left Tennessee next morning, May 10, having complied with the Secretary's further instructions to have "3000 good troops" follow him from Bragg's army as reinforcements for Pemberton.

Pemberton took new hope at the prospect of first-hand assistance from on high; now he could say, with a good deal more assurance than he had felt when he used the words the week before, "Think we will be all right." But there were flaws in the logic of his approach to the central problem, or at any rate errors in the conclusion to which that logic had led him. His assessment of Grant's intention was partly right, but it was also partly wrong: right, that is, in the conviction that what his opponent wanted and needed was a supply base above Vicksburg, but wrong as to how he would go about getting what he wanted. By now Grant had nine of his ten divisions across the Mississippi and had reached the final stage of his week-long build-up for an advance, though not in the direction Pemberton had supposed and planned for.

McPherson had been shifted eight miles east to Rocky Springs, leaving Hankinson's Ferry to be occupied by Sherman, two of whose three divisions were with him, while McClernand was in position along the road between those two points. In connection with the problem of supply, Grant had been collecting all the transportation he could lay hands on, horses, mules, oxen, and whatever rolled on wheels, ever since the Bruinsburg crossing. The result was a weird conglomeration of vehicles, ranging from the finest plantation carriages to ramshackle farm wagons, with surreys and buckboards thrown in for good measure, all piled to the dashboards and tailgates with supplies — mainly crates of ammunition and hardtack, the two great necessities for an army on the move — constantly shuttling back and forth between the Grand Gulf steamboat landing and Rocky Springs, where Grant had established headquarters near McPherson. Sherman, being farthest in the rear, had a close-up view of vehicular confusion that seemed to him to be building up to the greatest traffic snarl in history, despite the fact that there was still not transportation enough to supply more than a fraction of the army's needs. It was his conclusion that Grant's headlong impatience to be up and off was plunging him toward a logistic disaster. By May 9 he could put up with it no longer. "Stop all troops till your army is partially supplied with wagons, and then act as quickly as possible," he advised his chief, "for this road will be jammed as sure as life if you attempt to supply 50,000 men by one single road." The prompt reply from Rocky Springs gave the redhead the shock of his military life. Previously he had known scarcely more of Grant's future plans than Pemberton knew from beyond the Big Black River, but suddenly the veil of secrecy was lifted enough to give him considerably more than a glimmer of what he had never suspected until now. "I do not calculate upon the possibility of supplying the army with full rations from Grand Gulf," Grant told him. "I know it will be impossible without constructing additional roads. What I do expect, however, is to get up what rations of hard bread, coffee, and salt we can, and make the country furnish the balance."

This clearly implied, if it did not actually state, that he intended to launch an invasion, much as Cortez and Scott had done in Mexico, without a base from which to draw supplies. And so he did. Back in December, returning through North Mississippi to Memphis after the destruction of his forward depot at Holly Springs, he had discovered that his troops could live quite easily off the country by the simple expedient of taking what they wanted from the farmers in their path. "This taught me a lesson," he later remarked, and now the lesson was about to be applied. Moreover, the success of Grierson, whose troopers had lacked for nothing in the course of a 600-mile ride that had "knocked the heart out of the state" — so Grant himself declared in passing along to Washington the news of the raid — was a nearer and more recent example of what might be accomplished along those lines. For his own part, in the course of his march from Bruinsburg through Port Gibson to Rocky Springs, he had observed that "beef, mutton, poultry, and forage were found in abundance," along with "quite a quantity of bacon and molasses." What was more, every rural commissary "had a run of stone, propelled by mule power, to grind corn for the owners and their slaves. All these [could be] kept running ... day and night ... at all plantations covered by the troops." He felt sure there would be enough food and forage of one sort or another for all his men and animals, leaving room in the makeshift train for ammunition and such hard-to-get items as salt and coffee, provided there were no long halts during which the local supplies would be exhausted. All that was required was that he keep his army moving, and that was precisely what he intended to do, from start to finish, for tactical as well as logistic reasons. His 45,000 effectives were roughly twice as many as Pemberton had behind the curved shield of the Big Black River; he was convinced that he could whip him in short order with a frontal attack. "If Blair were up now," he told Sherman, who was still awaiting the arrival of the division that had feinted at Haines Bluff, "I believe we could be in Vicksburg in seven days." But that would leave some 10,000 rebels alive in his rear at Jackson, which was connected by rail not only to Vicksburg but also to the rest of the Confederacy, so that reinforcements could be hurried there from Bragg and the East until they outnumbered him as severely as he had outnumbered Pemberton, thus turning the tables on him. His solution was to strike both north and east, severing the rail connection between Jackson and Vicksburg near the Big Black crossing, while simultaneously closing in on the capital. He would capture the inferior force at that place, if possible, but at any rate he would knock it out of commission as a transportation hub or a rallying point; after which he would be free to turn on Vicksburg unmolested, approaching it from the east and north, and thus either take the citadel by storm or else establish a base on the Yazoo from which to draw supplies while starving the cut-off defenders into surrender.

Sherman had much of this explained to him when he rode over to Rocky Springs that afternoon, in considerable perturbation, for what he called "a full conversation" with the army commander. But his doubts persisted, much as they had done after he had agreed to stage the Haines Bluff demonstration. "He is satisfied that he will succeed in his plan," he said of Grant in a letter urging Blair to hasten his crossing from Hard Times, "and, of course, we must do our full share." Though he would "of course" co-operate fully in carrying out his chief's design, he wanted it understood from the start — and placed indelibly on the record — that he was doing so with something less than enthusiasm and against his better judgment. Grant by now was accustomed to his lieutenant's mercurial ups and downs, and he did not let them discourage him or influence his thinking. The following day, May 10 — the Sunday Joe Johnston left Tullahoma for Jackson — he heard again from Banks, who informed him, in a letter written four days ago at Opelousas, that he was making steady progress up the Teche, clearing out the rebels on his flank, and expected to turn east presently for Port Hudson. "By the 25th, probably, and by the 1st certainly, we will be there," he promised. Convinced more than ever that he had done right not to wait for Banks, Grant replied that he was going ahead on his own. Previously he had told him nothing of his plans, not even that he would not be meeting him; but now he did, on the off-chance that Banks might be of assistance. "Many days cannot elapse before the battle will begin which is to decide the fate of Vicksburg," he wrote, "but it is impossible to predict how long it may last. I would urgently request, therefore, that you join me or send all the force you can spare to co-operate in the great struggle for opening the Mississippi River." Similarly, at this near-final moment, he got off a dispatch to the general-in-chief, announcing that he was leaving Banks to fend for himself against Port Hudson while the Army of the Tennessee cut loose from its base at Grand Gulf and plunged inland in order to come upon Vicksburg from the rear. "I knew well that Halleck's caution would lead him to disapprove of this course," he subsequently explained; "but it was the only one that gave any chance of success." Besides, such messages were necessarily slow in transmission, having to be taken overland from Hard Times to Milliken's Bend, then north by steamboat all the way to Cairo before they could be put on the wire, and Grant saw a certain advantage in this arrangement. "The time it would take to communicate with Washington and get a reply would be so great that I could not be interfered with until it was demonstrated whether my plan was practicable."

This done, he turned to putting the final touches to the plan he had evolved. McClernand would move up the left bank of the Big Black, guarding the crossings as he went, and strike beyond Fourteen Mile Creek at Edwards Station, on the railroad sixteen miles east of Vicks-

burg. McPherson would move simultaneously against Jackson, and Sherman would be on call to assist either column, depending on which ran into the stiffest resistance. On the 11th, Grant advanced all three to their jump-off positions: McClernand on the left, as near Fourteen Mile Creek as possible "without bringing on a general engagement," Sherman in the center, beyond Cayuga, and McPherson on the right, near Utica. "Move your command tonight to the next crossroads if there is water," Grant told McPherson, "and tomorrow with all activity into Raymond. . . . We must fight the enemy before our rations fail, and we are equally bound to make our rations last as long as possible."

Before dawn the following morning, May 12, they were off. The second phase of the campaign designed for the capture of Vicksburg was under way.

Advancing through a rugged and parched region, McClernand's troops found that the only way they could quench their thirst, aggravated by the heat of the day and the dust of the country roads, was to drive the opposing cavalry beyond Fourteen Mile Creek, which was held by a rebel force covering Edwards Station, some four miles to the north. By midafternoon they had done just that. "Our men enjoyed both the skirmish and the water," the commander of the lead division re-

ported. Sherman, coming up on the right, accomplished this same purpose by throwing "a few quick rounds of cannister" at the gray vedettes,
who promptly scampered out of range. Pioneers rebuilt a bridge the
Confederates had burned as they fell back, and several regiments crossed
the creek at dusk, establishing a bridgehead while the two corps went
into bivouac on the south bank, prepared to advance on Edwards in the
morning.

But that was not to be. McPherson, when within two miles of
Raymond at 11 o'clock that morning, had encountered an enemy force
of undetermined strength, "judiciously posted, with two batteries of artillery so placed as to sweep the road and a bridge over which it was
necessary to pass." This was in fact a single brigade of about 4000 men,
recently arrived from Port Hudson under Brigadier General John
Gregg, who had come out from Jackson the day before, under orders
from Pemberton to cover the southwest approaches to the capital. Informed that the Federals were moving on Edwards, over near the Big
Black River, he assumed that the blue column marching toward him
from Utica was only "a brigade on a marauding excursion," and he was
determined not only to resist but also, if possible, to slaughter the marauders. The result was a sharp and — considering the odds — surprisingly hot contest, in which seven butternut regiments took on a whole
Union corps. McPherson threw Logan's division against the wooded enemy position, only to have it bloodily repulsed. While the other two
were coming forward, Logan rallied in time to frustrate a determined
counterattack and follow it up with one of his own. By now, however,
having learned what it was he had challenged — and having suffered
514 casualties, as compared to McPherson's 442 — Gregg had managed
to disengage and was withdrawing through Raymond. Five miles to the
east, one third of the distance to Jackson, he met Brigadier General
W. H. T. Walker, who had marched out to join him with a thousand
men just arrived from South Carolina. Gregg halted and faced about,
ready to try his hand again; but there was no further action that day.
Entering Raymond at 5 o'clock, McPherson decided to stop for the
night. "The rough and impracticable nature of the country, filled with
ravines and dense undergrowth, prevented anything like an effective use
of artillery or a very rapid pursuit," he explained in a sundown dispatch
to the army commander.

Grant was seven miles away, at the Dillon plantation on Fourteen
Mile Creek with Sherman, and when he learned the outcome of the battle whose guns he had heard booming, five miles off at first, then fading
eastward into silence, he revised his over-all plan completely. Edwards
could wait. If Jackson was where the enemy was — and the determined
resistance at Raymond seemed to indicate as much — he would go after
him in strength; he would risk no halfway job in snuffing out a segment
of the rebel army concentrated near a rail hub that gave it access to

reinforcements from all quarters of the South. Accordingly, at 9.15 he sent orders assigning all three of his corps commanders new objectives for tomorrow and prescribing that each would begin his march "at daylight in the morning." McPherson would move against Clinton, on the railroad nine miles north, then eastward that same distance along the right-of-way to Jackson. Sherman would turn due east from his present bivouac at Dillon, swinging through Raymond so as to come upon the objective from the south. McClernand, after detaching one division to serve as a rear guard in the event that the Confederates at Vicksburg attempted to interfere by crossing the Big Black, would come along behind Sherman and McPherson, prepared to move in support of either or both as they closed in on the Mississippi capital. Such were Grant's instructions, and presently he had cause to believe that he had improvised aright. Two days ago McPherson had passed along a rumor that "some of the citizens in the vicinity of Utica say Beauregard is at or near Jackson." If the Charleston hero was there it was practically certain he had not come alone. And now there arrived a second dispatch from McPherson, headed 11 p.m. and relaying another rumor that heavy Confederate reinforcements were moving against him out of Jackson, intending to fight again at Raymond soon after sunup. He did not know how much fact there was in this, he added, but he would "try to be prepared for them." Grant had confidence in McPherson, especially when he was forewarned as he was now, and did not bother to reply. Besides, whether it was true or false that the rebels were marching in force to meet him west of their capital, he already had made provisions to counter such a threat by ordering all but one of his ten divisions, some 40,000 men in all, to move toward a convergence on that very objective "at daylight in the morning."

All three columns moved on schedule. By early afternoon McPherson was in Clinton, nine miles from Jackson, and Sherman was six miles beyond Raymond, about the same distance from the Mississippi capital. A lack of determined resistance seemed to indicate that last night's rumor of heavy reinforcements was in error, and this, plus reports from scouts that Pemberton had advanced in force to the vicinity of Edwards, caused Grant to modify his strategy again. McPherson was instructed to spend the rest of the day wrecking the railroad west of Clinton, then resume his eastward march at first light tomorrow, May 14, tearing up more track as he went. Sherman, half a dozen miles to the south, would regulate his progress so that both corps would approach the Jackson defenses simultaneously. McClernand, instead of following along to furnish unneeded support, would turn north at Raymond and march on Bolton Depot, eight miles west of Clinton, occupying a strong position in case Pemberton attempted a farther advance along the railroad toward his threatened capital. There was of course the possibility that the Confederate commander might lunge southward,

across Fourteen Mile Creek, with the intention of attacking the Federal
army's rear and severing its connection with Grand Gulf: in which case
he would be removing himself from the campaign entirely, at least for
the period of time required for him to discover that he had plunged into
a vacuum. For Grant not only had no supply line; he had no rear,

either, in the sense that Pemberton might suppose. Such rear as
Grant had he had brought with
him, embodied in McClernand,
who now had orders to take up
a position at Bolton, astride the
railroad about midway between
Vicksburg and Jackson, facing
west. Moreover, once the capital had fallen and the blue army
turned its attention back to its
prime objective, the blufftop
citadel forty-five miles away,
what was now its rear would

automatically become its front; McClernand, already in position for an
advance, once more would take the lead, with Sherman and McPherson
in support. For all the improvisatorial nature of his tactics, Grant, like
any good chess player, was keeping a move or two ahead of the game. ·

By midmorning of May 14, slogging eastward under a torrential
rain that quickly turned the dusty roads into troughs of mud, Sherman
was within three miles of Jackson. At 10 o'clock, while peering through
the steely curtain of the downpour to examine the crude fortifications to
his front, he heard the welcome boom of guns off to the north; Mc-
Pherson was on schedule and in place. While Sherman reconnoitered
toward Pearl River for an opening on the flank, McPherson deployed
for a time-saving frontal attack, to be launched astride the railroad. He
waited an hour in the rain, lest the cartridge boxes of his troops be filled
with water, like buckets under a tap, when they lifted the flaps to remove their paper-wrapped ammunition, and then at 11 o'clock, the rain
having slacked to a drizzle at last, ordered his lead division forward
across fields of shin-deep mud. The rebel pickets faded back to the shelter of their intrenchments, laying down a heavy fire that stopped the
bluecoats in their tracks and flung them on their faces in the mud. By
now it was noon. McPherson impatiently reformed his staggered line,
having lost an even 300 men, and sent the survivors forward again. This
time they found the rebel infantry gone. Only a handful of cannoneers
had remained behind to serve the seven guns left on line and be captured by McPherson's jubilant soldiers. Sherman had the same experience, two miles to the south, except that he found ten guns in the abandoned works he had outflanked. Not only were his spoils thus greater

than McPherson's; his casualties were fewer, numbering only 32. The Confederates, under Gregg and Walker, who had fallen back from east of Raymond the night before, had lost just over 200 men before pulling out of their trenches to make a hairbreadth getaway to the north. The Battle of Jackson was over, such as it was, and Grant had taken the Mississippi capital at a bargain price of 48 killed, 273 wounded, and 11 missing.

He was there to enjoy in person the first fruits of today's sudden and inexpensive victory. Sherman, riding in from the south — and noting with disapproval some "acts of pillage" already being committed by early arrived bluecoats under the influence "of some bad rum found concealed in the stores of the town" — was summoned by a courier to the Bowman House, Jackson's best hotel, where he found Grant and McPherson celebrating the capture of Jeff Davis's own home-state capital, the third the South had lost in the past two years. From the lobby they had a view, through a front window, of the State House where the rebel President had predicted, less than six months ago, that his fellow Mississippians would "meet and hurl back these worse than vandal hordes." Quick as the two generals had been to reach the heart of town, riding in ahead of the main body, they were slower than the army commander's young son Fred. His mother and brother had gone back North after the second running of the Vicksburg batteries, but Fred had stayed on to enjoy the fun that followed, wearing his father's dress sword and sash — which the general himself had little use for, and almost never wore — as badges of rank. Grant, an indulgent parent, later explained that the boy "caused no trouble either to me or his mother, who was at home. He looked out for himself and was in every battle of the campaign. His age, then not quite thirteen, enabled him to take in all he saw, and then to retain a recollection of it that would not be possible in more mature years." Fred's recollection of the capture of Jackson was saddened, however, by his failure to get a souvenir he badly wanted. He and a friendly journalist had seen from the outskirts of town a large Confederate flag waving from its staff atop the golden dome of the capitol. Mounted, they hurried ahead of the leading infantry column, tethered their horses in front of the big stone building, and raced upstairs — only to meet, on his way down, "a ragged, muddy, begrimed cavalryman" descending with the rebel banner tucked beneath his arm. For Fred, a good measure of the glory of Jackson's capture had departed, then and there.

Grant could sympathize with the boy's disappointment, but he had just been handed something considerably more valuable to him than the lost flag or even the seventeen guns that had been taken in the engagement that served as prelude to the occupation of the capital. Charles Dana arrived in mid-celebration with a dispatch just delivered by a courier from Grand Gulf. Signed by the Secretary of War and dated

May 5, it had been sent in response to a letter in which Dana had given him a summation of Grant's plan "to lose no time in pushing his army toward the Big Black and Jackson, threatening both and striking at either, as is most convenient. . . . He will disregard his base and depend on the country for meat and even for bread." Now Stanton replied:

> General Grant has full and absolute authority to enforce his own commands, to remove any person who, by ignorance, inaction, or any cause, interferes with or delays his operations. He has the full confidence of the Government, is expected to enforce his authority, and will be firmly and heartily supported; but he will be responsible for any failure to exert his powers. You may communicate this to him.

There was more here than met the eye. Stanton of course had authority over Halleck, so that if — or rather, as Grant believed from past experience, *when* — the time came for the general-in-chief to protest that Grant had disobeyed orders by abandoning Banks and striking out on his own, he would find — if indeed he had not found already — that Stanton, and presumably Lincoln as well, had approved in advance the course Grant had adopted. Nor was that all. Dana, having long since taken a position alongside the army commander in his private war against McClernand, had been keeping the Secretary copiously posted on the former congressman's military shortcomings, large and small, and feeling him out as to what the administration's reaction would be when Grant decided the time had come for him to swing the ax. Now the answer was at hand. Grant not only had "full and absolute authority" to sit in judgment; he would in fact be held "responsible for any failure to exert his powers" in all matters pertaining to what he considered his army's welfare and the progress of what Stanton called his "operations," whether against the rebels or McClernand.

It was no wonder then — protected as he now was from the wrath of his immediate superior, as well as from the machinations of his ranking subordinate — that he was in good spirits during the hotel-lobby victory celebration. All around him, meanwhile, the town was in a turmoil. "Many citizens [had] fled at our approach," one Federal witness later recalled, "abandoning houses, stores, and all their personal property, without so much as locking their doors. The Negroes, poor whites, and it must be admitted some stragglers and bummers from the ranks of the Union army, carried off thousands of dollars worth of property from houses, homes, shops and stores, until some excuse was given for the charge of 'northern vandalism,' which was afterwards made by the South. The streets were filled with people, white and black, who were carrying away all the stolen goods they could stagger under, without the slightest attempt at concealment and without let or hindrance from citizens or soldiers. . . . In addition . . . the convicts of the penitentiary, who had been released by their own authorities, set all the buildings connected with that prison on fire, and their lurid flames added to the holocaust elsewhere prevailing." He observed that "many calls were made upon [Grant] by citizens asking for guards to protect their private property, some of which perhaps were granted, but by far the greater number [of these petitioners] were left to the tender mercies of their Confederate friends."

After all, Grant had not brought his army here to protect the private property of men in revolution against the government that army represented; nor, for that matter, had it ever been his custom to deny his soldiers a chance at relaxation they had earned, even though that relaxation sometimes took a rather violent form. His purpose, rather, was to destroy all public property such as might be of possible comfort to the Confederacy. This applied especially to the railroads, the wrecking of which would abolish the Mississippi capital as a transportation hub, at least through the critical period just ahead. But that other facilities were not neglected was observed by a witness who testified that "foundries, machine shops, warehouses, factories, arsenals, and public stores were fired as fast as flames could be kindled." Sherman was the man for this work, Grant decided, and he gave him instructions "to remain in Jackson until he destroyed that place as a railroad center and manufacturing city of military supplies."

Meanwhile there was the campaign to get on with; Pemberton was hovering to the west, already on the near side of the Big Black, and beyond him there was Vicksburg, the true object of all this roundabout marching and such bloodshed as had so far been involved. McPherson was told to get his corps in hand and be prepared to set out for Bolton Depot at first light tomorrow to support McClernand, whose corps was no longer the army's rear guard, but rather its advance. Having attended to this, Grant joined Sherman for a little relaxation of his own; namely, a tour of inspection to determine which of the local business establishments would be spared or burned. In the course of the tour they came upon a cloth factory which, as Grant said later, "had not ceased work on account of the battle nor for the entrance of Yankee troops." Outside the building "an immense amount of cotton" was stacked in bales; inside, the looms were going full tilt, tended by girl operatives, weaving bolts of tent cloth plainly stamped C.S.A. No one seemed to notice the two generals, who watched for some time in amused admiration of such oblivious industry. "Finally," Grant said afterwards, "I told Sherman I thought they had done work enough. The operatives were told they could leave and take with them what cloth they could carry. In a few minutes cotton and factory were in a blaze."

This done, Grant returned to the Bowman House for his first

night's sleep on a mattress in two weeks. Joe Johnston, he was told, had occupied the same room the night before.

✗ 3 ✗

Johnston — not Beauregard, as rumor had had it earlier — had arrived at dusk the day before, at the end of a grueling three-day train ride from Tennessee by way of Atlanta, Montgomery, Mobile, and Meridian, only to find the Mississippi capital seething with reports of heavy Union columns advancing from the west. As night closed in, a hard rain began to fall, shrouding the city and deepening the Virginian's gloom still further: as was shown in a wire he got off to Seddon after dark. "I arrived this evening finding the enemy's force between this place and General Pemberton, cutting off communication. I am too late." To Pemberton, still on the far side of the Big Black, he sent a message advising quick action on that general's part. To insure delivery, three copies were forwarded by as many couriers. "I have lately arrived, and learn that Major General Sherman is between us, with four divisions, at Clinton," Johnston wrote. "It is important to re-establish communications, that you may be reinforced. If practicable, come up in his rear at once. To beat such a detachment would be of immense value. The troops here could cooperate. All the strength you can quickly assemble should be brought. Time is all important."

He had at Jackson, he presently discovered, only two brigades of about 6000 men with which to oppose the 25,000 Federals who were knocking at the western gates next morning. After a sharp, brief skirmish and the sacrifice of seventeen guns to cover a withdrawal, he retreated seven miles up the Canton road to Tugaloo, where he halted at nightfall, unpursued, and sent another message to Pemberton, from whom he had heard nothing since his arrival, informing him that the capital had been evacuated. He was expecting another "12,000 or 13,000" troops from the East, he said, and "as soon as [these] reinforcements are all up, they must be united to the rest of the army. I am anxious to see a force assembled that may be able to inflict a heavy blow upon the enemy.... If prisoners tell the truth, the force at Jackson must be half of Grant's army. It would decide the campaign to beat it, which can only be done by concentrating, especially when the remainder of the eastern troops arrive." He himself could do little or nothing until these men reached him, reducing the odds to something within reason, but he did not think that Pemberton should neglect any opportunity Grant afforded meanwhile, particularly in regard to his lines of supply and communication. "Can he supply himself from the Mississippi?" Johnston asked. "Can you not cut him off from it, and above all, should he be compelled to fall back for want of supplies, beat him?"

This last was in accord with Pemberton's own decision, already arrived at before the second message was received. The first, delivered by one of the three couriers that morning at Bovina Station, nine miles east of Vicksburg, had taken him greatly by surprise. He had expected Johnston to come to his assistance in defense of the line along or just in front of the Big Black; yet here that general was, requesting him "if practicable" to come to *his* assistance by marching against the enemy's rear at Clinton, some twenty miles away. Pemberton replied that he would "move at once with the whole available force," explaining however that this included only 17,500 troops at best, since the remaining 9000 under his command were required to man the Warrenton-Vicksburg-Haines Bluff defenses, as well as the principal crossings of the Big Black, which otherwise would remain open in his rear, exposing the Gibraltar of the West to sudden capture by whatever roving segment of the rampant blue host happened to lunge in that direction. "In directing this move," he felt obliged to add, by way of protest, "I do not think you fully comprehend the position Vicksburg will be left in; but I comply at once with your request."

So he said. However, when he rode forward to Edwards, where his mobile force of three divisions under Loring, Stevenson, and Bowen was posted four miles east of the Big Black, he learned that a Union column, reportedly five divisions strong — it was in fact McClernand's corps, with Blair attached as guard for the wagon train — was at Raymond, in position for a northward advance on Bolton. If Pemberton marched on Clinton, as Johnston suggested, ignoring this threat to his right flank as he moved eastward along the railroad, he would not only be leaving Vicksburg and the remaining two divisions under Major Generals M. L. Smith and John H. Forney in grave danger of being gobbled up while his back was turned; he would also be exposing his eastbound force to destruction at the hands of the other half of the Northern army. Perplexed by this dilemma, and mindful of some advice received two days ago from Richmond that he "add conciliation to the discharge of duty" — "Patience in listening to suggestions ... is sometimes rewarded," Davis had added — he decided the time had come for him to call a council of war, something he had never done before in all his thirty years of military service. Assembling the general officers of the three divisions at Edwards Station shortly after noon, he laid Johnston's message before them and outlined the tactical problems it posed. Basically, what he had to deal with was a contradiction of orders from above. As he understood the President's wishes, he was not to risk losing Vicksburg by getting too far from it, whereas Johnston was suggesting a junction of their forces near Jackson, forty miles away, in order to engage what he called a "detachment" of four — in fact, five — divisions, without reference to or apparent knowledge of the five-division column now at Raymond, both of which outnumbered the Confederates at Edwards. Pemberton, on the other hand, did not strictly agree with either of his two superiors, preferring to await attack in a prepared position near or behind the Big Black River, with a chance of following up a repulse with a counterattack designed to cut off and annihilate the foe. These three views could not be reconciled, but neither did he consider that any one of them could be ignored; so that, like the nation at large, this Northerner who sided with the South was torn and divided against himself. That was his particular nightmare in this nightmare interlude of his country's history. According to an officer on his staff, the Pennsylvanian's trouble now and in the future was that he made "the capital mistake of trying to harmonize instructions from his superiors diametrically opposed to each other, and at the same time to bring them into accord with his own judgment, which was averse to the plans of both."

Nor was the council of much assistance to him in finding a way around the impasse. Though a majority of the participants favored complying with Johnston's suggestion that the two forces be united, they were obliged to admit that it could not be accomplished by a direct march on Clinton, which was plainly an invitation to disaster. Meanwhile Pemberton's own views, as he told Johnston later, "were strongly expressed as unfavorable to any advance which would remove me from my base, which was and is Vicksburg." Apparently he limited himself to this negative contention. But finally Loring — known as "Old Blizzards" since his and Tilghman's spirited repulse of the Yankee gunboats above Greenwood — suggested an alternate movement, southeast nine miles to Dillon, which he believed would sever Grant's connection with Grand Gulf and thus force him either to withdraw, for lack of supplies, or else to turn and fight at a disadvantage in a position of Pemberton's choice. Stevenson agreed, along with others, and Pemberton, though he disliked the notion of moving even that much farther from Vicksburg, "did not, however, see fit to put my own judgment and opinions so far in opposition as to prevent a movement altogether." He approved the suggestion, apparently for lack of having anything better to offer, and adjourned the council after giving the generals instructions to be ready to march at dawn. At 5.40, on the heels of the adjournment, he got off a message informing Johnston of his intentions. "I shall move as early tomorrow morning as practicable with a column of 17,000 men," he wrote, explaining the exact location of Dillon so that Johnston would have no trouble finding it on a map which was enclosed. "The object is to cut the enemy's communications and to force him to attack me, as I do not consider my force sufficient to justify an attack on the enemy in position or to attempt to cut my way to Jackson."

Johnston received this at 8.30 next morning, May 15, by which time he had withdrawn another three miles up the Canton road, still farther from the intended point of concentration at Clinton. Though the message showed that Pemberton had anticipated the Virginian's still unreceived suggestion that he attempt to "cut [Grant] off from [the Mississippi]," Johnston no longer favored such a movement. "Our being compelled to leave Jackson makes your plan impracticable," he replied, and repeated — despite Pemberton's objection to being drawn still farther from his base — his preference for an eastward march by the mobile force from Vicksburg: "The only mode by which we can unite is by your moving directly to Clinton, informing me, that [I] may move to that point with about 6000 troops. I have no means of estimating the enemy's force at Jackson. The principal officers here differ very widely, and I fear he will fortify if time is left him. Let me hear from you immediately."

Evidently Johnston believed that Grant was going to hole up in the Mississippi capital and thus allow him time to effect a junction between the Vicksburg troops and his own, including the "12,000 or 13,000" reinforcements expected any day now from the East. If so, he was presently disabused. A reply from Pemberton, written early the following morning but not delivered until after dark, informed him that the advance on Dillon — badly delayed anyhow by the need for building a bridge across a swollen creek — had been abandoned, in accordance with his wishes, and the direction of march reversed. It was Pemberton's intention, as explained in the message, to move north of the railroad, swing wide through Brownsville to avoid the mass of Federals reported to be near Bolton, and converge on Clinton as instructed. "The order of countermarch has been issued," he wrote, and followed a description of his proposed route with the words: "I am thus particular, so that you may be able to make a junction with this army."

The Vicksburg commander at last had abandoned his objections to what Johnston had called "the only mode by which we can unite." He was, or soon would be, moving east toward his appointed destination. But there was an ominous postscript to the message, written in evident haste and perhaps alarm: "Heavy skirmishing is now going on to my front."

What that portended Johnston did not know; but Grant did. Before he retired to the hotel room his adversary had occupied the night before the fall of Jackson, he received from McPherson one of the three copies of Johnston's message urging Pemberton to "come up in [Sherman's] rear at once." This windfall was the result of a ruse worked some months ago by Hurlbut, who banished from Memphis, with considerable fanfare, a citizen found guilty of "uttering disloyal and threatening sentiments," though he was in secret, as Hurlbut knew, a thoroughly loyal Union man. The expulsion, along with his continued expression of secessionist views after his removal to the Mississippi capital, won him the sympathy and admiration of the people there: so much so,

indeed, that he was one of the three couriers entrusted with copies of
Johnston's urgent message. He delivered it, however, not to Pemberton
but to McPherson, who passed it promptly along to Grant. "Time is all
important," the Virginian had written. Grant agreed. By first light next
morning, May 15, McPherson was marching west from the capital, leaving Sherman to accomplish its destruction while he himself moved toward a junction with McClernand, who had been instructed simultaneously by Grant: "Turn all your forces toward Bolton station, and
make all dispatch in getting there. Move troops by the most direct road
from wherever they may be on the receipt of this order."

McPherson's three divisions had seventeen miles to go, and Mc-
Clernand's four — five, including Blair — were variously scattered,
from Raymond back to Fourteen Mile Creek. Each corps got one division to Bolton by late afternoon — Hovey and Logan, in that order —
while the others camped along the roads at sundown. Carr and Osterhaus were three miles south, with A. J. Smith between them and Raymond, where Blair was. Brigadier Generals John McArthur and
Marcellus Crocker, commanding McPherson's other two divisions, were
bivouacked beside the railroad leading back to Clinton. Riding out from
Jackson to that point before nightfall, Grant ordered McClernand to
move on Edwards in the morning, supported by McPherson, but
warned him "to watch for the enemy and not bring on an engagement
unless he felt very certain of success." The fog of war, gathering again
to obscure the Confederate purpose, had provoked this note of caution;
but it was dispersed once more at 5 o'clock next morning, when two
Union-sympathizing employes of the Vicksburg-Jackson Railroad were
brought to Grant at Clinton. They had passed through Pemberton's
army in the night, they said, and could report that it was moving east
of Edwards with a strength of about 25,000 men. Though this was in
fact some 7500 high, it was still some 10,000 fewer than Grant had on
hand. But he was taking no unavoidable chances. Deciding to ignore
Johnston, who by now was a day's march north of Jackson at Calhoun
Station, he ordered Sherman to "put one division with an ammunition
train on the road at once, with directions to its commander to march
with all possible speed until he comes upon our rear." The remaining
division was to hurry its demolition work and follow along as soon as
might be. The orders to McClernand and McPherson were unaltered; all
that was changed by this second dispersal of the war fog was the weight
of the blow about to be delivered. Now that he knew Pemberton's
strength and had him spotted, Grant intended to hit him with everything he had.

At about the time the railroad men were telling all they knew,
McClernand started forward in high spirits. "My corps, again, led the
advance," he was to say proudly in a letter giving his friend Lincoln an
account of the campaign. Such was indeed the case. Three roads led

west from the vicinity of Bolton to a junction east of Edwards, and McClernand used all three: Hovey on the one to the north, Osterhaus and Carr on the one in the middle, and Smith on the one to the south. Blair followed Smith, and McPherson's three divisions followed Hovey. Rebel cavalry was soon encountered, gray phantoms who fired and scampered out of range while the blue skirmishers flailed the woods with bullets. Then at 7.30, five miles short of Edwards, Smith came upon a screen of butternut pickets and dislodged them, exposing a four-gun battery, which he silenced. He wanted to plunge on, despite the signs that the high ground ahead was occupied in strength, but McClernand told him to hold what he had till Blair came up to keep his exposed left flank from being turned. Immediately on the heels of this, a rattle of gunfire from the north signified that Osterhaus and Hovey had also come upon johnnies to their front. McClernand inspected the rebel position as best he could from a distance and, finding it formidable, decided to hang on where he was until the situation could be developed. Having obeyed Grant's instructions "to watch for the enemy," he was also mindful of the injunction "not [to] bring on an engagement unless he felt very certain of success." At this point, with his various columns a mile or two apart and facing a wooded ridge a-swarm with graybacks, he was not feeling very certain about anything at all. What he mainly felt was lonely.

Countermarching in obedience to the message received early that morning from Johnston, Pemberton had been warned by his outriders of the Union host advancing westward along the three roads from Bolton and Raymond. When this danger was emphasized by the "heavy skirmishing" mentioned in the postscript to his reply that he was moving north and east toward a junction at Clinton, he knew he had a fight on his hands, wanted or not, and to avoid the risk of being caught in motion, strung out on the road to Brownsville, he hastily put his troops in position for receiving the attack he knew was coming. Whether his choice of ground was "by accident or design," as Grant ungenerously remarked, there could be no doubt that Pemberton chose well. Just south of the railroad and within a broad northward loop of rain-swollen Baker's Creek, a seventy-foot eminence known as Champion Hill — so called because it was on a plantation belonging to a family of that name — caused the due-west road from Bolton to veer south around its flank, joining the middle road in order to cross a timbered ridge that extended southward for three miles, past the lower of the three roads along which the enemy was advancing. Pemberton placed Stevenson's division on the hill itself, overlooking the direct approach from Bolton, and Bowen's and Loring's divisions along the ridge, blocking the other two approaches. Here, in an opportune position of great natural strength, he faced as best he could the consequences of his reluctant and belated compliance with his superior's repeated suggestion that he abandon the security of his prepared lines, along and just in front of the Big Black, for an attack on the Federal "detachment" supposed to be at Clinton. Now, however, as the thing turned out, it was Pemberton who was about to be attacked, a dozen miles short of his assigned objective. And here, precisely midway between Vicksburg and Jackson, both of which were twenty-two miles away, was fought what at least one prominent western-minded historian was to call "the most decisive battle of the Civil War."

Grant did not much like the look of things when he came riding out from Bolton and reached the front, where the road veered south beyond the Champion house, to find Hovey exchanging long-range shots with the enemy on the tall hill just ahead. It seemed to him, as he said later, that the rebels "commanded all the ground in range." However, unlike McClernand on the two roads to the south, he was not content to hold his own while waiting for the situation to develop more or less of its own accord. Logan's division having arrived, he sent it to the right, to prolong the line and feel for an opening in that direction. This was about 10 o'clock; he preferred to wait for Crocker to come up and lend the weight of McPherson's second division to the attack. But Hovey by now was hotly engaged, taking punishment from the batteries on the height and protesting that he must either go forward or fall back. Grant unleashed him. A former Indiana lawyer, of whom it was said that he had taken to the army "just as if he expected to spend his life in it," Hovey drove straight up the steep acclivity to his front, flinging back successive Confederate lines, until he reached and seized the eleven guns that had been pounding him from near the crest. His men were whooping with delight, proud but winded, when they were struck in turn by a powerful counterattack launched from a fringe of woods along the crest. "We ran, and ran manfully," one among them declared, explaining how he and his fellows had been swept back from the captured guns and down the slope they had climbed. Reinforced by Crocker's lead brigade, which had just arrived under Colonel George Boomer, they managed to hang on at the foot of the hill; but only by the hardest. One officer called the fighting there "unequal, terrible, and most sanguinary." For half an hour, he said, the troops "on each side took their turn in driving and being driven."

It was obvious that Hovey, who had left about one third of his division lying dead or wounded on the hillside, could not hold out much longer unassisted. Then one of the survivors looked over his shoulder and saw the army commander speaking to the colonel in charge of Crocker's second brigade, which was coming forward along the road behind them. "I was close enough to see his features," the man was to recall. "Earnest they were, but sign of inward movement there was none." This was the Grant of Belmont, Donelson, and Shiloh, reacting to adversity here as he had reacted there. If the face was "cool and calculating," the soldier observed, it was also "careful and half-cynical." He could not catch the spoken words across the distance, but they were as characteristic as the calm, enigmatic mask or the habitual cigar stump that was wedged between its teeth. "Hovey's division and Boomer's brigade are good troops," Grant was saying. "If the enemy has driven them he is not in good plight himself. If we can go in again here and make a little showing, I think he will give way."

But it developed that a good deal more than this one additional brigade would have to join the melee at the base of Champion Hill if Grant was to make what he called "a little showing." With Mc-Pherson's third division still too far away to be of help in time, he had to call on Logan, who had been sent to probe the rebel left. And this, as Grant admitted later, was the salvation of Pemberton today. Logan had ridden around the north end of the hill, where the terrain was more open and gently rolling. He was sitting on horseback, surveying the scene, when a private who had wandered on his own came up to him and remarked laconically, gesturing off to the right: "General, I've been over the rise yonder, and it's my idea that if you'll put a regiment or two over there you'll get on their flank and lick 'em easy." Logan took a look for himself and saw that the man was right; Pemberton's left was "in the air" and the way to his rear was practically unobstructed, including the single bridge over Baker's Creek by which he could fall back. Just then, however, the order to return and support the hard-pressed Hovey was received; Logan had to defer pressing the advantage the amateur tactician had discovered. Learning of this when it was too late to take full advantage of the maneuver, Grant remarked with hindsight: "Had Mc-Clernand come up with reasonable promptness, or had I known the ground as I did afterwards, I cannot see how Pemberton could have escaped with any organized force."

The reference to McClernand was something more, this time, than merely another point scored in the private war Grant waged on paper against the former congressman from his home state. Pemberton, observing the lack of enemy aggressiveness to the south, had reinforced his staggered left by shifting troops northward from his center, which was disposed along the ridge. Bowen brought them to Stevenson's assistance on the run, arriving just in time to launch the savage counterattack that drove Hovey's exultant soldiers back down the hill. Like Grant, however, Pemberton was finding that he would need more than this to keep up the pressure or even hold what he had won; so he sent for Loring. That general — referred to as "a scared turkey" by a member of Stonewall Jackson's staff during the Romney controversy, two Christmases ago, which had almost resulted in Jackson's retirement from the army and which had been settled only with Loring's transfer to the West — was already in a state of agitation because Bowen's departure had left him alone on the ridge, with four blue divisions in plain sight. When the summons came for him to follow Bowen he declined. It would be suicidal, he protested. All this time, the pressure against Stevenson was mounting, and when Logan added the weight of his division it became unsupportable. Old Blizzards moved at last, in response to repeated calls from Pemberton; but too late. He was scarcely in motion northward, about 4 o'clock, when the whole Confederate left flank gave way. Stevenson's men fell back in a panic, and though Pemberton managed to rally them with a personal appeal, the damage was done. The eleven retaken guns were lost again, this time for good, and Bowen's division — having, as one officer remarked, "sustained its reputation by making one of its grand old charges, in which it bored a hole through the Federal army" — now found itself unsupported and nearly surrounded; whereupon it "turned around and bored its way back again," following Stevenson's pell-mell flight down to Baker's Creek, where it formed a rear-guard line in an attempt to hold off the bluecoats until Loring too had made his escape across the stream. Darkness fell and there was still no sign of Loring. Bowen waited another two hours, still maintaining his position, then gave it up and crossed in good order, burning the bridge when his last man was safe on the west bank.

Casualties here, after three hours of skirmishing and four of actual battle, had been much the heaviest of the campaign. Grant had lost 2441 men, Pemberton 3624, including prisoners cut off in the retreat — plus 11 guns and, as it turned out, all of Loring's division. Finding his path along the ridge blocked by victorious Federals, he swung west, then back south, and after a brief skirmish in which Lloyd Tilghman was killed by a cannonball while covering the withdrawal, made a rapid getaway around McClernand's open flank. By the following evening he was in Crystal Springs, twenty-five miles south of Jackson, and two days later he was with Johnston at Canton, an equal distance north of the capital. Except for the loss of Tilghman, whose courage and ability had been proved at Fort Henry and Fort Pemberton, Loring's disappearance was more a source of mystery than regret for the army of which he had lately been a part, since he had contributed little to the battle except to assist in the show of strength that immobilized McClernand. Grant felt much the same way about McClernand, whose 15,000-man command — including Blair but not Hovey, who fought beyond McClernand's control and suffered almost half the army's casualties — had lost a total of 17 dead and 141 wounded in the course of what a brigade commander with McPherson called "one of the most obstinate and murderous conflicts of the war." Despite the fact that not a single man had been killed in three of the four divisions to the south, elation over the victory scored by the three divisions to the north was tinged with sorrow at its cost. "I cannot think of this bloody hill without sadness and pride," Hovey was to say, and an Illinois soldier, roaming the field when the fighting was over, was struck by the thought that no moral solution had been arrived at as a result of all the bloodshed. "There they lay," he said of the dead and wounded all around him, "the blue and the gray intermingled; the same rich, young American blood flowing out in little rivulets of crimson; each thinking he was in the right."

Grant was more interested just now in military solutions, and he believed he had reached one. "We were now assured of our position between Johnston and Pemberton," he subsequently declared, "without a possibility of a junction of their forces." Others in his army believed they saw an even more profitable outcome of the struggle on Champion Hill. "Vicksburg must fall now," a participant wrote home that night; "I think a week may find us in possession. It may take longer," he added on second thought, "but the end will be the same."

While Pemberton's depleted army fell back through the darkness to a position covering the Big Black crossing, eight miles to the west, Grant let his soldiers sleep till dawn, by which time Wilson's engineers had the bridge over Baker's Creek rebuilt, then took up the pursuit. McClernand once more had the lead, though Blair was detached to rejoin Sherman, who by now was close at hand with his other two divisions. "We have made good progress today in the work of destruction," he had written Grant the day before, as he prepared to leave the Mississippi capital. "Jackson will no longer be a point of danger. The land is devastated for thirty miles around." Next morning — Sunday, May 17 — while Grant was crossing Baker's Creek to come to grips with Pemberton again, Sherman passed through Bolton and encountered other signs of devastation. Seeing some soldiers drawing water from a well in front of "a small hewn-log house" beside the road, he turned his horse in at the gate to get a drink. The place had been rifled, its furnishings wrecked and strewn about the yard, and though such acts of vandalism were fairly common at this stage of the campaign — brought on, so to speak, by an excess of skylark energy and delight that things were going so well for the army of invasion — this one appeared to have been committed with an extra measure of glee and satisfaction. When Sherman had one of the men hand him a book he saw lying on the ground beside the well, he found out why. It was a copy of the United States Constitution, with the name Jefferson Davis written on the title page. This was the property the Confederate President's brother had secured for him the year before, when Brierfield was occupied by Butler, and though in the course of his December visit Davis had expressed the hope that he would be spared further depredations, it had not turned out that way. For him, as for his septuagenarian brother, the blue pursuit had been unrelenting. "Joe Davis's plantation was not far off," Sherman later recalled. "One of my staff officers went there, with a few soldiers, and took a pair of carriage horses, without my knowledge at the time. He found Joe Davis at home, an old man, attended by a young and affectionate niece; but they were overwhelmed with grief to see their country overrun and swarming with Federal troops."

Grant meanwhile was pushing west. About 7 o'clock he came upon Pemberton's new position — and found it even stronger, in some respects, than the one the rebels had occupied "by accident or design" the day before. This time, however, it was clearly by design. Not only had the position been prepared overnight for just such an emergency as the Confederates now faced; it was here, in fact, that Pemberton had wanted to do his fighting in the first place. The railroad bridge, which had been floored to provide for passage of his artillery and wagons, was at the apex of a horseshoe bend of the Big Black, whose high west bank afforded the guns emplaced along it an excellent field of fire out over the low-lying eastern bank and the mile-long line of rifle pits already dug across the open end of the horseshoe. Parapeted with bales of cotton brought from surrounding plantations, the line was a strong one, even without the concentric support of the guns emplaced to its rear, its front being protected by a shallow bayou that abutted north on the river and south on an impenetrable cypress brake. Whatever came at the men in these pits would have to come straight up the narrow railroad embankment, a suicidal prospect in the face of all that massed artillery, or across the rain-swollen bayou, beyond which open fields stretched for nearly half a mile, allowing the attackers little or no cover except for a single copse of woods about three hundred yards in front of the far left, where guns were also grouped in expectation. Still unaware that Loring had skedaddled, Pemberton held this intrenched bridgehead in hopes that Old Blizzards would show up in time for a share in the impending fight at the gates of Vicksburg, which was less than a dozen miles back down the road.

What showed up instead was the Yankees. One look at the position his opponent had selected — Pemberton, after all, was a trained engineer, with a reputation for skill in the old army — told Grant that he stood an excellent chance of suffering the bloodiest of repulses if he attempted a frontal attack. Fortunately, though, he had instructed Sherman to swing north of Edwards for a crossing at Bridgeport, five miles upstream; so that all Grant had to do here, for the present, was keep up a show of strength to hold Pemberton in place while Sherman got his three divisions over the river above and came down on his flank. But McClernand had other ideas. Troubled perhaps by his poor showing yesterday — though he would not hesitate presently to claim a lion's share of the credit for the Champion Hill success, on grounds that Hovey's division was from his corps — he moved vigorously today, sending Carr and Osterhaus, the Pea Ridge companions, respectively north and south of the railroad to confront the rebels crouched behind their cotton parapets. An assault was a desperate thing to venture against the dug-in Confederates and all those high-sited batteries in their rear, he knew, but he was quite as determined as Grant to "make a little showing," if not a big one. So was Brigadier General Michael Lawler, commanding Carr's second brigade, which had worked its way into the copse on the far right. A big man, over 250 pounds in weight and so large of girth that he had to wear his sword belt looped over one shoulder, Lawler was Irish, forty-nine years old, and lately an Illinois farmer. His favorite Tipperary maxim, "If you see a head, hit it," was much in his mind as he peered across the chocolate-colored bayou at the rebel intrenchments three hundred yards away. Many heads were visible there, inviting him to hit them, and at last he could bear it no longer. Stripped to his shirt sleeves because of the midday heat, he stood up, swinging his sword, and ordered his four regiments forward on the double. The bayou was shoulder-deep in places, but the Iowa and Wisconsin soldiers floundered straight across it in what a reporter called "the most perilous and ludicrous charge I witnessed during the war," and came mud-plastered up to the enemy line with a whoop, having suffered 199 casualties in the three minutes that had elapsed since they left the copse. The loss was small compared to the gain, however, for the rebels broke rearward, avoiding contact, only to find that the bridge had been set afire in their rear to keep the close-following bluecoats from surging across in their wake. Lawler's reward was 1200 prisoners — more men, he said, than he himself had brought into action —out of a final total of 1751 Confederates killed and captured, along with 18 guns, when the other brigades took fire from his example and rushed forward, breaking the gray line all down its length. Grant's losses were 276 killed and wounded, plus 3 missing, presumably left at the bottom of the bayou now in his rear.

Across the way, Pemberton had watched the disintegration of his skillfully drawn line and the quick subtraction of a brigade from his dwindling army. Neither was truly catastrophic; he still held the high west bank of the river, and the bridge the Federals might have used for a crossing was burning fiercely in the noonday sunlight; but he was depressed by the failure of his men to hold a position of such strength. If they would not stand fast here, where would they stand fast? Years later, a member of his staff was to say: "The affair of Big Black bridge was one which an ex-Confederate participant naturally dislikes to record." It was unpleasant to remember, and it had been even more unpleasant to observe. Presently, moreover, word came from upstream that Sherman had forced a crossing at Bridgeport, capturing the dozen pickets on duty at that point. There was nothing for it now but to continue the retreat or be outflanked. Pemberton gave the necessary orders and the westward march got under way, as it had done after yesterday's bloodier action, except that this time there would be no halt until Vicksburg itself was reached. Then what? He did not know how well his troops would fight with their backs to the wall, but this most recent action was not an encouraging example of their mettle. Some thirty hours ago he had had 17,500 effectives in his mobile force, and now he was down to a good deal less than half that many. In fact it was nearer a third, 5375 having been killed, wounded, or captured, while as many more had wandered off with Loring. As he rode westward, accompanied by his chief engineer, young Major Samuel Lockett, Pemberton's distress increased and his confidence touched bottom. "Just thirty years ago," he said at last, breaking a long and painful silence, "I began my military career by receiving my appointment to a cadetship at the U.S. Military Academy, and today — that same date — that career is ended in disaster and disgrace." Lockett tried to reassure the general by reminding him that two fresh divisions stood in the Vicksburg intrenchments, which had been designed to withstand repeated assaults by almost any number of men. Besides, he said, Joe Johnston would be reinforced at Canton in the event of a siege, and would come to the beleaguered city's relief with all the skill for which he was famous, North and South. "To all of which," the major recalled afterwards, "General Pemberton replied that my youth and hopes were the parents of my judgment; he himself did not believe our troops would stand the first shock of an attack."

A dispatch had already gone to Johnston that morning, announcing the results of yesterday's battle and warning that Haines Bluff would have to be abandoned if the Big Black position was outflanked or overrun. Accordingly, as the retreat got under way, orders were sent for the garrison on the Yazoo to fall back, all but two companies, who were to forward all stores possible and destroy the rest, "making a show of force until the approach of the enemy by land should compel them to retire." Provisions were much on Pemberton's mind, despite his dejection, and he issued instructions that, from Bovina on, "all cattle, sheep, and hogs belonging to private parties, and likely to fall into the hands of the enemy, should be driven within our lines." Similarly, corn was pulled from the fields along the way, "and all disposable wagons applied to this end." If it was to be a siege, food was likely to be as vital a factor as ammunition, and he did all he could in that respect. The march continued, accompanied by the lowing of cows, the bleating of sheep, and the squealing of pigs, steadily westward. For all the Confederates knew, Sherman might have moved fast around their flank and beaten them to the goal. Then up ahead, as Pemberton was to remember it years later, "the outlines of the hill city rose slowly through the heated dust — Vicksburg and security. Passing raddled fields turning colorless from the powdered earth that rose beneath their tramp, the gray soldiers slacked off the turnpikes along the high ground until they came inside the city's breastworks. As word carried down the crooked line of march that the race to Vicksburg had been won, the footsore remnants in the rear flooded down the pike."

Sunset made a red glory over the Louisiana bayous; "The sky faded to a cool green and it was dark." Pemberton and his aides worked through the night, seeing to the comfort of the troops who had fought today and yesterday, bivouacked now in rear of the intrenchments, and inspecting the front-line defenses manned by the two divisions which had remained in the city all this time. Dawn gave light by which to check the overlapping fields of fire commanded by the 102 guns, light and heavy, emplaced along the semicircular landward fortifications. Mid-morning brought reports from scouts that the two companies left at Haines Bluff were on their way to Vicksburg, having complied with the order to hold out as long as possible. Heavy columns of Federals were close behind them, while other blue forces were hard on the march from Bovina. Before they arrived — as they presently did, to begin the investment — a messenger came riding in with a reply to yesterday's dispatch to Johnston, who had moved southwest from Canton to a position northeast of Brownsville. Pemberton's spirits had risen considerably since his confession of despair as he fell back from the Big Black the day before, but what his superior had to say was scarcely of a nature to raise them further. For one thing, the Virginian said nothing whatsoever about relief, either now or in the future. As he saw it, the choice had been narrowed to evacuation or surrender.

May 17, 1863.

LIEUTENANT GENERAL PEMBERTON:
Your dispatch of today ... was received. If Haines Bluff is untenable, Vicksburg is of no value and cannot be held. If, therefore, you are invested at Vicksburg, you must ultimately surrender. Under such circumstances, instead of losing both troops and place, we must, if possible, save the troops. If it is not too late, evacuate Vicksburg and its dependencies, and march them to the northeast.

Most respectfully, your obedient servant,
J. E. JOHNSTON, General.

Even if Pemberton had wanted to follow this advice — which he did not, considering it in violation of orders from the Commander in Chief that the place be held at all costs — compliance was altogether beyond his means. Before he had time for more than brief speculation as to what effect these words might have on his chances of survival, Union guns were shelling his outer works. The siege had begun, and Grant was jockeying for positions from which to launch an all-out assault, intending to bring the three-week-old campaign, which had opened on his birthday, to the shortest possible end.

Yesterday's rout on the Big Black had seemed to indicate what the result of one hard smash at the rebel lines would be, and Grant's spirits had risen more or less in ratio to the droop of his opponent's. If roads could be found, he said as he watched the enemy abandon the high western bank, he intended to advance in three columns of one corps each, "and have Vicksburg or Haines Bluff tomorrow night." While Wilson and his engineers were collecting materials for replacing the burned railroad bridge, he rode up to Bridgeport and found Sherman hard at work laying India-rubber pontoons for a crossing in force. Soon after dark the first of his three divisions started over, their way lighted by pitch pine bonfires on both banks. Grant and his red-haired lieutenant sat on a log and watched the troops move westward over the Big Black, faces pale in the firelight and gun barrels catching glints from the flames as "the bridge swayed to and fro under the passing feet." Sherman was to remember it so. A water-colorist of some skill back in the days when there had been time for such diversions, he thought the present scene "made a fine war picture."

By daybreak all three divisions were across. Riding south to see whether McClernand and McPherson had done as well, Grant left instructions for Sherman to march northwest in order to interpose between Vicksburg and the forts on the Yazoo. By 10 o'clock this had been done. A detachment sent northward found Haines Bluff unoccupied, its big guns spiked, and made contact with the Union gunboats on the river below, signaling them to steam in close and tie up under the frowning bluff that had defied them for so long. Grant now had the supply base he wanted, north of the city. Presently he came riding up, to find his friend Sherman gazing down from the Walnut Hills at the Chickasaw Bayou region below, from which he had launched his bloody and fruitless assault against these heights five months ago. Up to now, the Ohioan had had his reservations about this eighth attempt to take or bypass Vicksburg, saying flatly, "I tremble for the result. I look upon the whole thing as one of the most hazardous and desperate moves of this or any other war." But now his doubts were gone, replaced by enthusiasm: as was shown when he turned to Grant, standing quietly by, and abruptly broke the silence.

"Until this moment I never thought your expedition a success," he said; "I never could see the end clearly until now. But this is a campaign. This is a success if we never take the town."

Grant shared his friend's enthusiasm, if not his verbal exuberance, with regard to a situation brought about by a combination of careful strategy, flawlessly improvised tactics, sudden marches, and hard blows delivered with such triphammer rapidity that the enemy had never been given a chance to recover the balance he lost when the blue army, feinting coincidentally at Haines Bluff, swarmed ashore at Bruinsburg, forty-five air-line miles away. At no time in the past three weeks, moreover, had the outlook been so bright as it was now. All three corps had crossed the Big Black, the final natural barrier between them and their goal, and were converging swiftly upon the hilltop citadel by three main roads so appropriate to their purpose that they might have been surveyed with this in mind. Sherman advanced from the northeast on the Benton road, McPherson from due east, along the railroad and the Jackson turnpike, and McClernand from the southeast on the Baldwin's Ferry road. By nightfall, after a few brief skirmishes along the ill-organized line of rebel outposts — invariably abandoned at the first suggestion of real pressure — the lead elements of all three columns were in lateral contact with each other and in jump-off positions for tomorrow's assault. Next morning, May 19, while they completed their dispositions, the men were in high spirits.

They were in fact, like Sherman, "a little giddy with pride" at the realization of all they had accomplished up to now. In the twenty days since they crossed the Mississippi, they had marched 180 miles to fight and win five battles — Port Gibson, Raymond, Jackson, Champion Hill, Big Black River — occupy a Deep South capital, inflict over 7000 casualties at a cost of less than 4500 of their own, and seize no less than fifty pieces of field artillery, not to mention two dozen larger pieces they found spiked in fortifications they outflanked. In all this time, they had not lost a gun or a stand of colors, and they had never failed to take an assigned objective, usually much more quickly than their commanders expected them to do. And now, just ahead, lay the last and largest of their objectives: Vicksburg itself, the ultimate prize for which the capture of all those others had served as prelude. Their belief that they would carry the place by storm, here and now, was matched by Grant, who issued his final orders before noon. "Corps commanders will push forward carefully, and gain as close position as possible to the enemy's works, until 2 p.m.; at [which] hour they will fire three volleys of artillery from all the pieces in position. This will be the signal for a general charge of all the army corps along the whole line." A closing sentence, intended to forestall the lapse of discipline that would attend a too-informal victory celebration, expressed the measure of his confidence that the assault would be successful, bringing the campaign to a triumphant close today: "When the works are carried, guards will be placed by all division commanders to prevent their men from straggling from their companies."

At the appointed hour, the guns boomed and the blue clots of troops rushed forward, shoulder to shoulder, cheering as they vied for the honor of being first to scale the ridge: whereupon, as if in response to the same signal, a long low cloud of smoke, torn along its bottom edge by the pinkish yellow stabs of muzzle flashes, boiled up with a great clatter from the rebel works ahead. The racket was so tremendous that no man could hear his own shouts or the sudden yelps of the wounded alongside him. What was immediately apparent, however, amid a confusion of sound so uproarious that it was as if the whole mad scene were being played in pantomime, was that the assault had failed almost as soon as it got started. Sherman, watching from a point of vantage near the north end of the line, put it simplest in a letter he wrote home that night: "The heads of the columns have been swept away as chaff thrown from the hand on a windy day." Others, closer up, had a more gritty sense of what had happened. Emerging into the open, an Illinois captain saw "the very sticks and chips, scattered over the ground, jumping under the hot shower of rebel bullets." Startled, he and his company plunged forward, tumbled into a cane-choked ravine at the base of the enemy ridge, and hugged the earth for cover and concealment. All up and down the line it was much the same for those who had not scattered rearward at the first burst of fire; once within point-blank musket range, there was little the attackers could do but try to stay out of sight until darkness gave them a chance to pull back without inviting a bullet between the shoulder blades. As they lay prone the fire continued, cutting the stalks of cane, one by one, so that "they lopped gently upon us," as if to assist in keeping them hidden. Through the remaining hours of daylight they stayed there, with bullets twittering just above the napes of their necks. Then they returned through the gathering dusk to the jump-off positions they had left five hours ago. Reaching safety after a hard run, the captain and other survivors of his company "stopped and took one long breath, bigger than a pound of wool."

Pemberton was perhaps as surprised as the bluecoats were at their abrupt repulse. In reporting to the President — the message would have to be smuggled out, of course, before it could be put on the wire for Richmond — that his army was "occupying the trenches around Vicksburg," he added proudly: "Our men have considerably recovered their morale." Meanwhile he strengthened his defenses and improved the disposition of his 20,000 effectives. M. L. Smith's division had the left, Forney's the center, and Stevenson's the right, while Bowen's was held in immediate reserve, under orders to be prepared to rush at a moment's notice to whatever point needed bolstering. There was a crippling shortage of intrenching tools, only about five hundred being on hand. "They were entirely inadequate," an engineer officer later declared, but "the men soon improvised wooden shovels [and used] their bayonets as picks." They had indeed "considerably recovered," now that they had stopped running, and they were hungry for revenge for the humiliations they had been handed, particularly day before yesterday on the Big Black River. If the Yankees would keep coming at them the way they had come this afternoon, the Confederates hoped they would keep it up forever.

In point of fact, that was pretty much what Grant had in mind. He had suffered 942 casualties and inflicted less than 200, thus coming close to reversing the Big Black ratio, but he still thought the ridge could be carried by assault. Conferring next morning with his corps commanders he found them agreed that this first effort had failed, in Sherman's words, "by reason of the natural strength of the position, and because we were forced by the nature of the ground to limit our attacks to the strongest part of the enemy line, viz., where the three principal roads entered the city." Nothing could be done about the first of these two drawbacks, but the second could be corrected by careful reconnaissance. Better artillery preparations would also be of help, it was decided, in softening up the rebel works; moreover, the navy could add the weight of its metal from the opposite side of the ridge, Porter having returned from a two-week expedition up the Red River to Alexandria, where he had met Banks coming north from Opelousas on May 6. Grant told McClernand, Sherman, and McPherson to spend today and tomorrow preparing "for a renewed assault on the 22d, simultaneously, at 10 a.m." Riding his line while the work was being pushed, he found the men undaunted by their repulse the day before, though they were prompt to let him know they were weary of the meat-and-vegetables diet on which they had been subsisting for the past three weeks. Turkey and sweet potatoes were fine as a special treat, it seemed, but such rich food had begun to pall as a regular thing. A private looked up from shoveling, recognized Grant riding by, and said in a pointed but conversational tone: "Hardtack." Others took up the call, on down the line, raising their voices with every repetition of the word, until finally they were shouting with all their might. "Hardtack! Hardtack!" they yelled as the army commander went past. "Hardtack! Hardtack!" Finally he reined in his horse and informed all those within earshot that the engineers were building a road from the Yazoo steamboat landing, "over which to supply them with everything they needed." At this, as he said later, "the cry was instantly changed to cheers." That night there was hardtack for everyone, along with beans, and coffee to wash it down. The soldiers woke next morning strengthened for the work that was now at hand.

For the first time in history, a major assault was launched by commanders whose eyes were fixed on the hands of watches synchronized the night before. This was necessary in the present case because the usual signal guns would not have been heard above the din of the preliminary bombardment, which included the naval weapons on both flanks, upstream and down, and six mortar boats already engaged for the past two days in what one defender contemptuously called "the grand but nearly harmless sport of pitching big shells into Vicksburg." All night the 13-inch mortars kept heaving their 200-pound projectiles into the checkerboard pattern of the city's streets and houses, terrifying citizens huddled under their beds and dining-room tables. ("Vertical fire is never very destructive of life," the same witness remarked. "Yet the howling and bursting shells had a very demoralizing effect on those not accustomed to them.") Then at dawn the 200 guns on the landward side chimed in, raising geysers of dirt on the ridge where the Confederates were intrenched and waiting. At 9.30, in compliance with Grant's request, Porter closed the range with four gunboats from below and took the lower water batteries under fire. He was supposed to keep this up until 10.30, half an hour past the scheduled time for the infantry assault to open, but since he could see no indication that the army had been successful in its storming attempt, he kept up the fire for an extra hour before dropping back downriver and out of range. One ironclad, the *Tuscumbia*, was severely battered and forced to retire before the others. Otherwise, though he reported that this was altogether the hottest fire his boats had yet endured, Porter suffered little damage in the bows-on fight, aside from a few men wounded. He could not see, however, that he had accomplished much in the way of punishing the defenders. Nor was there any evidence that the army had done any better.

As a matter of fact, the army had done a good deal worse, though not for lack of trying. At the appointed hour the men of all three corps rushed forward, the advance waves equipped with twenty-foot scaling ladders to be used against steep-walled strongpoints, of which there were many along the ridge ahead. "The rebel line, concealed by the parapet, showed no sign of unusual activity," Sherman observed from his point of vantage to the north, "but as our troops came in fair view, the enemy rose behind their parapet and poured a furious fire upon our lines. . . . For about two hours we had a severe and bloody battle, but at every point we were repulsed." It was much the same with McPherson and McClernand, to the south, who also lost heavily as a result of these whites-of-their-eyes tactics employed by the Confederates. At several points, left and right and center, individual groups managed to effect shallow penetrations, despite what an Illinois colonel called "the most murderous fire I ever saw," but were quickly expelled or captured by superior forces the enemy promptly brought to bear from his mobile reserve. Those bluecoats who crouched in the ravines and ditches at the base of the ridge, taking shelter there as they had done three days ago, were dislodged by the explosion in their midst of 12-inch shells which the defenders rolled downhill after lighting the fuzes. On McClernand's front a heavier lodgment was effected at one point, and the general, taking fire at the sight of his troops flaunting their banners on the rebel works, sent word to Grant that he had "part possession of two forts, and the stars and stripes are floating over them." If the other two corps "would make a diversion in my favor," he thought he could enlarge his gains and perhaps score an absolute breakthrough. At any rate, he earnestly declared, "a vigorous push ought to be made all along the line."

Grant was with Sherman when the message reached him. "I don't believe a word of it," he said. Sherman protested that the note was official and must be credited. Though he had just called off his own attack, admitting failure, he offered to renew it at once in the light of this appeal from McClernand. Grant thought the matter over, then told the redhead he "might try it again" at 3 o'clock, if no contrary orders reached him before that time. Riding south, he detached one of McPherson's divisions to support McClernand and authorized a resumption of the attack on the center as well. Promptly at 3, Sherman launched his promised second assault, but found it "a repetition of the first, equally unsuccessful and bloody." McPherson had the same unpleasant experience. McClernand, still afire with hope, threw the borrowed division into the fray — though not in time to maintain, much less widen or deepen, the penetration of which he had been so proud. A whooping counterattack by Colonel T. N. Waul's Texas Legion killed or captured all but a handful of Federals at that point. By sundown the firing had died to a sputter, and at nightfall the survivors crept back across the corpse-pocked fields to the safety of the lines they had left with such high hopes that morning. Some measure of their determination and valor was shown by a comparison of their losses today with those of three days ago. The previous assault had ended with two stands of colors left on the forward slope of the enemy ridge; this time there were five. Moreover, the casualties exceeded this five-two ratio. Less than a thousand men had fallen the time before, including 165 killed or missing, whereas this time the figures went above three thousand — 3199, to be exact — with 649 in the killed-or-missing category. In other words, Grant had lost in the past three days almost as many soldiers as he had lost in the past three weeks of nearly continuous battle and maneuver which had brought him within sight of the ramparts of Vicksburg only to be repulsed.

He was furious. "This last attack only served to increase our casualties without giving any benefit whatever," he wrote some twenty years later, still chagrined. Quick as ever to shift the blame for any setback or evidence of shortcoming — at Belmont it had been overexcited "higher officers"; at Donelson it had been McClernand; at Shiloh

it had been Prentiss and Lew Wallace, although the former most likely
had saved him from defeat; at Iuka it had been Rosecrans and the wind
— he notified Halleck, two days after the second Vicksburg repulse:
"The whole loss for the day will probably reach 1500 killed and
wounded. General McClernand's dispatches misled me as to the real
state of facts, and caused much of this loss. He is entirely unfit for the
position of corps commander, both on the march and on the battlefield.
Looking after his corps gives me more labor and infinitely more uneasiness than all the remainder of my department." And yet, on the day of
battle itself, he included that general's misleading claims in his own dispatch informing Halleck of the outcome. "Vicksburg is now completely
invested," he declared. "I have possession of Haines Bluff and the Yazoo;
consequently have supplies. Today an attempt was made to carry the
city by assault, but was not entirely successful. We hold possession,
however, of two of the enemy's forts, and have skirmishers close under
all of them. Our loss was not severe." As he wrote, his optimism grew;
for that was the reverse of the coin. He would no more admit discouragement than he would entertain self-blame. "The nature of the ground
about Vicksburg is such that it can only be taken by a siege," he judged,
but added: "It is entirely safe to us in time, I would say one week if the
enemy do not send a large army upon my rear."

He did not regret having made the assaults; he only regretted
that they had failed. Besides, he subsequently explained, his high-spirited
troops had approached the gates of Vicksburg with a three-week cluster
of victories to their credit; they would never have settled down willingly to the tedium of siege operations unless they had first been given
the chance to prove that the place could not be taken by storm. Now
that this had been demonstrated, though at the rather excessive price of
4141 casualties, they took to spadework with a will, constructing their
own complex system of intrenchments roughly parallel to those of the
rebels, which in a few places were not much more than fifty yards away.
As they delved in the sandy yellow clay of the hillsides or drew their
beads on such heads as appeared above the enemy parapets, they were
encouraged by news of tangential victories, particularly on the part of
the navy, which was on a rampage now that the outlying Confederate
defenses had been abandoned. An expedition made up of the *DeKalb*
and three tinclads, all under Lieutenant Commander John Walker, had
been sent up the Yazoo on May 20, the day after the first assault, and returned on the 23d, the day after the second, to report that the rebels
had set their Yazoo City navy yard afire at the approach of the Union
vessels, the flames consuming three warships under construction on the
stocks, for an estimated loss of $3,000,000. This meant that there would
be no successor to the *Arkansas*, which was welcome news indeed. But
Porter was unsatisfied; he sent the expedition back upriver the next
morning. This time Walker steamed to within a dozen miles of Fort

Pemberton, destroying steamboats and sawmills as he went, then came back downstream to push 180 miles up the winding Sunflower River, where he caught and burned still more fugitive rebel steamboats. Returning this second time, he could report that these streams were no longer arteries of supply for the Confederates below the confluence of the Tallahatchie and the Yalobusha, nearly one hundred air-line miles from the beleaguered Vicksburg bluff.

Pemberton took the news of this without undue distress. After all, the Yazoo and the Sunflower were no longer of much interest to him; the Father of Waters was now his sole concern, and only about a dozen miles of that. "I have decided to hold Vicksburg as long as possible," he had replied to Johnston's last-minute dispatch urging evacuation, "with the firm hope that the Government may yet be able to assist me in keeping this obstruction to the enemy's free navigation of the Mississippi River. I still conceive it to be the most important point in the Confederacy." His outlook improved with the repulse of the first Federal assault, and on the eve of the second he was asking: "Am I to expect reinforcements? From what direction, and how soon? . . . The men credit and are encouraged by a report that you are near with a large force. They are fighting in good spirits, and the reorganization is complete." After the second repulse, however, the defenders were faced with an unpleasant problem. For three days — six, in the case of those who had fallen in the first assault — Grant's dead and injured lay in the fields and ditches at the base of the Confederate ridge, exposed to the fierce heat of the early Mississippi summer. The stench of the dead, whose bodies were swollen grotesquely, and the cries of the wounded, who suffered the added torment of thirst, were intolerable to the men who had shot them down; yet Grant would not ask for a truce for burial or treatment of these unfortunates, evidently thinking that such a request would be an admission of weakness on his part. Finally Pemberton could bear it no longer. On the morning of May 25 he sent a message through the lines to the Union commander: "Two days having elapsed since your dead and wounded have been lying in our front, and as yet no disposition on your part of a desire to remove them being exhibited, in the name of humanity I have the honor to propose a cessation of hostilities for two hours and a half, that you may be enabled to remove your dead and dying men." To Pemberton's relief, Grant at last "acceded" to this proposal. At 6 p.m. all firing was suspended while the Federals came forward to bury the dead where they lay and bring comfort to such few men as had survived the three-day torture. This done, they returned through the darkness to their lines and the firing was resumed with as much fury as before.

In nothing was Grant more "unpronounceable" than in this. He would berate, and in at least one case attack with his fists, any man he saw abusing a dumb animal; he had, it was said to his credit, no stomach for suffering; he disliked above all to ride over a field where there had been recent heavy fighting; he would not eat a piece of meat until it had been cooked to a char, past any sign of blood or even pinkness. Yet this he could do to his own men, this abomination perhaps beyond all others of the war, without expressed regret or apparent concern. However, this too was the reverse of a coin, the other side of which was his singleness of purpose, his quality of intense preoccupation with what he called "the business," meaning combat. He took his losses as they came — they had, in fact, about been made up already with the arrival that week of a division of reinforcements from Memphis, and would be more than made up with the arrival, early the following week, of a second such division, while four more were being alerted even now for. the trip downriver from Tennessee, Missouri, and Kentucky to bring his mid-June total to 71,000 effectives — for the sake of getting on with the job to which he had set his hand. Long ago in Mexico, during a lull in the war, he had written home to the girl he was to marry: "If we have to fight, I would like to do it all at once and then make friends." He felt that way about it still, and now that he was calling the turn, he wanted no interludes or delays; he wanted it finished, and he believed the finish was in sight. "The enemy are now undoubtedly in our grasp," he told Halleck the day before the burial truce. "The fall of Vicksburg and the capture of most of the garrison can only be a question of time."

This was not to say there would be no more setbacks and frustrations. There would indeed, war being the chancy thing it was, and Grant knew it: which perhaps was why he had dropped his prediction, made two days before, that the fall of the city would be accomplished within "I would say one week." And in fact there was one such mishap three days later, two days after the burial truce, this time involving the navy. In the course of drawing his lines for the siege, Sherman had begun to suspect, from the amount of artillery fire he drew, that the Confederates were shifting guns from their upper water batteries to cover the landward approaches, particularly on their far left. Requested by Grant to test the facts of the case, Porter on May 27 sent the *Cincinnati* to draw the fire of the guns "if still there," covering her movements with four other ironclads at long range. She started downriver at 7 o'clock in the morning, commanded by Lieutenant G. M. Bache, and by 10 the matter had been settled beyond doubt. Not only were the guns still there, but they sank the *Cincinnati*. Rounding to in order to open fire, she took a pair of solids in her shell room and a third in her magazine. As she tried to make an upstream escape, a heavy shot drove through her pilot house and her starboard tiller was carried away, along with all three flagstaffs. Hulled repeatedly by plunging fire, she began filling rapidly. Bache, with five of his guns disabled in short order, tried to get beyond range and tie the vessel up to the east bank before she sank, but could not make it. She went down in three fathoms of water, still within range of the enemy guns, and what remained of her crew had to swim for their lives. The total loss, aside from the *Cincinnati* herself, was 5 killed, 14 wounded, and 15 missing, presumed drowned.

Convinced that Bache and his crew had done their best under disadvantageous circumstances, Porter accepted the loss of the ironclad — the third since his arrival in early December — as one of the accidents of war, and did not relax on that account his pressure against the rebels beleaguered on their bluff. He already had the approval of Grant for his conduct of naval affairs. Replying to a message in which the admiral informed him that Banks, although he had wound up his West Louisiana campaign at last, would "not [be] coming here with his men. He is going to occupy the attention of Port Hudson, and has landed at Bayou Sara, using your transports for the purpose," Grant told Porter: "I am satisfied that you are doing all that can be done in aid of the reduction of Vicksburg. There is no doubt of the fall of the place ultimately, but how long it will be is a matter of doubt. I intend to lose no more men, but to force the enemy from one position to another without exposing my troops."

✕ 4 ✕

Banks had done a good deal more by now than merely "occupy the attention of Port Hudson." Crossing the Mississippi on the day after Grant's second repulse at Vicksburg, he completed his investment of the Louisiana stronghold on May 26, and next morning — simultaneous with the sinking of the *Cincinnati*, 240 winding miles upriver — launched his own all-out assault, designed to bring to a sudden and victorious end a campaign even more circuitous than Grant's. That general had covered some 180 miles by land and water before returning to his approximate starting point and placing his objective under siege, whereas Banks had marched or ridden about three times that far, as the thing turned out, to accomplish the same result. However, not only was the distance greater; the numerical odds had been tougher, at least at the start. Back in mid-March, when Farragut ran two ships past the fuming hundred-foot bluff, Banks had maneuvered on the landward side, only to discover that the defenders had more men inside the works than he had on the outside. This gave him pause, as well it might, and while he pondered the problem he learned that Grant, whom he had expected to join him in reducing Port Hudson as a prelude to their combined movement against Vicksburg, was stymied north of the latter place, involved in a series of canal and bayou experiments which seemed likely to delay him for some time. Thinking it over, Banks decided to accomplish his assignment on his own. If he could not take Port Hudson, he would do as Grant was trying to do upriver. He would go around it.

It was not only that he was disinclined to wait and share the glory, politically ambitious though he was. He also believed he could not, and with cause. Nearly half of the 35,000 troops in his department were nine-month volunteers whose enlistments would be expiring between May and August; they would have to be used before summer or not at all. However, there was about as much need for caution as there was for haste, since more than half of this total, long- and short-term men alike, were required to garrison Baton Rouge, New Orleans, and various other points along the Mississippi and the Gulf. As a result of these necessary smaller detachments, his five divisions were reduced to about 5000 men each. Three of the five were with him near Port Hudson, under Major General C. C. Augur and Brigadier Generals William Emory and Cuvier Grover, while the fourth was at New Orleans under Brigadier General Thomas W. Sherman. Leaving Augur to hold Baton Rouge, Banks set out downriver with the other two on March 25 to join Godfrey Weitzel, commanding his fifth division at Brashear City, near Grand Lake and the junction of the Atchafalaya River and Bayou Teche. Back in January, Weitzel had ascended the former stream for a few miles, intending to establish an alternate route, well removed from the guns of Port Hudson, from the mouth of Red River to the Gulf. In this he had failed, not so much because of interference from Richard Taylor's scratch command of swamp-bound rebels, which he had thrown into precipitate retreat, but mainly because he had found the Atchafalaya choked with brush at that season of the year. Banks believed that this time he would succeed, and he hoped to abolish Taylor as a continuing threat. He intended in fact to capture him, bag and baggage, having worked out his plans with that in mind.

Taylor had about 4000 troops between the Teche and the Atchafalaya, his flanks protected right and left by two captured Union warships, the gunboat *Diana* and the armed ram *Queen of the West*, the former having been ambushed and seized that week near Pattersonville, when she imprudently ventured up the bayou, and the latter having been brought down from the Red River the week before to prevent her destruction or recapture by Farragut after his run past Port Hudson. Banks had four Gulf Squadron gunboats with which he planned to neutralize these two turncoat vessels, and he intended to bag Taylor's entire land force by sending one division from his 15,000-man command across Grand Lake to land in the rear of the rebels while he engaged them in front with his other two divisions. Hemmed in and outnumbered nearly four to one, Taylor would have to choose between surrender and annihilation. On April 11, in accordance with his design, Banks moved Emory and Weitzel from Brashear across the Atchafalaya to Berwick, and while they were advancing up the left bank of the Teche next day, skirmishing as they went, Grover put his troops aboard transports, escorted by the quartet of gunboats, and set out across the lake for a landing on the western shore within a mile of Irish Bend, an eastward loop of the Teche, control of which would place him squarely athwart the only Confederate line of retreat. Despite some irritating delays, the maneuver seemed to be going as planned; the skirmishing continued in front and Grover got his division ashore six miles in the enemy rear; Banks anticipated a Cannae. But Taylor got wind of what was up and reacted fast. Leaving a handful of men to put up a show of resistance to the two blue divisions in his front, he swung rearward with the rest to attack Grover and if possible drive him into the lake. On the 13th heavy fighting ensued. The shoestring force managed to delude and delay Emory and Weitzel while the main body fell on Grover. Though the latter was not driven into the lake, he was held in check while Taylor withdrew up the Teche in the darkness, foiling the plans so carefully laid for his destruction. In three days of intermittent action the Federals had lost 577 killed and wounded, the Confederates somewhat less, although there was considerable disagreement between the two commanders, then and later, as to the number of prisoners taken on each side, Taylor afterwards protesting that Banks had claimed the capture of more men than had actually opposed him.

Whatever the truth of his claims in this regard, and despite his failure to bring off the Cannae he intended, there could be no doubt that Banks, after a season of rather spectacular defeats in Virginia at the hands of Stonewall Jackson, had won his first clear-cut victory in the field. And next day, when he received word that the *Diana* and the *Queen* had been destroyed — the former burned by the rebels, who could not take her with them up the narrow Teche, and the latter sunk by the four Union gunboats, who blew her almost literally out of the water as soon as she entered Grand Lake and came within their range — his elation knew no bounds. Moreover, two of the gunboats steamed forthwith up the Atchafalaya and found it open to navigation all the way to the mouth of the Red, fifty miles above Port Hudson. This meant that Banks had the bypass he had been seeking, though of course it would be of small practical use until Vicksburg had likewise been bypassed or reduced. Since there was no news that Grant had succeeded in any of his experimental projects in that direction, the Massachusetts general decided to explore some vistas he saw opening before him as a result of Taylor's defeat and withdrawal. Within two weeks New Orleans would have been returned to Federal control a solid year, and yet this principal seaport of the South had even less commerce with the outside world today than she had enjoyed in the days of the blockade runners, mainly because the rebel land forces had her cut off from those regions that normally supplied her with goods for shipment. One of the richest of these lay before him now: the Teche. Return of the Teche country to Union control, along with its vast supplies of cotton, salt, lumber, and foodstuffs, would restore New Orleans to her rightful place among the world's great ports and would demonstrate effectively, as one observer pointed out, "that the conquests of the national armies instead of destroying trade were calculated to instill new life into it." There was one drawback. Such a movement up the long riverlike bayou stretching north almost to Alexandria, even though unopposed, might throw him off his previously announced schedule, which called for a meeting with Grant at Baton Rouge on May 10 for a combined attack, first on Port Hudson and then on Vicksburg. But Banks decided the probable gains were worth the risk. Besides, May 10 was nearly a month away, and he hoped to have completed his conquest of the region before then. If not, then Grant could wait, just as he had kept Banks waiting all this time.

Eager for more victories now that he had caught the flavor, the former Bay State governor put his three divisions on the march up the right bank of the Teche without delay. Two days later — April 16: Porter's bluejackets were steeling themselves for their run past the Vicksburg batteries that night, and Grierson's troopers would ride out of La Grange the following morning — he entered New Iberia and pushed on next day to the Vermilion River, which branched southward from the Teche near Vermilionville. Finding Taylor's rear guard drawn up on the opposite bank to contest a crossing, the bluecoats forced it with a brief skirmish, rebuilt the wrecked bridge, and on April 20 marched into Opelousas, evacuated two days earlier by the Louisiana government

which had moved there a year ago when Farragut steamed upriver from New Orleans and trained his guns on Baton Rouge. Taylor did not challenge the occupation of this alternate capital, but continued to fall back toward Alexandria, having received from Kirby Smith at Shreveport, his Transmississippi headquarters, a message expressing "gratification at the conduct of the troops under your command" and congratulating Taylor for the skill he had shown "in extricating them from a position of great peril." Banks called a halt in order to rest his men for a few days and consolidate his gains, which were considerable. Conquest of the Teche had brought within his grasp large quantities of lumber, 5000 bales of cotton, many hogsheads of sugar, an inexhaustible supply of salt, and an estimated 20,000 head of cattle, mules, and horses. He later calculated the value of these spoils to have been perhaps as high as $5,000,000 and pointed out that even this liberal figure should be doubled, since the goods it represented had not only come into Federal hands but had also been kept from the Confederates beyond the Mississippi, for whom they had been in a large part intended. Nor was that all. There were human spoils as well. Back in New Orleans the year before, Ben Butler had begun to enlist freedmen and fugitive slaves in what he called his Corps d'Afrique; now Banks continued this recruitment in the Teche. Two such regiments were organized at Opelousas, with about 500 men in each. Styled the 1st and 3d Louisiana Native Guards, the former was composed of "free Negroes of means and intelligence," with colored line officers and a white lieutenant colonel in command, while the latter was made up largely of ex-slaves whose officers were all white. There was considerable speculation, in the army of which they were now a part, as to how they would behave in combat — when and if they were exposed to it, which many of their fellow soldiers thought inadvisable — but Banks was willing to abide the issue until it had been settled incontrovertibly under fire.

Taylor by now had reached the Red at Gordon's Landing, where the *Queen of the West* had been blasted and captured back in February, thirty miles below Alexandria. Renamed Fort De Russy, the triple-casemated battery had held the low bluff against all comers, and on May 4 its staunchness was proved again when it was attacked by the two gunboats that had come up the Atchafalaya from Grand Lake after sinking the *Queen*. Leading the way, however, was the *Albatross*, which had got past Port Hudson with Farragut in mid-March. She closed the range to five hundred yards and kept up a forty-minute bombardment, supported by the other two ships at longer range, before dropping back with eleven holes punched in her hull and most of her spars and rigging shot away. Fifty miles downriver next morning, having given up hope of reducing the fort on their own, the three ships met Porter — who, after completing the ferrying of Grant's two lead divisions across the Mississippi, had taken possession of Grand Gulf three days ago — coming up the Red with three of his ironclads, a steam ram, and a tug. This seemed quite enough for the task of reduction, but when he reached Fort De Russy late that afternoon, prepared to throw all he had at the place, he found it abandoned, its casemates yawning empty. Threatened from the rear by Banks, who had ended his Opelousas rest halt and resumed his northward march beyond the headwaters of the Teche, the garrison had retreated to avoid capture. Porter continued on to Alexandria next day, May 6, to find that Taylor had also fallen back from there. A couple of hours later, Banks marched in at the head of his three-division column. He was in fine spirits, still wearing his three-week-old aura of victory, and Porter was impressed — particularly by the outward contrast between this new general and the one he had been working alongside for the past four months around Vicksburg. "A handsome, soldierly-looking man," the admiral called the former Speaker of the House, "though rather theatrical in his style of dress." The impression was one of nattiness and sartorial elegance; Banks in fact was something of a military dude. "He wore yellow gauntlets high upon his wrists, looking as clean as if they had just come from the glove-maker; his hat was picturesque, his long boots and spurs were faultless, and his air was that of one used to command. In short, I never saw a more faultless-looking soldier."

Banks was about as proud as he was dapper, and with cause. His Negro recruits more than made up — in numbers at any rate, though it was true their combat value was untested — for the casualties he had suffered in the course of his profitable campaign up the Teche, and his present position at Alexandria gave him access to the entire Red River Valley, a region quite as rich as the one he had just traversed, and far more extensive. With elements already on the march for Natchitoches, fifty air-line miles upriver, and Taylor still fading back from contact, he saw more vistas opening out before him. He also realized, however, that they were unattainable just yet. "The decisive battle of the West must soon be fought near Vicksburg," Kirby Smith was telling a subordinate even now. "The fate of the Trans-Mississippi Department depends on it, and Banks, by operating here, is thrown out of the campaign on the Mississippi." The Massachusetts general agreed, although unwillingly, that he must first turn back east to resume his collaboration with Grant for the reduction of Vicksburg and Port Hudson. Then perhaps, with the Mississippi unshackled throughout its length, he would return up the Red to explore those new vistas stretching all the way to Texas. Grant meanwhile, having won the Battle of Port Gibson, crossed Bayou Pierre, and put his three divisions into jump-off positions for the advance on Jackson, was calling urgently for Banks to join him at once in front of Vicksburg; "But I must say, without qualifications," the latter replied on May 12, "that the means at my disposal do not leave me a shadow of a chance to accomplish it." Though he was "dying with a kind of vanishing hope to see [our] two armies acting together against the strong places of the enemy," he had "neither water nor land transportation to make the movement by the river or by land. The utmost I can accomplish," he told Grant, "is to cross for the purpose of operating with you against Port Hudson."

Once more having reached a decision he wasted no time. Two days later, ending a week's occupation in the course of which he sent no less than 2000 spoils-laden wagons groaning south, he began his withdrawal from Alexandria. The march prescribed was via Simmesport for a crossing at Bayou Sara, a dozen miles above Port Hudson, but Banks himself did not accompany the three divisions on their overland trek; he went instead by boat, first down the Red, then down the Atchafalaya to Brashear City, where he caught a train for New Orleans. With him rode the fifty-two-year-old Emory, whose health had failed in the field and who had been succeeded by Brigadier General Halbert Paine, fifteen years his junior and the only non-West Pointer in Banks's army with so much rank — aside from Banks himself, of course — though he could claim the distinction of having shared a law office with Lincoln's friend Carl Schurz before the war. In New Orleans, Banks gave Emory the task of defending the city with a stripped-down garrison left behind by Thomas Sherman, who was instructed to put most of his men aboard transports bound for Baton Rouge to join Augur for an advance on Port Hudson. As Banks planned it, the two divisions marching north from Baton Rouge would converge on the objective at the same time as the three marching south from Bayou Sara. For all the omnivorous reading he had done since his days as a bobbin boy in his home-state spinning mills, he may or may not have known that in thus intending to unite two widely divided columns on the field of battle he was attempting what Napoleon had called the most difficult maneuver in the book. If so, nonprofessional though he was, he showed no qualms beyond those normally involved in getting some 20,000 troops from one place — or in this case two places — to another. What was more, he brought it off. Advancing simultaneously north and south, the two bodies converged on schedule, May 25. Next day they completed their investment, and the following morning they launched an all-out assault on the 7000 rebels penned up inside Port Hudson.

Like Pemberton, who was nine years his senior, Franklin Gardner was a northern-born professional who married South — his father-in-law was ex-Governor Alexander Mouton, who presided over the legislative body that voted Louisiana out of the Union — then went with his wife's people when the national crisis forced a choice. New York born and Iowa raised, the son of a regular army colonel who had been Adjutant General during the War of 1812, he had graduated from West Point in the class of '43, four places above Ulysses Grant and one below Christopher Augur, whose division was part of the blue cordon now drawn around the bastion Gardner was defending. A brigadier at Shiloh and with Bragg in Kentucky, he had been promoted to major general in December, shortly before his fortieth birthday, and sent to command the stronghold Breckinridge had established at Port Hudson after being repulsed at Baton Rouge in August. By early April his strength had risen beyond 15,000 men, but it had since been whittled down to less than half that as a result of levies by the department commander, reacting to upriver pressure from Grant while Banks was off in the Teche. On May 4, in response to what turned out to be Pemberton's final call, Gardner set out for Jackson with all but a single brigade, only to receive on May 9 at Osyka, just north of the Mississippi line, a dispatch instructing him to return at once to Port Hudson and hold it "to the last," this being Pemberton's interpretation of the President's warning that "both Vicksburg and Port Hudson [are] necessary to a connection with Trans-Mississippi." Gardner did as he was told, and got back there barely ahead of Banks. His strength report of May 19 — the date of Grant's first assault on the Vicksburg intrenchments, 120 air-line miles upriver — showed an "aggregate present" of 5715 in his three brigades, plus about one thousand artillerists in the permanent garrison. That was also the date on a message Joe Johnston addressed to Gardner from north of the Mississippi capital, which had fallen on the day after his arrival the week before: "Evacuate Port Hudson forthwith, and move with your troops toward Jackson to join other troops which I am uniting. Bring all the fieldpieces that you have, with their ammunition and the means of transportation. Heavy guns and their ammunition had better be destroyed, as well as the other property you may be unable to remove." By the time the courier got there, however, he found a ring of Federal steel drawn tightly around the blufftop fortress. He could only report back to Johnston that Port Hudson, like Vicksburg 240 roundabout miles upriver, was besieged.

The Union navy had reappeared ahead of the Union army. On May 4, meeting Porter at the mouth of the Red, Farragut gave over his blockade duties from that point north and steamed back down the Mississippi to Port Hudson. For three days, May 8-10, he bombarded the bluff from above and below, doing all he could to soften it up for Banks, who was still at Alexandria. Upstream were the *Hartford* and the *Albatross,* patched up since her recent misfortune at Fort De Russy, while the downstream batteries were engaged by the screw sloops *Monongahela* and *Richmond,* the gunboat *Genesee,* and the orphaned ironclad *Essex,* which had been downriver ever since her run past Vicksburg the summer before. Coming overland down the western bank, Farragut conferred with Banks on his arrival from New Orleans, May 22. The rebels had given him shell for shell, he said, and shown no sign of weakening under fire, but he assured the general that the navy would continue to do its share until the place had been reduced. Banks thanked him and proceeded to invest the bluff on its landward side, north and east and south, depending on the fleet to see that the beleaguered garrison made no westward escape across the river and received no reinforcements or supplies from that direction. Assisted meanwhile by Grierson's well-rested troopers, who had ridden up from Baton Rouge with the column from the south, he drew his lines closer about the rebel fortifications. On May 26, with ninety guns in position opposing Gardner's thirty-one, he issued orders for a full-scale assault designed to take the place by storm next morning. Weitzel, Grover, and Paine were north of the Clinton railroad, which entered the works about midway, Augur and Sherman to the south. The artillery preparation would begin at daybreak, he explained, augmented by high-angle fire from the navy, and the five division commanders would "dispose their troops so as to annoy the enemy as much as possible during the cannonade by advancing skirmishers to kill the enemy's cannoneers and to cover the advance of the assaulting column." This was somewhat hasty and Banks knew it, but he had reasons for not wanting to delay the attempt for the sake of more extensive preparations. First, like Grant eight days ago at Vicksburg, he believed the rebels were demoralized and unlikely to stand up under a determined blow if it were delivered before they had time to recover their balance. Second, and more important still, he was anxious to wind up the campaign and return to New Orleans; Emory was already complaining that he was in danger of being swamped by an attack from Mobile, where the Confederates had some 5000 men — twice as many as he himself had for the defense of the South's first city — or from Brashear, to which Taylor was free to return now that Banks had left the Teche. This was indeed a two-pronged danger; in fact, despite the cited lack of transportation, it had been the real basis for the Massachusetts general's refusal to join Grant in front of Vicksburg. However, for all his haste, the special orders he distributed on the 26th for the guidance of his subordinates in next day's operation were meticulous and full. Attempting to forestall confusion by assigning particular duties, he included no less than eleven numbered paragraphs in the order, all of them fairly long except the last, which contained a scant half-dozen words: "Port Hudson must be taken tomorrow."

At first it appeared that the order would be carried out, final paragraph and all; but around midmorning, when the thunder of the preliminary bombardment subsided and Weitzel went forward according to plan, driving the rebel skirmishers handsomely before him, he found that this unmasked their artillery, which opened point-blank on his troops with murderous effect. The bluecoats promptly hit the dirt and hugged it while their own batteries came up just behind them and unlimbered, returning the deluge of grape and canister at a range of two hundred and fifty yards. Crouched under all that hurtling iron and lead from front and rear, the men were badly confused and lost what little sense of direction they had retained during their advance through a maze of obstructions, both natural and man-made. "The whole fight took place in a dense forest of magnolias, mostly amid a thick undergrowth, and among ravines choked with felled and fallen timber, so that it was difficult not only to move but even to see," a participant was to recall, adding that what he had been involved in was not so much a battle or a charge as it was "a gigantic bush-whack." Paine and Grover, moving out in support of Weitzel, ran into the same maelstrom of resistance, with the same result. So did Augur, somewhat later, when his turn came to strike the Confederate center just south of the railroad. But all was strangely quiet all this while on the far left. At noon Banks rode over to look into the cause of this inaction, and found to his amazement that Tom Sherman had "failed utterly and criminally to bring his men into the field." The fifty-two-year-old Rhode Islander was at lunch, surrounded by "staff officers all with their horses unsaddled." As usual, despite the multiparagraphed directive, someone — in this case about 3500 someones, from the division commander down to the youngest drummer — had not got the word. Nettled by the dressing-down Banks gave him along with peremptory orders to "carry the works at all hazards," Sherman got his two brigades aligned at last and took them forward shortly after 2 o'clock. He rode at their head, old army style; but not for long. A conspicuous target, he soon tumbled off his horse, and the surgeons had to remove what was left of the leg he had been shot in.

Command of the division passed to Brigadier General William Dwight, who had resigned as a West Point cadet ten years ago to go into manufacturing in his native Massachusetts at the age of twenty-one, but had returned to military life on the outbreak of the war. However, for all the youth and vigor which had enabled him to survive three wounds and a period of captivity after being left for dead on the field of Williamsburg a year ago next month, Dwight could do no more than Sherman had done already. His pinned-down men knew only too well that to attempt to rise, with all those guns and rifles trained on them from behind the red clay parapets ahead, would mean at best a trip back to the surgery where the doctors by now were sawing off their former commander's leg. To attempt a farther advance, either here or on the east, was clearly hopeless; yet Banks was unwilling to call it a day until he had made at least one more effort. Weitzel's division, which had opened the action that morning around to the north, had gained more ground than any of the other four, causing one observer to remark that if he had "continued to press his attack a few minutes longer he would probably have broken through the Confederate defense and taken their whole line in reverse." Now that the defenders were alert and had the attackers zeroed in, that extra pressure would be a good deal harder to exert, but Banks at any rate thought it worth a try. Orders were sent to the far right for a resumption of the assault, and were passed along to the colonel commanding the two regiments lately recruited in the Teche, the 1st and 3d Louisiana Native Guards. Held in reserve till now, they were about to receive their baptism of fire: a baptism which, as it turned out, amounted to total immersion. A Union staff officer who watched them form for the attack described what happened. "They had hardly done so," he said, "when the extreme left of the Confederate line opened on them, in an exposed position, with artillery and musketry and forced them to abandon the attempt with great loss." However, that was only part of the story. Of the 1080 men in ranks, 271 were hit, or one out of every four. They had accomplished little except to prove, with a series of disjointed rushes and repulses over broken ground and through a tangle of obstructions, that the rebel position could not be carried in this fashion. And yet they had settled one other matter effectively: the question of whether Negroes would stand up under fire and take their losses as well as white men. "It gives me pleasure to report that they answered every expectation," Banks wrote Halleck. "In many respects their conduct was heroic. No troops could be more determined or more daring."

Yet this was but a fraction of the day-long butcher's bill, which was especially high by contrast; 1995 Federals had fallen, and only 235 Confederates. In reaction, Banks told Farragut next day that Port Hudson was "the strongest position there is in the United States." Though he frankly admitted, "No man on either side can show himself without being shot," he was no less determined than he had been before the assault was launched. "We shall hold on today," he said, "and make careful examinations with reference to future operations." That morning — unlike Grant after his second repulse, five days earlier at Vicksburg — he had requested "a suspension of hostilities until 2 o'clock this afternoon, in order that the dead and wounded may be brought off the field." Gardner consented, not only to this but also to a five-hour extension of the truce when it was found that the grisly harvest required a longer time for gleaning. Meanwhile Banks was writing to Grant, bringing him up to date on events and outlining the problem as he saw it now. "The garrison of the enemy is 5000 or 6000 men," he wrote. "The works are what would ordinarily be styled 'impregnable.' They are surrounded by ravines, woods, valleys, and bayous of the most intricate and labyrinthic character, that make the works themselves almost inaccessible. It requires time even to understand the geography of the position. [The rebels] fight with determination, and our men, after a march of some 500 or 600 miles, have done all that could be expected or required of any similar force." A postscript added an urgent request: "If it be possible, I beg you to send me at least one brigade of 4000 or 5000 men. This will be of vital importance to us. We may have to abandon these operations without it." No such reinforcements would be coming either now or later from Grant, who had his hands quite full upriver; but Banks had no real intention of abandoning the siege. "We mean to harass the enemy night and day, and to give him no rest," he declared in a message to Farragut that same day, and he followed this up with another next morning: "Everything looks well for us. The rebels attempted a sortie upon our right last evening upon the cessation of the armistice, but were smartly and quickly repulsed." Two days later, May 31, when the admiral informed him that three Confederate deserters had stated that "unless reinforcements arrive they cannot hold out three days longer," Banks replied: "Thanks for your note and the cheering report of the deserters. We are closing in upon the enemy, and will have him in a day or two."

So he said. But presently a dispatch arrived from Halleck, dated June 3, which threatened to cut the ground from under the besieging army's feet. Like Grant, and perhaps for the same reasons, Banks had kept the general-in-chief in the dark as to his intentions until it was too late for interference, and Old Brains expressed incredulity at the second-hand reports of what had happened. "The newspapers state that your forces are moving on Port Hudson instead of co-operating with General Grant, leaving the latter to fight both Johnston and Pemberton. As this is so contrary to all your instructions, and so opposed to military principles, I can hardly believe it true." That it was true, however, was shown by a bundle of letters he received that same day from Banks, announcing his intention to move southeast from Alexandria. "These fully account for your movement on Port Hudson, which before seemed so unaccountable," Halleck wrote next morning. But he still did not approve, and he said so in a message advising Banks to get his army back on what the general-in-chief considered the right track. "I hope that you have ere this given up your attempt on Port Hudson and sent all your spare forces to Grant. . . . If I have been over-urgent in this matter, it has arisen from my extreme anxiety lest the enemy should concentrate all his strength on one of your armies before you could unite, whereas if you act together you certainly will be able to defeat him." Banks bristled at being thus lectured to. It irked him, moreover, that the authorities did not seem to take into account the fact that he was the senior general on the river. If any reproach for nonco-operation was called for, it seemed to him that it should have been aimed at Grant. "Since I have been in the army," he replied in mid-June, when the second message reached him, "I have done all in my power to comply with my orders. It is so in the position I now occupy. I came here not only for the purpose of co-operating with General Grant, but by his own suggestion and appointment." In time Halleck came round. "The reasons given by you for moving against Port Hudson are satisfactory," he conceded in late June. "It was presumed that you had good and sufficient reasons for the course pursued, although at this distance it seemed contrary to principles and likely to prove unfortunate." If this was not altogether gracious, Banks did not mind too much. He considered that he had already disposed of Halleck's bookish June 4 argument with a logical rebuttal, written by coincidence on the same day: "If I defend New Orleans and its adjacent territory, the enemy will go against Grant. If I go with a force sufficient to aid him, [bypassing Port Hudson,] my rear will be seriously threatened. My force is not large enough to do both. Under these circumstances, my only course seems to be to carry this post as soon as possible, and then to join General Grant. . . . I have now my heavy artillery in position, and am confident of success in the course of a week."

Here again he underestimated the rebel garrison's powers of resistance; Port Hudson was not going to fall within a month, much less a week. Gardner had drawn his semicircular lines with care, anchoring both extremities to the lip of the hundred-foot bluff overlooking the river, and had posted his troops for maximum effect, whatever the odds.

North of the railroad there were two main forts, one square, the other pentagonal, with a small redoubt between them, all three surrounded and tied together by a network of trenches, occupied by two brigades under Colonels I. G. W. Steedman and W. R. Miles. Brigadier General William Beall, a Kentucky-born West Pointer, had his brigade, which was as big as the other two combined, disposed to the south along a double line of bastions, the largest of which surmounted the crest of a ridge and was called the Citadel because it dominated all the ground in that direction. These various major works, together with their redans, parapets, ditches, and gun emplacements, were mutually supporting, so that an advance on one invited fire from those adjoining it. Banks had discovered this first, to his regret, while launching the May 27 assault. Since then, he had limited his activities mainly to long-range bombardments and the digging of lines of contravallation, designed to prevent a breakout and to protect his troops from sorties. After two weeks of this, in the course of which a considerable number of his men were dropped by snipers, he grew impatient and ordered a probing night action which he characterized as an endeavor "to get within attacking distance of the works in order to avoid the terrible losses incurred in moving over the ground in front." Informed that the sudden lunge was to be preceded by a twenty-hour bombardment, Farragut, whose ships by now were getting low on ammunition, protested mildly that he did not think the constant shelling did much good. "After people have been harassed to a certain extent, they become indifferent to danger, I think," he said. But he added: "We will do all in our power to aid you." That power was not enough, as it turned out. At 3 o'clock in the morning, June 11, the blue infantry crept quietly forward under cover of darkness — and found the defenders very much on the alert. Though some men got through the abatis and up to the hostile lines, once the alarm was sounded they were quickly driven back, while those who chose not to run the gauntlet to regain their jump-off positions were taken captive. Except for lengthening the Federal casualty lists and increasing Confederate vigilance in the future, the action had no effect on anything whatsoever, so far as Banks and his shovel-weary, sniper-harassed men could discern: least of all on the siege, which continued as before.

His spirits were revived, however, by a message received two days later from Dwight, who reported that he had interrogated a quartet of Confederate deserters and had learned from them that the garrison, reduced by sickness to 3200 infantry and 800 artillerymen, was down to "about five days' beef." There were "plenty of peas, plenty of corn," but "no more meal." Starvation was staring the rebels in the face. In fact, a Mississippi regiment was said to be in such low spirits that it "drove about 50 head of cattle out of the works about a week ago," intending thereby to hasten the inevitable end. In short, Dwight wrote, "The troops generally wish to surrender, and despair of relief." Next morning, June 13, Banks decided to test the validity of this report. His plan, as he explained it to Farragut, whose co-operation was requested, was to "open a vigorous bombardment at exactly a quarter past eleven this morning, and continue it for exactly one hour.... The bombardment will be immediately followed by a summons to surrender. If that is not listened to, I shall probably attack tomorrow." The guns roared on schedule, then stopped at the appointed time, and Banks sent forward under a white flag his demand for instant capitulation. "Respect for the usages of war, and a desire to avoid unnecessary sacrifice of life, impose on me the necessity of formally demanding the surrender of the garrison of Port Hudson." That was the opening sentence of the page-long "summons," and it was balanced by another very like it at the close: "I desire to avoid unnecessary slaughter, and I therefore demand the immediate surrender of the garrison, subject to such conditions only as are imposed by the usages of civilized warfare. I have the honor to be, sir, very respectfully, your most obedient servant, *N. P. Banks*, Major General, Commanding." The Confederate reply was prompt and a good deal briefer. "Your note of this date has just been handed to me, and in reply I have to state that my duty requires me to defend this position, and therefore I decline to surrender. I have the honor to be, sir, very respectfully, your most obedient servant, *Frank. Gardner*, Major General, Commanding C. S. Forces."

Banks had said that if his demands were not "listened to" he probably would launch a second full-scale assault next morning, all along the line. At daybreak, following a vigorous one-hour cannonade which apparently served little purpose except to warn the Confederates he was coming, he did just that. When the smoke cleared it was found that he had suffered the worst drubbing of the war, so far at least as a comparison of the casualties was concerned. On the far left, Dwight was misdirected by his guides, with the result that he was blasted into retreat before he even knew he was exposed. In the center, Augur and Paine attacked with vigor and were bloodily repulsed when they struck what turned out to be the strongest point of the enemy line, the priest-cap near the Jackson road; Paine himself fell, badly wounded, and was carried off the field. On the right, Grover and Weitzel were stopped in midcareer when it was demonstrated that no man could clear the fire-swept ridge along their front and live. "In examining the position afterward," a Union officer declared, "I found [one] grass-covered knoll shaved bald, every blade cut down to the roots as by a hoe." By noon it was apparent that the assault had failed in every sector. All that had been accomplished was a reduction of the range for the deadly snipers across the way, and the price exacted was far beyond the worth of a few yards of shell-torn earth. There was hollow mockery, too, in the respective losses, North and South. The Federals had 1792 killed, wounded, and missing subtracted from their ranks, while the Confederates had lost an over-all total of 47.

Four weeks of siege, highlighted by two full-scale assaults and one abortive night attack, had cost Banks more than 4000 casualties along his seven concave miles of front. His men, suspecting that they had inflicted scarcely more than one tenth as many casualties on the enemy, were so discouraged that the best he could say of them, in a note to Farragut that evening, was that they were "in tolerable good spirits." Presently, though, even this was more than he could claim. "The heat, especially in the trenches, became almost insupportable, the stenches quite so," a staff major later recalled. "The brooks dried up, the creek lost itself in the pestilential swamp, the springs gave out, and the river fell, exposing to the tropical sun a wide margin of festering ooze. The illness and mortality were enormous." Counting noses four days after the second decisive repulse, Banks reported that he was down to 14,000 effectives, including the nine-month volunteers whose enlistments were expiring. This too was a source of discontent, which reached the stage of outright mutiny in at least one Bay State regiment, and the reaction was corrosive. Men whose time was nearly up did not "feel like desperate service," Banks told Halleck, while those who had signed on for the duration did not "like to lead where the rest will not follow." Old Brains had a prescription for that, however. "When a column of attack is formed of doubtful troops," he answered, "the proper mode of curing their defection is to place artillery in their rear, loaded with grape and canister, in the hands of reliable men, with orders to fire at the first moment of disaffection. A knowledge of such orders will probably prevent any wavering, and, if not, one such punishment will prevent any repetition of it in your army."

This was perhaps reassuring, though in an unpleasant sort of way, since it showed the general-in-chief to be considerably more savage where blue rebels were concerned than he had ever been when his opponents wore butternut or gray. However, Banks had even larger problems than mutiny on his hands by then. Emory was crying havoc in New Orleans, which he protested was in grave danger of being retaken by the rebels any day now. "The railroad track at Terre Bonne is torn up. Communication with Brashear cut off," he notified Banks on June 20, adding: "I have but 400 men in the city, and I consider the city and the public property very unsafe. The secessionists here profess to have certain information that their forces are to make an attempt on the city." Five days later — by which date Port Hudson had been under siege a month — he declared that the rebels bearing down on him were "known and ascertained to be at least 9000, and may be more.... The city is quiet on the surface, but the undercurrent is in a ferment." "Something must be done for this city, and that quickly," he insisted four days later.

His anxiety continued to mount in ratio to his estimate of the number of graybacks moving against him, until finally he said flatly: "It is a choice between Port Hudson and New Orleans.... My information is as nearly positive as human testimony can make it that the enemy are 13,000 strong, and they are fortifying the whole country as they march from Brashear to this place, and are steadily advancing. I respectfully suggest that, unless Port Hudson is already taken, you can only save this city by sending me reinforcements immediately and at any cost." What was more, he said, the danger was not only from outside New Orleans. "There are at least 10,000 fighting men in this city (citizens) and I do not doubt, from what I see, that these men will, at the first appearance of the enemy within view of the city, be against us to a man. I have the honor to be &c. *W. H. Emory*, Brigadier General, Commanding."

But Banks had no intention of loosening his grip on the upriver fortress, which he believed — despite the nonfulfillment of all his earlier predictions — could not hold out much longer. Emory would have to take his chances. If it came to the worst and New Orleans fell, Farragut would steam down and retake it with the fleet that would be freed for action on the day Port Hudson ran up the white flag. Meanwhile the signs were good. On June 29, no less than thirty deserters stole out of the rebel intrenchments and into the Union lines, and though by now Banks knew better than to judge the temper of the garrison by that of such defectors, he was pleased to learn from those who arrived in the afternoon that their dinner had been meatless. In the future, they had been told, the only meat they would get would be that of mules. Judging by the adverse reaction of his own troops to a far more palatable diet, Banks did not think the johnnies would be likely to sustain their morale for long on that. However, one of the butternut scarecrows brought with him a copy of yesterday's *Port Hudson Herald*, which featured a general order issued the day before by Gardner, "assuring the garrison that General Johnston will soon relieve Vicksburg, and then send reinforcements here." The southern commander declared as well, Banks pointed out in passing the news along to Halleck, "his purpose to defend the place to the last extremity."

Confident none the less "of a speedy and favorable result" — so at least he assured the general-in-chief — Banks kept his long-range batteries at work around the clock, determined to give the Confederates no rest. The fire at night was necessarily blind, but that by day was skillfully directed by an observer perched on a lofty yardarm of the *Richmond*, tied up across the river from the bluff. He communicated by wigwag with a battery ashore, which also had a signalman, and the two kept up a running colloquy, not only to improve the marksmanship, but also to relieve the tedium of the siege.

"Your fifth gun has hit the breastwork of the big rifle four times. Its fire is splendid. Can dismount it soon."

"You say our fifth gun?"

"Yes, from the left." But the next salvo brought a shift of attention. "Your sixth gun just made a glorious shot. . . . Let the sixth gun fire 10 feet more to the left."

"How now about the fifth and sixth guns?"

"The sixth gun is the bully boy."

"Can you give it any directions to make it more bully?"

"Last shot was little to the right."

Just then, however, the cannoneers were forced to call a halt. "Fearfully hot here," the battery signalman explained. "Several men sunstruck. Bullets whiz like fun. Have ceased firing for a while, the guns are so hot. Will profit by your directions afterward." Presently they resumed firing, though with much less satisfactory results, according to the observer high in the rigging of the *Richmond*.

"Howitzer shell goes 6 feet over the guns every shot; last was too low, little too high again." Exasperated, he added: "Can't they, or won't they, depress that gun?"

"Won't, I guess. . . . Was that shot any better, and that?"

"Both and forever too high."

"We will vamose now. Come again tomorrow."

"Nine a.m. will do, will it not?"

"Yes; cease signaling."

✗ 5 ✗

The forces threatening New Orleans were no such host as Emory envisioned, but they were under the determined and resourceful Richard Taylor, who earlier, though much against his will, had struck at Grant's supposedly vital supply line opposite Vicksburg. "To break this would render a most important service," Pemberton had told Kirby Smith in early May, in one of his several urgent appeals for help across the way. Returning to Alexandria as soon as Banks pulled out, Taylor prepared to move at once back down the Teche, threaten New Orleans, and thereby "raise such a storm as to bring General Banks from Port Hudson, the garrison of which could then unite with General Joseph Johnston in the rear of General Grant." On May 20, however, before he could translate his plan into action, he received instructions from Smith directing him to march in the opposite direction. "Grant's army is now supplied from Milliken's Bend by Richmond, down the Roundaway and Bayou Vidal to New Carthage," the department commander explained, and if Taylor could interrupt the flow of supplies along this route, the

Federal drive on Vicksburg would be "checked, if not frustrated." He sympathized with Taylor's desire "to recover what you have lost in Lower Louisiana and to push on toward New Orleans," Smith added, "but the stake contended for near Vicksburg is the Valley of the Mississippi and the Trans-Mississippi Department; the defeat of General Grant is the *terminus ad quem* of all operations in the West this summer; to its attainment all minor advantages should be sacrificed." Taylor agreed as to the object, but not as to the method, much preferring his own. However, as he said later, "remonstrances were of no avail." He turned his back on New Orleans, at least for the present, and set out up the Tensas, where he was joined by a division of about 4000 men under Major General John G. Walker, a Missourian lately returned from Virginia, where he had commanded a division in Lee's army and was one of the many who could fairly be said to have saved the day at Sharpsburg.

Debarking June 5 on the east bank of the Tensas, some twenty-five miles west of Grant's former Young's Point headquarters, Taylor sent his unarmed transports back downstream to avoid losing them in his absence. Next day he surprised and captured a small party of Federals at Richmond, midway between the Tensas and the Mississippi, only to learn that Grant had established a new base up the Yazoo, well beyond the reach of any west-bank forces, and was no longer dependent on the one at Milliken's Bend. "Our movement resulted, and could result, in nothing," Taylor later admitted. All the same, he carried out his instructions by attacking, at dawn of the 7th, both Young's Point and Milliken's Bend, sending a full brigade against each. Like Banks, Grant had been recruiting Negroes, but since he intended to use them as laborers rather than as soldiers, he had given them little if any military training apart from the rudiments of drill. Surprised in their camps by the dawn attacks, they panicked and fled eastward over the levee to the protection of Porter's upstream flotilla. The gunboats promptly took up the quarrel, blasting away at the exultant rebels, and Taylor, observing that the panic was now on the side of the pursuers, ordered Walker to retire on Monroe, terminus of the railroad west of Vicksburg, while he himself went back down the Tensas and up the Red to Alexandria. Once there, he returned his attention to Banks and New Orleans, glad to have done with what he called "these absurd movements" against a supposedly vital supply line which in fact had been abandoned for nearly a month before he struck it.

Though the losses had been unequal — 652 Federals had fallen or were missing, as compared to 185 Confederates — Grant was not disposed to be critical of the outcome. Agreeing with Porter that the rebels had got "nothing but hard knocks," he was more laconic than reproachful in his mid-June report of the affair: "In this battle most of the troops engaged were Africans, who had little experience in the use of firearms. Their conduct is said, however, to have been most gallant, and I doubt not but with good officers they will make good troops." Anyhow, this was beyond the circle of his immediate attention, which was fixed on the close-up siege of Vicksburg itself. Six divisions had been added by now to his original ten, giving him a total of 71,000 effectives disposed along two lines, back to back, one snuggled up to the semicircular defenses and the other facing rearward in case Joe Johnston got up enough strength and nerve to risk an attack from the east. Three divisions arrived in late May and early June from Memphis, the first of which, commanded by Brigadier General Jacob Lauman, was used to extend the investment southward, while the other two, under Brigadier Generals Nathan Kimball and William Sooy Smith, made up a fourth corps under Washburn, now a major general, and were sent to join Osterhaus, who had been left behind to guard the Big Black crossings while the two assaults were being launched. Frank Herron, who at twenty-five had won his two stars at Prairie Grove to become the Union's youngest major general, arrived from Missouri with his division on June 11 and extended the line still farther southward to the river, completing Grant's nine-division bear hug on Pemberton's beleaguered garrison. The final two were sent by Burnside from his Department of the Ohio. Commanded by Brigadier Generals Thomas Welsh and Robert Potter, they constituted a fifth corps under Major General John G. Parke and raised the strength of the rearward-facing force to seven divisions. "Our situation is for the first time in the entire western campaign what it should be," Grant had written Banks in the course of the build-up. And now that it was complete, so was his confidence as to the outcome of the siege, which he expressed not only in official correspondence but also in informal talks with his officers and men. "Gen. Grant came along the line last night," an Illinois private wrote home. "He had on his old clothes and was alone. He sat on the ground and talked with the boys with less reserve than many a little puppy of a lieutenant. He told us that he had got as good a thing as he wanted here."

One item he would have liked more of was trained engineers. Only two such officers were serving in that capacity now in his whole army. However, as one of them afterwards declared, this problem was solved by the "native good sense and ingenuity" of the troops, Middle Western farm boys for the most part, who showed as much aptitude for such complicated work as they had shown for throwing bridges over creeks and bayous during the march that brought them here. According to the same officer, "Whether a battery was to be constructed by men who had never built one before, [or] a sap-roller made by those who had never heard the name ... it was done, and after a few trials well done." Before long, a later observer remarked, "those who had cut wood only for stoves would be speaking fluently of gabions and fascines; men who had patiently smoothed earth so that radishes might grow better would be talking affectionately of terrepleins for guns." In all of this they were inspired by the same bustling energy and quick adaptability on the part of the generals who led them; for one thing that characterized Grant's army was the youth of its commanders. McClernand, who was fifty-one, was the only general officer past fifty. Of the twenty-one corps and division commanders assigned to the Army of the Tennessee in the course of the campaign, the average age was under forty. And that promotion had been based on merit was indicated by the fact that the average age of the nine major generals was as low as that of the dozen brigadiers; indeed, excepting McClernand, it was better than one year lower. Moreover, nine of these twenty-one men were older than Grant himself, and this too was part of the reason for his confidence in himself and in the army which had come of age, so to speak, under his care and tutelage. He considered it more than a match for anything the Confederates could bring against him — even under Joe Johnston, whose abilities he respected highly. One day a staff officer expressed the fear that Johnston was planning to fight his way into Vicksburg in order to help Pemberton stage a breakout; but Grant did not agree. "No," he said. "We are the only fellows who want to get in there. The rebels who are in now want to get out, and those who are out want to stay out. If Johnston tries to cut his way in we will let him do it, and then see that he don't get out. You say he has 30,000 men with him? That will give us 30,000 more prisoners than we now have."

This was not to say that the two repulsed assaults had taught him nothing. They had indeed, if only by way of confirming a first impression that the rebel works were formidable. One officer, riding west on the Jackson road, had found himself confronted by "a long line of high, rugged, irregular bluffs, clearly cut against the sky, crowned with cannon which peered ominously from embrasures to the right and left as far as the eye could see." Beyond an almost impenetrable tangle of timber felled on the forward slopes, "lines of heavy rifle pits, surmounted with head-logs, ran along the bluffs, connecting fort with fort, and filled with veteran infantry." The approaches, he said, "were frightful enough to appall the stoutest heart." Sherman agreed, especially after the two assaults which had cost the army more than four thousand casualties. "I have since seen the position at Sevastopol," he wrote years later, "and without hesitation I declare that at Vicksburg to have been the more difficult of the two." Skillfully constructed, well sited, and prepared for a year against the day of investment, the fortifications extended for seven miles along commanding ridges and were anchored at both extremities to the lip of the sheer 200-foot bluff, north and south of the beleaguered city. Forts, redoubts, salients, redans, lunets, and bastions had been erected or dug at irregular intervals along the line, protected by overlapping fields of fire and connected by a complex of trenches, which in turn were mutually supporting. There simply was no easy way to get at the defenders. Moreover, Grant's three-to-one

numerical advantage was considerably offset, not only by the
necessity for protecting his rear
from possible attacks by the
army Johnston was assembling
to the east, but also by the fact
that, because of the vagaries of
the up-ended terrain, his line of
contravallation had to be more
than twice the length of the line
he was attempting to confront.
"There is only one way to account for the hills of Vicksburg," a Confederate soldier had
said a year ago, while helping to
survey the present works. "After
the Lord of Creation had made
all the big mountains and ranges
of hills, He had left on His
hands a large lot of scraps.
These were all dumped at Vicksburg in a waste heap." One of
Grant's two professional engineers was altogether in agreement, pronouncing the Confederate position "rather an intrenched camp than a fortified

place, owing much of its strength to the difficult ground, obstructed by
fallen trees to its front, which rendered rapidity of movement and *en-
semble* in an assault impossible."

Yet even this ruggedness had its compensations. Although the
hillsides, as one who climbed them said, "were often so steep that their
ascent was difficult to a footman unless he aided himself with his hands,"
the many ravines provided excellent cover for the besiegers, and Grant
had specified in his investment order: "Every advantage will be taken
of the natural inequalities of the ground to gain positions from which to
start mines, trenches, or advance batteries." With the memory of slaughter fresh in their minds as a result of their two repulses, the men dug
with a will. Knowing little or nothing at the outset of the five formal
stages of a siege — the investment, the artillery attack, the construction
of parallels and approaches, the breaching by artillery or mines, and the
final assault — they told one another that Grant, having failed to go
over the rebel works, had decided to go under them instead. Fortunately
the enemy used his artillery sparingly, apparently conserving ammunition for use in repelling major assaults, but snipers were quick to shoot

at targets of opportunity: in which connection a Federal major was to recall that "a favorite amusement of the soldiers was to place a cap on the end of a ramrod and raise it just above the head-logs, betting on the number of bullets which would pass through it within a given time." Few things on earth appealed to them more, as humor, than the notion of some butternut marksman flaunting his skill when the target was something less than flesh and blood. Mostly, though, they dug and took what rest they could, sweating in their wool uniforms and cursing the heat even more than they did the snipers. Soon they were old hands at siege warfare. "The excitement . . . has worn away," a lieutenant wrote home from the trenches in early June, "and we have settled down to our work as quietly and as regularly as if we were hoeing corn or drawing bills in chancery."

Life in the trenches across the way — though the occupants did not call them that; they called them "ditches" — was at once more sedentary and more active. With their own 102 guns mostly silent and Grant's opposing 220 roaring practically all the time, they did nearly as much digging as the bluecoats, the difference being that they did it mainly in the same place, time after time, repairing damages inflicted by the steady rain of shells. Nor were they any less inventive. "Thunder barrels," for example — powder-filled hogsheads, fuzed at the bung — were found to be quite effective when rolled downhill into the enemy parallels and approaches. Similarly, such large naval projectiles as failed to detonate, either in the air or on contact with the ground, could be dug up, re-fuzed, and used in the same fashion to discourage the blue diggers on the slopes. However, despite such violent distractions, after a couple of weeks of spadework the two lines were within clod-tossing distance of each other at several points, and this resulted in an edgy sort of existence for the soldiers of both sides, as if they were spending their days and nights at the wrong end of a shooting gallery or in a testing chamber for explosives. "Fighting by hand grenades was all that was possible at such close quarters," a Confederate was to recall. "As the Federals had the hand grenades and we had none, we obtained our supply by using such of theirs as failed to explode, or by catching them as they came over the parapet and hurling them back."

Resistance under these circumstances implied a high state of morale, and such was indeed the case. Grant's heavy losses in his two assaults — inflicted at so little cost to the defenders that, until they looked out through the lifting smoke and saw the opposite hillsides strewn with the rag-doll shapes of the Union dead, they could scarcely believe a major effort had been made — convinced them that the Yankees could never take the place by storm. What was more, they had faith in "Old Joe" Johnston, believing that he would raise the siege as soon as he got his troops assembled off beyond the blue horizon, whereupon the two gray forces would combine and turn the tables on the besiegers. Until then, as they saw it, all that was needed was firmness against the odds, and they stood firm. Thanks to Pemberton's foresight, which included pulling corn along the roadside and driving livestock ahead of the army during its march from the Big Black, food so far was more plentiful inside the Confederate lines than it was beyond them. The people there were the first to feel the pinch of hunger; for the Federals, coming along behind the retreating graybacks, had consumed what little remained while waiting for roads to be opened to their new base on the Yazoo. "The soldiers ate up everything the folks had for ten miles around," a Union private wrote home. "They are now of necessity compelled to come here and ask for something to live upon, and they have discovered that they have the best success when the youngest and best-looking one in the family comes to plead their case, and they have some very handsome women here." This humbling of their pride did not displease him; it seemed to him no more than they deserved. "They were well educated and rich before their niggers ran away," he added, but adversity had brought them down in the world. "If I was to meet them in Illinois I should think they were born and brought up there."

Whether this last was meant as a compliment, and if so to whom, he did not say. But at least these people beyond the city's bristling limits were not being shot at; which was a great deal more than could be said of those within the gun-studded belt that girdled the bluff Vicksburg had been founded on, forty-odd years ago, by provision of the last will and testament of the pioneer farmer and Methodist parson Newitt Vick. In a sense, however, the bluff was returning to an earlier destiny. All that had been here when Vick arrived were the weed-choked ruins of a Spanish fort, around which the settlement had grown in less than two generations into a bustling town of some 4500 souls, mostly devoted to trade with planters in the lower Yazoo delta but also plagued by flatboat men on the way downriver from Memphis, who found it a convenient place for letting off what they called "a load of steam" that would not wait for New Orleans. As it turned out, though, the ham-fisted boatmen with knives in their boots and the gamblers with aces and derringers up their sleeves were mild indeed compared to what was visited upon them by the blue-clad host sent against them by what had lately been their government. Now the bluff was a fort again, on a scale beyond the most flamboyant dreams of the long-departed Spaniards, and the residents spent much of their time, as one of them said, watching the incoming shells "rising steadily and shiningly in great parabolic curves, descending with ever-increasing swiftness, and falling with deafening shrieks and explosions." The "ponderous fragments" flew everywhere, he added, thickening the atmosphere of terror until "even the dogs seemed to share the general fear. On hearing the descent of a shell, they would dart aside [and] then, as it exploded, sit down and howl in a pitiful manner." Children, on the other hand, observed the uproar with

wide-eyed evident pleasure, accepting it as a natural phenomenon, like
rain or lightning, unable to comprehend — as the dogs, for example, so
obviously did — that men could do such things to one another and to
them. "How is it possible you live here?" a woman who had arrived to
visit her soldier husband just before the siege lines tightened asked a citizen, and was told: "After one is accustomed to the change, we do not
mind it. But becoming accustomed: that is the trial." Some took it
better than others, in or out of uniform. There was for instance a
Frenchman, "a gallant officer who had distinguished himself in several
severe engagements," who was "almost unmanned" whenever one of
the huge mortar projectiles fell anywhere near him. Chided by friends
for this reaction, he would reply: "I no like ze bomb: I cannot fight him
back!" Neither could anyone else "fight him back," least of all the civilians, many of whom took refuge in caves dug into the hillsides. Some of
these were quite commodious, with several rooms, and the occupants
brought in chairs and beds and even carpets to add to the comfort,
sleeping soundly or taking dinner unperturbed while the world outside
seemed turned to flame and thunder. "Prairie Dog Village," the blue
cannoneers renamed the city on the bluff, while from the decks of ironclads and mortar rafts on the great brown river, above and below, and
from the semicircular curve of eighty-nine sand-bagged battery emplacements on the landward side, they continued to pump their steel-
packaged explosives into the checkerboard pattern of its streets and
houses.

Like the men in the trenches, civilians of both sexes and all ages
were convinced that their tormentors could never take Vicksburg by
storm, and whatever their fright they had no intention of knuckling under to what they called the bombs. For them, too, Johnston was the one
bright hope of deliverance. Old Joe would be coming soon, they assured each other; all that was needed was to hold on till he completed
his arrangements; then, with all the resources of the Confederacy at his
command, he would come swooping over the eastern horizon and
down on the Yankee rear. But presently, as time wore on and Johnston
did not come, they were made aware of a new enemy. Hunger. By
mid-June, though the garrison had been put first on half and then on
quarter rations of meat, the livestock driven into the works ahead of the
army back in May had been consumed, and Pemberton had his foragers
impress all the cattle in the city. This struck nearer home than even the
Union shells had done, for it was no easy thing for a family with milk-
thirsty children to watch its one cow being led away to slaughter by a
squad of ragged strangers. Moreover, the army's supply of bread was
running low by now, and the commissary was directed to issue instead
equal portions of rice and flour, four ounces of each per man per day,
supplementing a quarter-pound of meat that was generally stringy or
rancid or both. When these grains ran low, as they soon did, the experi-

ment was tried of baking bread from dough composed of equal parts of corn and dried peas, ground up together until they achieved a gritty consistency not unlike cannon powder. "It made a nauseous composition," one who survived the diet was to recall with a shudder, "as the corn meal cooked in half the time the peas meal did, so the stuff was half raw.... It had the properties of india-rubber, and was worse than leather to digest." Soon afterwards came the crowning indignity. With the last cow and hog gone lowing and squealing under the sledge and cleaver, still another experiment was tried: the substitution of mule meat for beef and bacon. Though it was issued, out of respect for religious and folk prejudices, "only to those who desired it," Pemberton was gratified to report that both officers and men considered it "not only nutritious, but very palatable, and in every way preferable to poor beef." So he said; but soldiers and civilians alike found something humiliating, not to say degrading, about the practice. "The rebels don't starve with success," a Federal infantryman observed jokingly from beyond the lines about this time. "I think that if I had nothing to eat I'd starve better than they do." Vicksburg's residents and defenders might well have agreed, especially when mule meat was concerned. Even if a man refused to eat such stuff himself, he found it disturbing to live among companions who did not. It was enough to diminish even their faith in Joe Johnston, who seemed in point of fact a long time coming.

Though at the outset the Virginian had sounded vigorous and purposeful in his assurance of assistance, Pemberton himself by now had begun to doubt the outcome of the race between starvation and delivery. "I am trying to gather a force which may attempt to relieve you. Hold out," Johnston wrote on May 19, and six days later he made this more specific: "Bragg is sending a division. When it comes, I will move to you. Which do you think is the best route? How and where is the enemy encamped? What is your force?" Receiving this last on May 29 — the delay was not extreme, considering that couriers to and from the city had to creep by darkness through the Federal lines, risking capture every foot of the way — the Vicksburg commander replied as best he could to his superior's questions as to Grant's dispositions and strength. "My men are in good spirits, awaiting your arrival," he added. "You may depend on my holding the place as long as possible." After waiting nine days and receiving no answer, he asked: "When may I expect you to move, and in what direction?" Three more days he waited, and still there was no reply. "I am waiting most anxiously to know your intentions," he repeated. "I have heard nothing from you since [your dispatch of] May 25. I shall endeavor to hold out as long as we have anything to eat." Three days more went by, and then on June 13 — two weeks and a day since any word had reached him from the world outside — he received a message dated May 29. "I am too weak to save Vicksburg," Johnston told him. "Can do no more than attempt to save you and your garrison. It will be impossible to extricate you unless you co-operate and we make mutually supporting movements. Communicate your plans and suggestions, if possible." This was not only considerably less than had been expected in the way of help; it also seemed to indicate that Johnston did not realize how tightly the Union cordon was drawn about Vicksburg's bluff. In effect, the meager trickle of dispatches left Pemberton in a position not unlike that of a man who calls on a friend to make a strangler turn loose of his throat, only to have the friend inquire as to the strangler's strength, the position of his thumbs, the condition of the sufferer's windpipe, and just what kind of help he had in mind. So instead of "plans and suggestions," Vicksburg's defender tried to communicate some measure of the desperation he and his soldiers were feeling. "The enemy has placed several heavy guns in position against our works," he replied on June 15, "and is approaching them very nearly by sap. His fire is almost continuous. Our men have no relief; are becoming much fatigued, but are still in pretty good spirits. I think your movement should be made as soon as possible. The enemy is receiving reinforcements. We are living on greatly reduced rations, but I think sufficient for twenty days yet."

Having thus placed the limit of Vicksburg's endurance only one day beyond the Fourth of July — now strictly a Yankee holiday — Pemberton followed this up, lest Johnston fail to sense the desperation implied, with a more outspoken message four days later: "I hope you will advance with the least possible delay. My men have been thirty-four days and nights in the trenches, without relief, and the enemy within conversation distance. We are living on very reduced rations, and, as you know, are entirely isolated." He closed by asking bluntly, "What aid am I to expect from you?" This time the answer, if vague, was prompt. On June 23 a courier arrived with a dispatch written only the day before. "Scouts report the enemy fortifying toward us and the roads blocked," Johnston declared. "If I can do nothing to relieve you, rather than surrender the garrison, endeavor to cross the river at the last moment if you and General Taylor communicate." To Pemberton this seemed little short of madness. Taylor had made his gesture against Young's Point and Milliken's Bend more than two weeks ago; by now he was all the way down the Teche, intent on menacing New Orleans. But that was by no means the worst of Johnston's oversights, which was to ignore the presence of the Union navy. The bluejacket gun crews would have liked nothing better than a chance to try their marksmanship on a makeshift flotilla of skiffs, canoes, and rowboats manned by the half-starved tatterdemalions they had been probing for at long range all these weeks. Besides, even if the boats required had been available, which they were not, there was the question of whether the men in the trenches were in condition for such a strenuous effort. They looked well enough to a casual eye, for all their rags and hollow-eyed gauntness, but it was observed that they tired easily under the mildest exertion and could serve only brief shifts when shovel work was called for. The meager diet was beginning to tell. A Texas colonel reported that many of his men had "swollen ankles and symptoms of incipient scurvy." By late June, nearly half the garrison was on the sick list or in hospital. If Pemberton could not see what this meant, a letter he received at this time — June 28: exactly one week short of the date he had set, two weeks ago, as the limit of Vicksburg's endurance — presumed to define it for him in unmistakable terms. Signed "Many Soldiers," the letter called attention to the fact that the ration now had been reduced to "one biscuit and a small bit of bacon per day," and continued:

> The emergency of the case demands prompt and decided action on your part. If you can't feed us, you had better surrender us, horrible as the idea is, than suffer this noble army to disgrace themselves by desertion. I tell you plainly, men are not going to lie here and perish, if they do love their country dearly. Self-preservation is the first law of nature, and hunger will compel a man to do almost anything.... This army is now ripe for mutiny, unless it can be fed. Just think of one small biscuit and one or two mouthfuls of bacon per day. General, please direct your inquiries in the proper channel, and see if I have not stated the stubborn facts, which had better be heeded before we are disgraced.

★　★　★

"Grant is now deservedly the hero," Sherman wrote home in early June, adding characteristically — for his dislike of reporters was not tempered by any evidence of affection on their part, either for himself or for Grant, with whom, as he presently said, "I am a second self" — that his friend was being "belabored with praise by those who a month ago accused him of all the sins in the calendar, and who next will turn against him if so blows the popular breeze. Vox populi, vox humbug."

In point of fact, however, once the encompassing lines had been drawn, the journalists could find little else to write about that had not been covered during the first week of the siege. And it was much the same for the soldiers, whose only diversion was firing some fifty to one hundred rounds of ammunition a day, as required by orders. Across the way — though the Confederates lacked even this distraction, being under instructions to burn no powder needlessly — the main problem, or at any rate the most constant one, was hunger; whereas for the Federals it was boredom. "The history of a single day was the history of all the others," an officer was to recall. Different men had different ways of trying to hasten the slow drag of time. Sherman, for instance, took horseback rides and paid off-duty visits to points of interest roundabout, at

least one of which resulted in a scene he found discomforting, even painful. Learning that the mother of one of his former Louisiana Academy
cadets was refugeeing in the neighborhood — she had come all the way
from Plaquemine Parish to escape the attentions of Butler and Banks,
only to run spang into Grant and Sherman — he rode over to tender his
respects and found her sitting on her gallery with about a dozen
women visitors. He introduced himself, inquired politely after her son,
and was told that the young man was besieged in Vicksburg, a lieutenant of artillery. When the general went on to ask for news of her
husband, whom he had known in the days before the war, the woman
suddenly burst into tears and cried out in anguish: "You killed him at
Bull Run, where he was fighting for his country!" Sherman hastily denied
that he had "killed anybody at Bull Run," which was literally true, but by
now all the other women had joined the chorus of abuse and lamenta-
tion. This, he said long afterwards, "made it most uncomfortable for me,
and I rode away."

Other men had other spare-time diversions. Grant's, it was said,
was whiskey. Some denied this vehemently, protesting that he was a
teetotaler, while some asserted that this only appeared to be the case because of his low tolerance for the stuff; a single glass unsteadied him,
and a second gave him the glassy-eyed look of a man with a heavy load
on. He himself seemed to recognize the problem from the outset, if only
by the appointment and retention of John A. Rawlins as his assistant
adjutant general. A frail but vigorous young man, with a "marble pallor"
to his face and "large, lustrous eyes of a deep black," Rawlins at first
had wanted to be a preacher, but had become instead a lawyer in Galena,
where Grant first knew him. His wife had died of tuberculosis soon after
the start of the war, and he himself would die of the same disease before
he was forty, but the death that seemed to have affected him most had
been that of his father, an improvident charcoal burner who had died at
last of the alcoholism that had kept him and his large family in poverty
all his life. Rawlins, a staff captain at thirty and now a lieutenant colonel
at thirty-two, was rabid on the subject of drink. He was in fact blunt in
most things, including his relationship with Grant. "He bossed everything
at Grant's headquarters," Charles Dana later wrote, adding: "I have
heard him curse at Grant when, according to his judgment, the general
was doing something that he thought he had better not do." Observing
this, many wondered why Grant put up with it. Others believed they
knew. "If you hit Rawlins on the head, you'll knock out Grant's brains,"
they said. But they were wrong. Rawlins was not Grant's brain; he was
his conscience, and a rough one, too, especially where whiskey was concerned. "I say to you frankly, and I pledge you my word for it," he had
written eighteen months ago to Elihu Washburne, the general's congressional guardian angel, "that should General Grant at any time become an intemperate man or an habitual drunkard, I will notify you

immediately, will ask to be removed from duty on his staff (kind as he has been to me) or resign my commission. For while there are times when I would gladly throw the mantle of charity over the faults of my friends, at this time and from a man of his position I would rather tear the mantle off and expose the deformity." Grant had cause to believe that Rawlins meant it. And yet, despite the danger to his career and despite what a fellow staffer called Rawlins' "insubordination twenty times a day," he kept him on, both for his own good and the army's.

Since writing to Washburne, however, the adjutant had either changed his mind about disturbing the mantle or else he had been singularly forgetful. Despite periodic incidents thereafter, in which Grant was involved with whiskey, Rawlins limited his remarks to the general himself, apparently in the belief that he could handle him. And so he could, except for lapses. Anyhow, there was never any problem so long as Mrs Grant was around; "If she is with him all will be well and I can be spared," he later confided to a friend. The trouble seemed in part sexual, as in California nine years ago, and it was intensified by periods of boredom, such as now. Three weeks of slam-bang fighting and rapid maneuver had given way to the tedium of a siege, and Mrs Grant had been six weeks off the scene. On June 5 Rawlins found a box of wine in front of the general's tent and had it removed, ignoring Grant's protest that he was saving it to toast the fall of Vicksburg. He learned, moreover, that the general had recently accepted a glass of wine from a convivial doctor. These were danger signs, and there were others that evening. Rawlins sat down after midnight and wrote Grant a letter. "The great solicitude I feel for the safety of this army leads me to mention, what I had hoped never again to do, the subject of your drinking. ... Tonight when you should, because of the condition of your health if nothing else, have been in bed, I find you where the wine bottle has just been emptied, in company with those who drink and urge you to do likewise, and the lack of your usual promptness and decision, and clearness in expressing yourself in writing conduces to confirm my suspicion." Rawlins himself had become rather incoherent by now, whether from anger or from sorrow; but the ending was clear enough. Unless Grant would pledge himself "[not] to touch a single drop of any kind of liquor, no matter by whom asked or under what circumstances," Rawlins wanted to be relieved at once from duty in the department. Grant, however, left early next morning — apparently before the letter reached him — on a tour of inspection up the Yazoo River to Satartia, near which he had posted a division in case Johnston came that way. The two-day trip, beyond the sight and influence of Rawlins, became a two-day bender.

Dana went with him, and on the way upriver from Haines Bluff they met the steamboat *Diligent* coming down. Grant hailed the vessel, whose captain was a friend of his, transferred to her, and had her turned back upstream for Satartia. Aboard was Sylvanus Cadwallader, a Chicago *Times* correspondent on the prowl for news. It was he who had ridden into Jackson with Fred Grant in mid-May, when they lost the race for the souvenir flag atop the capitol, and it was he who was to leave the only detailed eyewitness account of Grant on a wartime bender — specifically the two-day one which already was under way up the Yazoo. In some ways, for Cadwallader at least, it was more like a two-day nightmare. "I was not long in perceiving that Grant had been drinking," he wrote long afterwards, "and that he was still keeping it up. He made several trips to the bar room of the boat in a short time, and became stupid in speech and staggering in gait." The reporter of course had heard rumors of Grant's predilection, but this was the first time he had seen him show it to the extent of intoxication. Alarmed by the general's "condition, which was fast becoming worse," he tried to get the captain and a lieutenant aide to intervene. Neither would; so Cadwallader undertook to do it himself. He got Grant into his stateroom, locked the door, "and commenced throwing bottles of whiskey which stood on the table, through the windows, over the guards, into the river." Grant protested, to no avail; the reporter "firmly, but good-naturedly declined to obey," and finally got him quieted. "As it was a very hot day and the stateroom almost suffocating, I insisted on his taking off his coat, vest and boots, and lying down on one of the berths. After much resistance I succeeded, and soon fanned him to sleep."

But that was only the beginning. Shortly before dark, when the *Diligent* neared Satartia, she met two gunboats steaming down, and a naval officer came aboard to warn that it was not safe for the unarmed vessel to proceed. Dana — who later reported tactfully in his *Recollections* that "Grant was ill and went to bed soon after we started" — knocked on the stateroom door to ask whether the boat should turn back. Grant, he said, was "too sick to decide," and told him: "I will leave it to you." Now that he was awake, however, though still not "recovered from his stupor," Cadwallader said, the general took it into his head "to dress and go ashore," despite the naval officer's warning. Once more the reporter prevailed, and got him back to bed. While he slept, the *Diligent* returned downstream in the darkness to Haines Bluff. Next morning, according to Dana, Grant was "fresh as a rose, clean shirt and all, quite himself," when he came out to breakfast. "Well, Mr Dana," he observed, "I suppose we are at Satartia."

Cadwallader relaxed his guard, despite the 25-mile geographical error, presuming that "all necessity for extra vigilance on my part had passed," and was profoundly shocked to discover, an hour later, "that Grant had procured another supply of whiskey from on shore and was quite as much intoxicated as the day before." Again the reporter managed to separate the general from his bottle, only to have him insist on proceeding at once to Chickasaw Bayou. This would have brought them there "about the middle of the afternoon, when the landing would have been alive with officers, men, and trains from all parts of the army." Conferring with the captain as to the best means by which to avoid exposing Grant to "utter disgrace and ruin," Cadwallader managed to delay the departure so that they did not arrive until about sundown, when there was much less activity at the landing. As luck would have it, however, they tied up alongside a sutler boat whose owner "kept open house to all officers and dispensed free liquors and cigars generously." Alarmed at the possibilities of disaster, the reporter slipped hastily over the rail, warned the sutler of what was afoot, and "received his promise that the general should not have a drop of anything intoxicating on his boat." Back aboard the *Diligent*, Cadwallader helped the escort to unload the horses for the five-mile ride to army headquarters northeast of Vicksburg; but when this was done he looked around and could find no sign of Grant. Fearing the worst, he hurried aboard the sutler boat "and soon heard a general hum of conversation and laughter proceeding from a room opening out of the ladies' cabin." There he saw his worst fears realized. The sutler was seated at "a table covered with bottled whiskey and baskets of champagne," and Grant was beside him, "in the act of swallowing a glass of whiskey." Cadwallader once more intervened, insisting that "the escort was waiting, and it would be long after dark before we could reach headquarters." Grant came along, though he plainly resented the interruption. His horse was a borrowed one called Kangaroo "from his habit of rearing on his hind feet and making a plunging start whenever mounted." That was his reaction now; for "Grant gave him the spur the moment he was in the saddle, and the horse darted away at full speed before anyone was ready to follow." The road was crooked, winding among the many slews and bayous, but the general more or less straightened it out, "heading only for the bridges, and literally tore through and over everything in his way. The air was full of dust, ashes, and embers from campfires, and shouts and curses from those he rode down in his race." Cadwallader, whose horse was no match for Kangaroo, thought he had lost his charge for good. But he kept on anyhow, hoping against hope, and "after crossing the last bayou bridge three-fourths of a mile from the landing," caught up with him riding sedately at a walk. Finding that Grant had become "unsteady in the saddle" as a result of the drink or drinks he had had from the sutler, and fearing "discovery of his rank and situation," the reporter seized Kangaroo's rein and led him off into a roadside thicket, where he helped the general to dismount and persuaded him to lie down on the grass and get some sleep. While Grant slept Cadwallader managed to hail a trooper from the escort, whom he instructed to go directly to headquarters "and report at once to Rawlins — and no one else — and say to him that I want an ambulance with a careful driver."

Waking before the ambulance got there, Grant wanted to resume his ride at once, but the reporter "took him by the arm, walked him back and forth, and kept up a lively rather one-sided conversation, till the ambulance arrived." Then there was the problem of getting the general into the curtained vehicle, which he refused to permit until, as Cadwallader said, "we compromised the question by my agreeing to ride in the ambulance also, and having our horses led by the orderly." They reached headquarters about midnight to find the dark-eyed Rawlins and Colonel John Riggin, another staff officer, "waiting for us in the driveway." The reporter got out first, "followed promptly by Grant," who now gave him perhaps the greatest shock of the past two days. "He shrugged his shoulders, pulled down his vest, 'shook himself together,' as one just rising from a nap, and seeing Rawlins and Riggin, bid them good night in a natural tone and manner, and started to his tent as steadily as he ever walked in his life." Cadwallader turned to Rawlins, who was pale with rage — "The whole appearance of the man indicated a fierceness that would have torn me into a thousand pieces had he considered me to blame" — and said he was afraid, from what they had just seen, that the adjutant would think it was he, not Grant, who had been drinking. "No, no," Rawlins said through clenched teeth. "I know him, I know him. I want you to tell me the exact facts, and all of them, without any concealment. I have a right to know them, and I will know them."

He heard them all, from start to finish, but he never reported the incident to Washburne, any more than Dana did to the War Department, not only out of loyalty and friendship, but also perhaps on reflecting that if anything brought about Grant's removal, or even his suspension during an inquiry, command of the army would pass automatically to McClernand, whom they both despised. As for Cadwallader, despite assurances from Rawlins — "He will not send you out of the department while I remain in it," the adjutant told him — he spent an anxious night, "somewhat in doubt as to the view of the matter Gen. Grant would take next day," and "purposely kept out of his way for twenty-four hours to spare him the mortification I supposed he might feel." As it turned out, he need not have worried. "The second day afterward I passed in and out of his presence as though nothing unusual had occurred. To my surprise he never made the most distant allusion to [the matter] then, or ever afterward." From that time on, he said, it was "as if I had been regularly gazetted a member of his staff." Passes from Grant enabled the reporter to go anywhere he wanted; he could requisition transportation and draw subsistence from quartermaster and commissary authorities; his tent was always pitched near Grant's, and his dispatches often were sent in the official mail pouch; in short, he "constantly received flattering personal and professional favors and attentions shown to no one else in my position." All this was in return for his respecting a confidence which he kept for more than thirty years. In 1896, a seventy-year-old sheep raiser out in California, he wrote his memoirs, including an account of Grant's two-day trip up the Yazoo and back. For nearly sixty years they remained in manuscript, and when at last they were published, ninety years after the war was over, they were attacked and the writer vilified by some of the general's long-range admirers, who claimed that what Cadwallader called "this Yazoo-Vicksburg adventure" never happened.

At any rate, no harm had resulted from the army commander's two-day absence from headquarters, drunk or sober. The repulse of Taylor at Milliken's Bend and Young's Point by the gunboats, on the second day, increased Grant's confidence rather than his fretfulness, which in fact seemed to be cured. "All is going on here now just right," he wrote to a friend on June 15, and added: "My position is so strong that I feel myself abundantly able to leave it and go out twenty or thirty miles with force enough to whip two such garrisons." He had small use for Pemberton, characterizing him as "a northern man [who] got into bad company." Nor did he fear Joe Johnston. Though he respected his ability, he said he did not believe the Virginian could save Vicksburg without "a larger army than the Confederates now have at any one place." Next day, moreover, the watchful eye of former congressman Frank Blair enabled Grant to dispose of his third opponent, John McClernand, and thus wind up the private war he had been waging all this time. Scanning the columns of the Memphis *Evening Bulletin,* Blair spotted a congratulatory order McClernand had issued to his corps, claiming the lion's share of the credit for the victory he foresaw. Blair sent the clipping to Sherman, who forwarded it to Grant next day, calling it "a catalogue of nonsense" and "an effusion of vain-glory and hypocrisy . . . addressed not to an army, but to a constituency in Illinois." He also cited a War Department order, issued the year before, "which actually forbids the publication of all official letters and reports, and requires the name of the writer to be laid before the President of the United States for dismissal."

Grant had waited half a year for this, passing over various lesser offenses in hopes that one would come along which would justify charges that could not fail to stick. But now that he had it he still moved with deftness and precision, completing the adjustment of the noose. That same day, June 17, he forwarded the clipping to McClernand with a note: "Inclosed I send you what purports to be your congratulatory address to the Thirteenth Army Corps. I would respectfully ask if it is a true copy. If it is not a correct copy, furnish me one by bearer, as required both by regulations and existing orders of the Department." Next day McClernand acknowledged the validity of the clipping. "I am prepared to maintain its statements," he declared. "I regret that my adjutant did not send you a copy as he ought, and I thought he had." With the noose now snug, Grant sprang the trap: "Major General John A. McClernand is hereby relieved from command of the Thirteenth Army Corps. He will proceed to any point he may select in the state of Illinois and report by letter to Headquarters of the Army for orders." Grant signed the order after working hours, supposing that it would be delivered the following morning, but when James Wilson came in at midnight and heard what was afoot — there was bad blood between him and McClernand; the two had nearly come to blows a couple of weeks ago — he urged Rawlins to let him deliver the order in person, without delay, lest something come up — a rebel sortie at dawn, for example, which might enable McClernand to distinguish himself as he had done at Shiloh — to cause its suspension or cancellation. Rawlins agreed, and Wilson put on his dress uniform, summoned the provost marshal and a squad of soldiers, and set out through the darkness for McClernand's headquarters. Arriving about 2 o'clock in the morning, he demanded that the general be roused. Presently he was admitted to McClernand's tent, where he found the former congressman seated at a table on which two candles burned. Apparently he knew what to expect, for he too was in full uniform and his sword lay before him on the table. Wilson handed him the order, remarking that he had been instructed to see that it was read and understood. McClernand took it, adjusted his glasses, and perused it. "Well, sir, I am relieved," he said. Then, looking up at Wilson, whose expression did not mask his satisfaction, he added: "By God, sir, we are both relieved!"

He did not intend to take this lying down, but he soon found that Grant had played the old army game with such skill that his opponent was left without a leg to stand on. "I have been relieved for an omission of my adjutant. Hear me," McClernand wired Lincoln from Cairo on his way to Springfield, their common home. From there he protested likewise to Halleck, suggesting the possible disclosure of matters that were dark indeed: "How far General Grant is indebted to the forbearance of officers under his command for his retention in the public service, I will not undertake to state unless he should challenge it. None know better than himself how much he is indebted to that forbearance." That might be, but it was no help to the general up in Illinois; Grant challenged nothing, except to state that he had "tolerat[ed] General McClernand long after I thought the good of the service demanded his removal." In time, there came to Springfield a letter signed "Your friend as ever, A. Lincoln," in which the unhappy warrior was told: "I doubt whether your present position is more painful to you than to myself. Grateful for the patriotic stand so early taken by you in this life-and-death struggle of the nation, I have done whatever has appeared practicable to advance you and the public interest together." However: "For me to force you back upon Gen. Grant would be forcing him to resign. I cannot give you a new command, because we have no forces except such as already have commanders." In short, the President had nothing to offer his fellow-townsman in the way of balm, save his conviction that a general was best judged by those "who have been with him in the field. . . . Relying on these," Lincoln said in closing, "he who has the right needs not to fear."

This was perhaps the unkindest cut of all, since McClernand knew only too well what was likely to happen to his reputation if judgment was left to Sherman and McPherson and their various subordinate commanders, including the army's two remaining ex-congressmen Blair and Logan. Among all these, and on Grant's staff, there was general rejoicing at his departure. Major General Edward O. C. Ord, who had fought under Grant at Iuka, had just arrived to take charge of a sixth corps intended to consist of the divisions under Herron and Lauman; instead, he replaced McClernand. Three days later, on June 22, Sherman was given command of the rearward line, which was strengthened by shifting more troops from in front of Vicksburg. "We want to whip Johnston at least 15 miles off, if possible," Grant explained. Steele succeeded Sherman, temporarily, and the siege went on as before. No less than nine approaches were being run, all with appropriate parallels close up to the enemy trenches, so that the final assault could be launched with the lowest possible loss in lives. Mines were sunk under rebel strong-points, and on June 25 two of these were exploded on McPherson's front, the largest just north of the Jackson road. It blew off the top of a hill there, leaving a big, dusty crater which the attackers occupied for a day and then abandoned, finding themselves under heavy plunging fire from both flanks and the rear. The mine accomplished little, but contributed greatly to the legend of the siege by somehow lofting a Negro cook, Abraham by name, all the way from the Confederate hilltop and into the Federal lines. He landed more or less unhurt, though terribly frightened. An Iowa outfit claimed him, put him in a tent, and got rich charging five cents a look. Asked how high he had been blown, Abraham always gave the same answer, coached perhaps by some would-be Iowa Barnum. "Donno, massa," he would say, "but tink bout tree mile."

Mostly, though, the weeks passed in boredom and increasing heat, under whose influence the Confederates appeared to succumb to a strange apathy during the final days of June. A Federal engineer remarked that their defense "was far from being vigorous." It seemed to him that the rebel strategy was "to wait for another assault, losing in the meantime as few men as possible," and he complained that this had a bad effect on his own men, since "without the stimulus of danger . . . troops of the line will not work efficiently, especially at night, after the novelty has worn off." Another trouble was that they foresaw the end of the siege, and no man coveted the distinction of being the last to die. Not that all was invariably quiet. Occasionally there were flare-ups, particularly where the trenches approached conjunction, and the snipers continued to take their toll. Though the losses were small, the suffering was great. "It looked hard," a Wisconsin soldier wrote, "to see six or eight poor fellows piled into an ambulance about the size of Jones's meat wagon and hustled over the rough roads as fast as the mules could trot and to see the blood running out of the carts in streams almost." Taunts were flung as handily as grenades, back and forth across the lines, the graybacks asking, "When are you folks going to come on into town?" and the bluecoats replying that they were in no hurry: "We are holding you fellows prisoner while you feed yourselves." There was much fraternization between pickets, who arranged informal truces for the exchange of coffee and tobacco, and the same Federal engineer reported that the enemy's "indifference to our approach became at some points almost ludicrous." Once, for example, when the blue sappers found that as a result of miscalculation a pair of approach trenches would converge just inside the rebel picket line, the two sides called a cease-fire and held a consultation at which it was decided that the Confederates would pull back a short distance in order to avoid an unnecessary fire fight. At one stage of the discussion a Federal suggested that the approaches could be redesigned to keep from disturbing the butternut sentries, but the latter seemed to think that it would be a shame if all that digging went to waste. Besides, one said, "it don't make any difference. You Yanks will soon have the place anyhow."

Grant thought so, too. By now, in fact — though he kept his soldiers burrowing, intending to launch his final assault from close-up positions in early July — he was giving less attention to Pemberton than he was to Johnston, off in the opposite direction, where Sherman described him as "vibrating between Jackson and Canton" in apparent indecision. Blair had reported earlier, on returning from a scout, that "every man I picked up was going to Canton to join him. The negroes told me their masters had joined him there, and those who were too old to go, or who could escape on any other pretext, told me the same story." This had a rather ominous sound, as if hosts were gathering to the east, but Grant was not disturbed. He had access, through the treacherous courier, to many of the messages that passed between his two opponents. He knew what they were thinking, what the men under them were thinking, and what the beleaguered citizens were thinking. He spoke of their expectations in a dispatch he sent Sherman on June 25, the day the slave Abraham came hurtling into the hands of the Iowans: "Strong faith is expressed by some in Johnston's coming to their relief. [They] cannot believe they have been so wicked as for Providence to allow the loss of their stronghold of Vicksburg. Their principal faith seems to be in Providence and Joe Johnston."

By then — the fortieth day of siege — it had been exactly a month since the man in whom Vicksburg's garrison placed its "principal faith" assured Pemberton: "Bragg is sending a division. When it joins I will come to you." The division reached him soon afterwards, under Breckinridge, and was combined with the three already at hand under

Loring, French, and Walker; Johnston's present-for-duty strength now totaled 31,226 men, two thirds of whom had joined him since his arrival in mid-May. But he found them quite deficient in equipment, especially wagons, and deferred action until such needs could be supplied. In the interim he got into a dispute with the Richmond authorities, protesting that he had only 23,000 troops, while Seddon insisted that the correct figure was 34,000. Finally the Secretary told him: "You must rely on what you have," and urged him to move at once to Pemberton's relief. But Johnston would not be prodded into action. "The odds against me are much greater than those you express," he wired on June 15, and added flatly: "I consider saving Vicksburg hopeless." Shocked by his fellow Virginian's statement that he considered his assignment an impossible one, Seddon took this to mean that Johnston did not comprehend the gravity of the situation or the consequences of the fall of the Gibraltar of the West, which in Seddon's eyes meant the probable fall of the Confederacy itself. It seemed to him, moreover, that the general — in line with his behavior a year ago, down the York-James peninsula — was moving toward a decision not to fight at all, and to the Secretary this was altogether unthinkable. "Your telegram grieves and alarms me," he replied next day. "Vicksburg must not be lost without a desperate struggle. The interest and honor of the Confederacy forbid it. I rely on you still to avert the loss. If better resources do not offer, you must hazard attack. It may be made in concert with the garrison, if practicable, but otherwise without; by day or night, as you think best." Still Johnston would not budge. "I think you do not appreciate the difficulties in the course you direct," he wired back, "nor the probabilities or consequences of failure. Grant's position, naturally very strong, is intrenched and protected by powerful artillery, and the roads obstructed. . . . The defeat of this little army would at once open Mississippi and Alabama to Grant. I will do all I can, without hope of doing more than aid to extricate the garrison." Fairly frantic and near despair over this prediction that the Father of Waters was about to pass out of Confederate hands, severing all practical connection with the Transmississippi and its supplies of men and food and horses, Seddon urged the general "to follow the most desperate course the occasion may demand. Rely upon it," he told him, "the eyes and hopes of the whole Confederacy are upon you, with the full confidence that you will act, and with the sentiment that it were better to fail nobly daring than, through prudence even, to be inactive. . . . I rely on you for all possible to save Vicksburg."

But no matter what ringing tones the Secretary employed, Johnston would not be provoked into what he considered rashness. "There has been no voluntary inaction," he protested; he simply had "not had the means of moving." By then it was June 22. Two days later he received a message from Pemberton, suggesting that he get in touch with Grant and make "propositions to pass this army out, with all its arms and equipages," in return for abandoning Vicksburg to him. Johnston declined, not only because he did not believe the proposal would be accepted, but also because "negotiations with Grant for the relief of the garrison, should they become necessary, must be made by you," he replied on June 27. "It would be a confession of weakness on my part, which I ought not to make, to propose them. When it becomes necessary to make terms, they may be considered as made under my authority." In other words, any time Pemberton wanted to throw in the sponge, it would be all right with Johnston. However, he prefaced this by saying that the Pennsylvanian's "determined spirit" encouraged him "to hope that something may yet be done to save Vicksburg," and two days later, June 29, "field transportation and other supplies having been obtained," he put his four divisions on the march for the Big Black, preceded by a screen of cavalry.

He had never been one to tilt at windmills, nor was he now. The march — or "expedition," as he preferred to call it — "was not undertaken in the wild spirit that dictated the dispatches from the War Department," he later explained, and added scornfully: "I did not indulge in the sentiment that it was better for me to waste the lives and blood of brave soldiers 'than, through prudence even,' to spare them." He never moved until he was ready, and then his movements were nearly always rearward. The one exception up to now had been Seven Pines, which turned out to be the exception that proved the rule, for it had cost him five months on the sidelines, command of the South's first army, and two wounds that were still unhealed a year later. Moreover, it had resulted in his present assignment, which was by no means to his liking, though his resultant brusqueness was reserved for those above him on the ladder of command, never for those below. To subordinates he was invariably genial and considerate, and they repaid him with loyalty, affection, and admiration. "His mind was clear as a bell," a staff officer had written from Jackson to a friend, two weeks ago, while the build-up for the present movement was still in progress. "I never saw a brain act with a quicker or more sustained movement, or one which exhibited a finer sweep or more striking power. . . . I cannot conceive surroundings more intensely depressing. Yet amidst them all, he preserved the elastic step and glowing brow of the genuine hero."

Desperation never rattled him; indeed, it had rather the opposite effect of increasing his native caution. And such was the case now as he approached the Big Black, beyond which Grant had intrenched a rearward-facing line. On the evening of July 1, Johnston called a halt between Brownsville and the river, and spent the next two days reconnoitering. Convinced by this "that attack north of the railroad was impracticable," he "determined, therefore, to make the examinations necessary for the attempt south of the railroad." On July 3, near Birdsong's Ferry, he wrote Pemberton that he intended "to create a diversion, and thus enable you to cut your way out if the time has arrived for you to do this. Of that time I cannot judge; you must, as it depends upon your condition. I hope to attack the enemy in your front [on] the 7th. . . . Our firing will show you where we are engaged. If Vicksburg cannot be saved, the garrison must."

Next morning, however, before he took up the march southward he noticed a strange thing. Today was the Fourth — Independence Day — but the Yankees over toward Vicksburg did not seem to be celebrating it in the usual fashion. On this of all days, the forty-eighth of the siege, the guns were silent for the first time since May 18, when the bluecoats filed into positions from which to launch their first and second assaults before settling down to the digging and bombarding that had gone on ever since; at least till now. Johnston and his men listened attentively, cocking their heads toward the beleaguered city. But there was no rumble of guns at all. Everything was quiet in that direction.

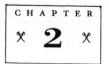
Stars in Their Courses

★ ✕ ☆

WHATEVER LACK OF NERVE OR INGENUITY
had been demonstrated in Mississippi throughout the long hot hungry
weeks that Vicksburg had shuddered under assault and languished under
siege, there had been no shortage elsewhere in the Confederate States of
either of these qualities on which the beleaguered city's hopes were hung.
Indeed, a sort of inverse ratio seemed to obtain between proximity
and daring, as if distance not only lent enchantment but also encouraged
boldness, so far at least as the western theater was concerned. A case in
point was Beauregard, 650 air-line miles away on the eastern seaboard.
Charleston's two-time savior was nothing if not inventive: especially
when he had time on his hands, as he did now. In mid-May, with the
laurels still green on his brow for the repulse of Du Pont's ironclad
fleet the month before, he unfolded in a letter to Joe Johnston — with
whom he had shared the triumph of Manassas, back in the first glad summer of the war, and to whom, under pressure from Richmond, he had
just dispatched 8000 of his men — a plan so sweeping in its concept that
the delivery of the Gibraltar of the West, whose plight had started him
thinking along these lines, was finally no more than an incidental facet of
a design for sudden and absolute victory over all the combinations
whereby the North intended to subjugate the South. According to his
"general views of the coming summer campaign," propounded in the
letter to his friend, Johnston would be reinforced by troops from all the
other Confederate commanders, who would stand on the defensive, east
and west, while Johnston joined Bragg for an all-out offensive against
the Union center, wrecking Rosecrans and driving the frazzled remnant of his army beyond the Ohio. Johnston would follow, picking up
10,000 recruits in Middle Tennessee and another 20,000 in Kentucky,
and if this threat to the Federal heartland had not already prompted a
withdrawal by the bluecoats from in front of Vicksburg, he could march
west to the Mississippi, above Memphis, "and thus cut off Grant's com-

munications with the north." When the besiegers moved upriver, as they would be obliged to do for want of supplies, Johnston would draw them into battle on a field of his choice, "and the result could not be doubtful for an instant." With Grant thus disposed of, the victorious southern Army of the Center, some 150,000 strong by then, could split in two, one half crossing the big river to assist Kirby Smith and Price in the liberation of Louisiana and Missouri, while the other half joined Lee in Virginia to complete "the terrible lesson the enemy has just had at Chancellorsville." Meanwhile, by way of lagniappe, a fleet of special torpedo boats would be constructed in England, from designs already on hand at Charleston, to steam westward across the Atlantic and "resecure" the Mississippi, upwards from its mouth. The war would be over: won.

Thus Beauregard. But after waiting five weeks and receiving no sign that his suggestions had been received, much less adopted, he felt, as he told another friend, "like Samson shorn of his locks." Time was slipping away, he complained in a postscript to his retained copy of the letter, despite the fact that "the whole of this brilliant campaign, which is only indicated here, could have been terminated by the end of June." On July 1 he heard at last from Johnston, though only on an administrative matter and without reference to his proposals of mid-May. Assuming that the original must have gone astray, he sent him at once a copy of the letter, together with the postscript stressing the need for haste in the adoption of the plan which he called brilliant. "I fear, though, it is now too late to undertake it," he admitted, and added rather lamely: "I hope everything will yet turn out well, although I do not exactly see how."

Nothing came of the Creole general's dream of reversing the blue flood, first in the center and then on the left and right; but others with easier access to the authorities in Richmond had been making similar, if less flamboyant, proposals all the while. Longstreet for example, on his way to rejoin Lee in early May, hard on the heels of Chancellorsville and the aborted Siege of Suffolk, outlined for the Secretary of War a plan not unlike Beauregard's, except that it had the virtue of comparative simplicity. It was Old Peter's conviction "that the only way to equalize the contest was by skillful use of our interior lines," and in this connection he proposed that Johnson give over any attempt to go directly to Pemberton's assistance and instead reinforce Bragg at Tullahoma, while Longstreet, with his two divisions now en route from Suffolk, moved by rail to that same point for that same purpose; Rosecrans would be swamped by overwhelming numbers, and the victors then could march for the Ohio. Grant's being the only force that could be used to meet this threat, his army would be withdrawn upriver and Vicksburg thereby would be relieved. . . . Seddon listened attentively. Though he liked the notion of using Hood and Pickett to

break the enemy's grip on the Mississippi south of Memphis, he preferred
the more direct and still simpler method of sending them to Jackson for a
movement against Grant where he then was. However, this presupposed the approval of Lee: which was not forthcoming. Lee replied that
he would of course obey any order sent him, but he considered the suggestion less than wise. "The adoption of your proposition is hazardous,"
he wired Seddon, "and it becomes a question between Virginia and the
Mississippi." The date was May 10; Stonewall Jackson died that afternoon. But Lee suppressed his grief in order to expand his objections to
the Secretary's proposal in a letter that same Sunday. He not only
thought the attempt to rescue Pemberton by sending troops from Virginia unduly risky; he also considered it unnecessary. "I presume [the
reinforcements] would not reach him until the last of this month," he
wrote. "If anything is done in that quarter, it will be over by that
time, as the climate in June will force the enemy to retire."

Seddon doubted that climate alone would be enough to cause the
Federals to abandon, even for a season, their bid for source-to-mouth
control of the Mississippi. Whatever Lee might think of Grant, the Secretary considered him "such an obstinate fellow that he could only be
induced to quit Vicksburg by terribly hard knocks." In fact, that had
been his objection to Longstreet's claim that a strike at Rosecrans
would abolish the threat downriver; Grant might simply ignore the
provocation and refuse to loosen his grip. Davis agreed. Moreover, he
shared Seddon's reservations about Johnston, who had just been ordered
to Jackson, as a deliverer of hard knocks. Between them, under pressure
of the knowledge that something had to be done, and done quickly,
now that the bluecoats were on the march in Pemberton's rear, the President and the Secretary decided that the time had come for a high-level
conference to determine just what that something was to be. On May
14, the day Johnston abandoned the Mississippi capital to Union occupation, they summoned Lee to Richmond for a full discussion of the problem.

He arrived next day, which was one of sorrow and strain for the
whole Confederacy; Stonewall Jackson was being buried, out in the
Shenandoah Valley, and Joe Johnston was retreating to Canton while
Grant turned west for a leap at Vicksburg from the rear. Davis and
Seddon hoped that, face to face with Lee, they might persuade him to
continue the risk of facing Hooker with a depleted army, so that Longstreet could join Johnston for a strike at Grant. However, they found
him still convinced that such an attempt, undertaken for the possible
salvation of Mississippi for a season, would mean the loss of Virginia
forever; and that for him was quite unthinkable. "Save in defense of my
native State, I never again desire to draw my sword," he had said two
years ago, on the day he resigned from the U.S. Army. Apparently he
still felt that way about it: with one refinement. His proposal now —

for he agreed that something drastic had to be done to reverse the blue flood of conquest in the center and on the far left of the thousand-mile Confederate line of battle — was that he launch a second invasion of the North. The first, back in September, had come to grief in Maryland because of a combination of mishaps, not the least of which had been McClellan's luck in finding the lost order issued by Lee when he snapped at the bait left dangling at Harpers Ferry. This time, though, he would profit by that experience. He would march without delay into Pennsylvania, deep in Washington's rear, where a victory might well prove decisive, not only in his year-long contest with the Army of the Potomac, in which he had never lost a major battle, but also in the war. It might or might not cause the withdrawal of Grant from in front of Vicksburg, but at least it would remove the invaders from the soil of Virginia during the vital harvest season, while at best it would accomplish the fall of the northern capital and thus encourage the foreign intervention which Davis long had seen as the key to victory over the superior forces of the Union. . . . The President and Seddon were impressed. Having heard Lee out, Davis asked him to return the following morning for a presentation of his views to the entire cabinet.

That too was a critical day for the young republic. Before it was over, Grant had thrown Pemberton into retreat from Champion Hill, continuing his lunge for the back door of Vicksburg, and Banks had ended his week-long occupation of Alexandria in order to move against Port Hudson. Lee spent most of it closeted with Davis and the cabinet at the White House, presenting his solution to the national crisis. He spoke not in his former capacity as military adviser to the President, and certainly not as general-in-chief — no such office existed in the Confederacy; Halleck's only counterpart was Davis, or at least a fraction of him — but rather as commander of the Department of Northern Virginia. Having rejected the notion of reinforcing Vicksburg — "The distance and the uncertainty of the employment of the troops are unfavorable," he told Seddon — Lee based his present advice on what was good or bad for his department and the soldiers in his charge. "I considered the problem in every possible phase," he subsequently explained, "and to my mind, it resolved itself into a choice of one of two things: either to retire to Richmond and stand a siege, which must ultimately have ended in surrender, or to invade Pennsylvania." Placed in that light, the alternatives were much the same as if the cabinet members were being asked to choose between certain defeat and possible victory. In fact, "possible" became *probable* with Robert E. Lee in charge of an invasion launched as the aftermath of Fredericksburg and Chancellorsville, triumphs scored against the same adversary and against longer odds than he would be likely to encounter when he crossed the Potomac with the reunited Army of Northern Virginia. Seddon and Benjamin, Secretary of the Treasury Christopher G. Memminger,

Attorney General Thomas H. Watts, and Secretary of the Navy Stephen R. Mallory all agreed with the gray-bearded general "whose fame," as one of them said, "now filled the world." They were not only persuaded by his logic; they were awed by his presence, his aura of invincibility. And this included Davis, who had seldom experienced that reaction to any man.

It did not include Postmaster General John H. Reagan. He was by no means persuaded by Lee, and such awe as he felt for any living man was reserved for Jefferson Davis, whom he considered self-made and practical-minded like himself. Born in poverty forty-five years ago in Tennessee, Reagan had been a schoolteacher and a Mississippi plantation overseer before he was eighteen, when he moved to Texas with all he owned tied up in a kerchief. Passing the bar, he had gone into Lone Star politics and in time won election to Congress, where service on the postal committee prepared him for his present assignment. In this he already had scored a singular triumph, unequaled by any American postmaster in the past seventy-five years or indeed in the next one hundred. Under Reagan's watchful eye, the Confederate postal department did not suffer an annual deficit, but yielded a clear profit. He accomplished this mainly by forcefulness and vigor, and now he employed these qualities in an attempt to persuade Davis and his fellow cabinet members that no victory anywhere, even in Washington itself, could offset the disaster that would result from the loss of the Mississippi. The only man present whose home lay beyond that river, he said plainly that he thought Lee was so absorbed in his masterful defense of Virginia that he did not realize the importance of the Transmississippi, which would be cut off from the rest of the country with the fall of Vicksburg. It had been claimed that Lee's advance might result in Grant's withdrawal to meet the challenge, but Reagan did not believe this for an instant. Grant was committed, he declared. The only way to stop him from accomplishing his object was to destroy him, and the only way to destroy him was to move against him with all possible reinforcements, including Longstreet's two divisions from Lee's army. As for the talk of co-operation expected from those with antiwar sentiments in the North — this too had been advanced as an argument for invasion; the peace movement had been growing beyond the Potomac — Reagan agreed with Beauregard as to "the probability that the threatened danger to Washington would arouse again the whole Yankee nation to renewed efforts for the protection of their capital." In short, he saw everything wrong with Lee's plan and everything right about the plan it had superseded. Grant was the main threat to the survival of the Confederacy, and it was Grant at whom the main blow must be aimed and struck.

Davis and the others heard both men out, and when the two had had their say a vote was taken. In theory, the cabinet could reject Lee's proposal as readily as that of any other department commander, Bragg or

Pemberton or Beauregard, for example, each of whom was zealous to protect the interests of the region for which he was responsible. But that was only in theory. This was Lee, the first soldier of the Confederacy — the first soldier of the world, some would assert — and this was, after all, a military decision. The vote was five to one, in the general's favor. Davis concurring, it was agreed that the invasion would begin at the earliest possible date.

Pleased with the outcome and the confidence expressed, Lee went that evening to pay his respects to a Richmond matron who had done much to comfort the wounded of his army. As he took his leave, it seemed to a young lady of the house — much as it had seemed earlier to five of the six cabinet members — that he was clothed in glory. "It was broad moonlight," she was to write years later, "and I recall the superb figure of our hero standing in the little porch without, saying a last few words, as he swung his military cape around his shoulders. It did not need my fervid imagination to think him the most noble looking mortal I had ever seen. We felt, as he left us and walked off up the quiet leafy street in the moonlight, that we had been honored by more than royalty."

Again Reagan had a different reaction. Unable to sleep because of his conviction that a fatal mistake had been made that day at the White House, he rose before dawn — it was Sunday now, May 17; Pemberton would be routed at high noon on the Big Black, and Johnston was advising the immediate evacuation of Vicksburg — to send a message urging Davis to call the cabinet back into session for a reconsideration of yesterday's decision. Davis did so, having much the same concern for Mississippi as Lee had for Virginia — his brother and sisters were there, along with many lifelong friends who had sent their sons to help defend the Old Dominion and now looked to him for deliverance from the gathering blue host — but the result of today's vote, taken after another long discussion, was the same as yesterday's: five to one, against Reagan. Lee returned to the Rappahannock the following day, which was the first of many in the far-off Siege of Vicksburg.

The problems awaiting him at Fredericksburg were multitudinous and complex. Chancellorsville, barely two weeks in the past and already being referred to as "Lee's masterpiece," had subtracted nearly 13,000 of the best men from his army. Of these, in time, about half would be returning; but the other half would not. And of these last, as all agreed, the most sorely missed was Jackson. "Any victory would be dear at such a price," Lee declared. He found it hard to speak of him, so deep was his emotion at the loss. "I know not how to replace him," he said — and, indeed, he did not try. Instead he reorganized the army, abandoning the previous grouping of the infantry into two corps, of four divisions each, for a new arrangement of three corps, each with three divisions. The new ninth division thus required was created by detaching two brigades from A. P. Hill's so-called Light Division, the largest in the army, and combining them with two brought up from Richmond and North Carolina; Henry Heth, Hill's senior brigadier, was given command, along with a promotion to major general. Similarly, one division was taken from each of the two existing corps — Anderson's from the First and what was left of Hill's from the Second — in order to fill out the new Third. The problem of appointing corps commanders was solved with equal facility. Longstreet of course would remain at the head of the First Corps, whose composition was unchanged except for the loss of Anderson; McLaws, Pickett, and Hood were in command of their three divisions, as before. The Second Corps went to Richard S. Ewell, Jackson's former chief subordinate, who opportunely returned to the army at this time, having recovered from the loss of a leg nine months ago at Groveton. A. P. Hill got the new Third Corps, which was scarcely a surprise; Lee had praised him weeks ago to Davis as the best of his division commanders, and moreover a good half of the troops involved had been under him all along. Promotion to lieutenant general went to both Ewell and Hill. Jubal Early kept the division he had led since Ewell's departure, and W. Dorsey Pender succeeded Hill, under whom he had served from the outset. He was promoted to major general, as was Robert Rodes, who was confirmed as commander of the division that had spearheaded the flank attack on Hooker. Major General Edward Johnson, returning to duty after a year-long absence spent healing the bad leg wound he had suffered at McDowell, the curtain raiser for Jackson's Valley Campaign, completed the roster of corps and division commanders by taking over the Second Corps division which had been temporarily under Colston. The artillery was reshuffled, too, and the general reserve abolished, so that each corps now had five battalions; William Pendleton, the former Episcopal rector, retained his assignment as chief of the army's artillery, though the title was merely nominal now that the reserve battalions had been distributed, and he remained a brigadier. Stuart, on the other hand, gained three new brigades of Virginia cavalry, brought in from various parts of the state in order to add their weight to the three he already had for the offensive. As a result of all these acquisitions, supplemented by volunteers and conscripts forwarded from all parts of the nation as replacements for the fallen, the army was almost up to the strength it had enjoyed before the subtractions of Fredericksburg and Chancellorsville. Approximately 75,000 effectives — in round figures, 5000 artillery, 10,000 cavalry, and 60,000 infantry — stood in its ranks. The infantry order of battle was as follows:

I. LONGSTREET	II. EWELL	III. A. P. HILL
McLaws	Early	Anderson
Pickett	Johnson	Heth
Hood	Rodes	Pender

The arrangement seemed pat and apt enough, but there were those who had objections no less sharp for being silent. Longstreet for instance, perhaps chagrined that Lee had not consulted him beforehand, resented Hill's promotion over the head of McLaws, whom he considered better qualified for the job. Aside from that, Old Peter was of the opinion that the post should have gone to Harvey Hill, on duty now in his home state of North Carolina. "His record was as good as that of Stonewall Jackson," the Georgian later wrote, "but, not being a Virginian, he was not so well advertised." There was, he thought, "too much Virginia" on the roster — and there were, in fact, apparent grounds for the complaint. Of the fifteen most responsible assignments in the army, ten were held by natives of the Old Dominion, including Lee himself, Ewell and Hill, Stuart, Early and Johnson, Pickett, Rodes and Heth, and Pendleton. Georgia had two, Longstreet and McLaws; Texas had Hood, South Carolina Anderson, and North Carolina, which furnished more than a quarter of Lee's troops, had only the newly promoted Pender; while Mississippi and Alabama, which furnished three brigades apiece, had no representative on the list at all.

Lee too saw possible drawbacks and shortcomings to the arrangement, though not with regard to the states his leading generals came from. His concern was rather with the extent of the reorganization, which placed two of his three corps and five of his nine divisions under men who previously had served either briefly or not at all in their present capacities. Moreover, though his brigadiers were the acknowledged backbone of his army, six of the thirty-seven brigades were under new commanders, and another half dozen were under colonels whom he considered unready for promotion. This troubled him, though not as much as something else. Always in his mind was the missing Jackson, whose death had been the occasion for the shake-up now in progress and of whom he said, "I never troubled myself to give him detailed instructions. The most general suggestions were all that he needed." Lee's proposed solution was characteristically simple. "We must all do more than formerly," he told one general. And this applied as much to himself as it did to anyone; especially as far as "detailed instructions" were concerned. The sustaining factor was the army itself, the foot soldiers, troopers, and cannoneers who had never failed him in the year since the last day of May, 1862, when Davis gave him the command amid the half-fought confusion of Seven Pines. He was convinced, he declared within ten days of the anniversary of his appointment, "that our army would be invincible if it could be properly organized and officered." Of the troops themselves, the rank and file who carried the South's cause on their bayonets, he had no doubts at all. "There never were such men in an army before," he said. "They will go anywhere and do anything if properly led."

Another known quantity, or at any rate an assumed one, was

James Longstreet. "My old warhorse," Lee had called him after Sharpsburg, a battle which Old Peter had advised against fighting — "General," he had said to Lee on entering Maryland, "I wish we could stand still and let the damned Yankees come to us" — but which at least was fought in the style he preferred, with the Confederates taking up a strong defensive position against which the superior blue forces were shattered, like waves against a rock. Fredericksburg, where his corps had suffered fewer than 2000 casualties while inflicting about 9000, had confirmed his predilection in that respect, and he considered Chancellorsville the kind of flashy spectacle the South could ill afford. Facing what Lincoln called "the arithmetic," he perceived that four more such battles, in which the Confederates were outnumbered two to one and inflicted casualties at a rate of three for four, would reduce Lee's army to a handful, while Hooker would be left with the number Lee had had at the outset. Disappointed by the rejection of his proposal that he take Hood and Pickett west for an assault on Rosecrans, the burly Georgian listened with disapproval as Lee announced his intention to launch an offensive in the East. He protested, much as Reagan had done, but with no more success; Lee's mind was made up. So Longstreet contented himself with developing his theory — or, as he thought, advancing the stipulation — that the proposed invasion be conducted in accordance with his preference for receiving rather than delivering attack when the two armies came to grips, wherever that might be. As he put it later, quite as if he and Lee had been joint commanders of the army, "I then accepted his proposition to make a campaign into Pennsylvania, provided it should be offensive in strategy but defensive in tactics, forcing the Federal army to give us battle when we were in strong position and ready to receive them."

Lee heard him out with the courtesy which he was accustomed to extend to all subordinates, but which in this case was mistaken for a commitment. He intended no such thing, of course, and when he was told years later that Longstreet had said he so understood him, he refused to believe that his former lieutenant had made the statement. But Old Peter had said it, and he had indeed received that impression at the time; whereby trouble was stored up for all involved.

In any case, once Lee had completed the groundwork for his plans, he wasted no time in putting them into execution. Four days after his May 30 announcement of the army's reorganization, and just one month after Chancellorsville, he started McLaws on a march up the south bank of the Rappahannock to Culpeper, near which Hood and Pickett had been halted on their return from Suffolk. Rodes followed on June 4, and Early and Johnson the next day, leaving Hill's three divisions at Fredericksburg to face alone the Union host across the river. Hooker's balloons were up and apparently spotted the movement, for the bluecoats promptly effected a crossing below the town. It was rumored that Lee had expressed a willingness to "swap queens," Richmond for Washington, in case Hooker plunged south while his back was turned. However, the validity of the rumor was not tested; Hill reported the bridgehead was nothing he could not handle, and Lee took him at his word. Riding westward in the wake of Longstreet and Ewell, he joined them at Culpeper on June 7.

Stuart had been there more than two weeks already, getting his cavalry in shape for new exertions, and two days before Lee's arrival he had staged at nearby Brandy Station a grand review of five of his brigades, including by way of finale a mock charge on the guns of the horse artillery, which lent a touch of realism to the pageant by firing blank rounds as the long lines of grayjackets bore down on them with drawn sabers and wild yells. Stirred or frightened by this gaudy climax, several ladies fainted, or pretended to faint, in the grandstand which Jeb had had set up for them along one side of the field. To his further delight, the army commander agreed to let him restage the show for his benefit on the day after his arrival, though he insisted that the finale be omitted as a waste of powder and horseflesh. Despite this curtailment, the performance was a source of pride to the plumed chief of cavalry, who, as Lee wrote home, "was in all his glory." It was something more, as well; for another result of this second review was that he still had most of his 10,000 troopers concentrated near Brandy on June 9 for what turned out to be the greatest cavalry battle of the war.

Thirty-nine-year-old Alfred Pleasonton, recently promoted to major general as successor to Stoneman, had eight brigades of cavalry, roughly 12,000 men, grouped in three divisions under Brigadier Generals John Buford, David Gregg, and Judson Kilpatrick. All were West Pointers, like himself, and all were of the new hell-for-leather style of horsemen who had learned to care more for results than they did for spit and polish. Buford, the oldest, was thirty-seven; Gregg was thirty; Kilpatrick was twenty-seven. Supported by two brigades of infantry, Pleasonton moved upriver from Falmouth on June 8, with six of his brigades, which gave him a mounted force equal in strength to Stuart's, and crossed at dawn next morning at Beverly and Kelly's fords, above and below Rappahannock Station. Instructed to determine what Lee was up to, there in the V of the rivers where Pope had nearly come to grief the year before, he got over under cover of the heavy morning fog and surprised the rebel pickets, who were driven back toward Brandy, five miles away, with the blue riders hard on their heels. And so it was that Stuart, who had pitched his headquarters tent on Fleetwood Hill overlooking the field where the two reviews were held, got his first sight of the Yankees at about the same time he received the first message warning him that they were over the river at Beverly Ford. Two of his present five brigades, under Rooney Lee and Brigadier General William E. Jones, were already in that direction, contesting the advance. Fitz Lee's brigade was seven miles north, beyond the Hazel River, and the other two, under Wade Hampton and Brigadier General Beverly Robertson, were in the vicinity of Kelly's Ford, where Pelham had fallen twelve weeks ago today. Stuart sent couriers to alert the brigades to the north and south, then rode forward to join the fight Lee and Jones were making, about midway between Beverly Ford and Fleetwood Hill. However, he had no sooner gotten the situation fairly well in hand on that quarter of the field than he learned that another enemy column of equal strength had eluded the pickets at Kelly's Ford and was riding now into Brandy Station, two miles in his rear. The result, as he regrouped his forces arriving from north and south to meet the double threat, was hard fighting in the classic style, headlong charges met by headlong countercharges, with sabers, pistols, and carbines employed hand to hand to empty a lot of saddles. He lost Fleetwood Hill, retook it, lost it again, and again retook it. Near sundown, spotting rebel infantry on the march from Brandy — his own infantry had been engaged only lightly — Pleasonton fell back the way he had come, effecting an orderly withdrawal. He had lost 936 men, including 486 taken prisoner, as compared to the Confederate total of 523, but he was well satisfied with his troopers and their day's work on the rebel side of the Rappahannock.

Stuart expressed an equal if not greater satisfaction. After all, he retained possession of the field, along with three captured guns, and had inflicted a good deal more damage than he had suffered: except perhaps in terms of pride. For there could be no denying that he had been surprised, on his own ground, or that the Yankees had fought as hard — and, for that matter, as well — as his own famed gray horsemen, at least one of whom was saying, even now, that the bluecoats had been successful because he and his fellows had been "worried out," all the preceding week, by the grand reviews Jeb staged out of fondness for "military foppery and display." One thing was clear to Stuart at any rate. Such exploits as he hoped to perform in the future, enhancing his already considerable reputation, were going to be more difficult to bring off than those he had accomplished in the days when the blue troopers were comparatively inept. Doubtless his solution was the same as the army commander's. "We must all do more than formerly," Lee had said, and for Jeb this meant more, even, than the two rides around McClellan.

Approaching the field of battle that afternoon, Lee experienced the double shock of learning that his normally vigilant chief of cavalry had suffered a surprise and of seeing his son Rooney being carried to the rear with an ugly leg wound. However, he did not let either development change his plans for the march northward; which were as follows. While Longstreet remained at Culpeper, in position to reinforce Hill in case Hooker tried to swamp him, Ewell would move into and down the

Shenandoah Valley, preceded by Stuart's sixth brigade of cavalry, en route from Southwest Virginia under Brigadier General Albert Jenkins. When Ewell reached the Potomac, he was to cross into Maryland and strike out for Pennsylvania without delay. Longstreet then would advance northward, east of the Blue Ridge, thus preventing Union penetration of the passes, while Hill marched west from Fredericksburg and followed Ewell down the Valley and over the Potomac, to be followed in turn by Longstreet, who would leave Stuart to guard the Blue Ridge passes until the combined advance of 60,000 butternut infantry into Pennsylvania caused the Washington authorities to call the Army of the Potomac northward across the river from which it took its name.

Lee's plan was a bold one, but it had worked well against Lincoln and McClellan in September and it seemed likely to work as well against Lincoln and Hooker nine months later. The most questionable factor was Ewell, whose corps would not only set the pace for the rest of the army, but would also be the first to encounter whatever trouble lay in store for the Confederates in the North. In effect, this meant that he was being required to march and fight with the same fervor and skill as his former chief and predecessor, and whether he could ever become another Jackson was extremely doubtful, especially since he was not even the same Ewell, either to the ear or eye, who had fought under and alongside the dead Wizard of the Valley. In partial compensation for the loss of his leg — though this seemed in fact to bother him very little, either on horseback or afoot — he had made two acquisitions. One was religion, which tempered his language, and the other was a wife, which tempered his whole outlook. Formerly profane, he now was mild in manner. Formerly of modest means, he now was wealthy, having won the hand of a rich widow who in her youth had rejected his suit in order to marry a man with the undistinguished name of Brown. Now that she and her extensive property were in his charge, Old Bald Head could scarcely believe his luck, and sometimes he forgot himself so far as to introduce her as "My wife, Mrs Brown." Whether this new, gentled Ewell would measure up to such high expectations was the subject of much discussion around the campfires of all three corps, particularly his own; but it soon appeared that all the worry had been for nothing. Out in the Valley, the scene of former military magic, his firm grasp of strategy and tactics, coupled with a decisiveness of judgment, a good eye, and an eagerness to gather all the fruits of sudden victory, made it seem to former doubters that another Stonewall had indeed been found to lead the Second Corps and inspire the army.

He moved northward on the day after Stuart's fight at Brandy Station, entered the Valley by way of Chester Gap, and on June 13, having divided his corps at Front Royal the day before, marched on Winchester with Early and Johnson while Rodes and the cavalry struck at Berryville. Major General Robert Milroy had 5100 bluecoats at the former place, and Ewell was out to get them, along with an 1800-man detachment at the latter, ten miles east. As it turned out, the Berryville force made its getaway due to blunders by Jenkins, who was unfamiliar with the kind of work expected of horsemen in Lee's army, but the success of the operation against Winchester more than made up for the disappointment. Warned to fall back, Milroy chose to stand his ground, much as Banks had done in a similar predicament the year before. That hesitation had led to Banks's undoing, and so now did it lead to Milroy's. Charged by Early on the 14th from the west, he retreated northeastward in the darkness, only to be intercepted at dawn by Johnson some four miles up the Harpers Ferry road at Stevenson's Depot, where he was routed. The Union general managed to escape with a couple of hundred of his troopers, but his unmounted men had no such luck in outrunning their pursuers, who gathered them up in droves. Johnson himself — called "Old Clubby" by his soldiers because he preferred to direct their combat maneuvers with a heavy walking stick instead of a sword — asserted happily that he had taken thirty prisoners "with his opera glass" before he ended his private chase by falling off his horse and into Opequon Creek. Milroy was presently removed from command by Lincoln, but that was a rather superfluous gesture, since practically all of his command had already been removed from him by Ewell. The total bag, in addition to the infliction of 443 casualties on the immediate field of battle, was 700 sick and 3358 able-bodied prisoners, 23 fine guns, and some 300 well-stocked wagons: all at a cost of 269 Confederate casualties, less than fifty of whom were killed. Ewell's triumph over Milroy was even greater than Jackson's had been over Banks on that same field: a fact that was not lost on the men of the Second Corps, whose final doubts as to the worth of their new commander were forgotten. Moreover, like Stonewall, Old Bald Head did not sit down to enjoy in leisure the spoils and glory he had won. Pushing Jenkins forward to the Potomac before sundown, he had Rodes follow on June 16 for a crossing at Williamsport, Maryland, where a halt was called to allow the other two divisions to catch up for a combined advance into Pennsylvania.

Lee had already put the other two corps in motion. On June 15, while Ewell was gathering prisoners in the woods and fields near Winchester, Longstreet started north from Culpeper, and Hill — who reported that Hooker had abandoned his west-bank bridgehead and withdrawn his army from its camps around Falmouth the day before, apparently for a concentration at or near Manassas, where he would stand athwart Lee's path in case the unpredictable Virginian launched a direct drive on Washington from Culpeper — left Fredericksburg, under instructions to follow Ewell's line of march to the Potomac. Two days later, Lee himself moved north, establishing headquarters at Berryville on the 19th, while Stuart fought a series of thunderous cavalry engagements at Aldie, Middleburg, and Upperville, in all of which he was successful at keeping his hard-riding blue opponents from discovering what was afoot beyond the mountains that screened the Valley from the Piedmont. Pleased with Jeb's recovery of his verve, the army commander listened with sympathy to the cavalry chief's suggestion that he leave two brigades of horsemen to plug the gaps of the Blue Ridge and move with the other three into Hooker's rear, the better to annoy and delay him when he started north across the Potomac. Lee approved, in principle, but warned that once it became clear that Fighting Joe was crossing the river, Stuart "must immediately cross himself and take his place on our right flank," where he would be needed to screen the northward advance and keep the invading army informed of the movements of the defenders. Aware of his former cadet's fondness for adventure at any price, Lee sent him written instructions on June 22, repeating the warning that he must not allow himself to be delayed in joining the rest of the column when the time came. Next day, when Stuart reported the bluecoats lying quiet in their camps north of Manassas and suggested that a crossing of the Potomac to the east of them by his three mobile brigades would help to mislead Hooker as to Lee's intentions, Lee followed his first message with a second, re-emphasizing the need for close observance of the Federals, but adding: "You will, however, be able to judge whether you can pass around their army without hindrance, doing them all the damage you can, and cross the river east of the mountains. In either case, after crossing the river, you must move on and feel the right of Ewell's troops, collecting information, provisions, etc." The dispatch ended on a note of caution. "Be watchful and circumspect in all your movements," Lee told Stuart.

Meanwhile the infantry was marching rapidly. By June 24, Ewell's main body had cleared Hagerstown and his lead division was at Chambersburg, twenty miles beyond the Pennsylvania line, with orders to press on to the Susquehanna. Presumably the North was in turmoil, having been warned that the penetration would be deep. "It is said," the Richmond *Whig* had reported the week before, "that an artificial leg ordered some months ago awaits General Ewell's arrival in the city of Philadelphia." Hill and Longstreet crossed the Potomac that same day, at Shepherdstown and Williamsport, and Lee himself made camp that night on the south bank, opposite the latter place, intending to cross over in the morning. Before he did so, however, he received from the President a reply to a letter written two weeks before, in which Lee had made certain admissions in regard to the present national outlook and had suggested some maneuvers he thought might be available to the Confederacy, not only on the military but also on the diplomatic front. "Our resources in men are constantly diminishing," he had written, "and the disproportion in this respect between us and our enemies, if they continue united in their efforts to subjugate us, is steadily augmenting." This being so, he thought the proper course would be to promote division in the northern ranks by encouraging those who favored arbitration as a substitute for bloodshed. "Should the belief that peace will bring back the Union become general," Lee continued, "the war would no longer be supported, and that, after all, is what we are interested in bringing about. When peace is proposed to us, it will be time enough to discuss its terms, and it is not the part of prudence to spurn the proposition in advance, merely because those who wish to make it believe, or affect to believe, that it will result in bringing us back to the Union." If this was sly, it was also rather ingenuous, particularly in its assumption of such a contrast between the peoples of the North and South that the latter would be willing to resume fighting if negotiations produced no better terms than a restoration of the Union, whereas the former would be willing to concede the Confederacy's independence rather than have the war begin again. Perceiving the risk involved — after all, it might turn out the other way around — Davis contented himself with remarking that encouragement of the followers of the northern peace party was a commendable notion, especially now that a second invasion was being launched at them. Lee replied next morning, as he prepared to cross the Potomac, that he was "much gratified" by the President's approval of his views. He suggested, moreover, that Bragg at Tullahoma and Buckner at Knoxville take the offensive against the Union center and thus "accomplish something in Ohio." Beauregard, too, could share in the delivery of the all-out blow about to be struck for southern independence, Lee said, by bringing to Culpeper such troops as he could scrape together on the Seaboard for a feint at Washington. This "army in effigy," as Lee called it, would have at least a psychological effect, particularly with the Hero of Manassas at its head, since it probably would cause Lincoln to make Hooker leave a portion of his army behind when he started north to challenge the invaders of Pennsylvania. Of course, it was rather late for such improvisations, but Lee suggested them anyhow. "I still hope that all things will end well for us in Vicksburg," he said in closing, unaware that this was the day Grant exploded the mine that transferred the slave Abraham's allegiance to the Union. "At any rate, every effort should be made to bring about that result." And with that, having advanced such recommendations as he thought proper in connection with the supreme endeavor he was about to make with the Army of Northern Virginia, he mounted Traveler and rode in a heavy rain across the shallow Potomac.

This was the week of the summer solstice, and the land was green with promise as Lee rode northward, this day and the next. "It's like a hole full of blubber to a Greenlander!" Ewell had exclaimed as he passed this way the week before. Hill and Longstreet agreed, finding that his heavy requisitions of food and livestock had scarcely diminished the pickings all around. Marches were so rapid over the good roads that some outfits enjoyed "breakfast in Virginia, whiskey in Maryland, and supper in Pennsylvania." Struck by the contrast to the ravaged, fought-over region in which they had spent most of the past two years, the Confederates gazed wide-eyed at the lush fields and cattle and the prosperity of the citizens who tilled and tended them. A Texas private wrote home in amazement that the barns hereabouts were "positively more tastily built than two thirds of the houses in Waco." The sour looks of the natives had no repressive effect on the soldiers, who "would ask them for their names so we could write them on a piece of paper, so we told them, and put it in water as we knew it would turn to vinegar." Spirits were high all down the long gray column. "Och, mine contree!" the lean marchers called out to the stolid men along the roadside, or: "Here's your played-out rebellion!" The Pennsylvanians in turn were impressed by the butternut invaders, so different from their own well-turned-out militiamen, who had fallen back northward at the approach of Ewell's outriders the week before. "Many were ragged, shoeless, and filthy," a civilian wrote, but all were "well armed and under perfect discipline. They seemed to move as one vast machine." Others found that the obvious admiration the rebels felt for this land of plenty did not necessarily mean that they preferred it to their homeland. The farms were too close together for their liking, and they complained of the lack of trees and shade, which made the atmosphere seem cramped and unfit for leisure. Even the magnificent-looking horses, the great Percherons and Clydesdales, turned out to be a disappointment in the end. Consuming about twice the feed, they could stand only about half the hardship required of what one artilleryman called "our compact, hard-muscled little horses. . . . It was pitiful later," he added, "to see these great brutes suffer when compelled to dash off at full gallop with a gun, after pasturing on dry broom sedge and eating a quarter of feed of weevil-eaten corn." Nor was the qualified reaction limited to those from whom it might have been expected. A housewife, questioning a Negro body servant who was attending his North Carolina master on the march, tested his loyalty by asking him if he was treated well, and she got a careful answer. "I live as I wish," he told her, "and if I did not,

I think I couldn't better myself by stopping here. This is a beautiful country, but it doesn't come up to home in my eyes."

Apparently Lee felt much the same way about it, for at Chambersburg on June 27 — he had arrived the day before and pitched his headquarters tent just east of town in a roadside grove called Shetter's Woods, where the townspeople came in normal times for picnics and such celebrations as the one planned for the Fourth of July, a week from now — he told "a true Union woman" who asked him for his autograph: "My only desire is that they will let me go home and eat my bread in peace." He said this despite the fact that his ride northward had in some ways resembled a triumphal procession, beginning with a gift of fresh raspberries just after he crossed the Potomac. Though Marylanders noted that he had aged considerably in the ten months since his previous visit, the gray commander on the iron-gray horse still impressed them as quite the handsomest man they had ever seen. "Oh, I wish he was ours!" a girl who was waving a Union flag exclaimed with sudden fervor as he passed through Hagerstown, and in Pennsylvania when a civilian whispered in awe as he rode by, "What a large neck he has," a nearby Confederate was quick with an explanation: "It takes a damn big neck to hold his head." The "perfect discipline" remarked on by civilians as the butternut columns wound past their houses and left them unmolested was the result of a decision Lee had made before leaving Virginia. "I cannot hope that Heaven will prosper our cause when we are violating its laws," he said. "I shall therefore carry on the war in Pennsylvania without offending the sanctions of a high civilization and of Christianity." Accordingly, he had instructed his commissary officers to meet all the necessities of the army by formal requisition on local authorities or by direct purchase with Confederate money. Exhorting his troops "to abstain with most scrupulous care from unnecessary or wanton injury to private property," he issued at Chambersburg today a general order commending them for their good behavior so far on the march. "It must be remembered that we make war only upon armed men," he told them, "and that we cannot take vengeance for the wrongs our people have suffered without lowering ourselves in the eyes of all whose abhorrence has been excited by the atrocities of our enemies, and offending against Him to whom vengeance belongeth, without whose favor and support our efforts must all prove in vain."

In part these words were written, and enforced, with an eye to the encouragement of the northern peace movement. Whether anything would come of that remained to be seen, but the effect on the men to whom the order was addressed was all that could have been desired. No army had ever marched better or with so little straggling. Longstreet and Hill had their two corps in bivouac at Chambersburg and Fayetteville, six miles east, and their men were in excellent spirits, well rested and far better shod and clad and fed than they had been when they were up this way the year before. Ewell by now was well along with his independent mission; Early was within half a dozen miles of York, and the other two divisions were at Carlisle, a short day's march from the Susquehanna and Harrisburg, which Ewell had been authorized to capture if it "comes within your means." This now seemed likely, and Lee was prepared to follow with the other two corps as soon as Stuart arrived to shield his flank and bring him news of what the Federals were up to on the far side of the Potomac. But there was the rub; Lee had heard nothing from Stuart in three days. This probably meant that Jeb and his picked brigades were off on the "ride" Lee had authorized on the 23d, but he seemed either to have ignored the admonition to "take his place on our right flank," which was highly improbable, or else to have run into unforeseen difficulties: which might mean almost anything, including annihilation, except that it was hard to imagine the irrepressible Stuart being caught in any box he could not get out of. Still, the strain of waiting was beginning to tell on Lee, who spent much of his time poring over a large-scale map of western Maryland and southern Pennsylvania which Stonewall Jackson had had prepared that winter, with just such a campaign as the present one in mind.

Another legacy from Jackson was a sixty-one-year-old West Pointer named Isaac Trimble, one of his favorite brigadiers, who reported for duty to Lee in Shetter's Woods today, having recovered at last from a leg wound received ten months ago. "Before this war is over," he had told Stonewall, "I intend to be a major general or a corpse." His promotion having come through in April, he had been slated for command of the division that had gone to Edward Johnson, but his injuries had been so slow to heal — in part, no doubt, because of his age — that it had been necessary to go ahead without him. There could be no question of his superseding Old Clubby, who had done so well at Winchester, yet Lee had no intention of losing the services of so hard a fighter as this veteran of all the Second Corps victories from First through Second Manassas, even though there was no specific command to give him that was commensurate with his rank. Ewell was moving against Harrisburg, Lee told Trimble; "go and join him and help him take the place." Before he left, however, Lee drew him into conversation about the terrain just beyond the mountains to the east. Trimble, who had been chief engineer of a nearby railroad before the war, replied that there was scarcely a square mile in that direction that did not contain excellent ground for battle or maneuver. Lee seemed pleased at that, and he told why. "Our army is in good spirits, not overfatigued, and can be concentrated in twenty-four hours or less." Not having heard from Stuart to the contrary — as he surely would have done if such had been the case — he assumed that the Federals were still on the far side of the Potomac, and he outlined for Trimble his plans for their destruction. "When they hear where we are, they will make forced

marches to interpose their forces between us and Baltimore and Philadelphia. They will come up, probably through Frederick, broken down
with hunger and hard marching, strung out on a long line and much
demoralized. When they come into Pennsylvania, I shall throw an overwhelming force on their advance, crush it, follow up the success, drive
one corps back on another, and by successive repulses and surprises, before they can concentrate, create a panic and virtually destroy the
army."

Stirred by this vision of the Army of the Potomac being toppled
like a row of dominoes, Trimble said that he did not doubt the outcome
of such a confrontation, especially since the morale of the Army of
Northern Virginia had never been higher than it was now. "That is, I
hear, the general impression," Lee replied, and by way of a parting gesture he laid his hand on the dead Jackson's map, touching the region
just east of the mountains that caught on their western flanks the rays
of the setting sun. "Hereabouts we shall probably meet the enemy and
fight a great battle," he said, "and if God gives us the victory, the war
will be over and we shall achieve the recognition of our independence."

One of the place names under his hand as he spoke was the college
town of Gettysburg, just over twenty miles away, from which no less
than ten roads ran to as many disparate points of the compass, as if it
were probing for trouble in all directions.

★   ★   ★

At sundown of that same June 27, as Trimble said goodbye to Lee
and left for Carlisle to join Ewell, a courier left Washington aboard a
special train for Hooker's headquarters, established just that afternoon at
Frederick. Though he thus was risking capture by rebel cavalry, which
was known to be on the loose, the documents he carried would admit
of no delay. In the past ten months, the army had fought four major battles under as many different commanders — Bull Run under Pope, Antietam under McClellan, Fredericksburg under Burnside, and Chancellorsville under Hooker — all against a single adversary, Robert Lee,
who could claim unquestionable victory in three out of the four: especially the first and the last, of which about the best that could be said
was that the Federal army had survived them. Now it was about to fight
its fifth great battle, and the import of the messages about to be delivered
was that it would fight it under still a fifth commander.

Not that Hooker had not done well in the seven weeks since
Chancellorsville. He had indeed: especially in the past few days, when
by dint of hard and skillful marching he managed to interpose his
100,000 soldiers between Lee and Washington without that general's
knowledge that the blue army had even crossed the river from which it
took its name. The trouble was that, despite his efforts to shift the
blame for the recent Wilderness fiasco — principally onto Stoneman

and Sedgwick and Howard's rattled Dutchmen — he could not blur a line of the picture fixed in the public mind of himself as the exclusive author of that woeful chapter. In early June, for example, the Chicago *Tribune* defined its attitude in an editorial reprinted in papers as far away as Richmond: "Under the leadership of 'fighting Joe Hooker' the glorious Army of the Potomac is becoming more slow in its movements, more unwieldy, less confident of itself, more of a football to the enemy, and less an honor to the country than any army we have yet raised." There was much in this that was unfair — particularly in regard to slowness, a charge Hooker had refuted once and would refute again — but it was generally known, in and out of army circles, that his ranking corps commander, Darius Couch, had applied for and been granted transfer to another department in order to avoid further service under a man he judged incompetent. Moreover, this mistrust was shared to a considerable extent by the authorities in Washington. Stanton and Halleck had never liked Joe Hooker, and Lincoln had sent him at the outset a letter which made only too clear the doubts that had attended his appointment. These doubts had been allayed for a time by the boldness and celerity of his movements preceding the May Day confrontation in the Wilderness, when he came unglued under pressure and revived them. Now they were back, and in force: as was shown by the day-to-day correspondence between himself and Lincoln, made voluminous by his determination to avoid all possible contact with Halleck, whom he regarded with reciprocal distaste.

On June 4, when Lowe's balloonists reported some Confederates gone from their camps across the Rappahannock, Hooker interpreted this as the opening movement of an offensive elsewhere, probably upriver, and reasoned that the most effective way to stop it was to launch one of his own, here and now. Next morning, after directing the establishment of a west-bank bridgehead for this purpose, he wired Lincoln that he thought his best move would be "to pitch into [Lee's] rear," and he asked: "Will it be within the sphere of my instructions to do so?" Lincoln replied promptly, to the effect that it would not. He had, he said, "but one idea which I think worth suggesting to you, and that is, in case you find Lee coming to the north of the Rappahannock, I would by no means cross to the south of it. . . . In one word, I would not take any risk of being entangled upon the river, like an ox jumped half over a fence and liable to be torn by dogs, front and rear, without a fair chance to gore one way or kick the other." Halleck followed this up with some advice of his own. "Lee will probably move light and rapidly," he warned. "Your movable force should be prepared to do the same." Hooker did as he was told, alerting his troops for a sidling movement up the north bank, but he maintained the bridgehead, not only as a possible means of learning what the enemy was up to, but also on the off-chance that the authorities might decide to give him his head after all. On June 10, hearing from Pleasonton that rebel infantry had been spotted in force at Brandy Station the day before, he showed that he too, though he considered the Washington defenses quite strong enough to withstand attack, was willing to risk a swap of queens in the presently deadly chess game. If Lee had taken a good part of his army west to Culpeper, Hooker wired Lincoln, "will it not promote the true interest of the cause for me to march to Richmond at once? . . . If left to operate from my own judgment, with my present information, I do not hesitate to say that I should adopt this course as being the most speedy and certain mode of giving the rebellion a mortal blow." Once more Lincoln was prompt in reply. Unlike Davis, who believed that the best defense of his capital was a threat to the enemy's, he was plainly horrified at this notion of removing the army from its present tactical position between Lee and Washington. Besides, he said, "If you had Richmond invested today, you would not be able to take it in twenty days; meanwhile your communications, and with them your army, would be ruined. I think Lee's army, and not Richmond, is your true objective point. If he comes toward the Upper Potomac, follow on his flank and on his inside track, shortening your lines whilst he lengthens his. Fight him, too, when opportunity offers. If he stays where he is, fret him and fret him."

Next morning Hooker began the movement north, conforming to the pattern set by Lee, but maintaining what Lincoln called the "inside track." This meant that he was required to keep between the Confederates and the capital in his rear, a limitation he found irksome. Moreover, though he knew the rebels had been reinforced for the campaign now fairly under way, his own army was far below the strength it had enjoyed when it marched on Chancellorsville. Nearly 17,000 men had fallen there, and an equal number of short-term enlistments had expired in the past six weeks. As a result of these subtractions, by no means offset by the trickle of recruits, barely 100,000 effectives left the familiar camps around Falmouth in the course of the next four days. To facilitate the march, which would be a hard one, he divided his army into two unequal wings, one led by John Reynolds, consisting of his own corps and those under Sickles and Howard, and the other by Hooker himself, consisting of those under Meade, Sedgwick, Slocum, and Hancock, who had succeeded Couch. "If the enemy should be making for Maryland, I will make the best dispositions in my power to come up with him," he assured Lincoln on June 14: only to receive from him a message sent at the same time. Foreseeing disaster in the present threat to Milroy, the Commander in Chief wanted something more from Fighting Joe than words of reassurance. "If the head of Lee's army is at Martinsburg and the tail of it on the Plank road between Fredericksburg and Chancellorsville," he wired, "the animal must be very slim somewhere. Could you not break him?" Strung out on the roads as he was by now, having abandoned the bridgehead he had held for more than a week, there was nothing Hooker could do for the present but keep marching, and that was what he did. Hancock's corps, the last to go, pulled out of Falmouth on June 15, the day that A. P. Hill left Fredericksburg and Ewell's lead division began its crossing of the Potomac. A simultaneous dispatch from Halleck, warning against "wanton and wasteful destruction of public property," snapped the string of Hooker's patience, and he got off an urgent wire to Lincoln: "You have long been aware, Mr President, that I have not enjoyed the confidence of the major general commanding the army, and I can assure you so long as this continues we may look in vain for success." This sounded as if he was saying he lacked confidence in himself, "the major general commanding the army," but it was Old Brains he meant, and Lincoln knew it. "To remove all misunderstanding," he replied, "I now place you in the strict military relation to General Halleck of a commander of one of the armies to the general-in-chief of all the armies. I have not intended differently, but as it seems to be differently understood, I shall direct him to give you orders and you to obey them."

The sting of this was somewhat relieved by a covering letter in which the Chief Executive explained that all he asked was "that you will be in such mood that we can get into our action the best cordial judgment of yourself and General Halleck, with my own poor mite added, if indeed he and you shall think it entitled to any consideration at all." However, it had begun to seem to Hooker that Lincoln's advice in regard to Lee — "fret him and fret him" — was also being applied in regard to himself, not only by the general-in-chief but also by the President, whose "poor mite" often made up in sharpness for what it lacked in weight. It seemed to Hooker that he was being goaded, and unquestionably he was. One after another his proposals had been dismissed as rash, or else they had been urged upon him only after subsequent instructions had placed his army in an attitude from which they could no longer be accomplished. Urgent appeals for reinforcements were rejected out of hand, as were others that his authority be extended to include the soldiers in the capital defenses. More and more, as the long hot days of hard and dusty marching went by, it came to seem to Fighting Joe that he commanded his army only in semblance, though it was clear enough at the same time that his was the head on which the blame would fall in event of the disaster he saw looming. Leapfrogging his headquarters northward, first to Dumfries and then to Fairfax, with no information as to what was occurring beyond his immediate horizon, he complained at last to Halleck, on June 24, that "outside of the Army of the Potomac I don't know whether I am standing on my head or feet." The next two days were spent crossing the Potomac at Edwards Ferry and effecting a concentration around Frederick. His plan was to strike westward into the Cumberland Valley, severing Lee's communications with Virginia, and for this he wanted the co-operation of the 10,000 men at Harpers Ferry, which was beyond the limits of his control, but which he thought should be evacuated before Lee turned and gobbled up the garrison as he had done in September. On the evening of June 26, believing that the authorities might have learned from that example — at least they had learned to post the troops on Maryland Heights, occupation of which had permitted the Confederates to take the place in short order the time before, along with some 12,000 men and 73 cannon — Hooker wired Halleck: "Is there any reason why Maryland Heights should not be abandoned after the public stores and property are removed?" Halleck replied next morning: "Maryland Heights have always been regarded as an important point to be held by us, and much expense and labor incurred in fortifying them. I cannot approve their abandonment, except in case of absolute necessity."

Convinced that the garrison was "of no earthly account" on its perch above the Ferry, Hooker decided to appeal through channels to Stanton and Lincoln. "All the public property could have been secured tonight," he wired back, "and the troops marched to where they could have been of some service. Now they are but a bait for the rebels, should they return. I beg that this may be presented to the Secretary of War and His Excellency the President." While waiting for an answer, he either decided the appeal should be strengthened or else he lost his head entirely. Or perhaps, having taken all he could take from above, he really wanted to get from under. At any rate, before the general-in-chief replied, Fighting Joe got off a second wire to him, hard on the heels of the first. "My original instructions require me to cover Harpers Ferry and Washington," it read. "I have now imposed upon me, in addition, an enemy in my front of more than my number. I beg to be understood, respectfully, but firmly, that I am unable to comply with this condition with the means at my disposal, and earnestly request that I may at once be relieved from the position I occupy." This was sent at 1 p.m. The long afternoon wore slowly away; the sun had set and night had fallen before he received an answer addressed to "Major General Hooker, Army of the Potomac." Whether the word *commanding* had been omitted by accident or design he could not tell. Nor was the body of the message at all conclusive on that point. "Your application to be relieved from your present command is received," Halleck told him. "As you were appointed to this command by the President, I have no power to relieve you. Your dispatch has been duly referred for Executive action."

The wire was headed 8 p.m. and that was where duplicity came in. Halleck knew that the special train had left Washington half an hour before that time, for the courier aboard it was Colonel James A. Hardie, his own assistant adjutant general, and Old Brains himself had written the documents he carried, one an order relieving Hooker of command

and the other a letter of instructions for his successor. Reaching Frederick well after midnight, Hardie did not wait for morning. Nor did he call first on Joe Hooker. Rather, he went directly to the tent of the man who would succeed him: George Meade.

This would come as something of a shock to the army, especially to Reynolds and Sedgwick, who ranked him, but no one was more surprised than Meade himself. His immediate reaction, on waking out of a sound sleep at 3 o'clock in the morning to find the staff officer standing beside his cot, was alarm. He thought he was about to be arrested. Sure enough, after a brief exchange of greetings, during which Meade wondered just what military sin he had committed, Hardie's first words were: "General, I'm afraid I've come to make trouble for you." And with that, changing the nature if not the force of the shock, he handed him Halleck's letter of instructions, which began: "You will receive with this the order of the President placing you in command of the Army of the Potomac."

Shortly before, in a letter to his wife, Meade had commented on "the ridiculous appearance we present of changing our generals after each battle," and only two days ago, amid rumors that Hooker was slated for removal, he had written her that he stood little chance of receiving the appointment, not only because he was outranked by two of his six fellow corps commanders, but also "because I have no friends, political or others, who press or advance my claims or pretensions." Yet now he had it, against all the odds, and with it a cluster of problems inherited on what was obviously the eve of battle. Partly, though — if he could believe what Halleck told him — these problems were reduced at the very outset. "You will not be hampered by any minute instructions from these headquarters," the letter read. "Your army is free to act as you may deem proper under the circumstances as they arise." His main duty would be to cover Washington and Baltimore. "Should General Lee move upon either of these places, it is expected that you will either anticipate him or arrive with him so as to give him battle." By way of stressing the fact that the new commander would have a free hand, Halleck added: "Harpers Ferry and its garrison are under your direct orders." Knowing the difficulties Hooker had encountered on this question, Meade could scarcely believe his eyes. "Am I permitted, under existing circumstances," he inquired by telegraph, later that same day, "to withdraw a portion of the garrison of Harpers Ferry, providing I leave sufficient force to hold Maryland Heights against a *coup de main?*" Promptly the reply came back: "The garrison at Harpers Ferry is under your orders. You can diminish or increase it as you think the circumstances justify."

Meanwhile the new commander had called on Hooker, who reacted to the order with as much apparent relief as Lincoln and Halleck had felt in issuing it. In fact, nothing in Fighting Joe's five-month tenure, in the course of which the army had experienced much of profit as well as pain, became him more than the manner in which he brought it to a close. Conferring with Meade on his plans and dispositions, he was co-operative and pleasant, except for one brief flare-up when Meade, looking over the situation map, remarked that the various corps seemed "rather scattered." Then Hooker quieted down, issued a farewell address urging support for his successor — "a brave and accomplished officer, who has nobly earned the confidence and esteem of this army on many a well-fought field" — and got into a spring wagon, alongside Hardie, for the ride to the railroad station. Meade shook his hand, stood for a moment watching the wagon roll away, then turned and entered the tent Hooker had just vacated. Presently he was interrupted by Reynolds, who had put on his dress uniform to come over and congratulate his fellow Pennsylvanian. This had a good effect on those who had wondered what his reaction would be: the more so because those closest to him knew that he had gone to Washington early that month, when it was rumored that Fighting Joe was about to get the ax, to tell Lincoln that he did not want the command — for which, with Couch gone, he was next in line — unless he was allowed more freedom of action than any of the army's five unfortunate chieftains had been granted up to then. Now, if not before, Reynolds had his answer, and he took it with aplomb. Sedgwick too arrived to offer congratulations and assurance of support, having managed to assuage the burning in his bosom which the announcement had provoked. News that it was Meade who would head the army, and not himself, had reached Uncle John while he was out for his morning ride. For him, as for most old soldiers, the tradition of seniority was a strong one. Putting the spurs to his horse, he led his staff on a hard gallop for some distance to relieve his agitation, then rode over to shake the hand of the man who had passed him by.

That hand was a busy one just now, getting the feel of the controls even as the vehicle was headed for a collision. Meade's own elevation called for other promotions and advancements beyond those recently conferred in the wake of Chancellorsville, which in turn had followed hard upon another extensive shake-up after bloody Fredericksburg. As a result, not one of the seven army corps was commanded now by the general who had led it into battle at Antietam, and the same was true of all but two of the nineteen infantry divisions — Humphreys' and Alpheus S. Williams' — only four of which were commanded by major generals: Doubleday, Birney, Newton, and Carl Schurz. Of the fifteen brigadiers in charge of divisions, seven had been appointed to their posts since early May: John C. Caldwell, Alexander Hays, James Barnes, Romeyn B. Ayres, Samuel W. Crawford, Horatio G. Wright, and Francis Barlow. Equally new to their positions were Hancock and George Sykes, successors to Couch and Meade as corps commanders. In fact, only Reynolds and Slocum had the same division commanders they had had at Chancellorsville: Doubleday, James S. Wadsworth, and John C. Robinson with the former, Williams and John W. Geary with the latter. Other drawbacks there were, too. In contrast to Lee, all of whose corps and division commanders were West Pointers except for one V.M.I. man, Meade had only fourteen academy graduates among the twenty-six generals who filled those vital positions in the Army of the Potomac. This meant that nearly half were nonprofessionals, and of these a number were political appointees: Dan Sickles for example, for whom Meade had small use, either military or private. He had, however, for whatever it was worth, a better geographical distribution among his generals than Lee had achieved. Eight were Pennsylvanians and seven were New Yorkers, while three were from Connecticut, two from Maine, two from Germany — Schurz and Adolf von Steinwehr, both of course in Howard's corps — and one each from Vermont, Massachusetts, Maryland, and Virginia. The revised order of battle was as follows:

I. REYNOLDS	II. HANCOCK	III. SICKLES	V. SYKES
Wadsworth	Caldwell	Birney	Barnes
Doubleday	Gibbon	Humphreys	Ayres
Robinson	Hays		Crawford

VI. SEDGWICK	XI. HOWARD	XII. SLOCUM
Wright	Barlow	Williams
Howe	Steinwehr	Geary
Newton	Schurz	

Doubtful as were the qualities of a sizable proportion of these men, one third of whom had been assigned to their current posts within the past eight weeks, none was more of a military question mark than the man who had just been given the most responsible job of all. This doubt was not so much because of any lack of experience; Meade had performed well, if not brilliantly, in combat as the commander of a brigade, a division, and a corps. If at Chancellorsville, through no fault of his own, he had been denied an appreciable share in the battle, at Fredericksburg his had been the only division to achieve even a brief penetration of the rebel line, and surely this had been considered by Lincoln — along with Reynolds' unacceptable stipulation and Sedgwick's alleged poor showing in early May, of which Hooker had complained — in making his choice as to who was to become the army's sixth commander. The question, rather, was whether Meade could inspire that army when pay-off time came round, as it was now about to do. He seemed utterly incapable of provoking the sort of personal enthusiasm McClellan and Hooker could arouse by their mere presence; Burnside and Pope, even the hapless McDowell, seemed downright gaudy alongside Meade, who gave an impression of professorial dryness and lack of juice. What he lacked in fact was glamour, not only in his actions and dispatches, but also in his appearance, which a journalist said was more that of "a learned pundit than a soldier." Two birthdays short of fifty, he looked considerably older, with a "small and compact" balding head, a grizzled beard, and outsized pouches under eyes that were "serious, almost sad," and "rather sunken" on each side of what the reporter charitably described as "the late Duke of Wellington class of nose." The over-all effect, although "decidedly patrician and distinguished," was not of the kind that brought forth cheers or a wholesale tossing of caps, particularly when it was known to be combined with a hair-trigger temper and a petulance which tested in turn the patience of his staff. "What's Meade ever done?" was a common response among the men — those outside his corps, at least — when they heard that he was their new commander. The general himself had few delusions on this score. "I know they call me a damned old snapping turtle," he remarked.

Whatever other shortcomings he might have, in addition to lacking glamour, it presently was shown that indecision was not one of them: at least not now, in these first hours. "So soon as I can post myself up, I will communicate more in detail," he had closed an early-morning telegram accepting the appointment to command. By midafternoon, having studied Hooker's plans and dispositions, along with intelligence reports on Lee — reports which, incidentally, turned out to be extremely accurate; "The enemy force does not exceed 80,000 men and 275 guns," he was told by Maryland observers who kept tally on what passed through Hagerstown, and this was within 5000 men and 3 guns of agreement with Lee's own figures, which included his scattered cavalry — Meade had decided on a course of action and had already begun to issue orders that would put it into execution. "I propose to move this army tomorrow in the direction of York," he wired Halleck at 4.45 p.m. This meant that he had rejected Hooker's plan for a westward strike at Lee's supply line. Moreover, the decision was made irrevocable by dispatches, not only recalling the units that had gone in that direction, but also ordering French to march eastward to Frederick with 7000 men while the remainder of the garrison served as train guards for the Harpers Ferry stores, which were to be removed at once to the capital defenses. Meade thus was adopting what had seemed to him at the outset the only proper course for him to take in conformity with his orders from above: "I must move toward the Susquehanna, keeping Washington and Baltimore well covered, and if the enemy is checked in his attempt to cross the Susquehanna, or if he turns toward Baltimore, to give him battle." Reynolds was retained as commander of the three corps in the lead on the swing north, and a warning order went out soon after sundown for the whole army to "be ready to march at daylight tomorrow.... Strong exertions are required."

That meant early reveille and breakfast in the dark, but the men had grown accustomed to this in the two weeks they had spent on the road since leaving the Rappahannock. All the same, and even though they had taken what Lincoln called the "inside track," the pace had been killing — Slocum's corps, as an extreme example, had covered thirty-three hot dusty miles in a single day while moving up to Fairfax — with the result that straggling had been worse than at any time since the berry-picking jaunt to First Bull Run, just three weeks short of two full years ago. For the most part, those who fell out managed to catch up at night and start out with their units in the morning, but enough had dropped out permanently, skulking in barns along the way, to bring the army's total down to 94,974 effectives of all arms. Then — on June 28, by coincidence a Sunday — had come a day of rest, occasioned by the change of commanders, and now they were off again. Although they did not know just where they were going, at any rate they were glad it was not back to the Old Dominion. "We have marched through some beautiful country," a colonel wrote home. "It is refreshing to get out of the barren desert of Virginia and into this land of thrift and plenty." One thing was practically certain, however, and this was that the road they now were taking led to battle. But that was all right, too, apparently, despite the tradition of defeat which had been lengthened under Burnside and Hooker and was a part of Meade's inheritance. "We felt some doubt about whether it was ever going to be our fortune to win a victory in Virginia," another soldier afterwards recalled, "but no one admitted the possibility of a defeat north of the Potomac."

★ ★ ★

For Lee, this same Sunday had been a day of puzzlement, mounting tension, and frustration. He not only did not know of the early-morning switch in blue commanders; he did not even know that for the past two days the whole Federal army had been on the same side of the Potomac as his own. Such ignorance might have been expected to be the opposite of disturbing — a maxim even described it as "bliss"— except that, as he knew only too well, having had occasion to prove it to several opponents, a lack of information was all too often the prelude to disaster. A recent prime example of this was Hooker, of whom Jackson had said on the ride to Guiney Station: "He should not have sent away his cavalry. That was his great blunder. It was that which enabled me to turn him, without his being aware of it, and to take him by the rear." Now Lee himself was in somewhat the same danger, and for somewhat the same reason. For the better part of a week he had heard nothing at all from Stuart, on whom he had always depended for information, or from any of his six brigades. One was at Carlisle with Ewell, approaching the Susquehanna; two were guarding the Blue Ridge passes, far to the south; while the other three, presumably, were off on another of those circumferential "rides" that had brought fame to their plumed leader. This last was not in itself the reason for Lee's anxiety. After all, he himself had authorized the adoption of such a course. What bothered him was the silence, which was as complete as if a sound-proof curtain had been dropped between him and his one best source of information. Scarcely an officer who approached him there in Shetter's Woods today escaped the question: "Can you tell me where General Stuart is?" or: "Where on earth is my cavalry?" or even: "Have you any news of the enemy's movements? What is the enemy going to do?"

No one had ever heard him ask such things before, for the simple reason that he had never needed to ask them; Stuart had generally supplied the answers in advance. And now, for lack of answers, he was obliged — as most of his opponents, to their distress in the course of the past year, had been obliged — to fall back on uninformed conjecture. This summoned up a host of alarming possibilities, including the danger that the bluecoats might be contemplating an attack on thinly defended Richmond or on his even more thinly defended supply line in the Cumberland Valley: both of which maneuvers had in fact been proposed by Hooker and disallowed by Lincoln. One would be about as unwelcome to Lee as the other in the present dispersed condition of his army, one third of which was a good forty miles from Chambersburg, where the remaining two thirds were in profitless bivouac and so completely stripped of cavalry that the foraging was being done by soldiers mounted on horses from the artillery and the wagon train. However, for all his inward anxiety, which he masked as best he could behind a show of being calm and even cheerful, Lee not only let his dispositions stand; he sent word for Ewell to continue the advance on Harrisburg, and prepared to move the rest of his army in that direction the following day, first Longstreet and then Hill, both of whom were put on the alert. "If the enemy does not find us," he explained, "we must try to find him, in the absence of the cavalry, as best we can." So he said, continuing the attempt to mask his growing concern. But still he asked all comers: "Can you tell me where General Stuart is?" and "Where on earth is my cavalry?"

Perhaps it was just as well, so far at least as his temper was concerned, that no one within range of his voice could give him the answer, which was not of a nature to relieve his qualms. In fact, it might well have upset him more than did the tantalizing silence. For even as he inquired of various callers as to the whereabouts of his cavalry on this Sunday afternoon, Stuart and the more than 5000 troopers of his three best brigades were on the northeast fringe of Washington, some seventy miles away. That was as the crow flew, moreover, and for anyone but a crow it would have been considerably farther, not only because Jeb had no more notion of Lee's whereabouts than Lee had of his, but also because a good many of those intervening miles were occupied by the Federal army, which Lee mistakenly assumed to be still south of the Potomac but which in fact was being alerted even now for a resumption of its northward march at dawn. This meant that Stuart would face tomorrow the same frustration he had faced today, and indeed for the past three days as well, in attempting to carry out his instructions to make contact with the right flank of the Confederate army of invasion; Hooker had stood in his path, and so would Meade. It had been that way from the outset, just after midnight June 24, when he first left Salem and moved east, beyond the Bull Run Mountains, to find a heavy column of blue infantry marching squarely athwart the route he had chosen for what was intended to be not only the greatest of all his "rides," but also indemnity for the ugly things some of the southern papers had been saying about him ever since the surprise they claimed he had suffered a couple of weeks ago at Brandy Station.

His plan, based on information that the bluecoats were inactive in their camps east of the mountains and were scattered over so wide an area that he would be able to push his way between two of their corps in order to get beyond them for a crossing of the Potomac in their rear, had been workable the day before, when the information was true; but it was true no longer. By coincidence, Hooker began his northward march to the Potomac shortly before Stuart emerged from Glasscock's Gap on the morning of June 25, and that was how it happened that Jeb found his progress blocked by a whole corps of Federals in motion across his front. Promptly he unlimbered the six guns he had brought along and began to shell the passing column, which extended north and south for a greater distance than the eye could follow. He thus was mindful of Lee's instructions to do the enemy "all the damage you can," but the admonition included in the same letter, that he was not to attempt his favorite maneuver unless he found he could do so "without hindrance," was ignored. Turning off to the south, he camped for the night near Buckland, intending to swing wide around the enemy rear next morning. However, dawn showed the Federals gone, and he rode east through Bristoe and Brentsville, not sighting a single bluecoat all day long, to bivouac just south of Occoquan Creek, which he crossed at Wolf Run Shoals next morning, June 27. In better than fifty hours he had covered less than forty miles of road, and he was about as far from the nearest Potomac ford as he had been when he started. Moreover, horses and men were beginning to show how hard they had been worked these past two weeks, fending off the aggressive blue troopers at such places as Middleburg and Aldie before undertaking their present exertions deep in the enemy rear. Frequent halts were necessary for rest and feeding, no matter how Stuart chafed when he remembered that his orders had been to cross the Potomac as soon as practicable after the 24th, three days ago.

Pressing northward, first through Fairfax Station, where he captured most of a 100-man detachment of New York cavalry, and then to Fairfax Court House, where he called a halt to let his hungry troopers "go through" several sutler shacks and graze their horses, he struck the

Leesburg-Alexandria turnpike and turned left along it for Dranesville, which he reached soon after sundown. Smoldering campfires were evidence that Federal infantry had recently passed this way and were still in the vicinity, guarding the better Potomac fords upstream; so he swung due north for a crossing at Rowser's Ford, which was deep and wide and booming. "No more difficult achievement was accomplished by the cavalry during the war," a staff officer later declared. The guns went completely out of sight, and the ammunition was distributed among the men, who kept it above water by carrying it over in their arms. By 3 o'clock in the morning, June 28 — as Meade awoke to find Hardie standing beside his cot — the entire command, one member said, "stood wet and dripping on the Maryland shore." Stuart let his troopers sleep till dawn, then resumed the march, mindful of his orders to "take position on General Ewell's right, place yourself in communication with him, guard his flank, keep him informed of the enemy's movements, and collect all the supplies you can for the use of the army." The trouble was he did not know Ewell's position, any more than he knew Lee's, except that Ewell would "probably move toward the Susquehanna." Jeb's decision to move in that direction, too, was easily arrived at. The whole Union army was to the west; the heavily-manned Washington defenses were to the east; all that was left — unless he gave the project up and retraced his steps southward, which apparently never crossed his mind — was north, and that was the way he went.

By midday he was in Rockville, a town on the National Road, which ran from Washington through Frederick, present headquarters of the Army of the Potomac, and thence on out to Ohio. Rockville was thus on the main Federal supply route, and scouts reported a train of 150 mule-drawn wagons on the way there from the capital, whose outskirts were less than a dozen miles away. Soon they came in sight and the raiders bore down on them, whooping in hungry anticipation of a feast. "The wagons were brand new, the mules fat and sleek, and the harness in use for the first time," one trooper later wrote. "Such a train we had never seen before and did not see again." Though almost half were captured at that first swoop, the other teamsters got their wagons turned around and took off down the road at a hard trot. For a time it looked as if they might be able to outrun the weary rebel horses, but presently a wagon overturned and caused a pile-up, blocking the road for all but about two dozen of the others, whose drivers continued their race for safety, still pursued, until the gray riders came within full view of Washington itself and abandoned the chase. Even without the ones that got away, the spoils were rich, including 400 teamsters, 900 mules, and 125 wagons loaded with hams, bacon, sugar, hardtack, bottled whiskey, and enough oats to feed the 5000 half-starved mounts of the raiders for several days. Much time was spent at Rockville, paroling the prisoners, feeding the horses, and accepting the admiring glances of some young ladies from a local seminary, who came out waving improvised Confederate flags and requesting souvenir buttons. While all this was going on, Stuart toyed with the notion of making a quick dash into the northern capital, but then rejected it regretfully — for lack of time, he subsequently explained — and resumed his northward march at sundown, hampered somewhat by the "one hundred and twenty-five best United States model wagons and splendid teams with gay caparisons" which he was determined to turn over to Lee, as a sort of super trophy of the ride, when and if he managed to find him.

A twenty-mile night march brought the raiders into Cooksville, where they captured another detachment of blue cavalry on the morning of June 29 before pushing on to Hood's Mill, a station on the B&O about midway between Baltimore and Frederick. While further disrupting the Federal lines of supply and communication by tearing up the tracks there and burning a bridge at Sykeston, three miles east, Stuart inquired of friendly Marylanders as to Ewell's whereabouts. None of them could tell him anything, but newspapers just in from the north reported Confederate infantry at York and Carlisle, moving against Wrightsville and Harrisburg; so Jeb pressed on to Westminster, fifteen miles north, on the turnpike connecting Gettysburg and Baltimore. Arriving in the late afternoon, he gobbled up another mounted blue detachment and made camp for the night. Scouts brought word that Union cavalry was in strength at Littletown, twelve miles ahead and just beyond the Pennsylvania line. Next morning — it was now the last day of June, the sixth he had spent out of touch with the rest of the army — he took the precaution of placing Fitz Lee on the left of the column, assigned Hampton to guard the captured wagons, and rode in the lead with Colonel John R. Chambliss, successor to the wounded Rooney Lee. His immediate objective, another fifteen miles to the north, was Hanover, where he would be able to choose between two good roads, one leading northwest to Carlisle and the other northeast to York, for a hook-up with one or the other of Ewell's reported columns of invasion. What he encountered first at Hanover, however, was a fight. It was an unequal affair, the enemy force amounting to no more than a single brigade, but what the blue horsemen lacked in numbers they made up for in vigor. A sudden charge struck and shattered the head of the gray column, and Stuart himself was obliged to take a fifteen-foot ditch jump to avoid being captured along with his blooded mare Virginia. "I shall never forget the glimpse I then saw of this beautiful animal away up in midair over the chasm," a staff officer later wrote, "and Stuart's fine figure sitting erect and firm in the saddle." Bringing up reserves, Jeb drove off the attackers, who in turn were reinforced by another brigade. No serious fighting ensued, however, for while the Federals seemed content to block the road to Gettysburg, a dozen miles to the west, Stuart wanted only to take the road to York, twenty miles to the northeast.

After some desultory long-range firing, the two forces drew apart, the Confederates still hampered by the train of captured wagons and some 400 prisoners, taken here and elsewhere in the past two days since leaving Rockville, where the previous 400 had been paroled.

This called for another night march, and the riders who made it remembered it ever after as a nightmare. "It is impossible for me to give you a correct idea of the fatigue and exhaustion of the men and beasts," a lieutenant afterwards said. "Even in line of battle, in momentary expectation of being made to charge, [the men] would throw themselves upon their horses' necks, and even to the ground, and fall to sleep. Couriers in attempting to give orders to officers would be compelled to give them a shake and a word, before they could make them understand." Reaching Dover soon after dawn of the hot first day of July, Stuart learned to his chagrin that there were no Confederates at York, six miles east. They had been there, two days ago, but now they were gone and no one would say where. So he turned the head of the column hard left toward Carlisle, 25 miles northwest, supposing that Ewell had ordered a concentration there. He was wrong: as he discovered when he approached the town that afternoon and found it occupied by Pennsylvania militia, who peremptorily rejected his demand for a surrender. Jeb and his road-worn troopers were in no shape for a fight, even with raw home guardsmen, one of his officers frankly admitted. "Weak and helpless as we were," he wrote home later, "our anxiety and uneasiness were painful indeed. Thoughts of saving the wagons now were gone, and we thought only of how we, ourselves, might escape." Contenting himself with a token long-range shelling of the U.S. cavalry barracks, the plumed commander was at a loss for a next move until well after nightfall, when two scouts who had left the column near York, with instructions to search westward for signs of the army, reported back to Stuart outside Carlisle. They had found Lee and the main body that day at Gettysburg, where a battle was in progress, and Lee had sent them to find and summon the long-absent Jeb, who thus was placed in the unusual position of having the army commander report to him the location of the infantry he had been ordered to get in touch with and protect.

At 1 o'clock in the morning, July 2 — one week, to the hour, since he first set out on the ride that was designed, in part, to retrieve his slipping reputation — Stuart had his troopers on the march for Gettysburg, which was thirty miles away by the nearest road. This was their fifth night march in the past eight days, and it was perhaps the hardest of them all. Southward the weary horses plodded, over Yellow Breeches Creek, through Mount Holly Pass, and across the rolling farmland of Adams County, of which Gettysburg was the county seat. The riders were so exhausted, it was noted, that one who tumbled from his mount slept sprawled across the fence that broke his fall. At dawn they still had miles to go, and even the indefatigable Jeb, though he still clung tenaciously to the train of captured wagons as the one substantial trophy of his ride, could see that a rest halt had to be called if he was to arrive with more than a remnant of his three brigades. It was late afternoon before he reached the field of the greatest battle of the war, having missed all of the first day and most of the second. Lee received him with an iciness which a staff officer found "painful beyond description."

Reddening at the sight of his chief of cavalry, the gray commander raised one arm in a menacing gesture of exasperation. "General Stuart, where have you been?" he said. "I have not heard a word from you in days, and you the eyes and ears of my army." Jeb wilted under this unfamiliar treatment and became so flustered that he played his trump card at the outset. "I have brought you 125 wagons and their teams, General," he announced: only to have Lee reply, "Yes, General, but they are an impediment to me now." Then suddenly Lee softened. Perhaps it was Stuart's obvious dismay or his somewhat bedraggled appearance after eight days in the saddle; or perhaps it was a recollection of all the service this young man had done him in the past. At any rate, a witness recalled years later, Lee's manner became one "of great tenderness" as he added: "Let me ask your help now. We will not discuss this longer. Help me fight these people."

The reason Stuart had encountered none of Ewell's men at York or Carlisle the day before — a Wednesday — was that Lee, acting on information that reached him Sunday night, had recalled them Monday morning. As it was, the tail of Early's column, marching westward on the road through East Berlin and Heidlersburg, had been less than ten miles from the head of Stuart's own at the time he took the risky ditch jump near Hanover on Tuesday. In fact, the foot soldiers had heard the guns of that brief engagement, but had not investigated because Lee, despite his repeated warning to Stuart to be on the lookout for Ewell, had neglected to warn Ewell to be on the lookout for Stuart: with the result that the cavalry's roundabout hegira was prolonged for two more days, including some thirty-odd hours beyond the opening of the battle, which in turn resulted from Lee's groping his way across the Pennsylvania landscape, deprived of his eyes and ears, as he said, and with little information as to the enemy's whereabouts or intentions. Because that ten-mile gap had been ignored — not only ignored, but unsuspected — whatever Lee encountered, good or bad, was bound to come as a surprise, and surprise was seldom a welcome thing in war. And so it was. Coincidents refused to mesh for the general who, six weeks ago in Richmond, had cast his vote for the long chance. Fortuity itself, as the deadly game unfolded move by move, appeared to conform to a pattern of hard luck; so much so, indeed, that in time men would say of Lee, as Jael had said of Sisera after she drove the tent peg into his temple, that the stars in their courses had fought against him.

Such information as he had, and it was meager, had come to him not from Robertson or Jones, whom Stuart had left to guard the Blue Ridge passes, nor from Jenkins, who was off with Ewell, but from a spy — "scout" was the euphemistic word — sent out some weeks before by Longstreet, with instructions to pick up what useful tips he could in the lobbies and barrooms of Washington. His name was Harrison, and no one knew much about him except that he was a Mississippian, bearded and of average height, with sloping shoulders, pale hazel eyes, and an abiding dislike of all Yankees. Lee, for one, apparently considered him unsavory and declined at first to see him when he was brought to Shetter's Woods that Sunday night. "I have no confidence in any scout," he said. Informed by a staff officer, however, that Harrison claimed the Federal army had crossed the Potomac — which Lee could scarcely credit, in the absence of any such report from Stuart — he changed his mind and sent for him, shortly before midnight. Travel-stained and weary, the spy told Lee that

he had been in Frederick that morning, having heard in Washington that Hooker had transferred his headquarters to that place. Arriving he had found it true. At least two corps were there, he said, and others were in the vicinity, with two more pushed out toward South Mountain. After observing all this he had procured a horse and ridden hard for Chambersburg to report to Longstreet, who had sent him on to Lee. Incidentally, he remarked in closing, Hooker had been replaced that day by Meade.

Lee reacted fast — as well he might — to this news that the blue army had been for the past two days on the same side of the Potomac as his own, one of whose corps, in addition to being divided itself, was thirty-odd miles away from the other two, which were threatened in turn by a possible movement against their rear. It was not so much that he feared for his supply line; he was prepared to abandon contact with Virginia anyhow. The trouble was, if the Federals crossed South Mountain and entered the lower Cumberland Valley — as Harrison had claimed they were about to do, and as Hooker in fact had intended — they would force Lee to conform, in order to meet the threat to his rear, and thus deprive him of the initiative he had to retain if he was to conduct the sort of campaign he had in mind. In the absence of his cavalry, moreover, the dispersed segments of his army were in danger of being surprised and swamped by overwhelming numbers: Meade, in short, might do to him what he had planned to do to Hooker — defeat him in detail. What was called for, in the face of this, was a rapid concentration of all his forces, preferably east of the mountains so as to compel the enemy to abandon the threat to his rear. Orders designed to effect this went out promptly. Ewell was instructed to give up his advance on Harrisburg and return at once to Chambersburg with all three of his divisions. Hill and Longstreet, who had just been alerted for a northward march to the Susquehanna, were told to prepare instead for a move on Cashtown, eighteen miles to the east and just beyond South Mountain; the former would start today — it was morning by now, June 29 — the latter tomorrow, which would keep the single road from being clogged. On second thought, and for the same purpose of avoiding a jam, Lee sent a follow-up message to Ewell, suggesting that he remain on the far side of the mountains and march directly to Cashtown or Gettysburg, another eight miles to the east. Simultaneously, couriers hurried south to urge Robertson and Jones to leave the Blue Ridge and join the army in Pennsylvania as soon as possible. A seventh brigade of cavalry, under Brigadier General John B. Imboden, assigned to Lee for use on the invasion but so far only used to guard the western approaches to the lower Cumberland Valley, was also summoned, but since it would be at least two days before these horsemen could get to Chambersburg, Lee told Longstreet to leave one division behind to protect the trains until Imboden arrived. Meanwhile the rest of the army would converge on Cashtown, from which point it could threaten both Washington and Baltimore, thus retaining the initiative by forcing the enemy to turn back east or remain there, in order to keep between the gray invaders and those two vital cities.

All this had been arranged within eight hours of Harrison's report to Lee. But neither the spy nor anyone else could tell him anything of Stuart, who had vanished as if into quicksand. However, an officer who arrived from the south that morning reported that he had met two cavalrymen who told him they had left Stuart on June 27, all the way down in Prince William County, on the far side of Occoquan Creek. Lee was startled to hear this, having learned from Harrison that Hooker had begun to cross the Potomac two full days before that time. Though he kept up a show of confidence for the benefit of subordinates — "Ah, General, the enemy is a long time finding us," he told a division commander; "If he does not succeed soon, we must go in search of him" — Lee was obviously disturbed, and he kept asking for news of Stuart from all callers, none of whom could tell him anything. One more item concerned him, though few of his lieutenants agreed that it should do so. They were saying that Meade was about as able a general as Hooker, but considerably less bold, and they were exchanging congratulations on Lincoln's appointment of another mediocre opponent for them. Lee, who had known the Pennsylvanian as a fellow engineer in the old army, did not agree. "General Meade will commit no blunder on my front," he said, "and if I make one he will make haste to take advantage of it."

While Longstreet marked time at Chambersburg, waiting for Hill to clear the road on which his three divisions were proceeding east to Cashtown, Ewell began his southward march from Carlisle. Greatly disappointed by the cancellation of his plan to occupy the Pennsylvania capital, which he saw as a fitting climax to the campaign that had opened so auspiciously at Winchester and continued for the next two weeks as a triumphal procession through one of the most prosperous regions of the North, Old Bald Head was puzzled by the apparent indecisiveness of his chief. Jackson's orders, enigmatic though they often were, had always been precise and positive; whereas Lee had not only reversed himself by ordering a return to Chambersburg, he had also modified this further by changing the objective to Cashtown or Gettysburg and leaving it up to the corps commander to choose between the two. Unaccustomed to such leeway, which Jackson had never allowed him on any account, Ewell deferred making a final choice until next day, when he would reach Middletown, aptly named because it was equidistant from both of these alternative objectives. Sending word for Early to head west from York and taking up the southward march himself with Rodes while Johnson came along behind with the spoils-laden wagon train, he was also nettled by Lee's additional instructions that if at any point he encountered what he judged to be a large force of the enemy, he was to avoid a general engagement, if practicable, until the other two corps were at hand. This seemed to Ewell a plethora of ifs, and he fumed under the added burden of responsibility, not only for the safety of his corps, but also for the safety of the army, in a situation which, for him at least, was far from clear. Much as he missed his amputated leg, he missed even more the iron guidance of the man under whom he had been serving when he lost it.

Those same precautionary instructions had gone of course to Hill, who was known to have little caution in his make-up. His policy, throughout his year of service under Lee — beginning with the attack that opened the Seven Days offensive, which he had started rolling for the simple reason that he could no longer abide the strain of standing idle — had been to pitch into whatever loomed in his path, with little or no regard for its strength or composition. This had stood the Confederacy in good stead from time to time, especially at Cedar Mountain, where he had saved Stonewall from defeat, and at Sharpsburg, where he had done the same for Lee, whose reference to him in the official report of that battle, "And then A. P. Hill came up," had become a byword in the army. Little Powell was the embodiment of the offensive spirit, here in Pennsylvania as well as back home in Virginia, and so were the troops of his command, who took a fierce pride in the fact. Completing the march to Cashtown that first day, Heth's division went into camp while the other two were still on the road, and hearing that Early's men had overlooked a supply of shoes while passing through Gettysburg the week before, Heth sent his lead brigade forward next morning, June 30, to investigate the rumor. Its commander, Brigadier General Johnston Pettigrew, mindful of Lee's warning not to bring on a battle until the whole army was at hand, prudently withdrew when he encountered Federal troopers along a creekbank west of town, not knowing what number of blue soldiers of all arms might be lurking in rear of the cavalry outposts. He returned to Cashtown late that afternoon, having put his men into bivouac about midway between there and Gettysburg, and reported on the day's events. Heth did not think highly of such wariness. What was more, he wanted those shoes. So he took Pettigrew to Hill and had him repeat the account of what he had seen. Hill agreed with Heth. "The only force at Gettysburg is cavalry," he declared, "probably a detachment of observation." Meade's infantry forces were still down in Maryland, he added, "and have not struck their tents."

Heth was quick to take him up on that. "If there is no objection," he said, "I will take my division tomorrow and go to Gettysburg and get those shoes."

"None in the world," Hill told him.

★　★　★

One strenuous objector was there, however, in the person of John Buford, a tough, Kentucky-born regular with a fondness for hard fighting and the skill to back it up. And though Hill was strictly correct in saying that the only bluecoats now in Gettysburg were cavalry, Buford's two brigades were formidable in their own right, being equipped with the new seven-shot Spencer carbine, which enabled a handy trooper to get off twenty rounds a minute, as compared to his muzzle-loading adversary, who would be doing well to get off four in the same span. Moreover, in addition to having five times the firepower of any equal number of opponents, these two brigades were outriders for the infantry wing under Reynolds, whose own corps was camped to-night within six miles of the town, while those under Howard and Sickles were close behind him. Meade had set up army headquarters just south of the state line at Taneytown, about the same distance from Reynolds as Reynolds was from Gettysburg, and all but one of his seven corps — Sedgwick's, off to the east at Manchester — were within easy marching distance of the latter place. He was, in fact, about as well concentrated as Lee was on this last night of June. The Confederates had the advantage of converging on a central point — Ewell at Heidlersburg and Longstreet in rear of Cashtown were each about ten miles from Gettysburg, and Hill was closer than either — whereas the Federals would be marching toward a point that was beyond their perimeter, but Meade had the advantage of numbers and a less congested road net: plus another advantage which up to now, except for the brief September interlude that ended bloodily at Sharpsburg, had been with Lee. The northern commander and his soldiers would be fighting on their own ground, in defense of their own homes.

His march north, today and yesterday, after the day spent getting the feel of the reins, had been made with the intention, announced to Halleck at the outset, "of falling upon some portion of Lee's army in detail" with the full strength of his own. His "main point," he said, was "to find and fight the enemy," since in his opinion "the attitude of the enemy's army in Pennsylvania presents us the best opportunity we have had since the war began." But this morning, receiving information "that the enemy are advancing, probably in strong force, on Gettysburg," he had begun to doubt that that was really what he wanted after all. "Much oppressed with a sense of responsibility and the magnitude of the great interests intrusted to me," as he wrote his wife, he had begun to think that his best course would be to take up a strong defensive position, covering Washington and Baltimore, and there await attack. It was his intention, he declared in a circular issued that afternoon, "to hold this army pretty nearly in the position it now occupies until the plans of the enemy shall have been more fully developed," adding that it was "not his desire to wear the troops out by excessive fatigue and marches, and thus unfit them for the work they will be called upon to perform." He found what he considered an excellent position along the south bank of Pipe Creek, just to the rear of his present headquarters at Taneytown, and he had his engineers start laying it out on the morning of July 1, planning to rally his army there in case Lee came at him in dead earnest. "The commanding general is satisfied that the object of the movement of the army in this direction has been accomplished," he announced in another circular, "viz. the relief of Harrisburg, and the prevention of the enemy's intended invasion of Philadelphia, &c. beyond the Susquehanna. It is no longer his intention to assume the offensive until the enemy's movements or position should render such an operation certain of success." If this was reminiscent of Hooker in the Wilderness, Meade went Fighting Joe one better by making it plain that every corps commander was authorized to initiate a retirement to the Pipe Creek line, not only by his own corps but also by the others, in the event that the rebels made a lunge at him: "The time for falling back can only be developed by circumstances. Whenever such circumstances arise as would seem to indicate the necessity for falling back and assuming this general line indicated, notice of such movement will be at once communicated to these headquarters and to all adjoining corps commanders."

That was a long way from the intention expressed two days ago, "to find and fight the enemy." But the fact was, Meade had already lost

control of events before he made this offer to abide by the decision
of the first of his chief subordinates who took a notion that the time had
come to backtrack. Even as the circular was being prepared and the
engineers were laying out the proposed defensive line behind Pipe Creek,
John Reynolds was committing the army to battle a dozen miles north
of the headquarters Meade was getting ready to abandon. And Reynolds
in turn had taken his cue from Buford, who had spread his troopers
along the banks of another creek, just west of Gettysburg; Willoughby
Run, it was called. "By daylight of July 1," he later reported, "I had
gained positive information of the enemy's position and movements, and
my arrangements were made for entertaining him until General Reynolds could reach the scene."

Buford was all business and hard action, now as always. A former
Indian fighter, he drove himself as mercilessly as he did his men, with the
result that he would be dead within six months, at the age of thirty-
seven, of what the doctors classified as "exposure and exhaustion." Convinced now that the fate of the nation was in his hands, here on the
outskirts of the little college town, the Kentuckian was prepared to act
accordingly. A journalist had recently described him as being "of a
good-natured disposition, but not to be trifled with," a "singular-looking
party . . . with a tawny mustache and a little, triangular gray eye, whose
expression is determined, not to say sinister." The night before, when
one of his brigade commanders expressed the opinion that the rebels
would not be coming in any considerable strength and that he would be
able to hold them off without much trouble, Buford had not agreed at
all. "No, you won't," he said. "They will attack you in the morning and
they will come booming — skirmishers three-deep. You will have to
fight like the devil until supports arrive."

✗ 2 ✗

That was how they came, three-deep and booming; Heth was on his
way to "get those shoes." In the lead today, by normal rotation of the
honor, was the Alabama brigade of Maryland-born James Archer. A
Princeton graduate who had discovered an aptitude for war in Mexico
and had gone on to become a U.S. Army captain and now a Confederate
brigadier at the age of forty-six, Archer had fought in every major battle under Lee, from the Seven Days through Chancellorsville, where he
led the charge on Hazel Grove that broke the back of the Federal defense. Hill had fallen sick in the night and was confined to his tent in
Cashtown this morning, too weak to mount a horse, but with Archer
out front he would have all the aggressiveness even he could desire
— as was presently demonstrated. Though Pettigrew had warned him
the previous evening that he was likely to run into trouble short of

Gettysburg, Archer moved his Alabamians rapidly eastward, down the Chambersburg Pike, until they topped a rise and came under fire, first from the banks of a stream in the swale below and then from the slopes of another north-south ridge beyond, on whose crest a six-gun battery was in action at a range of three quarters of a mile. That was about 8 o'clock. Archer ordered up a battery of his own, and while it took up the challenge of the guns across the way, he shook out a triple line of skirmishers, textbook style, and prepared to continue the advance. But Heth, who had come to the head of the column by now, decided to make doubly sure there would be no further delay. He called up a Mississippi brigade commanded by Brigadier General Joseph R. Davis, put it on the left of Archer, north of the pike, and sent them forward together, down into the shallow valley that was floored with the shimmering gold of ripened wheat fields. The two brigades started downhill through the standing grain, the skirmishers whooping and firing as they went. Just as the Deep South had led the way to secession — Alabama had been fourth and Mississippi second among the original seven states to leave the Union — so was it leading the way into the greatest battle of the war that had been provoked by that withdrawal.

Buford's troopers, back across Willoughby Run by now and in position on McPherson's Ridge, fired their carbines rapidly as the butternut riflemen came at them down the east side of Herr Ridge. But it was obvious to their general, who had a good view of the scene from the cupola of a Lutheran seminary on the crest of the next rearward ridge, about midway between Gettysburg and the one they were defending a mile from town, that his two brigades of dismounted men, one out of four of whom had to stay behind to hold the horses of the other three, were not going to be able to hang on long in the face of all that power. Moreover, reports had reached him from outposts he had established to the north, toward Heidlersburg, that substantial rebel forces were advancing from there as well. Unless Federal infantry came up soon, and in strength, he would have to pull out to avoid being swamped from both directions. At about 8.30, however, as he started down the ladder, perhaps to give the order to retire, he heard a calm voice asking from below: "What's the matter, John?" It was Reynolds, whom many considered not only the highest ranking but also the best general in the army. Buford shook his head. "The devil's to pay," he said, and he came on down the ladder. But when Reynolds asked if this meant that he could not hang on till the I Corps got there, most likely within an hour, the cavalryman said he reckoned he could; at any rate he would try. That was enough for Reynolds. He sent at once for Howard and Sickles, urging haste on the march to join him, then turned to an aide and gave him a verbal message for Meade at Taneytown. "Tell him the enemy are advancing in strong force, and that I fear they will get to the heights beyond the town before I can. I will fight them inch by inch, and if driven into the town I will barricade the streets and hold them back as long as possible."

He himself rode back to bring up Wadsworth's division, which was leading the march up the Emmitsburg Road, and guided it cross-country, over Seminary Ridge and up the Chambersburg Pike toward McPherson's Ridge, where by now, after two full hours of fighting, Buford's troopers were approaching both the crest of the ridge, uphill in their rear, and the limit of their endurance. Reynolds directed one of Wadsworth's two brigades to the right and the other to the left, to bolster the cavalry and oppose the rebel infantry coming at them. The race was close; he knew that unless he hurried he would lose it. Already the time was past 10 o'clock, and he could see Confederates among the trees of an apple orchard just to the left of where the pike went out of sight beyond the ridge. He turned in the saddle and called back over his shoulder to the infantry trudging behind him: "Forward, forward, men! Drive those fellows out of that! Forward! For God's sake, forward!" Those were his last words. He suddenly toppled from his horse and lay quite still, face-down on the soil of his native Pennsylvania. No one knew what had hit him — including Reynolds himself, most likely — until an aide saw the neat half-inch hole behind his right ear, where the rifle bullet had struck. When they turned him over he gasped once, then smiled; but that was all. He was dead at the age of forty-two, brought down by a rebel marksman in the orchard just ahead. "His death affected us much," a young lieutenant later wrote, "for he was one of the *soldier* generals of the army."

Beyond the ridge, Heth had decided by now that the time had come for him to press the issue with more than skirmishers. He passed the word and Davis and Archer went in with their main bodies, left and right of the turnpike, intending to overrun the rapid-firing blue troopers spread out on the slope before them. Archer's men were thrown into some disorder by a fence they had to climb just west of Willoughby Run, but at last they got over and splashed across the stream. As they started up McPherson's Ridge, however, the woods along the crest were suddenly filled with flame-stabbed smoke and the crash of heavy volleys. This was musketry, not sporadic carbine fire, and then they saw why. Not only were these new opponents infantry, but their black hats told the startled and stalled attackers that this was the Iron Brigade, made up of hard-bitten Westerners with a formidable reputation for hard fighting and a fierce pride in their official designation as the first brigade of the first division of the first corps of the first army of the Republic. Staggered by the ambush and outnumbered as they were, the butternut survivors perceived that the time had come to get out of there, and that was what they did. Splashing back across the stream, however, they piled up again at the high fence and were struck heavily on the outer flank by a Michigan regiment that had worked its way around through the woods to the south. Most got over, but about 75 Confederates were captured while awaiting their turn at the fence: including Archer, who was grabbed and mauled by a hefty private named Patrick Maloney. Exuberant over the size of his catch — as well he might be; no general in Lee's army had ever been captured before — Maloney turned Archer over to his captain, who refused to accept the sword that was offered in formal surrender. "Keep your sword, General, and go to the rear," he told him. "One sword is all I need on this line." A staff lieutenant who had taken no part in the fighting did not see it that way, however, and insisted on having the trophy even after the prisoner explained that it had been declined by the man who was entitled to it. Archer was furious, not only at this but also because of the roughing-up the big Irishman had given him; which accounted in part for his reaction when he was presented to Doubleday, who had succeeded Reynolds as corps commander. "Archer! I'm glad to see you," the New Yorker cried, striding forward with his hand out. They had been friends in the old army, but apparently that meant nothing to Archer now. "Well, I'm not glad to see you by a damn sight," he said coldly, and he kept his hand at his side.

North of the turnpike, the other half of Heth's attack had better success, at least at the start. Though Reynolds even in death had won his race on the Union left, where the Iron Brigade arrived in time to prepare for what was coming, the brigade on the right not only had a longer way to go, and consequently less time for getting set, it also found no covering woods along that stretch of McPherson's Ridge. Davis's men — five regiments scraped together from the Richmond defenses and the Carolina littoral, none of whom had worked together previously and only two of which had ever fought in Virginia — could see what lay before them, and they advanced with all the eagerness of green troops glad of a chance to demonstrate their mettle. One of the five was a North Carolina outfit whose colonel went down early in the charge, shot as he took up the fallen colors, and when another Tarheel officer bent over him to ask if he was badly hurt, he replied: "Yes, but pay no attention to me. Take the colors and keep ahead of the Mississippians." By then the whole line was going in on the double. On the crest ahead, the Federals wavered and then, as Wadsworth sought to forestall a rout by ordering a withdrawal, fell back hastily toward Seminary Ridge. Davis was elated. The President's nephew, he was aware of muttered complaints of nepotism, and he was happy to be proving his worth and his right to the stars on his collar. Yelling in anticipation of coming to grips with the fleeing bluecoats, the attackers swept over the crest of McPherson's Ridge and into the quarter-mile-wide valley beyond. There they funneled into the deep cut of an unfinished railroad bed, which seemed to offer an ideal covered approach to the Federal rear, but which in fact turned out to be a trap. Once in, they found the sides of the cut so high and steep that they could not fire out, and Doubleday, spotting the opportunity, quickly took advantage of it by sending two regiments over from south of the pike, where Archer had just been routed. "Throw down your muskets! Throw down your muskets!" the men in the cut heard voices calling from overhead, and they looked up into the muzzles of rifles slanted down at them from the rim above. Caught thus in a situation not unlike that of fish in a rainbarrel, some 250 graybacks surrendered outright, dropping their weapons where they stood, while casualties were heavy among those who chose to attempt escape by running the gauntlet westward. The reversal was complete. Davis and his survivors fell back across McPherson's Ridge, profoundly shaken by the sudden frown of fortune and considerably reduced from the strength they had enjoyed when they first came whooping over the crest, headed in the opposite direction. Here on the Confederate left, after so brave a beginning, the attackers had wound up with an even worse disaster than had been suffered on the right. Though Davis himself, unlike Archer, had avoided capture, a good half of his men had either been taken prisoner or shot, and the rest were too demoralized to be of any present use at all.

Doubleday was as elated as Davis had been, a short while back. Moreover, his hard-won feeling of security was strengthened by the arrival of the other two divisions of the corps, his own and Robinson's, and close on their heels came Howard, riding in advance of his own corps, which was coming fast and would be there within an hour. Eleven years younger than forty-four-year-old Doubleday, Howard assumed command of the field by virtue of his seniority. While the skirmishers of both armies kept up a racket down in the valley, banging away at each other from opposite banks of Willoughby Run, he reinforced Wadsworth on McPherson's Ridge and continued the long-range artillery duel with rebel batteries on Herr Ridge. It was noon by now; the XI Corps was arriving, under Schurz, and the lines were much the same as they had been four hours ago, when Buford's dismounted troopers were all that held them. Unquestionably, there were a great many butternut soldiers on the field — you could see them plainly across the valley, "formed in continuous double lines of battle," a staff man noted, adding that "as a spectacle it was striking" — but Howard believed he was ready for whatever came his way. Sickles ought to be arriving soon, and he had sent for Slocum as well; that would give him five more divisions, a total of eleven, perhaps by nightfall. . . . Just then, however, a shell burst in rear of the Union center, followed quickly by another and another, all with such startling accuracy that one regimental commander sent an angry complaint that the supporting guns were firing short. But those were not friendly shells, dropped in error; they were Confederate. A mile north of the Chambersburg Pike, the two eastern ridges merged at a dominant height called Oak Hill, and there an enemy battery was in action, signaling danger to the Federal right, which extended only about half that distance. Coming south across the fields around Oak Hill, directly toward the vulnerable flank, was another gray flood of rebel infantry. One-armed Howard, knowing he had to move fast to meet the threat, bent the north end of Doubleday's line back east, astride Seminary Ridge, and hurried the first two divisions of his own corps across the rolling farmland north of Gettysburg, with instructions for Schurz to form a new line there, at right angles to the first. They barely had time to arrive before the storm burst.

This new gray pressure was brought to bear by Rodes. Like Heth, he was going into battle for the first time as a major general, and just as his fellow Virginian had faced the test without his corps commander at hand to advise him, so too was Rodes on his own, not because Ewell lay sick in his tent, as had been the case with Hill, but because he preferred to ride near the tail of the column in his buggy. Old Bald Head was in a strange mood anyhow, confused by discretionary orders and aggrieved by the sudden abandonment of his advance on Harrisburg, just as he had the place within his grasp. At Middletown that morning, confronted with the necessity for choosing between his alter-nate objectives, he had had his mind made up for him at last by a note from Hill, informing him that the Third Corps was on its way to Gettysburg; so he had directed Rodes to take the left fork, which led there. Besides, that seemed a convenient point for a junction with Early who was marching from the west, while Johnson, off to the east with the train, could join them there by turning east when he reached Cashtown. By nightfall the corps would be reunited for the first time in a week, but until then Ewell preferred to allow all three division commanders to function independently. Rodes no doubt appreciated the confidence this implied. At any rate, hearing heavy firing up ahead at noon, he quickened the pace and reached Oak Hill about 1.30 to find a golden opportunity spread before him. On parallel ridges extending south from where he stood, Confederates and Federals were disposed in an attitude not unlike that of two animals who had just met and scrapped and then drawn back, still growling, for a better assessment of each other before coming to grips again. What attracted Rodes at first glance was the fact that the enemy flank, half a mile down the eastern ridge, was wide open to an oblique attack from the road along which his division was advancing. He would have to move fast, however, for already the near end of the Union line was beginning to curl back in response to his appearance, and reinforcements were pouring in large numbers from the streets of Gettysburg, taking up positions from which to defend it. This last was quite all right with Rodes. It was not the town he wanted, dead ahead; it was the blue force on the ridge to his right front. Accordingly, after posting one of his five brigades out to the left, with instructions to hold off the still-arriving defenders of the town in case they went over to the offensive — which they well might do; their number by now was larger than his own — he held another brigade in reserve and put the remaining three in line abreast, facing south, for a charge against the flank of the bluecoats on the ridge. All this was quickly done, with no time spared for a preliminary reconnaissance or even the advancement of a skirmish line. By 2 o'clock the alignment had been completed, and Rodes gave his three attack brigades the order to go forward.

They did go forward, but into chaos. Left on its own by the other two brigades — one stalled at the outset; the other drifted wide — the center brigade stepped in midstride into slaughter when a line of Federals, hidden till then, rose from behind a low stone wall, diagonal to the front, and killed or wounded about half of the advancing men with a series of point-blank volleys pumped directly into their flank. Such was the price they paid for the time Rodes saved by foregoing a reconnaissance. The survivors hit the ground alongside the fallen, some making futile attempts to return the decimating fire, while others began waving scraps of cloth in token of surrender. Observing this, their shaken commander, Brigadier General Alfred Iverson, sent word to Rodes that one whole regiment had raised the white flag and gone over to the enemy on first contact. Though Rodes did not credit the hysterical report, he saw only too clearly that he had the makings of a first-class disaster on his hands. Like Heth to the south, he had paid in disproportionate blood for the ready aggressiveness which in the past had been the hallmark of the army's greatest victories, but which now seemed mere rashness and the hallmark of defeat. It had been so for the captured Archer and for Davis, and now it was the same for Iverson, who was so demoralized by what he had seen, or thought he had seen, that he had to turn over to his adjutant the task of trying to extricate his shattered regiments.

It was at this critical juncture that Lee drew near. Riding through the mountains east of Chambersburg that morning, he had heard the rumble of guns in the distance and wondered what it meant. Hill, who had risen from his sickbed at the sound, pale and feeble though he was, and called for his horse in order to go forward and investigate, could tell Lee nothing more than he already knew — namely, that Heth had marched on Gettysburg, with Pender in support — nor could Anderson, whose division was just beyond Cashtown and within half a dozen miles of the ominous booming. Despite repeated warnings that a general engagement was to be avoided until the army was reunited, the noise up ahead was too loud, or anyhow too sustained, for a mere skirmish. Moreover, Lee was aware of Napoleon's remark that at certain edgy times a dogfight could bring on a battle, and it seemed to him that with his infantry groping its way across unfamiliar hostile terrain, in an attempt to perform the proper function of cavalry, this might well be one of those times. He was worried and he said so.

"I cannot think what has become of Stuart," he told Anderson. "I ought to have heard from him long before now. He may have met with disaster, but I hope not." As he spoke he gazed up the road, where the guns continued to rumble beyond the horizon. "In the absence of reports from him, I am in ignorance of what we have in front of us here. It may be the whole Federal army, or it may be only a detachment. If it is the whole Federal force, we must fight a battle here." For once, he did not seem pleased at the prospect of combat, and he spoke of a withdrawal before he knew what lay before him: "If we do not gain a victory, those defiles and gorges which we passed this morning will shelter us from disaster." And having used the word disaster twice within less than a minute, he hurried ahead, as Hill had done before him, to see for himself what grounds there might be for such forebodings.

About 2.30, after passing through Pender's division, which was formed for attack on both sides of the pike but was so far uncommitted, he ascended Herr Ridge to find the smoky panorama of a battle spread before him — a battle he had neither sought nor wanted. Heth had three brigades in line on the slope giving down upon Willoughby Run, and Lee now learned that he had attacked some three hours earlier, due east and on a mile-wide front, only to encounter Federal infantry whose presence he had not even suspected until he saw what was left of his two attack brigades streaming back from a bloody repulse. Since then, belatedly mindful of the warning not to bring on a battle, he had contented himself with restoring his shattered front while engaging the enemy guns in a long-range contest. Lee could see for himself the situation that had developed. Across the way, disposed along the two parallel ridges that intervened between the one on which he stood and Gettysburg, plainly visible two miles to the southeast, the Federals confronted Heth in unknown strength, their right flank withdrawn sharply in the direction of the town, from whose streets more bluecoats were pouring in heavy numbers, in order to meet a new Confederate threat from the north. This was Rodes, just arrived from Heidlersburg, Lee was told, and though his attack was opportune, catching the bluecoats end-on and almost unawares, he was making little headway because he had launched it in a disjointed fashion. At that point Heth came riding up, having heard that Lee was on the field. Anxious to make up for a slipshod beginning, he appealed to the commanding general to let him go back in.

"Rodes is heavily engaged," he said. "Had I not better attack?"

Lee was reluctant. "N-no," he said slowly, continuing to sweep the field with his glasses. It was not that he lacked confidence in Heth, who was not only a fellow Virginian and a distant cousin, but was also the only officer in the army, aside of course from his own sons, whom he addressed by his first name. It was because Lee still had no real notion of the enemy strength, except that it was obviously considerable, and he was by no means willing to risk the apparent likelihood of expanding a double into a triple repulse. "No," he said again, more decisively than before; "I am not prepared to bring on a general engagement today. Longstreet is not up."

But suddenly his mind was changed by what he saw before him. Rodes's right brigade, after drifting wide, came down hard on the critical angle where the Union line bent east, and his reserve brigade, committed after the wreck of Iverson, dislodged the Federals from their position behind the diagonal stone wall, while his left brigade recovered momentum and plunged into a quarter-mile gap between the two blue corps, north and west of Gettysburg. Assailed and outflanked, the eastward extension of Doubleday's line began to crumble as the men who had held it retreated stubbornly down Seminary Ridge. Simultaneously, Howard's two divisions under Schurz—his own, now led by Brigadier General Alexander Schimmelfennig, and Barlow's; the third, Von Steinwehr's, had been left in reserve on the other side of the town—were assaulted by a new gray force that came roaring down the Harrisburg Road—it was Early, arriving from York—to strike their right at the moment when Rodes was probing the gap beyond their left. As a result, this line too began to crumble, but much faster than the other.... On Herr Ridge, Lee saw much of this through his binoculars. Blind chance having reproduced in miniature the conditions of Second Manassas, with Chancellorsville thrown in for good measure, he dropped his unaccustomed cloak of caution and told Hill, who rode up just then, to send both Heth and Pender forward to sweep the field.

They did just that, but only after fierce and bloody fighting, particularly on McPherson's Ridge, south of the pike, where the Iron Brigade was posted. Unleashed at last, Heth's men went splashing across Willoughby Run and up the opposite slope, to and finally over the fuming crest. Heth himself did not make it all the way, having been unhorsed by a fragment of shell which struck him on the side of the head, knocked him unconscious, and probably would have killed him, too, except that the force of the blow was absorbed in part by a folded newspaper tucked under the sweatband of a too-large hat acquired the day before in Cashtown. Hundreds of others in both armies were not so fortunate. Told by Doubleday to maintain his position at all costs, Brigadier General Solomon Meredith, commander of the Iron Brigade, came close to following these instructions to the letter, although he himself, like Heth, was knocked out before the action was half over. The 24th Michigan, for example, had come onto the ridge with 496 officers and men; it left with 97. This loss of just over eighty percent was exceeded only by the regiment that inflicted it, Pettigrew's 26th North Carolina, whose two center companies set new records for battlefield losses that would never be broken, here or elsewhere; one took 83 soldiers into the fight and emerged with only 2 unhit, while the other went in with 91, and all were killed or wounded. Pender, sent forward by Hill as the struggle approached a climax, overlapped the south flank of the defenders and added the pressure that forced them off the ridge. The men of the Iron Brigade fell back at last — 600 of them, at any rate, for twice that many were casualties out of the original 1800 — ending the brief half hour of concentrated fury. "I have taken part in many hotly contested fights," Pettigrew's adjutant later declared, "but this I think was the deadliest of them all." Coming up in the wake of the attack he heard "dreadful howls" in the woods on the ridge, and when he went over to investigate he found that the source of the racket was the wounded of both sides. Several were foaming at the mouth, as though mad, and seemed not even to be aware that they were screaming. He attributed their reaction to the shock of having been exposed to "quick, frightful conflict following several hours of suspense."

Across the way, Ewell's two divisions were having a much easier time than Hill's. While Rodes was pressing Doubleday steadily southward down Seminary Ridge, widening the gap on the left of the line Schurz had drawn north of the town, Early struck hard at the far right of the Union front, which was exposed to just such a blow as the one that had crumpled that same flank at Chancellorsville, two months ago tomorrow. Most of the men opposing him had been through that experience, and now that they foresaw a repetition of it, they reacted in the same fashion. They broke and ran. First by ones and twos, then by squads and platoons, and finally by companies and regiments, they forgot that they had welcomed the chance to refute in action the ugly things the rest of the army had been saying about them; instead, they took off rearward in headlong flight. Barlow, a twenty-nine-year-old New York lawyer who had finished first in his class at Harvard and volunteered at the start of the war as a private in a militia company, tried desperately to rally the division he had commanded for less than six weeks, but was shot from his horse and left for dead on the field his men were quitting. It was otherwise with Schimmelfennig. A former Prussian officer, ten years older than Barlow and presumably that much wiser, he went along with the rush of his troops, all the way into Gettysburg, until he too was unhorsed by a stray bullet while clattering down a side street, and took refuge in a woodshed, where he remained in hiding for the next three days.

Yelling with pleasure at the sight of the blue flood running backwards across the fields as if the landscape had been tipped, the rebel pursuers cut down and gathered in fugitives by the hundreds, all at comparatively small cost to themselves, since but little of their fire was being returned. "General, where are your dead men?" an elated young officer called to Brigadier General John B. Gordon, whose six Georgia regiments had led the charge that threw the bluecoats into retreat before contact was established. Still intent on the pursuit, Gordon did not pause for an answer. "I haven't got any, sir!" he shouted as he rode past on his black stallion. "The Almighty has covered my men with his shield and buckler."

Lee observed from atop Herr Ridge the sudden climax of this latest addition to his year-long string of victories. Riding forward in the wake of Pender's exultant attack, which was delivered with the cohesive, smashing power of a clenched fist, he crossed McPherson's Ridge, thickly strewn with the dead and wounded of both armies, and mounted the opposite slope just as the Federals abandoned a fitful attempt to make a stand around the seminary. Ahead of him, down the remaining half mile of the Chambersburg Pike, they were retreating pell-mell into the streets of Gettysburg, already jammed with other blue troops pouring down from the north, under pressure from Ewell, as into a funnel whose spout extended south. Those who managed to struggle free of the crush, and thus emerge from the spout, were running hard down two roads that led steeply up a dominant height where guns were emplaced and the foremost of the fugitives were being brought to a halt, apparently for still another stand; Cemetery Hill, it was called because of the graveyard on its lofty plateau, half a mile from the town square. Another half mile to the east, about two miles from where Lee stood, there was a second eminence, Culp's Hill, slightly higher than the first, to which it was connected by a saddle of rocky ground, similarly precipitous and forbidding. These two hills, their summits a hundred feet above the town, which in turn was about half that far below the crest of Seminary Ridge, afforded the enemy a strong position — indeed, a natural fortress — on which to rally his whipped and panicky troops, especially if time was allowed for the steadily increasing number of defenders to improve with their spades the already formidable advantages of terrain. Lee could see for himself, now that he had what amounted to a ringside view of the action, that his victory had been achieved more as the result of tactical good fortune than because of any great preponderance of numbers, which in fact he did not have. Prisoners had been taken from two Union corps, six divisions in all, and they reported that the rest of the blue army was on the march to join them from bivouacs close at hand. Some 25,000 attackers, just under half of Lee's infantry, had faced 20,000 defenders, just over one fourth of Meade's, and the resultant casualties had done little to change the over-all ratio of the two armies, on and off the field. Nearly 8000 Confederates had fallen or been captured, as compared to 9000 Federals, about half of whom had been taken prisoner. It was clear that if the tactical advantage was not pressed, it might soon be lost altogether, first by giving the rattled bluecoats a chance to recompose themselves, there on the dominant heights just south of town, and second by allowing time for the arrival of heavy reinforcements already on the way. Moreover, both of these reasons for continuing the offensive were merely adjunctive to Lee's natural inclination, here as elsewhere, now as always, to keep a beaten opponent under pressure, and thus off balance, just as long as his own troops had wind and strength enough to put one foot in front of the other.

Ill though he was, ghostly pale and "very delicate," as one observer remarked, A. P. Hill was altogether in agreement that the new Federal position had to be carried if the victory was to be completed. But when Lee turned to him, there on Seminary Ridge, and proposed that the Third Corps make the attack, Little Powell declined. Anderson's division was still miles away; Heth's was shattered, the commander himself unconscious, and Pender's blown and disorganized by its furious charge and wild pursuit. The survivors were close to exhaustion and so was their ammunition, which would have to be replenished from the train back up the pike. Regretfully Hill replied that his men were in no condition for further exertion just now, and Lee, knowing from past experience that Hill invariably required of them all that flesh could endure, was obliged to accept his judgment. That left Ewell. Rodes had been roughly handled at the outset, it was true, but Early was comparatively fresh, had suffered only light casualties in driving the skittish Dutchmen from the field, and was already on the march through the streets of the town, rounding up herds of prisoners within half a mile of the proposed objective; besides which, it seemed fitting that the Second Corps continue its Jacksonian tradition of hard-legged mobility and terrific striking power, demonstrated recently at Winchester, a month after Stonewall was laid to rest nearby in the Shenandoah Valley, and redemonstrated here today in Pennsylvania. Having made the decision, Lee gave a staff officer oral instructions to take Ewell. As usual, not being in a position to judge for himself the condition of the troops or the difficulties the objective might present when approached from the north, he made the order discretionary; Ewell was "to carry the hill occupied by the enemy, if he found it practicable" — so Lee paraphrased the instructions afterwards in his formal report — "but to avoid a general engagement until the arrival of the other divisions of the army."

That was about 4.30; barely an hour had passed since Hill threw Pender into the follow-up attack on Seminary Ridge, sweeping it clear of defenders within less than half an hour, and a good four hours of daylight remained for Ewell's follow-up attack on Cemetery Hill, which would complete the victory by annihilating or driving the survivors from the scene before Meade could accomplish his convergence there.

Presently, as Lee continued to search the field for signs that the intended attack was under way, Longstreet arrived, riding well in advance of his troops, who had marked time short of Cashtown all morning, under instructions to yield the single eastward road to Johnson, who was hurrying to join the other divisions of the Second Corps. While Lee explained what had happened so far today, and pointed out the hill aswarm with bluecoats across the valley, Old Peter took out his binoculars and made a careful examination of the front. A broad low ridge, parallel to and roughly three quarters of a mile east of the one on which he stood, extended two miles southward from Cemetery Hill to a pair of conical heights, the nearer of which, called Little Round Top, was some fifty feet taller than the occupied hill to the north, while the farther, called simply Round Top, was more than a hundred feet taller still. On the map, and in the minds of students down the years, this complex of high ground south of Gettysburg conformed in general to the shape of a fishhook, with Round Top as the eye, Cemetery Ridge as the shank, Cemetery Hill as the bend, and Culp's Hill as the barb. Neither of the dominant heights to the south appeared to have been occupied yet by the enemy, though it was fairly clear that either would afford the Federals another rallying point in the event of another retreat. However, if this bothered Lee, he did not show it as he stood waiting for Ewell to open the attack from the north. Certainly it did not bother Longstreet, who had the look of a man whose prayers had been answered. Completing his survey of the field, he lowered his glasses, turned to his chief, and declared with evident satisfaction that conditions were ideal for pursuing the offensive-defensive campaign on which he presumed they had agreed before they left Virginia.

"If we could have chosen a point to meet our plans of operation," he said, "I do not think we could have found a better one than that upon which they are now concentrating. All we have to do is throw our army around by their left, and we shall interpose between the Federal army and Washington. We can get a strong position and wait, and if they fail to attack us we shall have everything in condition to move back tomorrow night in the direction of Washington, selecting beforehand a good position into which we can place our troops to receive battle next day. Finding our object is Washington and that army, the Federals will be sure to attack us. When they attack, we shall beat them, as we proposed to do before we left Fredericksburg, and the probabilities are that the fruits of our success will be great."

The southern commander's reaction to this proposed surrender of the initiative to Meade was immediate and decisive. "No," he said, and gestured with his fist in the direction of Cemetery Hill as he spoke. "The enemy is there, and I am going to attack him there."

"If he is there," Old Peter countered, unimpressed, "it will be because he is anxious that we should attack him: a good reason, in my judgment, for not doing so."

Lee still did not agree. He had made an auspicious beginning on his plan for toppling the Federal units piecemeal as they came up, like a row of dominoes, and he was determined to go ahead with it. "No," he said again. "They are there in position, and I am going to whip them or they are going to whip me."

For the present, Longstreet let it go at that, observing that his chief "was in no frame of mind to listen to further argument," but he resolved to return to the subject as soon as Lee had simmered down. "In defensive warfare he was perfect," he wrote years later. "When the hunt was up, his combativeness was overruling."

Just then a courier arrived with a message from Ewell, sent before the one from Lee had reached him. Rodes and Early believed they could take Cemetery Hill, he reported, if Hill would attack it simultaneously from the west. Lee replied that he was unable to furnish this support, except by long-range artillery fire, and after repeating his instructions for Ewell to take the height alone, if possible, added that he would ride over presently to see him. Once more Longstreet spoke up. Minute by minute, he had watched the number of bluecoats increasing on the hill, while those already there were making the dirt fly as they worked at improving the natural strength of the position. He was still opposed to the attack, he said, but if it was going to be made at all, it had better be made at once. Lee did not reply to this immediately. Instead, after sending the courier back to Ewell, he asked where the First Corps divisions were by now. McLaws was a couple of miles this side of Cashtown, Old Peter replied, with Hood somewhere behind him, awaiting road space on the pike. When Lee explained that he could not risk a general assault until these fresh units arrived, Longstreet again fell silent — whether in agreement or disagreement, he did not say — and soon rode off, apparently to hasten the march of the column whose head was half a dozen miles away.

It was now past 5.30 and the guns had stopped their growling on both sides. The staff officer returned to report that he had delivered the hour-old message to Ewell, but there was no other evidence that it had been received. Down below, the streets of the town were still crowded with Confederates, busy flushing Union fugitives out of cellars and back alleys, and there was no sign whatsoever that Ewell was preparing to launch the attack he had twice been told to make if he believed it would be successful. Meantime, the sun was dropping swiftly down the sky and the survivors of the two blue corps were hard at work improving their defenses. One welcome interruption there was, in the form of a pair of Stuart's troopers who brought word to Seminary Ridge of the skirmish near Hanover the day before, the fruitless grope toward York, and the subsequent decision to push on to Carlisle. Relieved to learn that Jeb had managed to avoid personal disaster, whatever trouble he might have made for others, Lee told the horsemen to ride the thirty miles north at once, with orders for the cavalry to rejoin the army as soon as possible. That could not be sooner than tomorrow, of course, but at least he could anticipate removal of the blindfold he had worn throughout the week of Stuart's absence. Near 7 o'clock, with sunset half an hour away and full darkness a good hour beyond that — which left just time enough, perhaps, for launching the attack on Cemetery Hill — Lee mounted Traveller and rode toward Gettysburg, intending not only to pay Ewell the visit he had promised, but also to discover for himself the reason for the long delay.

★ ★ ★

At Taneytown, a dozen miles from the hill where the men of the two wrecked blue corps were plying their shovels in frantic anticipation of the overdue assault, Meade had heard nothing of the eight-hour battle aside from the note in which Reynolds announced that he would "fight [the rebels] inch by inch ... and hold them back as long as possible." Not even the booming of the guns came through; for though the east wind carried their rumble as far as Pittsburgh, 150 miles to the west, it was not audible ten miles to the south, apparently having been absorbed by the Round Tops and the sultry air, which served as a soundproof curtain in that direction. In the early afternoon, however, a New York *Times* correspondent came riding back from Gettysburg on a lathered horse and requested the use of the army telegraph in order to file a story on the fighting. Taken at once to headquarters, he could only report that the conflict had been fierce, that the issue had been in doubt when he left, and that one among the many who had fallen was John Reynolds. All of this was a shock for Meade. Not only had he lost the officer on whom he had depended most for guidance during these first days of command, but one fourth of his army had been committed, perhaps beyond the possibil-

ity of disengagement, a hard day's march north of his chosen position
along Pipe Creek, which the engineers were still mapping and preparing
for occupation. Moreover, a 2 o'clock dispatch from Howard, confirming the newsman's statement and adding that he had sent for Sickles and
Slocum — which would mean the commitment, once they arrived, of
just over half the army — was followed by one from Buford, addressed
to Pleasonton, announcing that two enemy corps — two thirds of the
rebel army, it would seem — had made a junction on the heights northwest of town and seemed determined to press the issue to a conclusion,
however bloody. Outnumbered and outflanked on the left and right, the
defenders had been severely crippled, Buford added, by the untimely
death of Reynolds and the resultant loss of co-ordination all along the
line. "In my opinion," the cavalryman closed his dispatch, "there seems to
be no directing person. . . . P.S. We need help now."

The note was headed 3.20 p.m., by which time help had been on
the way for better than an hour: substantial help, moreover, though it
consisted of only one general and his staff. Hancock's corps had reached
Taneytown shortly before noon, and Meade had held it there while waiting to hear from Reynolds. When he heard instead of that general's
death, he told Hancock to turn his corps over to Gibbon and ride to Gettysburg as a replacement for their fellow Pennsylvanian, with full authority to assume command of all units there and recommend whether to reinforce or withdraw them. He himself would remain in Taneytown,
Meade said, to control the movements of the other corps and continue
work on the Pipe Creek line, which would be needed worse than ever in
the event of a northward collapse. Hancock was thirty-nine, a year
older than Sickles and six years older than Howard; all three had been
promoted to major general on the same day, back in November, but the
other two had been made brigadiers before him and therefore outranked
him still. When he suggested that this might make for trouble up ahead,
Meade showed him a letter from Stanton, stating that he would be sustained in such arrangements by the President and the Secretary of War.
So Hancock set out. He rode part of the way in an ambulance, thus
availing himself of the chance to study a map of the Gettysburg area,
which he had never previously visited though he was born and raised at
Norristown, less than a hundred miles away. Coming within earshot of
the guns, which swelled to a sudden uproar about 3.30, he shifted to
horseback and rode hard toward the sound of firing. At 4 o'clock, the
hour that Lee climbed Seminary Ridge to find a Confederate triumph
unfolding at his feet, Hancock appeared on Cemetery Hill, a mile southeast across the intervening valley, to view the same scene in reverse.
"Wreck, disaster, disorder, almost the panic that precedes disorganization, defeat and retreat were everywhere," a subordinate who arrived
with him declared.

One-armed Howard was there by the two-story arched brick

gateway to the cemetery, brandishing his sword in an attempt to stay the rout, but he was doing little better now than he had done two months ago at Chancellorsville, under similar circumstances. Von Steinwehr, an old-line Prussian and a believer in fortifications, had put his troops to digging on arrival, and the work had gone well, even though one of his two brigades had been called forward when the line began to waver north of town. The trouble was, there were so few men left to hold the hilltop, intrenched or not. Out of the 20,000 on hand for the battle, nearly half had fallen or been captured, while practically another fourth were fugitives who had had their fill of fighting: as was indicated by the fact that the provost guardsmen of a corps that came up two hours later herded ahead of them some 1200 skulkers encountered on the Baltimore Pike, which was only one of the three roads leading south. Fewer than 7000 soldiers — the equivalent of a single Confederate division — comprised the available remnant of the two wrecked Union corps, including the brigade that had remained in reserve on the hilltop all along. With all too clear a view of the jubilant mass of rebels in the town and on the ridge across the way, Howard foresaw an extension of the disaster, the second to be charged against his name in the past two months. Anxious as ever to retrieve his reputation, which had been grievously damaged in the Wilderness and practically demolished north of Gettysburg today, he was chagrined to hear from Hancock that Meade had sent him forward to take charge. "Why, Hancock, you cannot give orders here," he exclaimed. "I am in command and I rank you." When the other repeated that such were Meade's instructions all the same, he still would not agree. "I do not doubt your word, General Hancock," he said stiffly, "but you can give no orders while I am here." Possessed of a self-confidence that required no insistence on prerogatives, Hancock avoided having the exchange degenerate into a public squabble by pretending to defer to Howard's judgment in deciding whether to stand fast or fall back. "I think this is the strongest position by nature on which to fight a battle that I ever saw," he said, looking east and south along the fishhook line of heights from Culp's Hill to the Round Tops, "and if it meets with your approbation I will select this as the battlefield." When Howard replied that he agreed that the position was a strong one, Hancock concluded: "Very well, sir. I select this as the battlefield."

Howard later protested that he had selected and occupied Cemetery Hill as a rallying point long before Hancock got there. This was true; but neither could there be any doubt, when the time came for looking back, that it was the latter who organized the all-round defense of the position, regardless of who had selected it in the first place. Meade had chosen well in naming a successor to the fallen Reynolds. Fourteen months ago, in the course of his drive up the York-James peninsula, Mc-Clellan had characterized Hancock as "superb," and the word stuck; "Hancock the Superb," he was called thereafter, partly because of his handsome looks and regal bearing — "I think that if he were in citizen's clothes, and should give commands in the army to those who did not know him," one officer observed, "he would be likely to be obeyed at once"— but also because of his military record, which was known and admired by those below as well as by those above him. The army's craving for heroes, or at any rate a hero, had not been diminished by the fact that so many who supposedly qualified as such had melted away like wax dolls in the heat of combat; Hancock seemed an altogether likelier candidate. A Maine artilleryman, for example, recalling the Pennsylvanian's sudden appearance on Cemetery Hill, later asserted that his "very atmosphere was strong and invigorating," and added: "I remember (how refreshing to note!) even his linen clean and white, his collar wide and free, and his broad wrist bands showing large and rolling back from his firm, finely molded hands." Carl Schurz, who might have been expected to side with Howard, his immediate superior, found Hancock's arrival "most fortunate" at this juncture. "It gave the troops a new inspiration," he declared. "They all knew him by fame, and his stalwart figure, his proud mien, and his superb soldierly bearing seemed to verify all the things that fame had told about him. His mere presence was a reinforcement, and everybody on the field felt stronger for his being there."

His first order was for the troops to push forward to the stone walls that ran along the northern face of the hill, in order to present a show of strength and thus discourage an advance by the rebels down below. "I am of the opinion that the enemy will mass in town and make an effort to take this position," he told the captain of a battery posted astride the Baltimore Pike at the rim of the plateau, "but I want you to remain here until you are relieved by me or by my written order, and take orders from no one." It was clear to all who saw him that he meant business, and though Howard had chosen to defend only a portion of the hill, Hancock soon extended the line to cover it from flank to flank; after which he turned his attention to Culp's Hill. Half a mile to the east and slightly higher than the ground his present line was drawn on, that critical feature of the terrain had not been occupied, despite the obvious fact that Cemetery Hill itself could not be held if this companion height was lost. He told Doubleday to send a regiment over there at once. "My corps has been fighting, General, since 10 o'clock," the New Yorker protested, "and they have been all cut to pieces." Hancock replied: "I know that, sir. But this is a great emergency, and everyone must do all he can." With that he turned away, as if there could be no question of not obeying, and when he came back presently he found that Doubleday, whose regiments had been reduced to the size of companies in the earlier fighting, had sent Wadsworth's whole division to occupy the hill and the connecting saddle of high ground. It was, in fact, the shadow of a division, no larger than a small brigade, but the position was a strong one, heavily timbered and strewn with rocks that varied in size, as one defender wrote, "from a chicken coop to a pioneer's cabin." Moreover, the lead division of Slocum's corps soon arrived and was posted there, too. Feeling considerably more secure, Hancock got off a message to Meade in which he stated that he believed he could hold his ground till nightfall and that he considered his present position an excellent one for fighting a battle, "although somewhat exposed to be turned by the left."

Across the way, on Seminary Ridge, Longstreet was expressing that same opinion even now. The difference was that Old Peter was a subordinate, whereas Hancock was in actual command and therefore in a position to do something about it. Weak though the line was on those two hills to the north, he saw that it could not be held, even in strength, if those two commanding heights to the south — the Round Tops — were occupied by the enemy, whose batteries then would enfilade all the rest of the fishhook. And having noted this, he acted in accordance with his insight. Slocum's second division (but still not Slocum himself; he refused to come forward in person and take command by virtue of his rank, judging that Meade's plans for the occupation of the Pipe Creek line were being perverted by this affair near Gettysburg, which seemed to be going very badly. He would risk his men, but not his career; heads were likely to roll, and he was taking care that his would not be among them) was approaching the field soon after 5 o'clock, when its commander reported to Hancock near the cemetery gate. "Geary, where are your troops?" he was asked, and replied: "Two brigades are on the road advancing." Hancock gestured south, down Cemetery Ridge. "Do you see this knoll on the left?" He was pointing at Little Round Top. "That knoll is a commanding position. We must take possession of it, and then a line can be formed here and a battle fought.... In the absence of Slocum, I order you to place your troops on that knoll."

This was promptly done, and with the continuing forbearance of the Confederates, who obligingly refrained from launching the attack Hancock had predicted, Federal confidence gradually was restored. Here and there, along the heights and ridges, men began to say they hoped the rebels would come on, because when they did they were going to get a taste of Fredericksburg in reverse. Arriving with his lead division about 6 o'clock, Sickles was posted on the northern end of Cemetery Ridge, just in rear of Howard's and Doubleday's position on Cemetery Hill, which thus was defended in considerable depth. His other division would arrive in the night, as would Hancock's three under Gibbon, if Meade released them, to extend the line southward along the ridge leading down to the Round Tops. Once this had been done, the fishhook would be defended from eye to barb, and if Meade would also send Sykes and Sedgwick, reserves could be massed behind the high ground in the center, where they would have the advantage of interior lines in moving rapidly to the support of whatever portion of the convex front might happen to be under pressure at any time. All this depended on Meade, however, and when Slocum at last came forward at 7 o'clock (apparently he had decided to risk his reputation after all, or else he had decided that it was more risky to remain outside events in which his soldiers were involved) Hancock transferred the command to him and rode back to Taneytown to argue in person for a Gettysburg concentration of the whole army, nine of whose nineteen divisions were there already, with a tenth one on the way.

He arrived at about 9.30 to find his chief already persuaded by the message he had sent him four hours earlier. "I shall order up the troops," Meade had said, after brief deliberation, and orders had gone accordingly to Gibbon, Sykes, and Sedgwick, informing them that the Pipe Creek plan had been abandoned in favor of a rapid concentration on the heights just south of Gettysburg, where the other half of the army was awaiting their support. However, instead of going forward at once himself — there would be no time for a daylight reconnaissance anyhow — Meade decided to get some badly needed sleep. At 1 a.m. he came out of his tent, mounted his horse, and rode the twelve miles north with his staff and escort, a full moon floodlighting the landscape of his native Pennsylvania. At 3 o'clock, barely an hour before dawn, he dismounted at the cemetery gate, through which there was a rather eerie view of soldiers sprawled in sleep among the tombstones. Across the way, on the western ridge and down in the moon-drenched town below, he saw another sobering sight: the campfires of the enemy, apparently as countless as the stars. Slocum, Howard, and Sickles were there to greet him, and though he had seen but little of the position Hancock had so stoutly recommended, all assured him that it was a good one. "I am glad to hear you say so, gentlemen," Meade replied, "for it is too late to leave it."

By the time he had made a brief moonlight inspection of Culp's and Cemetery hills, dawn was breaking and Hancock's three divisions were filing into position on Cemetery Ridge, having completed their all-night march from Taneytown. Sykes had reached Hanover and turned west in the darkness; he would arrive within a couple of hours. Only Sedgwick's corps was not at hand, the largest of the seven. Uncle John had promised to make it from Manchester by 4 o'clock that afternoon, and though it seemed almost too much to hope that so large a body of men could cover better than thirty miles of road in less than twenty hours, Meade not only took him at his word; he announced that he would attack on the right, as soon as Sedgwick got there.

✗ 3 ✗

Lee's headquarters tents were pitched in a field beside the Chambersburg Pike, on the western slope of Seminary Ridge. When he rose from sleep, an hour before dawn — about the same time Meade drew rein beside the gate on Cemetery Hill — his intention, like his opponent's, was to attack on the right. He had arrived at this decision the previous evening, in the course of a twilight conference north of Gettysburg with Ewell, whom he found gripped by a strange paralysis of will, apparently brought on, or at any rate intensified, by Lee's stipulation that an assault on the blue-coats attempting a rally on the hilltop south of town, though much desired, not only could not be supported by troops outside his corps, as Ewell had requested, but also was to be attempted only if he found it "practicable," which Ewell interpreted as meaning that he must be certain of success. It occurred to him that in war few things were certain, least of all success; with the result that he refrained from taking any risk whatever. First he waited for Johnson, whose division did not come onto the field until past sundown, and finally he called the whole thing off, finding by then that the heights beyond the town bristled with guns and determined-looking infantry, deployed in overlapping lines, well dug in along much of the front, and heavily reinforced.

Though it was not Lee's way to challenge an assessment made by a general on ground which he himself had not examined, when he arrived for the conference he indicated his regret by expressing the hope that Ewell's decision would not apply to next day's operations. "Can't you, with your corps, attack on this front tomorrow?" he asked. Ewell said nothing; nor did Rodes, whose accustomed fieriness had been subdued by his narrow escape from disaster in his first action as a major general, and Johnson was not present. That left Early, who did not hesitate to answer for his chief that an offensive here on the left, after the Federals had spent the night preparing for such a move, would be unwise. However, he added, indicating the Round Tops looming dimly in the distance and the dusk, an attack on the right, with the mass of bluecoats concentrated northward to meet the expected threat from Ewell, offered the Confederates a splendid opportunity to seize the high ground to the south and assail the Union flank and rear from there. Ewell and Rodes nodded agreement, but when Lee replied: "Then perhaps I had better draw you around towards our right, as the line will be very long and thin if you remain here, and the enemy may come down and break through," Early again was quick to disagree. In his view, that would spoil the whole arrangement by allowing the foe to turn and give his full attention to the blow aimed at his rear. As for the integrity of the present line, Lee need have no qualms; whatever its shortcomings as a base from which to launch an offensive, the position was an excellent one for defense. Besides, Early went on to say, much captured material and many of the wounded could not be moved on such brief notice, not to mention the effect on morale if the troops were required to give up ground they had won so brilliantly today.

Lee heard him out, then pondered, head bent forward. The main thing he disliked about the proposal was that it would require a change in his preferred style of fighting, typified by Manassas, where he had used the nimble Second Corps to set his opponent up for the delivery of a knockout punch by the First Corps, whose specialty was power. Early was suggesting what amounted to a change of stance, which was neither an easy nor a wise thing for a boxer to attempt, even in training, let alone after a match was under way, as it was now. Head still bowed in thought, Lee mused aloud: "Well, if I attack from the right, Longstreet will have to make the attack." He raised his head. "Longstreet is a very good fighter when he gets in position and gets everything ready, but he is so slow." The extent of his perplexity was shown by this criticism of one subordinate in the presence of another, a thing he would never have done if he had not been upset at finding the commander of the Second Corps, famed for its slashing tactics under Jackson, content to fall back on the defensive with a victory half won. However, when Early, still speaking for his chief, who seemed to have lost his vocal powers along with those employed to arrive at a decision, assured him that the three divisions would be prompt to join the action as soon as the attack was launched across the way, Lee tentatively accepted the plan and rode back through the darkness to Seminary Ridge.

Once he was beyond the range of Early's persuasive tongue, however, his doubts returned. He reasoned that the blow, wherever it was to be delivered — and he had not yet decided on that point — should be struck with all the strength he could muster. If Ewell would not attempt it on the left, he would bring him around to the right, thus shortening the line while adding power to the punch. Accordingly, he sent him instructions to shift his three divisions west and south at once if he was still of the opinion that he could launch no drive from where they were. This not only restored Ewell's powers of speech; it brought him in person to army headquarters. Dismounting with some difficulty because of his wooden leg, he reported that Johnson had examined the Federal position on Culp's Hill and believed he could take it by assault. This changed the outlook completely; for if Culp's Hill could be taken, so could the main enemy position on Cemetery Hill, which it outflanked. Happy to return to his accustomed style, which was to use his left to set his opponent up for the knockout punch he planned to throw with his right, Lee canceled Ewell's instructions for a shift and directed instead that he remain where he was, with orders to seize the high ground to his front as soon as possible. By now it was close to midnight; Ewell rode back to his own headquarters north of Gettysburg. Lee pondered the matter further. Since Longstreet, who would deliver the major blow, was not yet up, whereas Ewell was already in position, he decided to time the latter's movements by the former's, and sent a courier after Ewell with instructions for him not to advance against Culp's Hill until he heard Longstreet open with his guns across the way. This done, Lee turned in at last to get some sleep, telling his staff as he did so: "Gentle-men, we will attack the enemy as early in the morning as practicable."

Rising at 3 a.m. he ate breakfast in the dark and went forward at first light to the crest of the ridge, preceded by a staff engineer whom he sent southward, in the direction of the Round Tops, to reconnoiter the ground where the main effort would be made. To his relief, as he focused his glasses on the enemy position, though he saw by the pearly light of dawn that the Federals still held Cemetery Hill in strength, the lower end of the ridge to the south appeared to be as bare of troops as it had been at sunset. Longstreet soon arrived to report that McLaws and Hood were coming forward on the pike, having camped within easy reach of the field the night before — all but one of Hood's brigades, which was on the way from New Guilford, more than twenty miles to the west. Pickett too was on the march, having been relieved by Im-boden the day before at Chambersburg, but could scarcely arrive be-fore evening. Glad at any rate to learn that Hood and McLaws were nearby, Lee then was startled to hear Old Peter return to yesterday's proposal that the Confederates maneuver around the Union left and thus invite attack instead of attempting one themselves against so formidable a position as the enemy now held. While Longstreet spoke, the force of his words was increased by the emergence on Cemetery Ridge of brigade after brigade of blue-clad soldiers, extending the line southward in the direction of the Round Tops. However, Lee rejected his burly lieuten-ant's argument out of hand, much as he had done the previous afternoon, although by sunup it was apparent that his plan for a bloodless occupa-tion of the enemy ridge would have to be revised. Longstreet lapsed into a troubled silence, and at that point A. P. Hill came up, still pale and weak from illness. Except to report that his whole corps was at hand, Anderson having arrived in the night, he had little to say. Heth was with him, his head wrapped in a bandage, too badly shaken by yesterday's injury to resume command of his division, which was to remain in re-serve today under Pettigrew, the senior brigadier. Hood rode up soon afterwards, ahead of his men. As he watched the bluecoats cluster thicker on the ridge across the mile-wide valley, Lee told him what he had told his corps commander earlier. "The enemy is here," he said, "and if we do not whip him, he will whip us." Hood interpreted this to mean that Lee intended to take the offensive as soon as possible, but Longstreet took him aside and explained in private: "The general is a little nervous this morning. He wishes me to attack. I do not wish to do so without Pickett. I never like to go into battle with one boot off."

Hood could see that both men were under a strain; but whatever its cause, it was mild compared to what followed presently. As the sun climbed swiftly clear of the horizon, Lee worked out a plan whereby he would extend his right down Seminary Ridge to a point beyond the en-emy left, then attack northeast up the Emmitsburg Road, which ran diagonally across the intervening valley, to strike and crumple the Union flank on Cemetery Ridge. Though he said nothing of this to Longstreet, who had expressed his disapproval in advance, he explained it in some detail to McLaws when he rode up shortly after 8 o'clock. "I wish you to place your division across this road," Lee told him, pointing it out on the map and on the ground. "I wish you to get there if possible without being seen by the enemy. Can you do it?" McLaws said he thought he could, but added that he would prefer to take a close-up look at the terrain in order to make certain. Lee replied that a staff engineer had been ordered to do just that, "and I expect he is about ready." He meant that the officer was probably about ready to report, but McLaws understood him to mean that he was about ready to set out. "I will go with him," he said. Before Lee could explain, Longstreet broke in, having overheard the conversation as he paced up and down. "No, sir," he said emphatically, "I do not wish you to leave your division." As he spoke he leaned forward and traced a line on the map, perpendicular to the one Lee had indicated earlier. "I wish your division placed so," he said. Quietly but in measured tones Lee replied: "No, General, I wish it placed just opposite." When the embarrassed McLaws repeated that he would like to go forward for a look at the ground his division was going to occupy, Longstreet once more refused to permit it and Lee declined to intervene further. So McLaws retired in some bewilderment to rejoin his troops and await the outcome of this unfamiliar clash of wills.

Presently the staff engineer, Captain S. R. Johnston, returned from his early-morning reconnaissance on the right, and his report was everything Lee could have hoped for. According to him, the Federals had left the southern portion of Cemetery Ridge unoccupied, along with both of the Round Tops. When Lee asked pointedly, "Did you get there?" — for the information was too vital to be accepted as mere hearsay — Johnston replied that his report was based entirely on what he had seen with his own eyes, after climbing one of the spurs of Little Round Top. Lee's pulse quickened. This confirmed the practicality of his plan, which was for Longstreet to launch an oblique attack up the Emmitsburg Road, get astride the lower end of Cemetery Ridge, and then sweep northward along it, rolling up the Union flank in order to get at the rear of the force on Cemetery Hill, kept under pressure all this time by Ewell, who was to attack on the left, fixing the bluecoats in position and setting them up for the kill, as soon as he heard the guns open fire to the south. Moreover, while Lee was considering this welcome intelligence, Longstreet received a report that his reserve artillery, eight batteries which were to lend the weight of their metal to the assault, had just arrived. It was now about 9 o'clock. Except for Pickett's division and Brigadier General Evander Law's brigade, on the march respectively from Chambersburg and New Guilford, the whole First

Corps was at hand. Still, Lee did not issue a final order for the attack, wanting first to confer with Ewell and thus make certain that the Second Corps understood its share in the revised plan for the destruction of "those people" across the way.

Leaving Hill and Longstreet on Seminary Ridge, he rode to Ewell's headquarters north of Gettysburg, only to find that the general was off on a tour of inspection. Trimble was there, however, serving in the capacity of a high-ranking aide and advisor, and while they waited for Ewell to return he conducted Lee to the cupola of a nearby alms-house, which afforded a good view of the crests of Culp's and Cemetery hills, above and beyond the rooftops of the town below. Observing that the defenses on the two heights had been greatly strengthened in the course of the sixteen hours that had elapsed since Ewell first declined to attack the rallying Federals there, Lee said regretfully: "The enemy have the advantage of us in a short and inside line, and we are too much extended. We did not or could not pursue our advantage of yesterday, and now the enemy are in a good position." When Ewell at last returned, Lee repeated what he had told Trimble, stressing the words, "We did not or could not pursue our advantage," as if to impress Ewell with his desire that the Second Corps would neglect no such opportunity today. Though it was plain that the Union stronghold had been rendered almost impregnable to attack from this direction, he explained his overall plan in detail, making it clear that all three divisions here on the left were to menace both heights as soon as Longstreet's guns began to roar, and he added that the demonstration was to be converted into a full-scale assault if events disclosed a fair chance of success. This done, he rode back toward Seminary Ridge, along whose eastern slope two of Hill's divisions were already posted, well south of the Chambersburg Pike. Anderson's, which had not arrived in time for a share in yesterday's fight, was farthest south, under orders to join Longstreet's attack as it came abreast, rolling northward, and Pender's was to do the same in turn, simultaneously extending its left to make contact with the Second Corps southwest of Gettysburg. Heth's division, which was in about as shaken a state as its shell-shocked commander, would remain in reserve on the far side of Willoughby Run, not to be called for except in the event of the threat of a disaster.

It was just past 11 o'clock when Lee returned to Seminary Ridge, suffering en route from what an officer who rode with him called "more impatience than I ever saw him exhibit upon any other occasion," and gave Longstreet orders to move out. Observing his chief's disappointment at finding the two First Corps divisions still occupying the stand-by positions in which he had left them two hours earlier, Longstreet did not presume to suggest that he wait for Pickett — as he had told Hood he preferred to do, even though this would have postponed the attack until sundown at the soonest — but he did request a half-hour delay to allow for the arrival of Law, whose brigade was reported close at hand by now. Lee agreed, although regretfully, and when Law came up shortly before noon, completing a 24-mile speed march from New Guilford in less than nine hours, the two divisions lurched into motion, headed south under cover of Herr Ridge, which screened them from observation by enemy lookouts on the Round Tops. Apparently Meade had begun to rectify his neglect of those bastions, for signal flags were flapping busily from the summit of the nearer of the two. Lee was not disturbed by this, however. Now that the march was under way, his calm and confidence were restored. "Ah, well, that was to be expected," he said when scouts reported that the enemy left was being extended southward along Cemetery Ridge. "But General Meade might as well have saved himself the trouble, for we'll have it in our possession before night."

Longstreet's veterans agreed. The march was far from an easy one, the day being hot and water scarce, but they were accustomed to such hardships, which were to be endured as prelude to the delivery of the assault that would determine the outcome of the battle. Moreover, they considered it standard procedure that theirs was the corps selected for that purpose. "There was a kind of intuition, an apparent settled fact," one of its members later declared, "that after all the other troops had made their long marches, tugged at the flanks of the enemy, threatened his rear, and all the display of strategy and generalship had been exhausted in the dislodgment of the foe, and all these failed, then when the hard, stubborn, decisive blow was to be struck, the troops of the First Corps were called on to strike it." As it turned out, however, the march was a good deal harder and longer than they or anyone else, including Lee and Longstreet, had expected when they began it. The crow-flight distance of three miles, from their starting point near Lee's headquarters to their jump-off position astride the Emmitsburg Road just opposite the Round Tops, would be doubled by the necessity for taking a roundabout covered route in order to stay hidden from Meade, who would be able to hurry reinforcements to any portion of his line within minutes of being warned that it was threatened. Nor was that all. This estimated distance of six miles had to be redoubled in turn, at least for some of the marchers, when it was discovered that the movement eastward would be disclosed to the enemy if the butternut column passed over the crest of Herr Ridge here to the south where the woods were thin. Plainly upset by this sign of the guide's incompetence — but no more so than the guide himself, Captain Johnston of Lee's staff, who had neither sought nor wanted the assignment, who had not reconnoitered west of Seminary Ridge at all, and who later protested that he "had no idea that I had the confidence of the great General Lee to such an extent that he would entrust me with the conduct of an army corps moving within two miles of the enemy line" — Longstreet halted the column and reversed its direction of march, back northward to a point near the Chambersburg Pike again, where the ridge could be crossed under cover of heavy woods. Some time was saved by giving the lead to Hood, who had followed McLaws till then, but nearly two full hours had been wasted in marching and countermarching, only to return to the approximate starting point. Longstreet's anger soon gave way to sadness. A soldier who watched him ride past, "his eyes cast to the ground, as if in deep study, his mind disturbed," recorded afterwards that Old Peter today had "more the look of gloom" than he had ever seen him wear before.

Southward the march continued, under cover of McPherson's Ridge, then around its lower end, eastward across Pitzer's Run and through the woods to Seminary Ridge, which here approached the Emmitsburg Road at the point desired. The head of the column — Law's brigade, which by now had spent twelve blistering hours on the march — got there shortly after 3 o'clock. This was not bad time for the distance hiked, but the better part of another hour would be required to mass the two divisions for attack. Worst of all, as Hood's men filed in on the far right, confronting the rocky loom of Little Round Top, they saw bluecoats clustered thickly in a peach orchard half a mile to the north, just under a mile in advance of the main Federal line on Cemetery Ridge and directly across the road from the position McLaws had been assigned. This came as a considerable surprise. They were not supposed to be there at all, or at any rate their presence was not something that had been covered by Lee's instructions.

★ ★ ★

Neither was their presence in the orchard covered by any instructions from their own commander. In fact, at the time Hood's men first spotted them, Meade did not even know they were there, but supposed instead that they were still back on the ridge, in the position he had assigned to them that morning. Since 9 o'clock — six hours ago, and within six hours of his arrival — his dispositions for defense had been virtually complete. Slocum's two divisions, reunited by shifting Geary north from Little Round Top, occupied the southeast extremity of Culp's Hill, while Wadsworth's I Corps division was posted on the summit and along the saddle leading west to Cemetery Hill. There Howard's three divisions held the broad plateau, supported by the other two divisions of the First Corps, now under Virginia-born John Newton, whom Meade had ordered forward from Sedgwick's corps because he mistrusted Doubleday. Thus eight of the sixteen available divisions were concentrated to defend the barb and bend of the fishhook, with Sykes's three in general reserve, available too if needed. South of there, along the nearly two miles of shank, the five divisions under Hancock and Sickles extended the line down Cemetery Ridge to the vicinity of Little Round

Top, though the height itself remained unoccupied after Geary's early-morning departure. Buford's cavalry guarded the left flank, Gregg's the right, and Kilpatrick's the rear, coming west from Hanover.

Meade had established headquarters in a small house beside the Taneytown Road, half a mile south of Cemetery Hill and thus near the center of his curved, three-mile line. Here, once the posting of his men and guns had been completed, he busied himself with attempts to divine his opponent's intentions. With Ewell's three divisions in more or less plain view to the north, he expected the rebel attack to come from that direction and he had massed his troops accordingly. However, as the sun climbed swiftly up the sky, the apparent inactivity of the other two enemy corps disturbed him, knowing as he did that Lee was seldom one to bide his time. It seemed to him that the Virginian must have something up his sleeve — something as violent and bloody, no doubt, as Chancellorsville, where Hooker had been unhorsed — and the more he considered this possibility, the less he liked the present look of things. At 9.30, thinking perhaps the proper move would be to beat his old friend to the punch, he asked Slocum to report from Culp's Hill on "the practicability of attacking the enemy in that quarter." When Slocum replied an hour later that the terrain on the right, though excellent for defense, was not favorable for attack, Meade abandoned the notion of taking the offensive when Sedgwick arrived. In point of fact, he already had his chief of staff at work in the low-ceilinged garret of his headquarters cottage, preparing an order for retirement. Not that he meant to use it unless he had to, he explained later; but with so large a portion of Lee's army on the prowl, or at any rate out of sight, he thought it best to be prepared for almost anything, including a sudden necessity for retreat. At 3 o'clock, still with no substantial information as to his adversary's intentions, he wrote Halleck that he had his army in "a strong position for defensive." He was hoping to attack, he said, but: "If I find it hazardous to do so, or am satisfied the enemy is endeavoring to move by my rear and interpose between me and Washington, I shall fall back to my supplies at Westminster. . . . I feel fully the responsibility resting upon me," he added, "and will endeavor to act with caution."

At least one of his corps commanders — Sickles, whose two divisions were on the extreme left of the line — had serious reservations about the defensive strength of the position, at least so far as his own portion of it was concerned. Cemetery Ridge lost height as it extended southward, until finally, just short of Little Round Top, it dwindled to comparatively low and even somewhat marshy ground. Three quarters of a mile due west, moreover, the Emmitsburg Road crossed a broad knoll which seemed to Sickles, though its crest was in fact no more than twelve feet higher than the lowest point of the ridge, to dominate the sector Meade had assigned him. The only cover out there was afforded by the scant foliage of a peach orchard in the southeast corner of a junction formed by a dirt road leading back across the ridge; artillery from either side could bludgeon, more or less at will, that otherwise bald hump of earth and everything on it. But to Sickles, gazing uphill at it from his post on the low-lying far left of the army, the situation resembled the one that had obtained when his enforced abandonment of Hazel Grove caused the Union line to come unhinged at Chancellorsville, and he reasoned that the same thing would happen here at Gettysburg unless something more than skirmishers were advanced to deny the Confederates access to that dominant ground directly to his front. As the morning wore on and Meade did not arrive to inspect the dispositions on the left, Sickles sent word that he was grievously exposed. Meade, concerned exclusively with the threat to his right and having little respect anyhow for the former Tammany politician's military judgment, dismissed he warning with the remark: "Oh, generals are apt to look for the attack to be made where they are." To Sickles this sounded more than ever like Hooker, and at midmorning he went in person to headquarters to ask if he was or was not authorized to post his troops as he thought best. "Certainly," Meade replied, "within the limits of the general instructions I have given you. Any ground within those limits you choose to occupy I leave to you." So Sickles rode back, accompanied by Henry Hunt, whom Meade sent along to look into the complaint, and though the artillerist rather agreed that it was valid, he also pointed out the danger of establishing a salient — for that was what it would amount to — so far in advance of the main line, so open to interdictory fire, and so extensive that the available troops would have to be spread thin in order to occupy it. In short, he declined to authorize the proposed adjustment, though he promised to discuss it further with the army commander and send back a final decision. As the sun went past the overhead and no word came from headquarters, Sickles continued to fume and fret. Learning finally that Buford's cavalry had been relieved from its duty of patrolling the left flank, which he believed exposed him to assault from that direction, he could bear it no longer. If Meade was blind to obvious portents of disaster, Sickles certainly was not. He decided to move out on his own.

At 3 o'clock, while Meade was writing Halleck that his position was a strong one "for defensive," the veterans of Hancock's corps, playing cards and boiling coffee along the northern half of Cemetery Ridge, taking it easy as the long hot day wore on and no attack developed, were surprised to hear drums rolling and throbbing, off to the left, and when they looked in that direction they saw Sickles' two divisions of better than 10,000 men advancing westward across the open fields in formal battle order, bugles blaring and flags aflutter, lines carefully dressed behind a swarm of skirmishers all across the front. "How splendidly they march!" one of the watchers cried, and another remarked in round-eyed admiration: "It looks like a dress parade, a review." The movement was so deliberate, so methodical in execution, that John Gibbon, sitting his horse alongside Hancock, who had dismounted, wondered if the II Corps had somehow failed to receive an order for a general advance. Hancock knew better. Leaning on his sword and resting one knee on the ground, he tempered his surprise with amusement at the sight of Old Dan Sickles leading his soldiers to the war. "Wait a moment," he said, and he smiled grimly as he spoke, "you'll see them tumbling back."

Some among Sickles' own officers were inclined to agree with this prediction: especially after they had reached and examined their new position, half a mile and more in front of the rest of the army. In ordering the maneuver, one brigadier observed, the corps commander had shown "more ardor to advance and meet the fight than a nice appreciation of the means to sustain it." Old soldiers reviewing the situation down the years expressed the same thought in simpler terms when they said that Sickles "stuck out like a sore thumb." Not only was there little cover or means of concealment, out here on the broad low hump of earth; there was also a half-mile gap between the extreme right of the salient and the left of Hancock's corps, back on the ridge. Moreover, Hunt's theoretical objection that Sickles did not have enough troops for the operation he proposed was sustained by the fact that his new line — extending from near the Cordori house, well up the Emmitsburg Road, to the peach orchard, where it bent sharply back to form an angle, and then across the southwest corner of a large wheat field, to end rather inconclusively in front of a mean-looking jumble of boulders known appropriately as the Devil's Den, just west of Little Round Top — was about twice the length of the mile-long stretch of ridge which now lay vacant in its rear. As a result, the position had little depth, practically no reserves or physical feature to fall back on, and was unsupported on both ends. To some, it seemed an outright invitation to disaster: an impression that was strengthened considerably, within half an hour of the march out, by a full-scale bombardment from rebel guns across the way, in the woods along the eastern slope of Seminary Ridge.

Riding down at last in response to the sudden uproar, Meade was appalled to see what Sickles had improvised here on the left. "General, I am afraid you are too far out," he said, understating the case in an attempt to keep control of his hair-trigger temper. Still in disagreement, Sickles insisted that he could maintain his position if he were given adequate support: a stipulation he had not made before. "However, I will withdraw if you wish, sir," he added. Meade shook his head as the guns continued to growl and rumble in the woods beyond the Emmitsburg Road. "I think it is too late," he said. "The enemy will not allow you." He was calculating his chances as he spoke. The situation had been greatly improved by the arrival of Sedgwick, whose three divisions now were filling up the Baltimore Pike, across Rock Creek, and onto the field, ending on schedule their long march from Manchester. They could replace Sykes in general reserve and thus free those three well-rested divisions to move in support of Sickles. "If you need more artillery, call on the reserve!" Meade shouted above the thunder of the bombardment. "The V Corps and a division of Hancock's will support you —"

But that was as far as he got. His horse reared in terror at the roar of a nearby gun and suddenly bolted, the bit in his teeth. For a moment all Meade's attention was on the fear-crazed animal, which seemed as likely to carry him into the enemy lines as to remain within his own, but presently he got him under control again and galloped off to order up supports for Sickles in the salient.

It was clear by now that they would be needed soon; for behind him, as he rode, he could hear above the uproar of the guns the unnerving quaver of the rebel yell, which signified all too clearly that Lee was launching another of those savage attacks that had won fame for him and his scarecrow infantry.

★   ★   ★

Although Lee's ready acceptance of the role of attacker seemed to indicate otherwise, the odds were decidedly with Meade. Sedgwick's arrival completed the concentration of the Army of the Potomac, which remained some 80,000 strong after deductions for stragglers and yesterday's casualties. Lee on the other hand, with Pickett's division and six of the seven cavalry brigades still absent, had fewer than 50,000 effectives on the field after similar deductions. Moreover, the tactical deployment of the two forces extended these eight-to-five odds considerably. Meade's 51 brigades of infantry and seven of cavalry were available for the occupation of three miles of line, which gave him an average of 27,000 men per mile, or better than fifteen to the yard — roughly twice as heavy a concentration as the Confederates had enjoyed at Fredericksburg — whereas Lee's 34 brigades of infantry and one of cavalry were distributed along a five-mile semicircle for an average of 10,000 men to the mile, or fewer than six per yard. As for artillery, Meade had 354 guns and Lee 272, or 118 to the mile, as compared to 54.

Nor were numbers the whole story. If the attacker enjoyed the advantage of being able to mass his troops for a sudden strike from a point of his choice along the extended arc, this was largely offset by the defender's advantage of being able to rush his ample reserves along the chord of that arc, first to bolster the threatened point and then to counterattack; so that the problem for Lee was not only to achieve a penetration, but also to maintain it afterwards in order to exploit it, which might prove an even greater difficulty. What was more, as he had warned Ewell the evening before, any thinning of the circumferential line to provide a striking force elsewhere would expose the weakened sector to being swamped and broken by the kind of powerful assault Meade could launch, more or less at will, from his interior lines. In short, if Sickles had exposed his two divisions to possible destruction by his occupation of the salient, the same might be said of Lee, in the light of all this, with regard to his whole army and the manner in which he had disposed it.

Longstreet had discerned a good deal of this at first glance; at any rate he had recognized the potentials of disaster, even though he had no access to figures comparing the tactical strengths of the two armies. The two positions were there to look at, Meade's and Lee's, and the only thing he liked about the latter was that it could be abandoned without much trouble. When Lee declined his suggestion that the Confederates move around the Federal left and take up a similar position of their own, thus reversing the present assignment of roles, Old Peter was dismayed. Failure by Hill and Ewell to complete the victory by driving the blue fugitives from the heights they had fallen back on, which was his second choice as a proper course of action, only increased his despondency. "It would have been better had we not fought at all than to have left undone what we did," he had said the night before, in response to a staff officer's exuberance over the day's success. Renewing his plea for a withdrawal this morning, the burly Georgian had been rebuffed again: whereupon he turned sulky. Though he had of course obeyed all orders given him, he had not anticipated them in the best tradition of the Army of Northern Virginia, with the result that he was partly to blame for the delays encountered in the course of the unreconnoitered flank march. As it approached its close, however, his spirits rose — as they always did in proximity to the enemy. Above all, by a sort of extension if not reversal of his native stubbornness, he was determined to carry out Lee's orders to the letter.

Just how determined Longstreet was in this respect was demonstrated to McLaws and Hood shortly after they halted their divisions in wooded jump-off positions due west of the Peach Orchard and the Devil's Den. McLaws rode forward, then dismounted and walked to the edge of the woods, about a quarter of a mile from the Emmitsburg Road, for a look at the ground over which his troops would be advancing. There in plain sight he saw two blue divisions, one posted north along the road and the other southeast in the direction of the Round Tops. "The view presented astonished me," he later recalled, "as the enemy was massed in my front, and extended to my right and left as far as I could see." Whatever validity they might have had when they were conceived, two miles away and something over five hours ago, Lee's plans for an attack up the Emmitsburg Road, in order to get astride the lower end of Cemetery Ridge, were obviously no longer practicable. Not only was the Union left not overlapped, as had been presupposed, but McLaws would be exposing his flank to end-on fire if he attacked in accordance with instructions. He notified Longstreet of this turn of events, only to be told that the orders were not subject to alteration. "There is no one in your front but a regiment of infantry and a battery of artillery," the staff man who brought this message informed him. McLaws replied that he knew better, having seen with his own eyes what was out there. But this had no effect. Three times he protested, and three times he was told to attack as ordered. And the same was true of Hood. Never in his military life had the sad-eyed blond young giant requested a modification of an order to attack, but he took one look at the situation and reacted much as McLaws was doing, half a mile to the north. Before protesting, however, he sent out scouts to search for an alternative to what appeared to him to be a suicidal venture. They promptly found one. All the country south of the Round Tops was unoccupied, they reported; Meade's far left was wide open to just such an attack as Lee had contemplated. So Hood sent word to Longstreet that it was "unwise to attack up the Emmitsburg Road, as ordered," and requested instead that he be allowed "to turn Round Top and attack the enemy in flank and rear."

Longstreet's reply — based, as he said later, on Lee's repeated earlier refusal to permit any maneuver around the enemy left — was brief and to the point: "General Lee's orders are to attack up the Emmitsburg Road." Supposing there must have been some misunderstanding, Hood repeated his request, and again his chief replied with that one sentence: "General Lee's orders are to attack up the Emmitsburg Road." By now Hood had been in position for nearly an hour, confronting the fissured tangle of the Devil's Den and the rocky frown of Little Round Top, and the longer he looked at what his men were being required to face, the more he became convinced that they were doomed. "In fact," he declared afterwards, "it seemed to me that the enemy occupied a position so strong — I may say impregnable — that, independently of their flank fire, they could easily repel our attack by merely throwing or rolling stones down the mountain side as we approached." Once more he urged Longstreet to grant him freedom to maneuver, only to have Old Peter deny him for still a third time: "General Lee's orders are to attack up the Emmitsburg Road." All that was lacking to complete the symbolism was a cockcrow. What came instead was a staff officer with peremptory instructions for him to go forward without delay, and while Hood was making last-minute adjustments in the alignment of his brigades, the corps commander himself rode up. It was 4 o'clock. With his troops already in motion, Hood made a fourth and final appeal for permission to maneuver around Round Top for a strike at the open flank and rear of the blue army. Longstreet still would not agree, though he did at least change the wording of his one-sentence reply. "We must obey the orders of General Lee," he said.

Lee's instructions called for the attack to be launched in echelon, from right to left, not only by divisions — first Hood, then McLaws, and finally Anderson, with Pender alerted to strike in turn if additional pressure was needed — but also by the brigades within those divi-

OAK HILL

PICKETT
(coming up)

RIDGE

CHAMBERSBURG PIKE

MUMMASBURG ROAD

CARLISLE ROAD

HARRISBURG ROAD

HETH

Willoughby Run

McPHERSON'S RIDGE

HAGERSTOWN ROAD

Lee Hq.

College

Gettysburg

Seminary

SEMINARY RIDGE

Plum Run

GETTYSBURG & HANOVER RAILROAD

YORK PIKE

JOHNSON
7 p.m.

HANOVER ROAD

EARLY
8 p.m.

BENNER'S
HILL

RODES

PENDER

HOWARD
CEMETERY
HILL

CULP'S
HILL

NEWTON

SLOCUM

Lee's
command
post

Cordori

Meade
Hq.

HANCOCK

ANDERSON
6 p.m.

BALTIMORE PIKE

Rock Creek

SYKES

POWERS
HILL

McLAWS
5 p.m.

SICKLES

SEDGWICK
(arriving)

PEACH
ORCHARD

CEMETERY RIDGE

WHEAT
FIELD

Plum Run

DEVIL'S
DEN

LITTLE
ROUND
TOP

HOOD
4 p.m.

EMMITSBURG ROAD

ROUND
TOP

TANEYTOWN ROAD

Half mile

Times of attack are
given to nearest hour;
Federal positions
shown as of 4 p.m.

sions, so that the attack would gather strength as it rolled northward. This meant that Law, on Hood's and therefore the army's right, would be the first to step off. And so he did, promptly at 4 o'clock: but not as ordered. If Longstreet would not disregard or modify Lee's instructions, nor Hood Longstreet's, Law — a month short of his twenty-seventh birthday and next to the youngest of Lee's generals — had no intention of exposing first the flank and then the rear of his troops to the destructive fire of the Yankees in the Devil's Den, as would necessarily be the case if he advanced with his left aligned on the Emmitsburg Road. His unwillingness was not the result of any lack of courage, a quality he had demonstrated on field after field, beginning with Gaines Mill, where his brigade had charged alongside Hood's to break Fitz-John Porter's apparently unbreakable triple line and give the Army of Northern Virginia its first victory. He would make whatever sacrifice was called for, but he saw that to advance as ordered would be to spill the blood of his five Alabama regiments to little purpose and with no chance of return. Consequently, in flat disobedience of orders, he charged due east, in a frontal not an oblique attack on the Devil's Den and Little Round Top itself, which he saw as the key to control of the field.

Brigadier General J. B. Robertson's Texas brigade conformed, being next in line, and the result, as Lee's far right and Meade's far left came to grips in that vine-laced maze of boulders and ravines, "was more like Indian fighting," one participant would recall, "than anything I experienced during the war." By the time Hood's other two brigades, both from Georgia and under Georgians, Brigadier Generals Henry L. Benning and G. T. Anderson, joined the melee in the Devil's Den, they found the conflict quite as confused as it was fierce. Hood was down, unhorsed by a shell fragment much as Heth had been the day before, except that he was struck in the arm and carried out of the battle on a stretcher. Such control as remained was on the company level, or even lower. "Every fellow was his own general," a Texan later wrote. "Private soldiers gave commands as loud as the officers; nobody paying any attention to either."

While this highly individualistic struggle was building toward a climax half a mile west of Little Round Top, Law gave twenty-seven-year-old Colonel William Oates instructions to veer southward with two regiments and flush a troublesome detachment of Union sharpshooters out of some woods at the foot of the steep northwest slope of Round Top. It was done in short order, though not without galling casualties; after which the five hundred survivors continued their uphill charge, scrambling hand over hand around and across huge boulders and through heavy underbrush, to call a halt at last on the lofty summit, panting for breath and wishing fervently that they had not sent their canteens off to be filled just before they received the order to advance. Unlike the lower conical hill immediately to the north, which had been cleared of timber in the fall and thus afforded an excellent all-round view of the countryside, this tallest of all the heights in Adams County — sometimes called Sugarloaf by the natives — was heavily wooded from base to crown, a condition detracting considerably from its tactical usefulness. Through the trees due north, however, just over a hundred feet below and less than half a beeline mile away, Oates could see the barren, craggy dome of Little Round Top, deserted except for a handful of enemy signalmen busily wagging their long-handled flags, while off to the left, on lower ground, smoke boiled furiously out of the rocks where the fight for the Devil's Den was raging at the tip of the left arm of the spraddled V drawn by Sickles, its apex in the Peach Orchard and its right arm extended for the better part of a mile up the Emmitsburg Road, south and west of the main Federal position along the upper end of Cemetery Ridge and on the dominant heights to the north and east, bend and barb of the fishhook Meade had chosen to defend. All this lay before and below the young Alabama colonel, who continued to look it over while his troops were catching their breath on the crest of Round Top. Victory seemed as clear to him, in his mind's eye, as the town of Gettysburg itself, which he could see through the drifting smoke, and the green fields rolling northward out of sight. He believed that with his present force he could hold this hilltop stronghold against the whole Yankee army, if necessary, so steep were the approaches on all sides, and if a battery of rifled guns could somehow be manhandled up here, piece by piece and part by part if need be, not a cranny of Meade's fishhook line would be tenable any longer than it would take a detail of axmen to clear a narrow field of fire. So he believed. But just then a courier arrived from Law with instructions for him to push on and capture Little Round Top. Oates protested briefly, to no avail, then got his parched and weary men to their feet — feet that had covered no less than thirty miles of road and mountainside since 3 o'clock that morning at New Guilford — and started them down the northern face of Round Top, intent on carrying out the order.

It did not seem to him that this would be too difficult, particularly after he crossed the wooded valley between the Round Tops and was joined by a third regiment of Alabamians and two of Texans who had fought their way eastward through the lower fringes of the Devil's Den. Earlier, looking down from the taller of the two peaks, he had seen that the lower was not only undefended but also unoccupied, except by a handful of signalmen, and the confidence he derived from this was strengthened as the uphill march began and then continued without an indication that a single enemy rifleman stood or crouched among the rocks ahead. Two thirds of the way up, however, as the butternut skirmishers approached a ledge that formed a natural bastion around the southwest face of the hill, a heavy volley of musketry exploded in their faces. Oates knew at once, from the volume of fire — he afterwards described it as the most destructive he had ever encountered — that it had been delivered by nothing less than a brigade, and probably a veteran one at that. This meant that he had a fight on his hands, against troops in a position that afforded the same advantages he had contemplated enjoying in defense of the hilltop he had just abandoned under protest that he could hold it against all comers with two regiments of about 500 badly winded men and no artillery at all. It was obvious here on Little Round Top, though, that a good many more men than that were shooting at him from the rocky ledge ahead, and what was more they had artillery, two guns spraying canister from the crest above and beyond them. As soon as he could establish a firing line of his own, the three Alabama regiments on the right and the two Texas regiments on the left, Oates gave the order for an all-out uphill charge to drive the Federals back on their guns and off the mountaintop.

That the blue defenders had taken position on Little Round Top, even as Oates was on his way down from the companion height to seize it, was due to the vigilance and perception of one man, a staff brigadier who, strictly speaking, had no direct command over troops at all. Gouverneur K. Warren, the army's thirty-three-year-old chief engineer, a frail-looking New Yorker, thin-faced and clean-shaven except for a drooped mustache and a tuft of beard just below his lower lip, had ridden over to inspect the hill's defenses at about the same time Meade's brief talk with Sickles was being interrupted by his horse's antic reaction to the rebel cannonade. Disturbed to find the high ground all but unoccupied, despite its obvious tactical value, Warren told the signalmen to keep up their wigwag activity, simply as a pretense of alertness, whether they had any real messages to transmit or not — which was why Oates had found them so busy when he looked down at them from across the valley — and quickly notified Meade of the grave danger to his left. Meade passed the word to Sykes, whose corps by now was in motion to reinforce Sickles, and Sykes passed it along to Barnes. Barnes, who at sixty-two was the oldest division commander in the army, was not with his troops at the time, but Colonel Strong Vincent, who at twenty-six was the army's youngest brigade commander, responded by marching at once to occupy the hill. Arriving less than a quarter of an hour before the Texans and Alabamians, he advanced his brigade — four regiments from as many different states, Pennsylvania, New York, Maine, and Michigan — to the far side of the crest, well downhill in order to leave room for reinforcements, and took up a stout position in which to wait for what was not long in coming. Warren meanwhile had ordered up two guns of First Lieutenant Charles Hazlett's battery, helping to manhandle them up the rocky incline and onto the summit. This done, he went in search of infantry supports, which he could see were about to be needed badly, and found Brigadier General Stephen

H. Weed's brigade of Ayres's division marching west on the road leading out to the Peach Orchard. When the commander of the rear regiment, Colonel Patrick O'Rorke — by coincidence it was the 140th
New York, which Warren himself had commanded before he moved up
to staff — protested that he and his men were under orders to join
Sickles, Warren did not waste time riding to the head of the column to
find Weed. "Never mind that, Paddy," he said. "Bring them up on the
double-quick, and don't stop for aligning. I'll take the responsibility."
O'Rorke did as Warren directed, and Weed soon followed with his other
three regiments, double-timing them as best he could up the steep,
boulder-clogged incline and over the crest, to find the struggle raging
furiously below him on the equally steep and rocky southwest face of
the fuming hill.

　　Vincent by then had fallen, shot through the heart as he ranged
up and down the firing line. "Don't yield an inch!" was his last command,
and though his men tried their hardest to do as he said, one officer was
to recall that, under the influence of no less than five charges and countercharges, "the edge of the fight swayed back and forward like a wave."
The conflict was particularly desperate on the far left, where the 20th
Maine, made up of lumberjacks and fishermen under Colonel Joshua
Chamberlain, a former minister and Bowdoin professor, opposed the 15th
Alabama, Oates's own regiment, composed for the most part of farmers.
Equally far from home — Presque Isle and Talladega were each 650
crowflight miles from Little Round Top, which lay practically on the
line connecting them — the men of these two outfits fought as if the
outcome of the battle, and with it the war, depended on their valor: as
indeed perhaps it did, since whoever had possession of this craggy height
on the Union left would dominate the whole fishhook position. "The
blood stood in puddles in some places on the rocks," Oates said later.
Losses were especially heavy among Federals of rank. O'Rorke, who
was barely twenty-three and an officer of much promise, having been
top man in the West Point class of '61, was killed along with more than
two dozen of his men in the first blast of musketry that greeted his arrival. Weed, coming up behind him with the rest of the brigade, was shot
in the head by a sniper down in the Devil's Den, and as Hazlett, who
was standing beside him directing the fire of his two guns, bent forward
to catch any last words the twenty-nine-year-old brigadier might utter,
he too was dropped, probably by the same long-range marksman, and
fell dead across Weed's body.

　　Casualties on the Confederate side were as heavy, if not heavier,
and increased steadily as blue reinforcements continued to come up, un-
matched by any on the downhill side. With all but one of the field officers
killed or wounded in the Texas regiments, and no replacements anywhere
in sight, Major J. C. Rogers, who had succeeded to leadership of the 5th
Texas by elimination, might have thought he had been forgotten by the

high command, except that presently a courier from division came up
the hillside, dodging from boulder to boulder among the twittering
bullets and screaming ricochets. He brought no expected word of reinforcements, but he did have a message from the wounded Hood's successor. "General Law presents his compliments," he told Rogers, "and
says to hold the place at all hazards." This was altogether too much for
the hard-pressed major. "Compliments, hell!" he roared above the clatter of battle. "Who wants compliments in such a damned place as this?
Go back and ask General Law if he expects me to hold the world in
check with the 5th Texas regiment!"

Oates could see that the struggle could have but one end if it continued at this rate, five regiments fighting uphill against eight who were
supported by artillery in defense of a position he had judged to be nearly
impregnable in the first place. So long as there was a hope of reinforcements he would fight — "Return to your companies; we will sell out as
dearly as possible," he told his captains — but presently, after the courier
arrived with nothing more substantial than Law's compliments, he ordered a withdrawal. Just as the word was passed, the Maine men
launched a bayonet attack. "When the signal was given we ran like a
herd of wild cattle," Oates later admitted.

Near the base of the hill they rallied, being joined by the rest of
Law's and Robertson's brigades, together with those of Anderson and
Benning, who had succeeded by now in driving the Federals out of the
Devil's Den, capturing three guns in the process. Not that the fighting
had abated; Sykes had brought up two of his divisions in support of
Sickles, with the result that the odds were as long down here as they
had been above. There on the lower western slopes of Little Round
Top the survivors began collecting rocks of all shapes and sizes, constructing a barricade to fight behind, and all the while the soldiers of
both armies kept up a hot fire, banging away at whatever showed itself
or perhaps at nothing at all. "Both sides were whipped," a Texas private
explained afterwards, "and all were mad about it."

McLaws was also engaged by now, in part at least, and though
this finally helped to relieve the pressure on the men who were fighting
for their lives at the base of the rocky hill, the wait had been a long one,
Longstreet having held him back in hopes that when he went forward at
last he would find the enemy line greatly weakened by the shift of
troops to meet Hood's attack on Little Round Top, which after all was
not the assigned objective. Such withholding tactics had made possible
the one-punch knockout Old Peter had scored at Second Manassas, a
year ago next month, and he planned to repeat that coup today. If this
was hard on Hood, whose men were thus required to absorb the single-
minded attention of the entire Federal left wing for more than an hour,
it was not easy on McLaws and his four brigade commanders, who were

burning to advance: particularly Barksdale, whose thirst for glory was as sharp in Pennsylvania as it had been on his great day at Fredericksburg, where Lee to his delight had let him challenge the whole Yankee army. From the eastern fringe of the woods in which his troops awaited the signal to move out, the Mississippian could see bluecoats milling about in the Peach Orchard, as if they had it in mind to advance against him, and a battery posted temptingly at the apex of the salient, less than six hundred yards away. "General, let me go; General, let me charge," he kept begging McLaws, who declined, being under orders to wait for corps to inform him when the time was ripe. Soon Longstreet came riding northward through the woods and drew rein to talk with McLaws. Born within a week of each other, forty-two years ago, the two Georgians had been classmates at West Point. Equally burly of form and shaggy of hair and beard, they even resembled one another, not only in looks but also in their deliberative manner. Barksdale approached them and renewed his plea. "I wish you would let me go in, General," he appealed to the corps commander; "I will take that battery in five minutes." Longstreet looked out at the guns in the orchard, then back at the tall, white-maned Mississippian, who was trembling with excitement. Old Peter liked Barksdale, who was half a year his junior but looked older because of the prematurely gray hair worn shoulder-length, and greatly admired his spirit; but he would not be hurried. "Wait a little," he said in a calm, deep voice. "We are all going in presently."

It was near 5.30 before he gave the signal that opened the secondary attack. McLaws went in as Hood had done, his brigades committed in echelon from the right, which meant that Barksdale had some more waiting to do, being stationed on the left. South Carolinians under Brigadier General J. B. Kershaw — one of the five generals the town of Camden was to contribute to the Confederacy before the war was over — went forward with a shout, headed straight for the big wheat field north of the Devil's Den, about midway between Little Round Top and the Peach Orchard. Longstreet walked out with them as far as the Emmitsburg Road, where he stopped and waved them on with his hat, adding his own deep-throated version of the rebel yell to the tumult. They struck the center of Birney's division, which was posted behind a low stone wall along the near edge of the shimmering field of wheat, with Barnes's two remaining brigades in close support. As the fighting mounted swiftly toward a climax, Brigadier General Paul J. Semmes — younger brother of the *Alabama's* captain — brought his Georgians out to join the stand-up fight, and behind them came the third brigade, still more Georgians, under Brigadier General W. T. Wofford, who had led them since the death of Tom Cobb in the sunken road at Fredericksburg. The Union line began to crumble under this added pressure, men dropping all along it and others scrambling rearward to get a head start in the race for safety.

Just then Semmes fell mortally wounded, which resulted in some confusion among his troops; but the loss was overbalanced at this critical point by one on the other side. Sickles was riding his line, erect on horseback, ignoring the whistle of bullets and the scream of shells, until one of the latter came along that could not be ignored because it struck his right leg, just above the knee, and left it hanging in shreds. He fell heavily to the ground, but kept cool enough to save his life by ordering a tourniquet improvised from a saddle strap. As he lay there, pale from the sudden loss of blood, his thigh bone protruding stark white against the red of mangled flesh, a staff officer rode up and asked solicitously, if superfluously: "General, are you hurt?" Normally, Sickles would have laughed at the simplicity of the question, but not now. "Tell General Birney he must take command," he replied. Lifted onto a stretcher, he heard through the waves of pain and shock that a rumor was being spread that he was dead; so he called the bearers to a halt while one of them lit a cigar for him, then rode the rest of the way to the aid station with it clenched at a jaunty angle between his teeth, puffing industriously at it by way of disproving the rumor that he had stopped breathing. Thus did Old Dan Sickles leave the war, to proceed in time to other fields of endeavor, including a well-publicized liaison with the deposed nymphomaniac Queen of Spain.

There was to be a great deal of discussion, beginning tonight and continuing down the years, as to whether his occupation of the salient, half a mile and more in front of the main Union line, had been a colossal blunder or a tactically sound maneuver. Whatever else it was or wasn't — and entirely aside from the fact that it helped to discourage Longstreet's men from attacking as Lee had ordered, straight up the Emmitsburg Road, which probably would have meant utter destruction for them if Sickles had stayed back on the ridge to tear their flank as they went by — the movement resulted at any rate in the wrecking of his corps, whose two divisions, formerly under Phil Kearny and Joe Hooker and therefore among the most famous in the army, were to suffer well over four thousand casualties in the two hours before sunset. The worst of the damage occurred when the line gave way at the western rim of the wheat field. "It is too hot; my men cannot stand it!" Barnes cried, and he ordered a retreat. Birney's were quick to follow, despite his efforts to stop them. But as the elated Confederates started forward, in close and hot pursuit, they were met by a fresh division under Caldwell, whom Hancock had alerted to stand by for trouble after predicting — quite accurately, as it turned out — that Sickles' troops would "come tumbling back" from the salient. Caldwell struck with all his strength, holding nothing in reserve. And now, though he lost three of his four brigade commanders, two of them killed on contact, it was the rebels who fell back through the trampled grain, the steam gone out of their drive. From Little Round Top to the northern edge of the wheat field, the fighting degenerated into a bloody squabble as regiment fought regiment, alternately driving and being driven. "What a hell is there down in that valley!" a Federal lieutenant exclaimed after viewing the carnage from up on Cemetery Ridge. Birney's men were out of it by then, such as remained uncaptured and alive, and now the turn had come of those with Humphreys in the orchard and strung out along the road northeast of there.

Longstreet's "presently" had begun to seem interminable to Barksdale and his soldiers, held under cover and straining at the leash all the time the other three brigades were taking on most of Birney's and Barnes's divisions and finally all of Caldwell's, which came in fresh to stop them short of the ridge. Though opinion was divided as to the distinguishing characteristics of these troops from the Deep South — a Virginia artilleryman, for example, having learned to feel secure whenever his battery had the support of the Mississippians, was to say that theirs was the brigade "I knew and loved best of all in Lee's army"; whereas a Chambersburg civilian, observing the various rebel outfits that passed through his town, decided quite to the contrary that "those from Mississippi and Texas were more vicious and defiant" than the rest — the men themselves not only would have considered both of these remarks complimentary, but also would have been hard put to say which compliment they preferred. Certainly their viciousness and defiance were apparent to the Federals in the orchard, just over a quarter-mile away, as they came running eastward out of the woods, unleashed at last and eager to come to grips. Barksdale was out in front of the whole line, his face "radiant with joy," as one observer remarked, to be leading what a Confederate lieutenant and a Union colonel referred to afterwards, respectively, as "the most magnificent charge I witnessed during the war" and "the grandest charge that was ever made by mortal man." His earlier assurance that he could "take that battery in five minutes" had sounded overconfident at the time, mainly because the stout rail fences on both sides of the Emmitsburg Road seemed likely to slow his advance while they were being torn down or climbed over. As it turned out, however, the fences were no deterrent at all. They simply vanished under the impact of the charging Mississippians, who reached the Peach Orchard even sooner than their general had predicted, whooping with delight as they swarmed over the battery and such of its defenders as had resisted the impulse to get out of the path of that savage assault. Four of the guns and close to a thousand prisoners were taken in one swoop, but that was only a part of what Barksdale was after. Still out front, hatless so that his long white hair streamed behind him as he ran, he shouted: "Forward, men! Forward!" pointing with his sword at the blue line half a mile ahead on Cemetery Ridge.

He did not make it that far, nor did any of his men. A Federal brigadier, watching the conspicuous figure draw nearer across the stony floor of the valley, assigned a whole company of riflemen the task of bringing him down; which they did. As for his men, the vigilant Hunt had prepared a reception for them by massing forty guns along the crest and down the slope of the ridge. Meade had seen to it that these batteries had infantry support by shifting troops southward from his over-crowded right, but the guns themselves, blasting the attackers wholesale as they came within easy range, turned out to be enough. Still they came on, overrunning the first line of artillery on the slope, where the cannoneers fought them with pistols and rammer staffs and whatever came to hand, and all the while the guns on the crest flung canister point-blank at them, mangling blue and gray alike. Finally, unsupported on the left or right, Barksdale's men fell back westward to a line along Plum Run, midway between the road and the ridge, leaving half their number dead or wounded on the field, including their commander. Scouts from a Vermont regiment were to bring him into their lines that night, shot through both legs and the breast, and he would die by morning, his thirst for glory slaked at last.

Hood and McLaws had done their worst, and the 15,000 men in their eight brigades, having taken on six full enemy divisions, together with major portions of three others — a total of 22 Federal brigades, disposed with all the advantages of the defensive and containing better than twice as many troops as came against them — were fought to a standstill along an irregular line stretching northward from the Round Tops to the Peach Orchard, anywhere from half a mile to a mile beyond the Emmitsburg Road, which had marked the line of departure. Proud of what his soldiers had accomplished against the odds, though he knew it was less than Lee had hoped for, Longstreet was to say: "I do not hesitate to pronounce this the best three hours' fighting ever done by any troops on any battlefield." The cost had been great — more than a third of the men in the two divisions had been hit; Hood would be out of combat for some time, a grievous loss, and Semmes and Barksdale forever — but so had been the gain: not so much in actual ground, though that had been considerable, as in its effect of setting the bluecoats up for the kill. Meade had been stripping his center, along with his right, to reinforce his left. And now the offensive passed to Hill, or more specifically to Richard Anderson, whose division was on the right, adjoining McLaws, and who now took up his portion of the echelon attack from a position directly opposite the weakened Union center.

In this as in the other two divisional attacks the brigades were to be committed in sequence from the right, and it opened with all the precision of a maneuver on the drill field. Nor was there any such delay as there had been in the case of McLaws, held in check by Longstreet while Hood's men were storming the Devil's Den and fighting for their lives on Little Round Top. At 6.20, when Barksdale's survivors began their withdrawal from the shell-swept western slope of Cemetery Ridge, Anderson sent Wilcox and his Alabamians driving hard for a section of the ridge just north of where the Mississippians had struck and been repulsed. Next in line, Colonel David Lang's small brigade of three Florida regiments followed promptly, supported in turn by Brigadier General Ambrose R. Wright's Georgians, who came forward on the left. But that was where the breakdown of the echelon plan began. Brigadier General Carnot Posey, having already committed three of his four Mississippi regiments as skirmishers, had not understood that he was to charge with the fourth, and his doubts became even graver when he discovered that his left would not be covered by Brigadier General William Mahone, who could not be persuaded that his Virginia brigade, posted all day in reserve, was intended to have a share in the attack. Wilcox by now had sent his adjutant back to ask for reinforcements, and Anderson had sent him on to Mahone with full approval of the request. But Mahone refused to budge. "I have my orders from General Anderson himself to stay here," he kept insisting, despite the staff man's protest that it was the division commander who had sent him. As a result, Posey advanced his single regiment only as far as the Emmitsburg Road, where he came under heavy artillery fire, and Wright, after pausing briefly to give the two laggard brigades a chance to catch up and cover his left, went on alone when he saw that the Mississippians would come no farther and that the Virginians had no intention of advancing at all.

The fault was primarily Anderson's. Missing the firm if sometimes heavy hand of Longstreet, under whom he had always fought before — except of course at Chancellorsville, where Lee himself had taken him in charge — he was unaccustomed to Hill's comparatively light touch, which allowed him to be less attentive to preparatory details. Furthermore, Hill had understood that his right division was more or less detached to Longstreet, whereas Longstreet had interpreted Lee's instructions merely to mean that Hill would be in support and therefore still in command of his own troops. Consequently, neither exercised any control over Anderson, who followed suit by leaving the conduct of the attack to his subordinates, with the result that it broke down in midcareer.

At this point, however, with Wilcox, Lang, and Wright driving hard for Cemetery Ridge, the question of blame seemed highly inappropriate. A more likely question seemed to concern a proper distribution of praise among the three attacking brigades for having pierced the Union center. Hancock certainly saw it in that light, and with good cause. Meade having placed him in command of the III Corps as well as his own when Sickles fell, he had sent one of his three divisions to reinforce the left an hour ago, and since then he had been using elements of the two remaining divisions to bolster the line along Plum Run, where McLaws was keeping up the pressure. As a result, he had found neither the time nor the means to fill the gap on his left, where Caldwell

had been posted until his departure, and the even larger gap that had
yawned beyond it ever since Sickles moved out to occupy the salient.
To his horror, Hancock now saw that Wilcox was headed directly for
this soft spot, driving the remnant of Humphreys' division pell-mell before him as he advanced, with Lang on his left and Wright on the left
of Lang. Gambling that no simultaneous attack would be launched
against his right, just below Cemetery Hill, Hancock ordered Gibbon
and Hays to double-time southward along the ridge and use what was
left of their commands to plug the gap the rebels were about to strike.

He hurried in that direction, ahead of his troops, and arrived in
time to witness the final rout of Humphreys, whose men were in full
flight by now, with Wilcox close on their heels and driving hard for the
scantly defended ridge beyond. As he himself climbed back up the slope
on horseback, under heavy fire from the attackers, Hancock wondered
how he was going to stop or even delay them long enough for a substantial line of defense to be formed on the high ground. Gibbon and
Hays "had been ordered up and were coming on the run," he later explained, "but I saw that in some way five minutes must be gained or we
were lost." Just then the lead regiment of Gibbon's first brigade came
over the crest in a column of fours, and Hancock saw a chance to gain
those five minutes, though at a cruel price.

"What regiment is this?" he asked the officer at the head of the
column moving toward him down the slope.

"First Minnesota," Colonel William Colvill replied.

Hancock nodded. "Colonel, do you see those colors?" As he
spoke he pointed at the Alabama flag in the front rank of the charging
rebels. Colvill said he did. "Then take them," Hancock told him.

Quickly, although scarcely a man among them could have failed
to see what was being asked of him, the Minnesotans deployed on the
slope — eight companies of them, at any rate; three others had been detached as skirmishers, leaving 262 men present for duty — and charging headlong down it, bayonets fixed, struck the center of the long gray
line. Already in some disorder as a result of their run of nearly a mile
over stony ground and against such resistance as Humphreys had managed to offer, the Confederates recoiled briefly, then came on again,
yelling fiercely as they concentrated their fire on this one undersized
blue regiment. The result was devastating. Colvill and all but three of his
officers were killed or wounded, together with 215 of his men. A captain
brought the 47 survivors back up the ridge, less than one fifth as many
as had charged down it. They had not taken the Alabama flag, but they
had held onto their own. And they had given Hancock his five minutes,
plus five more for good measure.

Those ten minutes were enough. By the time Wilcox reached the
foot of the ridge, with Lang bringing up his three regiments on the left,
Gibbon's division had taken position on the crest and was pouring heavy

volleys of musketry into the ranks of both brigades from dead ahead. Staggered by this, and torn on his unprotected right by fire from the massed batteries that had repulsed Barksdale half an hour before, Wilcox looked back across the valley and saw that his appeal for reinforcements had not been answered. Regretfully he ordered a retreat. So did Lang at the same time. And as the Alabamians and Floridians began their withdrawal from the base of the ridge, Wright's Georgians struck with irresistible force, some four hundred yards to the north. "On they came like the fury of a whirlwind," a Pennsylvania captain later recalled. The impetus of their drive carried them swiftly up the slope and into the breaking ranks of the defenders, then through the line of guns, whose cannoneers scattered, and onto the crest. They did not stay there long — Gibbon and Hays had them greatly outnumbered, as well as outflanked on the right and left, and Meade had already ordered another three divisions to converge on the threatened point from Cemetery Hill, three quarters of a mile to the north, and Culp's Hill, about the same distance across the eastern valley — but while they were there Wright believed that he had victory within his reach. On the reverse slope, bluecoats were streaming rearward across the Taneytown Road, and half a mile beyond it the Baltimore Pike was crowded with fugitives. Yet these were only the backwash of the battle. Nearer at hand, on the left and right, he saw heavy blue columns bearing down on him, and he saw too — like Wilcox and Lang before him, though they had achieved no such penetration of the main Union line — that to stay where he was, unsupported, meant capture or annihilation. He ordered a withdrawal, which was achieved only by charging a body of Federals who had gained his rear by now, and then fell back across the Emmitsburg Road, taking punishment all the way from the two dozen guns he had captured and then abandoned. Like Wilcox and Lang, Wright had lost nearly half his men in that one charge, and he found this a steep price to pay for one quick look at the Union rear, even though he believed ever after that the end of the war had been within his reach if only he had been supported while he was astride the crest of Cemetery Ridge, midway of the Yankee line and within plain sight of the cottage Meade was using as headquarters for his army.

The hard fact that no supports were at hand when the Georgians crested the ridge and stood poised there, silhouetted against the eastern sky for one brief fall of time as they pierced the enemy center, did not mean that none had been available. Though Posey and Mahone had hung back, declining for whatever reasons to go forward — the former calling a halt halfway across the valley and the latter refusing to budge from the shade of the trees on Seminary Ridge, directly behind Lee's command post — there still was Pender, whose division was to the Third Corps what Hood's and Johnson's were to the First and Second, the hardest-hitting and fiercest of the three. And yet Pender was not there after all: not Pender in person. Like Heth and Hood, at about the same time yesterday and earlier today, he had been unhorsed by a casual fragment of shell while riding his line to inspect and steady his men for their possible share in the attack then rolling northward. The wound in his leg, though ugly enough, was not thought to be very serious, or at any rate not fatal. But it was. Two weeks later the leg was taken off, infection having set in during the long ambulance ride back to Virginia, and he did not survive the amputation. "Tell my wife I do not fear to die," the twenty-nine-year-old North Carolinian said in the course of his suffering, which was intense. "I can confidently resign my soul to God, trusting in the atonement of our Lord Jesus Christ. My only regret is to leave her and our children." If this had the tone of Stonewall Jackson, under whom Pender had developed into one of the best of all Lee's generals despite his youth, his last words sounded even more like his dead chief: "I have always tried to do my duty in every sphere of life in which Providence has placed me." Few doubted afterwards that he would have done that duty here today at Gettysburg by leading his four brigades across the valley to assault the ridge just north of where Wright had struck it. There was in fact little to stop him once he got there. Not only had Hancock shifted his two divisions south to counter Anderson's attack; Meade had also moved Newton's two in that direction from their position supporting Howard on Cemetery Hill. But that was beside the point, as it turned out. The decision whether to join the charge had been discretionary anyhow, according to Lee's orders, and when Pender was hit and carried off the field, his temporary successor Brigadier General James Lane, having watched Anderson's two adjoining brigades falter, decided that it was no longer advisable for his troops to advance, since they would not be supported on the right. Moreover, A. P. Hill was not there at the time, having ridden northward to confer with Rodes, and did not urge Lane on.

With that, the three-hour-long assault on Cemetery Ridge broke down completely. Hood, McLaws, and Anderson — some 22,000 men in all, including the cannoneers — had tried their hands in sequence against a total of no less than 40,000 blue defenders. Better than 7000 of the attackers had fallen in the attempt, and all they had to show for this loss of one third of the force engaged was the Devil's Den, plus the Peach Orchard, which had been proved to be practically indefensible in the first place, and a few acres of stony ground on the floor of the valley between the ridges. "The whole affair was disjointed," a member of Lee's staff admitted later. "There was an utter absence of accord in the movements of the several commands."

The truth was, the army had slipped back to the disorganization of the Seven Days, except that here at Gettysburg there was no hard-core tactical plan to carry it through the bungling. There was in fact scarcely any plan at all, Lee's instructions for an attack up the Emmitsburg Road having been rejected out of necessity at the start. This, to-gether with the refusal of the Federals to panic under pressure, as they had done so often before when the graybacks came screaming at them, had stood in the way of victory. And yet, in light of the fact that each of the three attacking divisions in turn had come close to carrying the day, there was more to it than that. Specifically, there was Warren and there was Hancock, both of whom had served their commander in a way that none of Lee's chief lieutenants had served him. Warren had acted on his own to save Little Round Top and the battle, and Hancock had done the same to prevent a breakthrough, first at the lower end and then at the center of Cemetery Ridge; but no one above the rank of colonel — Oates, the exception, lacked the authority to make it count — had acted with any corresponding initiative on the other side. There was, as always, no lack of Confederate bravery, and the army's combat skill had been demonstrated amply by the fact that, despite its role as the attacker, it had inflicted even more casualties than it had suffered, yet these qualities could not make up for the crippling lack of direction from above and the equally disadvantageous lack of initiative just below the top.

Longstreet sensed a good part of this, of course — perhaps even his own share of the blame, at least to a degree — but once more his reaction was a strange one. Though he was saddened by the wounding of Hood and the death or capture of Barksdale, which he believed were the main reasons he had failed to break Meade's line, he was by no means as gloomy as he had been in the course of the roundabout march into position. "We have not been so successful as we wished," he told an in-quirer, and that was all he said. He seemed glad, for once, that his share of the fighting was over. If Hill had broken down, it was not his fault; he had small use for Little Powell anyhow. And now the battle passed to Ewell.

Stung by Lee's complaint that he had failed to "pursue our ad-vantage of yesterday," Ewell was eager to make a redemptive showing today, despite the difficulties of terrain on this northern quarter of the field. After Lee had departed he had kept busy, all through what was left of the morning and most of the afternoon, inspecting his three divi-sions, which were disposed along a convex arc on three sides of Gettys-burg, Rodes to the west, Early just south, and Johnson to the east, con-fronting the two dominant heights at the bend and barb of the Union fishhook. His instructions required him to guard the Confederate left, keeping as many bluecoats occupied there as possible, and to stage a vigorous demonstration, by way of insuring that effect, when Long-street's guns began to roar at the far end of the line. Moreover — and this was the prospect he found most attractive, in connection with his desire to make a showing — if Ewell decided that he could strike with a fair chance of success, he was to convert the demonstration into a real attack, driving the enemy from Cemetery and Culp's hills, which commanded the Taneytown Road and the Baltimore Pike, both vital to the Federals if they were thrown into retreat from these two northern heights and the ridge leading southward to the Round Tops. The wait was a long one, anxious as Ewell was, and some time after 4 o'clock, when the distant booming at last informed him that Longstreet's artillery preparation had begun, he decided to respond in the same fashion. Six batteries, held under cover till then by Major Joseph Latimer, Johnson's twenty-year-old chief of artillery, were sent to the crest of Benner's Hill, a solitary eminence one mile east of town, with orders to pummel Culp's Hill, half a mile southwest across the valley of Rock Creek. Ewell felt that this would not only serve as a "vigorous demonstration," fixing the blue defenders in position as required, but would also afford him an opportunity to study their reaction and thus determine the advisability of launching an all-out uphill infantry assault.

The answer was both sudden and emphatic, as might have been expected if a proper reconnaissance had been made. Benner's Hill was not only fifty feet lower than the height across the way; it was also bald, which meant that the two dozen guns found neither cover nor concealment when they went into action there, whereas the Federal cannoneers had spent the past twenty hours digging lunettes and piling up embankments to add to the security of their densely wooded battery positions. Lashing their teams up the reverse slope of the isolated hill, the Confederates opened fire from its crest soon after 5 o'clock, and within a few minutes of the prompt and wrathful response by the heavier guns directly across the valley, as well as by those a mile away on Cemetery Hill, it was obvious that there could be no doubt as to the outcome of the duel, but only as to how long it could be sustained against the odds. Starkly exposed on the naked summit, the gray gunners stood to their work under a deluge of hot metal and amid sudden pillars of smoke and flame reared by exploding caissons. After about an hour of this, Latimer, who was known as the "Boy Major" and was said to be developing fast into another Pelham, felt compelled to send word that his position was untenable, a thing he had never done before in the two years since he had interrupted his sophomore year at VMI to join the army. Johnson at once authorized him to withdraw all but four of the guns, which were to remain there in support of the attack Ewell had just ordered all three of his divisions to make, despite this graphic evidence of the fury they were likely to encounter as they approached the hilltop objectives he assigned them. Latimer's withdrawal was necessarily slow, his crews having been reduced to skeletons by the counterbattery fire, and he himself was mortally wounded before it was completed, a high price to pay for confirming what should have been apparent before the one-sided contest even began.

On the face of it, the infantry attempt seemed equally doomed. Actually this was not the case, however, for the paradoxical reason that Ewell had failed in his primary mission of holding the blue forces in position on his front. By 6 o'clock, when the attack order was issued, Meade had taken thorough alarm at the series of threats to his left and center, and by 7 o'clock, when the advance began against his right, he had shifted two of Newton's three divisions southward, together with all but a single brigade from the two divisions in Slocum's corps. All that remained by then on Cemetery Hill, which Early and Rodes were to assault in sequence from the north and the northwest, were the three battered divisions under Howard, while Culp's Hill was even more scantly held by Wadsworth's division of the I Corps, down to half its normal strength after yesterday's drubbing on Seminary Ridge, and the one brigade Slocum had left behind. That was where the paradox came in. If Ewell had succeeded in holding the departed bluecoats in position, as Lee had instructed him to do, the attack would have been as suicidal as any ever attempted by either army in the whole course of the war; but as it was, with the defenses manned only by Howard's jumpy Dutchmen, Wadsworth's thin line of survivors from the rout of the day before, and the single brigade from Geary's division, the chances of a Confederate breakthrough here on the north were considerably better than fair, despite the obvious difficulties of the terrain. For one thing, thanks to Meade's alarm at the unrelenting fury of the three-hour-long assault on the Round Tops and Cemetery Ridge, Ewell's troops outnumbered the defenders to their front, an advantage no other attacking force had enjoyed on any portion of the field today.

Johnson's division, which had arrived too late for a share in the battle yesterday, had remained in the same position for nearly twenty-four hours, a mile east of Gettysburg and north of the Hanover Road, its four brigades posted from right to left under Colonel J. M. Williams and Brigadier Generals John M. Jones, George H. Steuart, and James A. Walker. The men of the first were Louisianians, and the rest were nearly all Virginians, like Old Clubby himself, who took them forward at 7 o'clock, brandishing the post-thick hickory stick from which his nickname was derived. That left half an hour till sunset, but they had more than a mile to go and armpit-deep Rock Creek to cross before they came within musket range of their Culp's Hill objective. As a result, the sun was well down behind it by the time they came surging up the northeast slope, yelling fiercely as they approached the crest. They did not make it all the way; Wadsworth's troops, including the remnant of the Iron Brigade, were well dug in and quite as determined as they had been when they shattered Heth's attack the day before. Jones was wounded early in the fight, and his and Williams's men, unsupported because Walker and his famed Stonewall Brigade remained in reserve on the far side of the creek, had all they could do to keep from being driven off the hillside. Around to the left, Steuart had better luck, the trenches down the southern nose of the hill having yawned vacant ever since Slocum's departure, half an hour before the rebel advance got under way. The gray attackers swarmed into and along them, whooping as they swung northward in the twilight, apparently unopposed, only to strike a new line of fortifications, drawn at right angles to the old and occupied by the brigade Slocum had left behind. The struggle here was as bitter as on the right, and the defenders — five regiments of upstate New Yorkers under Brigadier General George S. Greene — fought with a determination every bit as grim as Wadsworth's.

Rhode-Island-born, with a seagoing son who had served as executive officer on the *Monitor*, Greene was sixty-two, a few months older than the ineffectual Barnes and therefore the oldest Federal on the field. "Old Man Greene," his soldiers called him, or sometimes merely "Pop," for though he had finished second in his class at West Point forty years ago, he affected an easy style of dress that made him look more like a farmer than a regular army man. What he was, in fact, was a civil engineer; he had left the service early to build railroads and design municipal sewage and water systems for Washington, Detroit, and several other cities, including New York, whose Central Park reservoir was his handiwork, along with the enlarged High Bridge across the Harlem River. Such experience, as he applied it now to laying out intrenchments, stood him and his 1300 men in good stead this evening on Culp's Hill. Rather than attempt to hold the empty trenches on his right with his one brigade, which would have stretched it beyond the breaking point, he had dug a traverse, midway of the line and facing south behind a five-foot-thick embankment of earth and logs. Here his troops fought savagely, holding their own against Steuart's frantic lunges, and were reinforced at last by two regiments Wadsworth was able to spare when the pressure eased on the north end of the hill. When the commander of the first of these reported to him on the firing line, the battle racket was so terrific that Greene had to give up trying to shout above the uproar, and instead wrote his name on a card which he handed to the colonel by way of identification. For two hours, from twilight well into darkness, the firing hardly slacked. Then gradually it did, dying away to a sputter of individual shots, as if by mutual agreement that the blind slaughter had grown pointless: as indeed it had. Johnson was forced to content himself with what was after all a substantial lodgment on the far Union right, and Greene was more or less satisfied that he had been able to keep it from being enlarged, though it was clear to the fighters on both sides that the lull would not last past daylight.

Although it started later and ended sooner, Early's attack on Cemetery Hill, launched when he heard Johnson open fire on the far left, not only accomplished a deeper penetration, but also came even closer than Wright's had done, two hours ago, to achieving a complete breakthrough and the consequent disruption of Meade's whole fishhook system of defense. His four brigades were from four different states, Virginia, Louisiana, North Carolina, and Georgia; Gordon commanded the last of these, and the other three were respectively under Brigadier Generals William Smith and Harry T. Hays and Colonel Isaac Avery. Smith had no share in the assault, having been posted two miles out the York Pike to fend off a rumored threat to the rear. Nor did Gordon, as the thing turned out; Early held him in reserve. But the North Carolinians and Louisianians did all they could, in fury and hard-handed determination, to make up for these subtractions. Hays advanced on the right and Avery on the left, headed straight for the steep northeast face of the hundred-foot hill, and neither brigade would be stopped. Avery fell at the outset, mortally wounded, but his men kept going, over and past three successive lines of bluecoats disposed behind stone walls, defying the frantic overhead fire of infantry and artillery massed on the summit. Hays, a Tennessee-born and Mississippi-raised New Orleans lawyer whose brigade had first won fame under Dick Taylor in the Shenandoah Valley, refused to be outdone, though he too had to contend with three successive blue lines, the first along the far side of a ravine at the foot of the hill, the second behind a stone wall halfway up, and the third in well-dug rifle pits just short of the crest, protected by an abatis of felled trees. Losses were surprisingly light, partly because the downhill-firing Federals tended to overshoot the climbing graybacks, but mostly, as Hays said later, because of "the darkness of the evening, now verging into night, and the deep obscurity afforded by the smoke." Another reason was that the defenders here were Howard's men, who had yesterday's disaster fresh in mind. Hays called no names, merely reporting that his troops, having taken the third Yankee line at small cost to themselves, "found many of the enemy who had not fled hiding in the pits for protection." While these were being rousted out and told to make their own way to the rear as prisoners, the two rebel brigades surged over the lip of the plateau, in hot pursuit of the fugitive survivors. One-armed Howard was there, again the unhappy witness of a scene that by now was becoming familiar. "Almost before I could tell where the assault was made," he afterwards declared, "our men and the Confederates came tumbling back together."

Once more, having failed to stem the rout, he was left with a choice of joining it or exposing himself to capture, along with the guns his cannoneers had abandoned when the attackers reached point-blank range. "At that time," Hays noted proudly, "every piece of artillery which had been firing upon us was silent." The Louisianians and Tarheels swarmed among them, in full possession of the Union stronghold at the bend of the three-mile fishhook. Like Wright before him, a mile to the south, though darkness permitted him no such view of the enemy rear, Hays experienced a feeling of elation as he looked about the plateau for

the reinforcements he had been told to expect. For a moment he thought
he saw them; heavy masses of infantry were coming up from the southwest in the gloom. He could not be sure they were not Federals, in
which case he would take them under fire, but he had been "cautioned
to expect friends" from that direction, either Longstreet or Hill, or
Rodes from his own corps. Even when they fired at him, dropping a
number of his men, he did not shoot back, not wanting to compound
the error if they were Confederates. They fired again and kept coming
on through the darkness; still he held his fire, perhaps remembering the
fall of Jackson in the Wilderness, two months ago tonight. A third volley
crashed, much nearer now, and he saw by the fitful glare of the muzzle
flashes that the uniforms were blue. A close look even showed the trefoil
insignia of the II Corps on the flat-top forage caps of the still advancing
Federals, whose "Clubs Are Trumps" motto Hays and his men knew
only too well from hard experience. They were, in fact, Colonel S. S. Carroll's brigade of Hancock's third division, and Hancock himself had sent
them. He had been talking just now with Gibbon in the twilight, gazing
westward from the point on Cemetery Ridge where Wright's breach
had been sealed, when the racket of Early's attack erupted on the north
slope of Cemetery Hill. "We ought to send some help over there," he
told Gibbon, who was acting as corps commander while his chief undertook the larger duties Meade had assigned him. As the uproar drew
nearer, signifying the progress of the attackers, Hancock added with
rapid decision: "Send a brigade. Send Carroll."

Carroll it was. And Hays, already staggered by the three un-
answered volleys — the third had been especially destructive, delivered
as it was at such close range — gave the order at last for his men to return the fire. This they did, glad to be released from hard restraint, and
kept it up as fast as they could ram cartridges and draw triggers, bringing the blue mass to a stumbling halt. Beyond it, however, Hays could
see other such masses forming in the flame-stabbed darkness; Howard's
fugitives were rallying to support the troops who had opened ranks to
let them through and then gone on to stop the rebels in their tracks.
Looking back over his shoulder for some sign that Gordon was advancing, and wishing fervently that at any moment he would see Rodes and
his five brigades come charging across the plateau from the west, Hays
held his own for a time against the odds, but then, abandoning all hope
of support, gave the necessary commands for a withdrawal. Unpursued
past the line of abandoned guns, the two brigades fell back in good
order, firing as they went, and called a halt at the bottom of the hill,
angry that neither Gordon nor Rodes had mounted the slope to help
them exploit the greatest opportunity of the day.

This lack of support — which, if supplied, might well have made
up for all the miscalculations and fumbled chances of the past two days
— resulted from a series of interrelated hesitations and downright fail-

ures of nerve on the part of several men. Early had withheld Gordon because he saw at the last moment that Rodes was not advancing on his right, and Rodes had called off his attack for the same reason, with regard to Lane. In a sense, it all went back to the fall of Pender and the curious defection of Mahone; or perhaps it went even further back than that, to the near escape from disaster Rodes had experienced yesterday. Restrained at first by a fear of being involved in another fiasco if he charged unsupported up Cemetery Hill, he now was prodded by a desire to retrieve what his restraint had cost him. When he heard the clatter of gunfire on the overhead plateau, which signified unmistakably that the blue defenses had been breached, he repented his inaction and decided to go forward anyhow, with or without support. But by the time he got his troops in position to advance — most of them had been waiting all day in Gettysburg itself, which meant that they had to be disentangled from the complex of streets and houses before they could form for attack — the hilltop clatter had subsided; Hays had brought his two brigades back down the northeast slope. Rodes took a careful, close-up look at the objective, which bristled with guns, and decided — no doubt wisely, at this late hour — that "it would be a useless sacrifice of life to go on." However, instead of bringing his five brigades back to their various starting points, he put them in line along the hollow of an old roadbed southwest of town, a position, he later reported, "from which I could readily attack without confusion." He did not explain why he had not done this sooner, in order to be able to move promptly in support of Hays, but he added: "Everything was gotten ready to attack at daybreak."

So he said. But for now the fighting was over, all but the final stages of Johnson's blind assault on Old Man Greene's well-engineered intrenchments, a mile across the way. Presently this too sputtered into silence, and moonlight glistened eerily on the corpse-strewn valleys and hillsides, its refulgence no longer broken by the fitful and ubiquitous pinkish-yellow stabs of muzzle flashes. Here and there, the wounded troubled the stillness with their cries for water and assistance, but for the most part the veterans of both armies were inured to this by now; they slept to rest their minds and bodies for tomorrow.

Thus ended the second day of what was already the bloodiest battle of the war to date, with no one knew how much more blood still to be shed on this same field.

★　★　★

Their lines drawn helter-skelter in the darkness, the soldiers could sleep; but not the two commanders and their staffs, who had the task of assessing what had been done today, or left undone, in order to plan for tomorrow. In this, the two reacted so literally in accordance with their native predilections — Lee's for daring, Meade's for caution —

that afterwards, when their separate decisions were examined down the tunnel of the years — which provides a diminished clarity not unlike that afforded by a reversed telescope — both would be condemned for having been extreme in these two different respects.

Lee had spent the battle hours at his command post on Seminary Ridge, midway of that portion of the line occupied by Hill's two divisions, and though this gave him a clear view of most of the fighting in the valley below and on the ridge across the way, he had made no attempt to control or even influence the action once the opening attack had been launched on the far right. An observer who was with him recorded that he sent only one message and received only one all afternoon, despite what another witness described as "an expression of painful anxiety" on his face as the assault rolled north toward its breakdown — just at the point where he stood, between Anderson and Pender, with Mahone's brigade taking it easy in the woods directly behind the command post — then shifted across to Culp's Hill and moved back toward him through the gathering dusk, only to stall again when it got to Rodes. Both breakdowns were particularly untimely, since in each case they had occurred at the moment when the echeloned build-up of pressure resulted at last in a penetration of the enemy defenses, hard by the point that had been scheduled to be struck next. If there was bitter mockery in these two near-successes, which had had to be abandoned for lack of support, there was also much encouragement in the over-all results of the five-hour contest. All that had been lacking, Lee perceived and later reported, was "proper concert of action." Substantial lodgments had been effected and maintained by Hood and Johnson, on the far right and far left; Meade was clamped as in a vise. Moreover, high ground along the Emmitsburg Road had been taken by McLaws in the vicinity of the Peach Orchard, which afforded good positions for the massing of artillery to support an attack on the enemy center or left center. It was just at that point, shortly before sundown and directly opposite the command post, that Lee had focused his binoculars to watch Wright's Georgians storm Cemetery Ridge, driving off the defending infantry and cannoneers, and then stand poised on the crest for a long moment, as if balanced on a knife blade, before they had to fall back for want of support. What had almost been achieved today could be achieved tomorrow, Lee believed, with "proper concert of action" and artillery support.

Basically, what he intended was a continuation of the tactics employed today. Longstreet and Ewell would strike simultaneously on the right and left, driving for the Taneytown Road and the Baltimore Pike, just in rear of their primary objectives, while Hill stood by to assist either or both in exploiting whatever opportunities proceeded from the exertion of this double pressure on an enemy Lee presumed was badly shaken by the headlong routs and heavy losses of the past two days. Not that there was no room for doubt or occasion for hesitation. There was indeed. If the fighting today had shown nothing else, it certainly had shown that this was a difficult undertaking. However, the situation was not without its compensations and attractions from the Confederate point of view. In at least one sense, the very strength of the close-knit Federal position worked to the disadvantage of the men who occupied it, and this was that any collapse at all was likely to be total and disastrous. Lee could never forget the breakthrough Hood and Law had scored a year ago at Gaines Mill, where they had launched a frontal assault on Turkey Hill under conditions not unlike those the army faced at Gettysburg. What he hoped for, in short, was a repetition of that exploit tomorrow: by Pickett.

That general had marched his three Virginia brigades to within three miles of the field by 6 o'clock, an hour and a half before sunset; but when he notified Lee of his arrival and asked if he was to press on and join the battle he could hear raging toward its climax just ahead, Lee had sent him instructions to go into bivouac where he was, apparently wanting the men to be fully rested for the work he already had in mind for them tomorrow. These 5000 soldiers would come a good deal short of making up for the nearly 9000 who had fallen here today, not to mention the nearly 8000 who had fallen or been captured the day before, but there were others to be taken into account in comparing the force of the blow he planned to strike with the one he had struck already, which had failed. In addition to Pickett, whose newly arrived division would supply the extra power Lee believed would insure an initial breakthrough, two of Hill's divisions and one of Ewell's had taken little or no part in the fighting today, and the same could be said of two of Anderson's brigades, two of Early's, and one of Johnson's. Longstreet alone had put in all the men he had on hand. In point of fact, only 16 of the army's 37 infantry brigades had been seriously engaged today, which left 21 presumably well rested for tomorrow. Moreover, Stuart's three veteran brigades of cavalry would also be available — two had arrived by sundown and the third was expected before sunrise — to harry the retreat of whatever remnant of the blue army survived the collapse that would attend the rapid exploitation of Pickett's breakthrough.... Such then were the factors that contributed to Lee's decision to renew the attack next morning. All this seemed not only possible but persuasive to a man who had determined to stake everything on one blow and whose confidence in his troops — "They will go anywhere and do anything, if properly led" — had been strengthened by the sight of what they had accomplished, rather than weakened by the thought of what they had failed to accomplish because of a lack of "concert" on the part of their commanders. Just as yesterday's successes had led to a continuation of the offensive today, so did today's successes — such as they were — lead to a continuation of the offensive tomorrow. And both were a part of what would be meant, in the years ahead, when it came to be said of Lee that the stars had fought against him in Pennsylvania.

By midnight, when he retired to his tent to get some sleep, his plans had been developed in considerable detail. A message had gone to Ewell, instructing him to open the action on the left at daybreak, and another to Hill, directing him to detach two brigades from Rodes to reinforce Johnson on Culp's Hill for that purpose, while Pendleton had been told to advance the artillery, under cover of darkness, into positions from which to support the attack on the left and right and center. No orders reached Longstreet, however; nor was Pickett alerted for the night march he would have to make if he was to have any share in the daybreak assault. Perhaps this was an oversight, or perhaps Lee had decided by then to attack at a later hour and thus give his troops more rest, though if so he neglected to inform Ewell of the change. In any event, none of the three corps commanders visited headquarters that evening to discuss their assignments for tomorrow; Lee neither summoned them nor rode out to see them, and though he sent instructions to Ewell and Hill, he did not get in touch with Longstreet at all, apparently being satisfied that the man he called his old warhorse would know what was expected of him without being told.

Across the way, on Cemetery Ridge, the northern leader was taking no such chances. An hour before Lee retired for the night, Meade assembled his corps commanders for a council of war in the headquarters cottage beside the Taneytown Road. He sent for them not only because he wanted to make sure they understood their duties for tomorrow, but also because he wanted to confer with them as to what those duties should be. Moreover, he wanted their help in solving a dilemma in which he had placed himself earlier that evening, the unguarded victim of his own enthusiasm. Elated by Warren's success in holding Little Round Top, as well as by Hancock's subsequent ejection of the rebels who pierced his center near sundown, he had gotten off an exultant message to Halleck. "The enemy attacked me about 4 p.m. this day," he wrote, "and, after one of the severest contests of the war, was repulsed at all points." This last was untrue and he knew it, though he might contend that, strictly speaking, neither the Devil's Den nor the Peach Orchard was an integral part of his fishhook system of defense. In any case, he closed the dispatch with a flat assurance: "I shall remain in my present position tomorrow, but am not prepared to say, until better advised of the condition of the army, whether my operations will be of an offensive or defensive character."

The courier had scarcely left with the message — it was headed 8 p.m. — when Johnson's attack exploded on the right. His troops swarmed into and along the trenches Slocum had vacated half an hour before, and while their advance was being challenged by Wadsworth and

Greene, Early struck hard at Cemetery Hill, driving Howard's panicky Dutchmen from the intrenchments on the summit. Thanks to Hancock, the nearer of these two dangers was repulsed, at least for the time, but the graybacks maintained the lodgment they had effected at the far end of the line. To Meade, this meant that his position — already penetrated twice today, however briefly, first left, then right of center — was gravely menaced at both extremities: from the Devil's Den, hard against Little Round Top, and on Culp's Hill itself. The inherent possibilities were unnerving. Though he ordered Slocum to return to the far right with all his troops and prepare to oust the rebels at first light, Meade now began to regret the flat assurance he had given Halleck that he would not budge from where he was. He foresaw disaster, and not without cause. Five days in command, he already had suffered about as many casualties as the bungling Hooker had lost in five whole months, and it appeared fairly certain that he was going to suffer a good many more tomorrow. In fact, considering what Lee must have learned today from his exploratory probes of the Union fishhook, it was by no means improbable that he had plans for breaking it entirely. And if that happened, the chances were strong that the Army of the Potomac would be abolished right here in its new commander's own home state. The more he thought about it, the more it seemed to Meade that the best way to avoid that catastrophe would be to pull out before morning and retire to the Pipe Creek line, which had seemed to him much superior in the first place. By now, moreover, his chief of staff had completed the formal orders for withdrawal; they could be issued without delay. As for his untimely assurance to Washington — "I shall remain in my present position tomorrow" — it occurred to him that a negative vote on the matter by his corps commanders would release him from his promise. Accordingly, he sent word for them to come to headquarters at once for a council of war.

All seven came, and more. Pleasanton was off on cavalry business — he later testified that he had been ordered to prepare for covering the withdrawal — but since Hancock and Slocum had brought Gibbon and Williams along, nine generals were present in addition to Meade and two staff advisers, Butterfield and Warren. A dozen men made quite a crowd in the little parlor, which measured barely ten feet by twelve and whose furnishings included a deal table in the center, with a cedar water bucket, a tin cup, and a pair of lighted candles on it, a somewhat rickety bed in one corner, and five or six chairs. These last were soon filled, as was the bed, which served as a couch, leaving three or four of the late arrivers, or their juniors, with nothing to sit on but the floor. A witness remarked afterwards that, for all their rank, those in attendance were "as modest and unpretentious as their surroundings" and "as calm, as mild-mannered, and as free from flurry or excitement as a board of commissioners met to discuss a street improvement." By

11 o'clock all were there. Meade opened the council by announcing that he intended to follow whatever line of action was favored by a majority of those present. Then he submitted three questions for a formal vote: "1. Under existing circumstances, is it advisable for this army to remain in its present position, or to retire to another nearer its base of supplies? 2. It being determined to remain in present position, shall the army attack or wait the attack of the enemy? 3. If we wait attack, how long?" As was the custom in such matters, the junior officer voted first, the senior last. From Gibbon through Slocum, with Butterfield keeping tally, all nine agreed that the army should neither retreat nor attack. Only on the third question was there any difference of opinion, and this varied from Slocum's "Stay and fight it out" to Hancock's "Can't wait long," which perhaps was some measure of how much fighting each had done already. At any rate, Meade had his answer. His lieutenants having declined to take him off the hook, the assurance he had given Halleck remained in effect. "Well, gentlemen," he said when all the votes were in, "the question is settled. We will remain here."

By now it was midnight. On the far side of the valley, Lee had retired, and on this side the Union council of war was breaking up. As the generals were departing to rejoin their commands, along and behind the three-mile curve of line, Meade stopped Gibbon, whose troops were posted on the nearby crest of Cemetery Ridge, due west of the headquarters cottage. "If Lee attacks tomorrow, it will be in your front," he told him. Gibbon asked why he thought so. "Because he has made attacks on both our flanks and failed," Meade said, "and if he concludes to try it again it will be on our center." Nearly a quarter-century later Gibbon recalled his reaction to this warning that it was his portion of the fishhook line that Lee would strike at: "I expressed the hope that he would, and told General Meade, with confidence, that if he did we would defeat him."

✗ 4 ✗

July 3; Lee rose by starlight, as he had done the previous morning, with equally fervent hopes of bringing this bloodiest of all his battles to a victorious conclusion before sunset. Two months ago today, Chancellorsville had thundered to its climax, fulfilling just such hopes against longer odds, and one month ago today, hard on the heels of a top-to-bottom reorganization occasioned by the death of Stonewall Jackson, the Army of Northern Virginia had begun its movement from the Rappahannock, northward to where an even greater triumph had seemed to be within its reach throughout the past forty-odd hours of savage fighting. Today would settle the outcome, he believed, not only of the battle — that went without saying; flesh and blood, bone and sinew and nerve could only stand so much — but also, perhaps, of the war; which, after all, was why he had come up here to Pennsylvania in the first place. He woke to a stillness so profound that one of Gibbon's officers, rolled in his blankets near a small clump of trees on Cemetery Ridge, two thirds of the way up the shank of the Union fishhook, heard the courthouse clock a mile away in Gettysburg strike three. Lee emerged from his tent soon afterwards, fully dressed for the fight, and shared a frugal breakfast with his staff. Three miles northwest, Pickett's men were stirring, too, in a grove of oaks where they had made camp beside the Chambersburg Pike at sundown. Well rested though still a little stiff from yesterday's long march, which had ended not in battle, as they had expected, but in bivouac, they were the shock troops Lee would employ today in an ultimate attempt to achieve the breakthrough he had been trying for all along. It was for this reason, this purpose, that he had withheld them from the carnage they might otherwise have arrived in time to share the day before.

With sunrise only an hour away, however, it was obvious that he had abandoned his plan for a dawn attack. A good two hours would be required for Pickett to move his three brigades from their present bivouac area and mass them in a jump-off position well down Seminary Ridge. For them to have any share in an attack at dawn, they had to have been in motion at least an hour ago, and Lee not only had not sent Pickett or his corps commander any word of his intentions; he did not even do so now. Perhaps, on second thought, he had reasoned that more deliberate preparations were required for so desperate an effort, including another daylight look at the objective, which the enemy might have reinforced or otherwise rendered impregnable overnight. Besides, the assault would necessarily be a one-shot endeavor; late was as good as early, and maybe better, since it not only would permit a more careful study of all the problems, but also would lessen the time allowed the Federals for mounting and launching a counterattack in event of a Confederate repulse. Or perhaps it was even simpler than that. Perhaps Lee merely wanted time for one more talk with the man he called his warhorse, whose three divisions he had decided to use in the assault. At any rate, it was Longstreet he set out to find as soon as he mounted Traveller in the predawn darkness and rode eastward up the reverse slope of Seminary Ridge, delaying only long enough to send a courier to Ewell with word that the proposed attack, though still designed as a simultaneous effort on the right and the far left, would be delayed until 10 o'clock or later.

From the crest of the ridge, as he gazed southeast to where the first pale streaks of dawn had just begun to glimmer, he was greeted by a sudden eruption of noise that seemed to have its source in the masked valley beyond Cemetery Hill. It was gunfire, unmistakably, a cannonade mounting quickly to a sustained crescendo; but whose? In the absence of reports, Lee could not tell, but he knew at once that one of two regrettable things had happened. Either his message had failed to reach Ewell in time, in which case his plan for the synchronization of the two attacks had gone awry, or else Meade had gotten the jump on him in that direction, leaving Ewell no choice whatsoever in the matter of when to fight.

In point of fact, it was something of both. The courier had not yet reached Second Corps headquarters (indeed, he had not had time to) and Meade *had* seized the initiative. Slocum, returning to the Federal right with both of his divisions before midnight, had massed them along the Baltimore Pike for the purpose of driving the Confederates from the lower end of Culp's Hill, where they had effected a lodgment soon after his sundown departure. At 3.45, accordingly, he opened with four batteries he had posted along the northern slope of Powers Hill, blasting away at the rebels crouched in the trenches his own men had dug the day before. For fifteen minutes he kept up the fire, taking care that the guns did not overshoot and drop their shells on Greene's troops just beyond, then paused briefly to survey the damage as best he could in the dim light. Apparently unsatisfied, he resumed the cannonade, joined now by a battery firing southeast from Cemetery Hill, and continued it for the better part of an hour, after which he intended to launch an infantry assault.

This time, though, it was the Confederates who got the jump on their opponents in this struggle for possession of the barb of the Union fishhook. Unable to bring artillery over Rock Creek and the rough ground he had crossed to gain the position he now held, Johnson had his men lie low among the rocks and in the trenches while the shells burst all around them. Then, as soon as the hour-long bombardment ended, he sent them surging forward, determined to gain control of the Baltimore Pike in accordance with last night's orders from Lee and Ewell. In this he was unsuccessful, though he gave it everything he had, including the added strength of the two brigades from Rodes, under Brigadier General Junius Daniel and Colonel Edward O'Neal. Slocum's troops refused to yield, and now that the graybacks were out of their holes the guns resumed their firing on the left and on the right, their targets clearly defined for them against the risen sun. Presently word arrived from Ewell that Lee had ordered a postponement of the attack here on the left so that it might be co-ordinated with Longstreet's on the right, which had been delayed; but Old Clubby, fighting less by now in hope of gain than for survival — to attempt even to disengage would be to invite destruction — no longer had any say-so in the matter. Unrelentingly severe, the contest degenerated into a series of brief advances and sudden repulses, first by one side, then the other. For better than five hours this continued, Slocum being reinforced by a brigade from Sedgwick's corps and Johnson adding Smith's brigade of

Early's division to his ranks, but neither could gain a decided advantage over the other, except in the weight of metal thrown. The unopposed Federal guns made the real difference, and they were what told in the end. By 10.30 the Confederates had been driven off Culp's Hill, approximately back to the line at its eastern base along Rock Creek, from which they had launched their attack the day before. Slocum, having recovered his lost trenches, was content to hold them, and Johnson was obliged to forgo any attempt to retake them. All he could do today he had done already, for the casualties in his seven brigades had been heavy and the survivors were fought to a frazzle. Whatever Longstreet was going to accomplish, around on the far side of the fishhook, would have to be accomplished on his own.

Lee had already taken this into account, however, and he had not seen in it any cause for cancellation of his plans. Ewell's share in them had been secondary anyhow, a diversionary effort designed to mislead his opponent into withholding reinforcements from that portion of the Federal line assigned to Longstreet for a breakthrough, with consequent disruption of the whole. If Meade had taken the offensive against Ewell, Lee's purpose might be served even better in that regard, since this would require the northern commander to employ more troops at the far end of his position than if he had remained on the defensive there. A more serious question was whether he could be prevented from turning the tables on the Confederates by scoring a breakthrough of his own, but Lee was no more inclined to worry about the possibility of such a mishap here at Gettysburg than Jackson had been at Fredericksburg, when he remarked of the soldiers now under fire on Culp's Hill, "My men have sometimes failed to take a position, but to defend one, never!" Lee might have said the same thing now, and he also might have added on Ewell's behalf, as Jackson had done on his own, "I am glad the Yankees are coming." At any rate, after pausing on the crest of Seminary Ridge to listen to the cannonade a mile across the way, he turned Traveller's head southward, noting with pleasure by the spreading light of dawn that Meade did not seem to have strengthened his center overnight, and continued his ride in search of Longstreet.

He found him shortly after sunrise, three miles down the line, in a field just west of Round Top. The burly Georgian had emerged at last from the gloom into which his heavy losses, following hard upon the rejection of his counsel, had plunged him the previous evening. Moreover, his first words showed the reason for this recovery of his spirits. "General," he greeted Lee, "I have had my scouts out all night, and I find that you still have an excellent opportunity to move around to the right of Meade's army and maneuver him into attacking us." Apparently he believed that yesterday's experience must have proved to the southern commander the folly of attempting to storm a position of great natural strength, occupied by a numerically superior foe who had demonstrated forcefully his ability to maintain it against the most violent attempts at dislodgment. But Lee was as quick to set Old Peter straight today as he had been the day before, and he did so with nearly the same words. "The enemy is there," he said, pointing northeast as he spoke, "and I am going to strike him." Longstreet's spirits took a sudden drop. He knew from Lee's tone and manner that his mind was quite made up, that no argument could persuade him not to continue the struggle on this same field. Accordingly, after giving instructions canceling the intended shift around the south end of the Federal line, Old Peter turned again to his chief to receive his orders for the continuation of the battle he did not want to fight, at least not here.

These orders only served to deepen his gloom still further. What Lee proposed was that Longstreet strike north of the Round Tops with his whole corps, now that Pickett was at hand, in an attempt to break the Union line on Cemetery Ridge. Essentially, this was what Old Peter had tried and failed to do the day before, after protesting to no avail, and he did not believe that his chances for success had been improved by the repulse already suffered, especially in view of the fact that all three of the attacking divisions had been fresh and up to full strength when they were committed yesterday, whereas two of the three Lee intended to employ today were near exhaustion and had lost no less than a third of their men by way of demonstrating that the attempt had been unwise in the first place. In opposing the selection of troops for the assault, Longstreet pointed out that to withdraw his two committed divisions from the vicinity of the Devil's Den and the Wheat Field would be to expose the right flank of the attacking column to assault by the bluecoats now being held in check in that direction. Lee thought this over briefly, then agreed. McLaws and Law would hold their ground; Pickett would be supported instead by two of Hill's divisions, and the point of attack would be shifted northward, from the left center to the right center of the enemy ridge, though this would afford the attackers less cover and a greater distance to march before they came to grips with the defenders on the far side of the nearly mile-wide valley.

Longstreet did some rapid calculations. Pickett had just under 5000 men, his division being the smallest in the army, and the chances were that Hill's would be no larger, if as large, after his losses of the past two days. That gave a rough total of 15,000 or less, and Longstreet did not believe this would be enough to do the job Lee had in mind. Perhaps he had reproached himself the night before for not having made a firmer protest yesterday against what he had believed to be an unwise assignment. If so, he made sure now, at the risk of being considered insubordinate, that he would have no occasion for self-reproach on that account tonight. "General," he told Lee in a last face-to-face endeavor to dissuade him from extending what he believed was an invitation to disaster, "I have been a soldier all my life. I have been with soldiers engaged in fights by couples, by squads, companies, regiments, divisions, and armies, and should know as well as anyone what soldiers can do. It is my opinion that no 15,000 men ever arrayed for battle can take that position."

Lee's reply to this was an order for Pickett to be summoned. He was to post his three brigades behind Seminary Ridge, just south of the army command post near the center of the line, and there await the signal to attack. Two of Anderson's brigades, those of Lang and Wilcox, already posted in the woods adjoining Pickett's assembly area, would be on call for his support if needed. On his left, north of the command post and also under cover of the ridge, Heth's four brigades — under Pettigrew, for Heth was still too jangled to resume command — would be massed for the same purpose, supported in turn by two brigades from Pender, who was also incapacitated. Longstreet was to be in over-all command of the attack, despite his impassioned protest that it was bound to fail, and would give the signal that would launch it, though only three of the eleven brigades involved were from his corps. The plan itself, as Lee explained it to his lieutenant while they rode northward for an inspection of the terrain and the units selected to cross it, had at least the virtue of simplicity. The objective was clearly defined against the skyline: a little clump of umbrella-shaped trees, four fifths of a mile away on Cemetery Ridge, just opposite the Confederate command post. Pickett and Pettigrew, each with two brigades in support, would align on each other as they emerged from cover and advanced, guiding on the distinctive landmark directly across the shallow valley from the point where their interior flanks would come together. By way of softening up the objective, the assault would be preceded by a brief but furious bombardment from more than 140 guns of various calibers: 80 from the First Corps, disposed along a mile-long arc extending from the Peach Orchard to the command post back on Seminary Ridge, and 63 from the Third Corps, strung out north of the command post, along the east slope of the ridge. This would be the greatest concentration of artillery ever assembled for a single purpose on the continent, and Lee appeared to have no doubt that it would pave the way for the infantry by pulverizing or driving off the batteries posted in support of the Union center.

Longstreet displayed considerably less confidence than did his chief as they rode north along the line McLaws had fallen back to in the darkness, after charging eastward across the wheat field and part way up the western slope of Cemetery Ridge. "Never was I so depressed as upon that day," Old Peter declared years later. Presently they came to Wofford, who proudly reported to Lee that his brigade had nearly reached the crest of the ridge the day before, just north of Little Round Top, in pursuit of the troops Dan Sickles had exposed. But when the army commander inquired if he could not go there again, the Georgian's jubilation left him.

"No, General, I think not," he said.

"Why not?" Lee asked, and Wofford replied:

"Because, General, the enemy have had all night to intrench and reinforce. I had been pursuing a broken enemy, and the situation now is very different."

Longstreet looked at Lee to see what effect this might have on him, but apparently it had none at all. The two men continued their ride northward, all the way to the sunken lane where Rodes's three remaining brigades were posted on the outskirts of Gettysburg, and then back south again. Twice they rode the full length of the critical front, and all this time Lee refused to be distracted by the clatter of Ewell's desperate back-and-forth struggle across the way, smoke from which kept boiling out of the hidden valley in rear of Lee's prime objective on Cemetery Ridge. He was leaving as little as possible to chance, including the posting of individual batteries for the preliminary bombardment.

Only once, in the three hours required for this careful examination of the ground over which the attack would pass, did he admit the possibility that it might not be successful, and this was when A. P. Hill, who joined him and Longstreet in the course of the reconnaissance, suggested that instead of using only eight of his thirteen brigades, as instructed, he be allowed to send his whole corps forward. Lee would not agree. "What remains of your corps will be my only reserve," he said, "and it will be needed if General Longstreet's attack should fail."

By now it was 9 o'clock; Pickett's three brigades of fifteen veteran regiments — 4600 men in all, and every one a Virginian, from the division commander down — were filing into position behind Seminary Ridge, there to await the signal which Longstreet, who would give it, believed would summon them to slaughter. Pickett himself took no such view of the matter. He saw it, rather, as his first real chance for distinction in this war, and he welcomed it accordingly, his hunger in that regard being as great as that of any man on the field, on either side. This was not only because he had missed the first two days of battle, marking time at Chambersburg, then eating road dust on the long march toward the rumble of guns beyond the horizon, but also because it had begun to appear to him, less than two years short of forty and therefore approaching what must have seemed the down slope of life, that he was in danger of missing the whole war. That came hard; for he had already had one taste of glory, sixteen years ago in Mexico, and he had found it sweet.

After a worse than undistinguished record at West Point — the class of 1846 had had fifty-nine members, including George McClellan and T. J. Jackson, and Pickett had ranked fifty-ninth — he went to war, within a year of graduation, and was the first American to scale the ramparts at Chapultepec, an exploit noted in official reports as well as in all the papers. Twelve years later he made news again, this time by defying a British squadron off San Juan Island in Puget Sound; "We'll make a Bunker Hill of it," he told his scant command; for which he was commended by his government and applauded by the press. Then came secession, and Pickett resigned his commission and headed home from Oregon. Arriving too late for First Manassas, he was wounded in the shoulder at Gaines Mill, just too early for a part in the charge that carried the day. That was a year ago this week, and he had seen no large-scale fighting since, not having returned to duty till after Second Manassas and Sharpsburg. At Fredericksburg his division had been posted in reserve, with scarcely a glimpse of the action and no share at all in the glory; after which, by way of capping the anticlimax, as it were, the Suffolk excursion had caused him to miss Chancellorsville entirely. But now there was Gettysburg, albeit the contest was two thirds over before he reached the field, and when he was offered this opportunity to deliver what Lee had designed as the climactic blow of the greatest battle of them all, he perceived at last what fate had kept in store for him through all these tantalizing months of blank denial. He grasped it eagerly, not only for his own sake, but also for the sake of the girl he called "the charming Sally," his letters to whom were always signed "Your Soldier."

So eager was he, indeed, that an English observer who saw him for the first time here today, just after Pickett learned of his assignment, described him as a "desperate-looking character." But the fact was he might have given that impression almost anywhere, on or off the field of battle, if only because of his clothes and his coiffure. Jaunty on a sleek black horse, he wore a small blue cap, buff gauntlets, and matching blue cuffs on the sleeves of his well-tailored uniform. Mounted or afoot, he carried an elegant riding crop. His boots were brightly polished and his gold spurs glinted sunlight, rivaling the sparkle of the double row of fire-gilt buttons on his breast. Of middle height, slender, graceful of carriage — "dapper and alert," a more familiar witness termed him, while another spoke of his "marvelous pulchritude" — he sported a curly chin-beard and a mustache that drooped beyond the corners of his mouth and then turned upward at the ends. To add to the swashbuckling effect, his dark-brown hair hung shoulder-length in ringlets which he anointed with perfume. There were those who alleged that he owed his rapid advancement to his friendship with the corps commander, which dated back to the peacetime army, rather than to any native ability, which in fact he had had little chance to prove. "Taking Longstreet's orders in emergencies," the corps adjutant would recall, "I could always see how he looked after Pickett, and made us give him things very fully; indeed, sometimes stay with him to make sure he did not go astray."

His three brigadiers were all his seniors in years, and one had been his senior in rank as well, until Pickett's October promotion to major general. James L. Kemper, the youngest, was just past his fortieth birthday. A former Piedmont lawyer and politician, twice elected speaker of the House of Delegates, he was the only nonprofessional soldier of the lot, and though he retained a fondness for high-flown oratory — "Judging by manner and conversation alone," an associate observed, "he would have been classed as a Bombastes Furioso" — his combat record was a good one, as was that of his troops, whose three previous commanders now commanded the three corps of the army. Kemper had been with the brigade from the outset, first at the head of a regiment, and had fought in all its battles, from First Manassas on. He and his men shared another proud distinction, dating back to what Southerners liked to refer to as the "earlier" Revolution; one of the five regiments was a descendant of George Washington's first command, and Kemper's grandfather had served as a colonel on the future President's staff. By contrast, though he too was of a distinguished Old Dominion family — one that had given the Confederacy the first of its seventy-seven general officers who would die of wounds received in action — Richard B. Garnett was a comparative newcomer to the division and had never led his present brigade in a large-scale battle. Forty-five years old, strikingly handsome, a West Pointer and a regular army man, he had advanced rapidly in the early months of the war and had succeeded Jackson as commander of the Stonewall Brigade. Then at Kernstown, where he ordered a withdrawal to avoid annihilation, had come tragedy; Jackson removed him from his post and put him in arrest for retreating without permission. Garnett promptly demanded a court-martial, convinced that it would clear him of the charge, but the case dragged on for months, interrupted by battle after battle — all of which he missed — until Lee took a hand in the matter, immediately after Sharpsburg, and transferred him to Longstreet's corps to take command of Pickett's brigade when that general, whom he had previously outranked, was promoted to command of the division. Neither Fredericksburg nor Suffolk brought Garnett the opportunity by which he hoped to clear his record of the Kernstown stain, and now in Pennsylvania he was not only limping painfully from an injury lately suffered when he was kicked in the knee by a horse; he was also sick with chills and fever. Medically speaking, he should have been in bed, not in the field, but he was determined to refute — with blood, if need be — the accusations Jackson had leveled against his reputation. The third and oldest of the three brigadiers, forty-six-year-old Lewis Armistead, was also something of a romantic figure, though less by circumstance than by inclination. A widower, twice brevetted for gallantry in Mexico, he was a great admirer of the ladies and enjoyed posing as a swain. This had earned him the nickname "Lo," an abbreviation of Lothario, which was scarcely in keeping with his close-

cropped, grizzled beard or receding hairline. He had, however, a senti-
mental turn of mind and fond memories of life in the old army. For
example, he and Hancock, who was waiting for him now across the way
though neither knew it, had been friends. "Hancock, goodbye," he had
said in parting, two years ago on the West Coast as he prepared to cross
the continent with Albert Sidney Johnston; "you can never know what
this has cost me." As he spoke he put both hands on his friend's shoulders,
and tears stood in his eyes. Now he and Dick Garnett stood together on
the crest of Seminary Ridge, looking out across the gently rolling valley
toward the little clump of umbrella-shaped trees which had been
pointed out to them as their objective, a mile away on Cemetery Ridge.
Both men were experienced soldiers, and both knew at a glance the ordeal they and their brigades would be exposed to when the signal came
for them to advance. Finally Garnett broke the silence. "This is a desperate thing to attempt," he said. Armistead agreed. "It is," he replied.
"But the issue is with the Almighty, and we must leave it in His hands."

Completing what was described as "a shady, quiet march" of
about five miles, southeast along the turnpike, then due south through the
woods along the far bank of a stream called Pitzer's Run, Pickett's men
were unaware of what awaited them beyond the screening ridge; or as
one among the marchers later put it, "No gloomy forebodings hovered
over our ranks." Not since Sharpsburg, nearly ten months ago, had the
troops in these fifteen regiments been involved in heavy fighting, and this
encouraged them to believe — quite erroneously, but after the custom of
young men everywhere — that they were going to live forever. Near
the confluence of Pitzer's and Willoughby Runs, they were halted and
permitted to break formation for a rest in the shade of the trees. The
sun had burned the early morning clouds away, and though the lack of
breeze gave promise of a sultry afternoon, the impression here in this
unscarred valley behind Seminary Ridge was of an ideal summer day,
no different from any other except in its perfection. "Never was sky or
earth more serene, more harmonious, more aglow with light and life,"
one among the loungers afterwards wrote. Presently they were called
back into ranks, told to leave their extra gear in the care of a single
guard from each regiment, and marched eastward over the crest of the
ridge, then down its opposite slope and into a wooded swale a couple of
hundred yards beyond, where they were halted. Here too they were
shielded from hostile observers by the low bulge of earth extending
northward from the Peach Orchard, along which they could see the
corps artillery disposed in a slow curve from the right, the cannoneers
silhouetted against the skyline directly in their front. Two brigades of
infantry were up there, too, under Wilcox, but Pickett's orders were for
his own troops to take it easy here in the swale, doing nothing that might
attract the enemy's attention. Soon after they were in position, Lee arrived and began to ride along the lines of reclining men. Mindful of

their instructions not to give away their presence, they refrained from cheering; but as the general drew abreast of each company, riding slowly, gravely past, the men rose and took off their hats in silent salute. Lee returned it in the same manner, the sunlight in his gray hair making a glory about his head.

If he seemed graver than usual this morning, he had cause. He had just come from making a similar inspection of the troops disposed northward along the densely wooded eastern slope of Seminary Ridge, where they too were waiting under cover for the signal to move out, and he had noticed that a good number of them wore bandages about their heads and limbs. "Many of these poor boys should go to the rear; they are not able for duty," he remarked. Drawing rein before one hard-hit unit, he looked more closely and realized, apparently for the first time, how few of its officers had survived the earlier fighting. "I miss in this brigade the faces of many dear friends," he said quietly. Riding away, he looked back once and muttered to himself, as if to fend off such tactical doubts as were provoked by personal sorrow: "The attack must succeed."

His choice of the half-dozen brigades that made up the left wing of the assault force — Heth's four, plus two from Pender — was doubly logical, in that all the troops so chosen were handy to the jump-off position and had not been engaged the day before, which not only lessened the chance of disclosing his intention to the enemy by their preliminary movements, but also was presumed to mean that they were fresh, or at any rate well rested, for the long advance across the valley and the subsequent task of driving the bluecoats off the ridge on the far side. What had not been taken into account, however — at least not until Lee saw for himself the thinned ranks and the bandaged wounds of the survivors — was the additional and highly pertinent fact that five of the six had suffered cruelly in the first day's fighting. Both division commanders were out of action, and only two of the six brigades were still under the leaders who had brought them onto the field. The one exception on both counts was Lane's brigade, which had not been heavily engaged and still had its original commander; but this was offset by the misfortune of the other brigade from Pender's division, which had lost its leader, Brigadier General Alfred Scales, together with all but two of its officers above the rank of captain and more than half of those of that rank or below. This was the unit Lee had paused in front of this morning to remark that he missed "the faces of many dear friends," and it was led now by Colonel William Lowrance, who never before had commanded anything larger than a regiment. Moreover, because Lee did not consider Lane experienced enough to succeed the wounded Pender, he had summoned old Isaac Trimble over from Ewell and put him in charge of the two brigades, though he too had never served in such a capacity before, despite his recent promotion to major general, and had

had no previous acquaintance, on or off the field of battle, with the troops he was about to lead across the valley in support of the four brigades under Pettigrew.

These last made up the first wave of the attack, here on the left, and they too had been more severely mauled in the earlier fighting than the army commander or his staff took into account. "They were terribly mistaken about Heth's division in the planning," Lee's chief aide declared afterwards. "It had not recovered, having suffered more than was reported on the first day." In point of fact, whether the planners knew it or not, the division had lost no less than forty percent of its officers and men. Ordinarily, this would have ruled out its employment as a fighting force, particularly on the offensive, until it had been reorganized and brought back up to strength; but in this case it had been selected to play a major role in the delivery of an attack designed as the climax of the army's bloodiest battle. Whether the choice proceeded from ignorance, indifference, or desperation (there was evidence of all three; Longstreet, while admitting his own profound depression, later said flatly that Lee had been "excited and off his balance") some measure of the condition of the division should have been perceived from the fact that only one of the original four commanders remained at the head of his brigade, and this was the inexperienced Davis, whose troops had lost so heavily when he led them into an ambush on the opening day. The captured Archer had been replaced by Colonel B. D. Fry, Colonel John M. Brockenbrough by Colonel Joseph Mayo, and Pettigrew by Colonel J. K. Marshall. All three were thus as new to command of their brigades as Pettigrew was to command of the division, which in turn had not been organized till after Chancellorsville and had gone into its first fight as a unit less than fifty hours ago. It had in all, after the cooks, the extra-duty men, and the lightly wounded were given rifles and brought forward into its ranks, about the same number of troops as Pickett had; that is, about 4600. Trimble had 1750 in the second line. If Wilcox and Lang added their 1400 to the assault, this Pickett-Pettigrew-Trimble total of just under 11,000 would be increased to roughly 12,500 effectives, a figure well below the 15,000 which the man in over-all command of the attack had already said would not be enough to afford him even the possibility of success.

In addition to Armistead and Garnett, who agreed that the maneuver was "a desperate thing to attempt," a good many other high-ranking officers had had a look at the ground in front by now, and their impressions were much the same. To a staff major, on a midmorning visit to the command post near the center, the long approach to the Union position across the shallow valley — more than half a mile out to the Emmitsburg Road, past a blue skirmish line "almost as heavy as a single line of battle," then another quarter-mile up the gradual slope of Cemetery Ridge, where the main enemy line was supported from the crest above by guns that could take the attackers under fire throughout most of their advance — resembled "a passage to the valley of death." Impressions mainly agreed, but reactions varied. For example, an artillerist observed that Pickett was "entirely sanguine of success in the charge, and was only congratulating himself on the opportunity," whereas Pettigrew seemed more determined than elated. Tomorrow would be his thirty-fifth birthday, and though his intellectual accomplishments were perhaps the highest of any man on the field — a scholar in Greek and Hebrew, fluent as well in most of the modern languages of Europe, he had made the best grades ever recorded at the University of North Carolina, where he had also excelled in fencing, boxing, and the single stick, then had traveled on the continent and written a book on what he had seen before returning to settle down to a brilliant legal career, only to have it interrupted by the war and the experience of being left for dead on the field of Seven Pines — he now was devoting his abilities to the fulfillment of his military duties. Slender and lithe of figure, with a neatly barbered beard, a spike mustache, and a dark complexion denoting his Gallic ancestry, Pettigrew was quite as eager as Pickett for distinction, but his eagerness was tempered by a sounder appreciation of the difficulties, since he had fought on this same field two days ago, against this newest version of the Army of the Potomac. Perhaps he recalled today what he had written after a visit to Solferino: "The invention of the Minié ball and the rifled cannon would, it was thought, abolish cavalry and reduce infantry charges within a small compass." On the other hand, if he was remembering his comments on that battle, fought four years ago in Italy, he might have drawn encouragement from the fact that in it the French had crushed the Austrian center, much as Lee intended to crush the Union center here today, with a frontal assault delivered hard on the heels of an intense bombardment.

The men themselves, though few of them had the chance to examine the terrain over which they would be advancing, knew only too well what lay before them; Lee and Longstreet had directed that they be told, and they had been, in considerable detail. "No disguises were used," one wrote afterwards, "nor was there any underrating of the difficult work at hand." They were told of the opportunities, as well as of the dangers, and it was stressed that the breaking of the Federal line might mean the end of the war. However, there were conflicting reports of their reaction. One declared that the men of Garnett's brigade "were in splendid spirits and confident of sweeping everything before them," while another recalled that when Mayo's troops, who were also Virginians, were informed of their share in the coming attack, "from being unusually merry and hilarious they on a sudden had become as still and thoughtful as Quakers at a love feast." Some managed to steal a look at the ground ahead, and like their officers they were sobered by what they saw. One such, a Tennessee sergeant from Fry's brigade, walked forward to the edge of the woods, looked across the wide open valley at the bluecoats standing toylike in the distance on their ridge, and was so startled by the realization of what was about to be required of him that he spoke aloud, asking himself the question: "June Kimble, are you going to do your duty?" The answer, too, was audible. "I'll do it, so help me God," he told himself. He felt better then. The dread passed from him, he said later. When he returned to his company, friends asked him how it looked out there, and Kimble replied: "Boys, if we have to go it will be hot for us, and we will have to do our best."

All this time, the waiting soldiers had been hearing the clatter of Ewell's fight beyond the ridge. By 10.30 it had diminished to a sputter and withdrawn eastward, indicating only too plainly how he had fared; Lee knew unmistakably, before any such admission reached him from the left, that what he had designed as a two-pronged effort had been reduced, by Ewell's failure, to a single thrust which the enemy would be able to oppose with a similar concentration of attention and reserves. However, he did not cancel or revise his plans in midcareer. That was not his way. Like Winfield Scott, on whose staff he had served in Mexico, he believed it "would do more harm than good," once the selected units were in position, for him to attempt to interfere. "It would be a bad thing if I could not rely on my brigade and division commanders," he told a Prussian observer three days later. "I plan and work with all my might to bring the troops to the right place at the right time. With that, I have done my duty." The same rule applied to a brisk skirmish that broke out, at 11 o'clock, around a house and barn on the floor of the valley, half a mile east-northeast of the command post and about midway between the lines. Confederate sharpshooters posted in the loft of the barn had been dropping Federal officers on the opposing ridge all morning, and finally two blue regiments moved out and drove the snipers back; whereupon Hill's guns opened thunderously with a half-hour bombardment. This in turn made the house and barn untenable for the new occupants, who set them afire and withdrew to their own lines, having solved the problem they had been sent to deal with. Lee watched from the command post and made no protest, either at the expenditure of ammunition, which was considerable, or at the resultant disclosure of the battery positions, which up to now the crews had been so careful to conceal. "I strive to make my plans as good as human skill allows," he told the Prussian inquirer, in further explanation of the hands-off policy he practiced here today, "but on the day of battle I lay the fate of my army in the hands of God."

By now it was noon, and a great stillness came down over the field and over the two armies on their ridges. Between them, the burning house and barn loosed a long plume of smoke that stood upright in the hot and windless air. From time to time some itchy-fingered picket would fire a shot, distinct as a single handclap, but for the most part the silence was profound. For the 11,000 Confederates maintaining their mile-wide formation along the wooded slope and in the swale, the heat was oppressive. They sweated and waited, knowing that they were about to be launched on a desperate undertaking from which many of them would not be coming back, and since it had to be, they were of one accord in wanting to get it over with as soon as possible. "It is said, that to the condemned, in going to execution, the moments fly," a member of Pickett's staff wrote some years later, recalling the strain of the long wait. "To the good soldier, about to go into action, I am sure the moments linger. Let us not dare say, that with him, either individually or collectively, it is that 'mythical love of fighting,' poetical but fabulous; but rather, that it is nervous anxiety to solve the great issue as speedily as possible, without stopping to count the cost. The Macbeth principle — *'Twere well it were done quickly* — holds quite as good in heroic action as in crime."

Colonel E. P. Alexander, a twenty-eight-year-old Georgian and West Pointer, had been up all night and hard at work all morning, supervising the movement into position of the 80 guns of the First Corps. By noon the job had been completed; the batteries were disposed along their mile-long arc, southward from the command post to the Peach Orchard and beyond, and the colonel, having taken time to breakfast on a crust of cornbread and a cup of sweet-potato coffee, was awaiting notification to fire the prearranged two-gun signal that would open the 140-gun bombardment. Young as he was, he had been given vital assignments from the outset of the war and had fought in all the army's major battles, first as Beauregard's signal officer, then as Johnston's chief of ordnance, and later as commander of an artillery battalion under Longstreet. Serving in these various capacities, he had contributed largely to the curtain-raising victory at Manassas, as well as to the subsequent effectiveness of Confederate firepower, and since his transfer from staff to line he had been winning a reputation as perhaps the best artillerist in Lee's army, despite the flashier performances of men like Latimer and Pelham. His had been the guns that defended Marye's Heights at Fredericksburg and accompanied Jackson on the flank march at Chancellorsville. However, his most challenging assignment came today from Longstreet, who instructed him to prepare and conduct the First Corps' share of the bombardment preceding the infantry attack. When the objective was shifted northward along Cemetery Ridge, after the early morning conference between Lee and Longstreet, Alexander rearranged his dispositions "as inoffensively as possible," seeking to hide his intentions from enemy lookouts on the heights, and took care to keep his crews from "getting into bunches." He listened with disapproval as Hill's 60-odd guns began their premature cannonade, northward along Seminary Ridge, and would not allow his own to join the action, lest they give

away the positions he had taken such pains to conceal. As the uproar
subsided and was followed by the silence that came over the field at
noon, he received an even greater shock from his own corps commander,
who informed him that he would be required to make the decision, not
only as to when the infantry attack was to begin, but also as to whether
it was to be launched at all. "If the artillery fire does not have the
effect to drive off the enemy or greatly demoralize him, so as to make
our effort pretty certain," Longstreet wrote in a message delivered by
an aide, "I would prefer that you should not advise Pickett to make the
charge. I shall rely a great deal upon your judgment to determine the
matter and shall expect you to let General Pickett know when the moment offers."

Alexander experienced a violent reaction to this sudden descent
of command responsibility. "Until that moment, though I fully recognized the strength of the enemy's position," he recalled years later, "I
had not doubted that we would carry it, in my confidence that Lee was
ordering it. But here was a proposition that *I* should decide the question.
Overwhelming reasons against the assault at once seemed to stare me in
the face." He replied at some length, declining the heavy burden Old
Peter appeared to be attempting to unload. "General," he protested, "I
will only be able to judge of the effect of our fire on the enemy by his
return fire, for his infantry is but little exposed to view and the smoke
will obscure the whole field. If, as I infer from your note, there is any
alternative to this attack, it should be carefully considered before opening our fire, for it will take all the artillery ammunition we have left to
test this one thoroughly, and if the result is unfavorable, we will have
none left for another effort. And even if this is entirely successful it can
only be so at a very bloody cost." Longstreet's answer was not long in
coming. Having failed to persuade the colonel to join him in resubmitting his protest that the charge was bound to fail — which was what he
had been suggesting between the lines of his rather turgid note — he
merely rephrased the essential portion of what he had said before.
"Colonel," he wrote, "The intention is to advance the infantry if the
artillery has the desired effect of driving the enemy's off, or having other
effect such as to warrant us in making the attack. When that moment ar-
rives advise General P., and of course advance such artillery as you can
use in aiding the attack."

This left one small loophole — "*if* the artillery has the desired
effect" — and Alexander saw it. No cannonade had ever driven Union
batteries from a prepared position, and he certainly had no confidence
that this one would accomplish that result. But before he replied this
second time he decided to confer with two men of higher authority than
his own. The first was his fellow Georgian A. R. Wright, who had
stormed the enemy ridge the day before, achieving at least a temporary
penetration, and could therefore testify as to the difficulty involved.

"What do you think of it?" Alexander asked him. "Is it as hard to get there as it looks?" Wright spoke frankly. "The trouble is not in going there," he said. "I was there with my brigade yesterday. There is a place where you can get breath and re-form. The trouble is to stay there after you get there, for the whole Yankee army is there in a bunch." Alexander took this to mean that the attack would succeed if it was heavily supported, and he-assumed that Lee had seen to that. Thus reassured, he went to see how Pickett was reacting to the assignment. He not only found him calm and confident, but also gathered that the ringleted Virginian "thought himself in luck to have the chance." So the colonel returned to his post, just north of the Peach Orchard, and got off a reply to Old Peter's second message. "When our fire is at its best," he wrote briefly, even curtly, "I will advise General Pickett to advance."

Word came soon afterwards from Longstreet: "Let the batteries open. Order great care and precision in firing."

By prearrangement, the two-gun signal was given by a battery near the center. According to a Gettysburg civilian, a professor of mathematics and an inveterate taker of notes, the first shot broke the stillness at exactly 1.07, following which there was an unpropitious pause, occasioned by a misfire. Nettled, the battery officer signaled the third of his four pieces and the second shot rang out. "As suddenly as an organ strikes up in church," Alexander would recall, "the grand roar followed from all the guns."

★　★　★

The firing was by salvos, for deliberate precision, and as the two-mile curve of metal came alive in response to the long-awaited signal, the individual pieces bucking and fuming in rapid sequence from right to left, a Federal cannoneer across the valley was "reminded of the 'powder snakes' we boys used to touch off on the Fourth of July." To a man, the lounging bluecoats, whose only concern up to then had been their hunger and the heat, both of which were oppressive, knew what the uproar meant as soon as it began. "Down! Down!" they shouted, diving for whatever cover they could find on the rocky forward slope of Cemetery Ridge. By now the rebel fire was general, though still by salvos within the four-gun units, and to Hunt, who was up on Little Round Top at the time, the sight was "indescribably grand. All their batteries were soon covered with smoke, through which the flames were incessant, whilst the air seemed filled with shells, whose sharp explosions, with the hurtling of their fragments, formed a running accompaniment to the deep roar of the guns." That was how it looked and sounded to a coldly professional eye and ear, sited well above the conflict, so to speak. But to Gibbon, down on the ridge where the shots were landing, the bombardment was "the most infernal pandemonium it has ever been my fortune to look upon." One of his soldiers, caught like him in the sudden deluge of fire and whining splinters, put it simpler. "The air was all murderous iron," he declared years later, apparently still somewhat surprised at finding that he had survived it.

In point of fact, despite the gaudiness of what might be called the fireworks aspect of the thing, casualties were few among the infantry. For the most part they had stone walls to crouch behind; moreover, they were disposed well down the slope, and this, as it turned out, afforded them the best protection of all. At first the fire was highly accurate, but as it continued, both the ridge and the batteries at opposite ends of the trajectory were blanketed in smoke, so that the rebel gunners were firing blind, just as Alexander had foretold. As the trails dug in, the tubes gained elevation and the shellbursts crept uphill, until finally almost all of the projectiles were either landing on the crest, where most of the close-support artillery was posted, or grazing it to explode in the rearward valley. "Quartermaster hunters," the crouching front-line soldiers called these last, deriving much satisfaction from the thought that what was meant for them was making havoc among the normally easy-living men of the rear echelon.

Havoc was by no means too strong a word, especially in reference to what was occurring around and in army headquarters. The small white cottage Meade had commandeered, immediately in rear of that portion of the ridge on which the rebels had been told to mass their hottest fire, became untenable in short order. Its steps were carried away by a direct hit at the outset, along with the supports of the porch, which then collapsed. Inside the house, a solid shot crashed through a door and barely missed the commanding general himself, while another plowed through the roof and garret, filling the lower rooms with flying splinters. Meade and his staff retired to the yard, where sixteen of their horses lay horribly mangled, still tethered to a fence; then moved into a nearby barn, where Butterfield was nicked by a shell fragment; and finally transferred in a body all the way to Powers Hill, where Slocum had set up the night before. Here at last they found a measure of the safety they had been seeking, but they were about as effectively removed from what was happening back on Cemetery Ridge, or was about to happen, as if they had taken refuge on one of the mountains of the moon.

Meanwhile, other rear-area elements had been catching it nearly as hard. Down and across both the Taneytown Road and the Baltimore Pike, fugitives of all kinds — clerks and orderlies, ambulance drivers and mess personnel, supernumeraries and just plain skulkers — were streaming east and south to escape the holocaust, adding greatly to the panic in their haste and disregard for order. Nor were such noncombatants the only ones involved in the confusion and the bloodshed. Returning to its post on the left, the VI Corps brigade that had been lent to Slocum that morning to assist in the retaking of Culp's Hill — he had not had to use it, after all — was caught on the road and lost 23 killed and wounded before it cleared the zone of fire. More important still, tactically speaking, the parked guns of the reserve artillery and the wagons of the ammunition train, drawn up in assumed safety on the lee side of the ridge, came under heavy bombardment, losing men and horses and caissons in the fury of the shellbursts, and had to be shifted half a mile southward, away from the point where they would be needed later. All in all, though it was more or less clear already that the gray artillerists were going to fail in their attempt to drive the blue defenders from the ridge, they had accomplished much with their faulty gunnery, including the disruption of army headquarters, the wounding of the chief of staff, and the displacement of the artillery reserve, not to mention a good deal of incidental slaughter among the rearward fugitives who had not intended to take any part in the fighting anyhow. Unwittingly, and in fact through carelessness and error, the Confederates had invented the box barrage of World War One, still fifty-odd years in the future, whereby a chosen sector of the enemy line was isolated for attack.

Awaiting that attack, crouched beneath what seemed a low, impenetrable dome of screaming metal overarching the forward slope of their isolated thousand yards of ridge, were three depleted divisions under Hancock, six brigades containing some 5700 infantry effectives, or roughly half the number about to be sent against them. This disparity of forces, occupying or aimed at the intended point of contact, was largely the fault of Meade, whose over-all numerical superiority was offset by the fact that his anticipations did not include the threat which this small segment of his army was about to be exposed to. Despite his midnight prediction to Gibbon that today's main rebel effort would be made against "your front," he not only had sent him no reinforcements; he had not even taken the precaution of seeing that any were made immediately available by posting them in proximity to that portion of the line. Daylight had brought a change of mind, a change of fears. He no longer considered that the point of danger, partly because his artillery enjoyed an unobstructed field of fire from there, but mostly because he recollected that his opponent was not partial to attacks against the center. As the morning wore on and Ewell failed to make headway on the right, Meade began to be convinced that Lee was planning to assault his left, and he kept his largely unused reserve, the big VI Corps, massed in the direction of the Round Tops. At 12.20, when Slocum sent word that he had "gained a decided advantage on my front, and hope to be able to spare one or two brigades to help you on some other part of the line," the northern commander was gratified by the evidence of staunchness, but he took no advantage of the offer. Then presently, under the distractive fury of the Confederate bombardment, which drove him in rapid, headlong sequence from house to yard, from yard to barn, and then from barn to hilltop, he apparently forgot it. Whatever defense of that critical thousand yards of ridge was going to be made would have to be made by the men who occupied it.

They amounted in all to 26 regiments, including two advanced as skirmishers, and their line ran half a mile due south from Ziegler's Grove, where Cemetery Hill fell off and Cemetery Ridge began. Gibbon held the center with three brigades, flanked on the left and right by Doubleday and Hays, respectively with one and two brigades; Gibbon had just over and Hays just under 2000 infantry apiece, while Doubleday had about 1700. For most of the long waiting time preceding the full-scale Confederate bombardment, these 5700 defenders had been hearing the Slocum-Johnson struggle for Culp's Hill, barely a mile away. At first it made them edgy, occurring as it did almost directly in their rear, but as it gradually receded and diminished they gained confidence. Finally it sputtered to a stop and was succeeded by a lull, which in turn was interrupted by the brief but lively skirmish for possession of the house and barn down on the floor of the western valley. The half-hour rebel cannonade that followed accomplished nothing, one way or the other, except perhaps as a bellow of protest at the outcome of the fight. By contrast, hard on the heels of this, the midday silence was profound. "At noon it became as still as the Sabbath day," a blue observer later wrote. He and his fellows scarcely knew what to make of this abrupt cessation, in which even the querulous skirmishers held their fire. "It was a queer sight to see men look at each other without speaking," another would recall; "the change was so great men seemed to go on tiptoe not knowing how to act." This lasted a full hour, during which they tried to improvise shelter from the rays of the sun and sought relief from the pangs of hunger. There was precious little of either shade or food, there on the naked ridge, but shortly after 1 o'clock, when the curtain of silence was suddenly ripped to tatters by the roar of what seemed to be all the guns in the world, they forgot the discomforts of heat and hunger, acute as these had been, and concentrated instead on a scramble for cover behind the low stone walls. However, as the pattern of shellbursts moved up the slope and stayed there — except for an occasional round, that is, that tumbled and fell short — they found that, once they grew accustomed to the whoosh and flutter of metal just overhead, the bombardment was not nearly so bad as it seemed. "All we had to do was flatten out a little thinner," one of the earth-hugging soldiers afterwards explained, "and our empty stomachs did not prevent that."

Despite the feeling of security that came from lying low, it seemed to another crouching there "that nothing four feet from the ground could live." Presently, however, he and his companions all along that blasted thousand yards of front were given unmistakable proof that such was not the case, at least so far as one man was concerned. As the bombardment thundered toward crescendo, they were startled to see Hancock, mounted on a fine black horse and trailed by most of his staff, riding the full length of his line amid the hiss and thud of plunging shells and solids. He rode slowly, a mounted orderly beside him displaying the swallow-tailed corps guidon. Resisting the impulse to weave or bob when he felt the breath of near misses on his face, the general only stopped once in the course of his excursion, and that was when his horse, with less concern for show than for survival, became unmanageable and forced him to take over the more tractable mount of an aide, who perhaps was not unhappy at the exchange since it permitted him to retire from the procession. Hancock resumed his ride at the same deliberate pace, combining a ramrod stiffness of backbone with that otherwise easy grace of manner expected of top-ranking officers under fire — a highly improbable mixture of contempt and disregard, for and of the rebel attempt to snuff out the one life he had — whereby the men under him, as one of them rather floridly explained, "found courage to endure the pelting of the pitiless gale." Intent on giving an exemplary performance, he would no more be deterred by friendly counsel than he would swerve to avoid the enemy shells that whooshed around him. When a brigadier ventured a protest: "General, the corps commander ought not to risk his life that way," Hancock replied curtly: "There are times when a corp commander's life does not count," and continued his ride along the line of admiring soldiers, who cheered him lustily from behind their low stone walls, but were careful, all the same, to remain in prone or kneeling positions while they did so.

Another high-ranking Federal was riding better than three times that length of line at the same time, but he did so less by way of staging a general show, as Hancock was doing to bolster the spirits of the men along his portion of the front, than by way of assuring conformity with Army Regulations. "In the attack," these regulations stated, "the artillery is employed to silence the batteries that protect the [enemy] position. In the defense, it is better to direct its fire on the advancing troops." It was the second of these two statements that here applied, and no one knew this better than Henry Hunt, who had been an artillery instructor at West Point and had spent the past two years in practical application, on the field of battle, of the theories he had expounded in the classroom. On Cemetery Hill, on Little Round Top, and along the ridge that ran between them, he had twenty batteries in position, just over one hundred guns that could be brought to bear on the shallow western valley and the ridge at its far rim. Just now there were no "advancing troops" for the long line of Union metal "to direct its fire on," but Hunt was convinced there soon would be, and his first concern — after observing, from his lofty perch at the south end of the line, the "indescribably grand" beginning of the Confederate bombardment — was that his cannoneers not burn up too much of their long-range ammunition in counterbattery fire, lest they run short before the rebel infantry made its appearance. Accordingly, after instructing Lieutenant B. F. Ritten-house to keep up a deliberate fire with his six-gun battery on Little Round Top, Hunt rode down onto the lower end of Cemetery Ridge and ordered Lieutenant Colonel Freeman McGilvery, commanding seven batteries of 37 guns from the artillery reserve, to refrain from taking up the enemy challenge until the proper time. The same in-structions went to Captain John G. Hazard, commanding the six II Corps batteries whose 29 guns were posted north of there, above and below the little umbrella-shaped clump of trees. On Cemetery Hill, completing the two-mile ride from Little Round Top, Hunt repeated what he had told Rittenhouse at the outset; Major T. W. Osborn was to keep up a deliberate counterbattery fire with the 29 guns of his six XI Corps batteries. By this arrangement, one third of the 101 guns were to do what they could to disconcert the rebel gunners by maintaining a crossfire from the high-sited extremities of the Federal position, while the remaining two thirds kept silent along the comparatively low-lying ridge that ran between them. However, it did not work out that way entirely. Completing his slow ride along his thousand-yard portion of the front, Hancock observed that his cannoneers were idle (if idle was quite the word for men who were hugging the earth amid a deluge of shells) and promptly countermanded Hunt's instructions. He did so, he explained afterwards, because he believed that his infantry needed the deep-voiced encouragement of the guns posted in close support on the crest of the ridge directly in their rear. Whatever comfort the blue foot soldiers derived from the roar and rumble in response to the fire of the rebel guns down in the valley, Hunt watched with disapproval as the half-dozen II Corps batteries came alive, but there was nothing he could do about it, since the corps commander had every right to do as he thought best with his own guns, no matter what any and all staff special-ists might advise.

All this time the Confederates kept firing, exploding caissons, dis-mounting guns, and maiming so many cannoneers — particularly in those batteries adjacent to the little clump of trees — that replacements had to be furnished from nearby infantry outfits, supposedly on a vol-unteer basis, but actually by a hard-handed form of conscription. "Vol-unteers are wanted to man the battery," a Massachusetts captain told his company. "Every man is to go of his own free will and accord. Come out here, John Dougherty, McGivern, and you Corrigan, and work those guns." For a solid hour the bombardment did not slacken, and when another half hour was added to this, still with no abatement, Mc-Gilvery ordered his seven batteries to open fire at last, convinced that by now the rebels must be getting low on ammunition and would have to launch their infantry attack, if they were going to launch it at all, before his own supply ran low. That was about 2.30; all the surviving

Union guns were in action, bucking and roaring along the whole two miles of line. From down in the valley, Alexander peered through the billowing smoke and it seemed to him that both enemy heights and the connecting ridge were "blazing like a volcano." On Cemetery Hill, where he availed himself of the excellent observation post established by the XI Corps chief of artillery, Hunt watched with gratification this tangible proof that, for all its prolonged fury, the rebel cannonade had failed to drive his gun crews from their pieces or the guns themselves from their assigned positions. It occurred to him, however, that in the light of this evidence, as plain from below as from above, the Confederates might not attempt their infantry assault at all, and he considered this regrettable. Standing beside him, Osborn suddenly asked: "Does Meade consider an attack of the enemy desirable?" When Hunt replied that the army commander had expressed a fervent hope that the rebels would try just that, "and he had no fear of the result," the major added: "If this is so, why not let them out while we are all in good condition? I would cease fire at once, and the enemy could reach but one conclusion, that of our being driven from the hill."

Hunt thought this over briefly, then agreed. Moreover, while the batteries on the hill fell silent one by one, he rode down onto Cemetery Ridge to increase the effectiveness of the ruse by passing the word along to the remaining two thirds of his guns. At closer range, however, he found the II Corps batteries so badly mauled by the rebel cannonade and so low on ammunition that he decided they might as well use up what few long-range rounds were still on hand. For example, Lieutenant Alonzo Cushing's battery, posted just north of the clump of trees, had only three of its six guns still in working order and only two of these in action, casualties having reduced the number of cannoneers to barely enough for two slim crews; Cushing himself, a twenty-two-year-old West Pointer from Wisconsin, had twice been hit by fragments of exploding shells, one of which had struck him in the crotch and groin. Despite the pain, he refused to leave the field or relinquish his command, and Hunt let him stay, together with his handful of survivors. A Rhode Island battery just south of the clump was in even worse shape, its ammunition practically exhausted, all of its officers dead or wounded, and barely enough men left to serve the three remaining guns; Hunt took a quick look at the wreckage and gave the survivors permission to withdraw, which they did in a rather helter-skelter fashion, being leaderless, but took their three guns with them. Riding on south, Hunt passed the cease-firing order along to McGilvery, down near the far end of the ridge, and finally to Rittenhouse, whose six guns had been firing all the while from Little Round Top. When the weary and badly cut-up batteries of the II Corps had gotten off their few remaining rounds, thus adding to the effectiveness of the pretense by giving the impression that the guns were being knocked out group by group, spasmodically, the whole Union line fell silent under the continuing rain of rebel projectiles.

That was about 2.45, and it soon became apparent that the ruse had worked, at least in part. Within another five or ten minutes, the Confederates also stopped firing, and what Osborn later referred to as "a singularly depressing silence" settled over the field. Whether the ruse had worked entirely would not be known until the enemy infantry started forward across the valley, but the Federal cannoneers were taking no chances that it had failed. The cooling tubes were swabbed to remove the gritty residue of powder and thus prepare them for the rapid-fire work that lay ahead, while in those batteries that had used up all their long-range ammunition, the pieces were carefully loaded with canister. Forty-four-year-old Alex Hays, a Pennsylvanian like his corps and army commanders, was certain that the rebs would soon be coming through the screening smoke. "Now, boys, look out; you will see some fun!" he called to the men of his two brigades, posted north of the clump of trees. In confirmation of his prediction, shortly after 3 o'clock, Warren wigwagged a message from the Little Round Top signal station, which afforded a clear view beyond the hump of earth that Sickles had claimed and lost the day before: "They are moving out to attack." Presently, all along the bend and shank of the Union fishhook, the waiting troops could see for themselves, through or below the rifting, lifting smoke, that what Warren had signaled was true. "Here they come!" men exclaimed as they caught sight of the long gray lines moving toward them across the shallow basin inclosed by the two ridges.

Reactions to this confrontation varied. "Thank God! Here comes the infantry!" one exuberant bluecoat cried. Though it was obvious at a glance that the attackers, moving steadily forward under their red and blue flags, outnumbered the defenders by no less than two to one, he and others like him looked forward to the slaughter, anticipating a Fredericksburg in reverse. A New Yorker, on the other hand, remembering the sight two days later, wrote in a home letter: "Beautiful, gloriously beautiful, did that vast array appear in the lovely little valley." Then he and his fellows — first the cannoneers, who took up their work with a will, and then the foot soldiers, no less eager — settled down to the task of transforming those well-dressed long gray lines into something far from beautiful.

There they came. And for them, advancing eastward over the gently undulating floor of the shallow valley, the relief of tension was as great as it was for the men awaiting their arrival on the ridge just under a mile across the way. In fact, if a comparison of losses was any measure of the strain, it was probably greater. The Federal infantry had suffered a good deal less from the bombardment than the Federal artillery had done, but for the Confederates, whose infantry was posted behind instead of in front of their fuming line of metal, it was the other way around. Both sides were overshooting, with the unequal result that the eastbound "overs" spared the bluecoats on the forward slope of their ridge, whereas a high proportion of their long shots landed squarely in the ranks of the gray soldiers drawn up to await the order to advance. Fewer than 200 of the former were hit, while the latter suffered approximately twice that number of casualties in the course of the nearly two-hour-long exchange. "Such a tornado of projectiles it has seldom been the fortune or misfortune of anyone to see," one of Pickett's veterans declared. It seemed to go on forever, he recalled, under a high hard hot blue sky that soon became "lurid with flame and murky with smoke," until presently the sun was in a red eclipse, "shadowing the earth as with a funeral pall," though this gave little relief from the heat, which was even more oppressive here in the swale than it was for the blue soldiers on the high ground in the distance. "Many a poor fellow thought his time had come," another grayback wrote. "Great big, stout-hearted men prayed — loudly, too." Stretcherbearers were kept on the run, answering the sudden, high-pitched yells of the wounded up and down the sweaty, mile-long formation. One of Kemper's men, attempting later to describe what he had been through, finally gave it up and contented himself with a four-word description of his ordeal by fire: "It was simply awful." Even so, not all the accustomed butternut risibility was suppressed. Near one badly pounded company, when a rabbit suddenly broke from a clump of bushes and went bounding for the rear: "Run, old hare," a man called after him. "If I was a old hare, I'd run too."

Officers of rank, commanders of the nine brigades and three divisions, kept moving among the waiting troops, seeking to encourage them by example, much as Hancock was doing at the same time across the way. However, the response was somewhat different on this side of the valley. When Longstreet rode along the front of Pickett's division and a round shot plowed the ground immediately under his horse's nose, the general kept the startled animal under control, "as quiet as an old farmer riding over his plantation on a Sunday morning, and looked neither to the right or left." Thus an admiring captain described the scene; but the men themselves, apparently resentful of the implication that they needed steadying, had a different reaction. "You'll get your old fool head knocked off!" one of them called out to him, while others shouted angrily: "We'll fight without you leading us!" Similarly, in Armistead's brigade, where the troops had been instructed to remain prone throughout the bombardment, there was resentment that their commander felt it necessary to move erect among them with encouraging remarks and a showy disregard for the projectiles whooshing past him. One soldier rose in protest, and when Armistead ordered him to lie back down, pointed out that he was only following his general's example. Armistead, however — like Hancock on the ridge across the valley — had a ready answer. "Yes, but never mind me," he said. "We want men with guns in their hands."

Out front, on the low bulge of earth crowned by the peach orchard Barksdale's men had seized the day before, Alexander had been watching all this time for evidence that the cannonade was accomplishing its mission, which was to wreck the enemy batteries or drive them from the ridge that was the infantry's objective. So far, although an hour had elapsed since his guns first opened, the young colonel had seen little that encouraged him to believe that he was going to succeed in his assignment. Volcano-like, the enemy ridge and its two flanking heights not only continued to return the fire directed at them, but presently that return fire grew more furious than ever, despite an occasional burst of flame and the sudden resultant erection of a pillar of smoke whose base marked the former location of a caisson. Earlier, Wright and Pickett had persuaded him that all Lee intended would be accomplished in short order. After more than an hour of steady firing, however, Alexander's doubts returned in strength. Moreover, the pressure of command responsibility grew heavier by the minute, until at last, as he wrote later, "It seemed madness to order a column in the middle of a hot July day to undertake an advance of three fourths of a mile over open ground against the center of that line." What was worse, another half hour reduced the ammunition supply to the point where the attack would have to be launched without delay if it was to have artillery support. Shortly after 2.30, with the counterbattery fire approaching crescendo, Alexander dispatched a courier with a note informing Pickett of the situation. "If you are to come at all, you must come at once, " he told him, "or we will not be able to support you as we ought. But the enemy's fire has not slackened materially and there are still 18 guns firing from the cemetery." This last had reference to the little clump of trees, which the colonel had been told was a cemetery, and though he was mistaken in this, his estimate as to the number of guns still active in that vicinity was accurate enough. And presently, as he kept peering through the smoke to catch the slightest encouraging reaction by the blue gunners in the distance, he observed with gratification that the Federals had ceased firing on the hill to the left, and soon afterwards he spotted a rearward displacement by some guns near the critical center. It was the battered Rhode Islanders, whom Hunt had given permission to withdraw their three surviving pieces, but in his elation — for the enemy fire continued to slacken all along the ridge and on both adjoining heights — Alexander persuaded himself that the withdrawal had been considerably more substantial than it was in fact. In other words, the blue ruse had worked far better than its authors would have any way of knowing until they saw the long gray lines of infantry advancing. He got off a second note to Pickett, hard on the heels of the first: "For God's sake come quick. The 18 guns have gone. Come quick or my ammunition will not let me support you properly."

Pickett by then had already acted on the first of the two dispatches. Glad to receive anything that might end the strain of waiting, he mounted his horse and rode at once to Longstreet, whom he found sitting on a snake rail fence out front, observing the bombardment. Dismounting, he handed him the note. Old Peter read it deliberately, but said nothing. "General, shall I advance?" Pickett asked eagerly. Longstreet, who later explained: "My feelings had so overcome me that I could not speak, for fear of betraying my want of confidence," responded with a silent nod. That was enough for the jaunty long-haired Virginian. "I am going to move forward, sir," he said. Then he saluted, remounted, and rode back to join his men.

Front and center of his division, he delivered from horseback what one of his officers called "a brief, animated address" which only those soldiers nearest him could hear but which ended on a ringing note: "Up, men, and to your posts! Don't forget today that you are from old Virginia!" There was, however, no disconcerting haste as the troops were placed in attack formation. For the most part, they simply rose to their feet and began to dress their regimental lines while their colonels passed among them repeating the instructions received from above: "Advance slowly, with arms at will. No cheering, no firing, no breaking from common to quick step. Dress on the center." In at least one outfit, a survivor would recall, one of the captains led in the singing of a hymn and a white-haired chaplain offered prayer. Nor was the step-off itself unduly precipitate. Pettigrew gave the signal on the left to the new leader of his old brigade: "Now, Colonel, for the honor of the good Old North State, forward!" The advance was somewhat ragged at first, as if the Virginians, Mississippians, Alabamians, and Tennesseans of his division supposed that the spoken order only applied to the Carolinians, but the laggard brigades soon restored the alignment by double-timing to catch up. Meanwhile, in the wooded swale to the south, others had taken up the cry. Armistead, whose brigade comprised the supporting line on the right, as Trimble's two did on the left, did not neglect the opportunity afforded for another display of determination. "Sergeant, are you going to plant those colors on the enemy works today?" he asked a nearby colorbearer, and when the sergeant gave the staunch expected answer, "I will try, sir, and if mortal man can do it, it shall be done," the general removed his wide-brimmed black felt hat, placed it on the point of his sword, and raised it high for all to see, shouting in a voice that carried from flank to flank of his brigade: "Attention, 2d Battalion, the battalion of direction! Forward, guide centerrr, *march!*" and led the way. Beyond the left, within the lower limits of the town of Gettysburg, onlookers from Rodes's division, seeing Pettigrew's troops emerge from the woods and begin their downhill march into the valley, called out to the Federal surgeons who had remained behind to tend the captured wounded of their army: "There go the men who will go through your damned Yankee line for you!"

Longstreet had preceded them out to the line of guns and was conferring with Alexander. Pleased though he had been at seeing the enemy artillery first slack then cease its fire, he was anything but pleased when he saw his own guns follow suit immediately after he gave Pickett the nod that would send him forth to what he himself had predicted would be slaughter. But his greatest surprise was at Alexander's explanation that he had suspended firing in order to save ammunition, being doubtful whether enough remained on hand for proper support of the infantry on its way across the valley. Old Peter was plainly horrified, despite the colonel's earlier statement that the supply was limited. "Go and stop Pickett right where he is, and replenish your ammunition!" he exclaimed. Now it was Alexander's turn to be surprised. "We can't do that, sir," he protested. "The train has but little. It would take an hour to distribute it, and meanwhile the enemy would improve the time." Longstreet made no reply to this. For a long moment he stood there saying nothing. Then he spoke, slowly and with deep emotion. "I do not want to make this charge," he said; "I do not see how it can succeed. I would not make it now but that General Lee has ordered it and expects it."

With that he stopped, gripped by indecision and regret, though in point of fact he had been given no authority to halt the attack even if he had so chosen. The young artillerist volunteered nothing further. Just then, however, the issue was settled for once and all by the appearance of Garnett's and Kemper's brigades from the swale behind the guns. Garnett was mounted, having been granted special permission to ride because of his injured knee and feverish condition, and Alexander went back to meet him; they had been friends out on the plains in the old army. Apparently the Virginian was experiencing a chill just now, for he wore an old blue overcoat buttoned close to his throat despite the July heat. Alexander walked beside the horse until they reached the slope leading down to the Emmitsburg Road and the Union ridge beyond. There he stopped and watched his friend ride on. "Goodbye," he called across the widening gap, and he added, as if by afterthought: "Good luck."

★   ★   ★

By now — some twenty or thirty minutes after the Union guns stopped firing, and consequently about half that long since Alexander followed suit — much of the smoke had been diffused or had drifted off, so that for the attackers, many of whom had stepped at a stride from the dense shade of their wooded assembly areas into the brilliant sunlight that dappled the floor of the valley, the result was not only dazzling to their eyes but also added to their feeling of elation and release. "Before us lay bright fields and fair landscape," one among them would recall.

It was not until the effect of this began to wear off, coincidental with the contraction of their pupils, that they saw at last the enormity of what was being required of them, and by then, although the vista afforded absolute confirmation of their direst apprehensions, the pattern of exhilaration had been set. Under the double influence of secondary inertia and terrific deliberation, the long gray lines came on, three brigades to the south under Pickett and six to the north under Pettigrew and Trimble, with a quarter-mile gap between the interior flanks of the two formations, the former composed of fifteen and the latter of twenty-seven regiments, all with their colors flying at more or less regular intervals along the rows of nearly 11,000 striding men. Harvey Hill was to say of the individual Confederate, as he had observed him in offensive action: "Of shoulder-to-shoulder courage, spirit of drill and discipline, he knew nothing and cared less. Hence, on the battlefield, he was more of a free-lance than a machine. Whoever saw a Confederate line advancing that was not crooked as a ram's horn? Each ragged rebel yelling on his own hook and aligning on himself." But Hill, though he was to see about as much combat as any general on either side before the war was over, was not at Gettysburg. If he had been, he would have had to cite it as the exception. Forbidden to step up the cadence or fire their rifles or even give the high-pitched yell that served at once to steady their own nerves and jangle their opponents', the marchers concentrated instead on maintaining their alignment, as if this in itself might serve to awe the waiting bluecoats and frighten them into retreat. And in point of fact, according to one among the watchers on the ridge across the way — a colonel commanding a brigade adjacent to the little clump of trees — it did at least produce the lesser of these two reactions. For him, the advancing graybacks had "the appearance of being fearfully irresistible," while a foreign observer, whose point of vantage was on the near side of the valley, used the same adjective to communicate the impression the attackers made on him: "They seemed impelled by some irresistible force." Out front with the rebel skirmishers, a captain had a closer view of the troops as they strode down the slope toward where he crouched, and he remembered ever afterwards the "glittering forest of bayonets," the two half-mile-wide formations bearing down "in superb alignment," the "murmur and jingle" of trouser-legs and equipment, and the "rustle of thousands of feet amid the stubble," which stirred up dust and chaff beneath and before them "like the dash of spray at the prow of a vessel."

They came on at a steady rate of about one hundred yards a minute, and before they had been three minutes in the open — barely clear of the line of friendly guns, whose cannoneers raised their hats in salute and wished them luck as they passed through — the Union batteries, as if in quick recovery from the shock of seeing them appear thus, massed for slaughter, began to roar. The gray lines dribbled rag-doll shapes, each of which left a gap where it had been while still in motion. Flags plunged with sudden flutters in the windless air, only to be taken up at once as the fallen colorbearers were replaced. This happened especially often in the regiments on the flanks, which came under galling long-range fire delivered in enfilade from the two heights, Cemetery Hill on the left and Little Round Top on the right. Pettigrew's troops had farther to go, since they had begun their march from Seminary Ridge itself, but this had been foreseen and allowed for; Pickett had been charged with closing the quarter-mile interval between the two formations, which would lengthen the distance his three brigades would have to cover in the course of their advance. Accordingly, once they were clear of the line of guns, in plain view of the little clump of trees just over half a mile ahead, he gave his troops the order, "Left oblique!" They obeyed it neatly, executing in midstride a half-face to the north, which, at every full step of their own, brought them half a step closer to the flank of the undeviating marchers on their left. All this time, both groups were taking losses, a more or less steady leakage of killed and wounded, who lay motionless where they fell or turned and hobbled painfully up the slope they had descended. Coming presently to a slight dip, about midway of the valley — a swale not deep enough to hide them from the enemy gunners, but conveniently parallel to the ridge that was their objective — Pickett's men received their second order, which was to halt, close up the gaps their casualties had left, and dress the line. They did so, once more with the deliberate precision of the drill field, but with the difference that such gaps continued to appear at an even more alarming rate as the Union gunners, delighted with this sudden transformation of a moving into a stationary target, stepped up their rate of fire. The result was the first evidence of confusion in the Confederate ranks. A soldier would look toward the comrade on his right, feeling meanwhile with his extended hand for the shoulder of the comrade on his left, and there would be a constant sidling motion in the latter direction, as men continued to fall all down the line, leaving additional gaps that had to be closed. This might have gone on indefinitely, or at any rate until there were no survivors left to dress or dress on, but at last the order came for them to continue the advance, still on the oblique.

This they did, to the considerable relief of most of the bluecoats on the ridge ahead, whose reaction to the maneuver was one of outrage, as if they had been exposed to a blatant indecency, such as the thumbing of a nose, though for others the feeling of revulsion was tempered by awe and incredulity. "My God, they're dressing the line!" some among the waiting infantry exclaimed, more by way of protest than applause. In the course of the ten- or fifteen-minute lull allowed by the enemy guns before the attackers first appeared on the far side of the valley, the defenders had improved the time by repairing what little damage had been done to their improvised earthworks by the rebel cannonade. Now there was nothing left to do but wait, and in some ways that was the hardest thing of all. In fact, some among them found it downright impossible. Despite the renewed Confederate bombardment, they stood up behind their low stone walls or their meager scooped-up mounds of dirt and began to shoot at the graybacks half a mile away, only to have their officers tell them gruffly to hold their fire until the Johnnies came within decent range. Hays, who was jumpy enough himself, being of an excitable nature, found a way to pass the time for the men of his two brigades; he put them through a few stiff minutes of drill in the manual of arms, despite the overhead hiss and flutter of going and coming projectiles. Meanwhile the Union cannoneers kept busy, at any rate those who had husbanded their long-range ammunition for the opportunity now at hand, including the men in a six-gun battery that came up with full limbers just as the lull was ending and replaced the departed Rhode Islanders in the position directly south of the clump of trees. Rittenhouse and Osborn had the best of it in this respect, slamming their shells in at angles that caught the advancing lines almost end-on, but others were by no means idle. "We had a splendid chance at them," one of McGilvery's captains later testified, "and we made the most of it." Watching the effects of this — the gnawed flanks and the plunging flags, the constantly recurring gaps all up and down the long gray front — the bluecoats cheered, and from time to time a man would holler "Fredericksburg!" elated by the thought that he was seeing, or was about to see, a repetition of that fiasco, though with certain welcome differences. On that field, for example, only the last four hundred yards of the attack had been made in full view of the defenders behind their wall of stone and dirt, yet not a single one of the attackers had come within twenty yards of the objective. Here the critical distance was more than three times as great, and the waiting soldiers took much consolation in the fact that the respective roles of the two armies, as attackers and defenders, had been reversed. "Come on, Blue Belly!" the rebs had yelled, but now it was the other way around; now it was the Federals who were yelling, "Come on, Johnny! Keep on coming!" even though the Confederates were bringing no blankets or overcoats along and their worn-out shoes would not be worth stripping from their corpses.

On Pickett's right, Kemper's brigade was taking cruel punishment from the half-dozen guns on Little Round Top, whose gunners tracked their victims with the cool precision of marksmen in a monstrous shooting gallery, except that in this case the targets were displayed in depth, which greatly increased the likelihood of hits. Moreover, the slightest excess in elevation landed their shots in Garnett's ranks "with fearful effect," as one of his officers would report, "sometimes as many as ten men being killed [or] wounded by the bursting of a single shell." But worse by far was the predicament of the troops on Pettigrew's left. Here Mayo's brigade — Virginians too, but fewer by half in number; their heavy losses at Chancellorsville had never been made up, and they had been under a series of temporary commanders for nearly a year, with the result that their morale had been known to be shaky even before the bloody action two days ago had taken its further toll — caught the end-on fire, not of six but of 29 high-sited guns, with correspondingly greater suffering and disruption. As they tottered forward under the merciless pounding from the batteries on Cemetery Hill, these unfortunates had all they could do to maintain their alignment and keep their four flags flying. Whereupon, about two hundred yards short of the Emmitsburg Road, having passed the still-hot ashes of the house and barn set afire by the forenoon bombardment, they were struck on the flank by a regiment of Ohioans from the Union skirmish line, whose colonel massed and launched them in an assault as unexpected as it was bold. The reaction of the Virginians — it was they who "on a sudden had become as still and thoughtful as Quakers at a love feast" when they first learned that the attack was to be made and that they were to have a share in it — was immediate and decisive. Despite their four-to-one numerical advantage and their well-earned heritage of valor, they took off rearward at a run, flags and all, to the considerable dismay of the onlookers who had told the Federal surgeons, "There go the men who will go through your damned Yankee line for you," and did not stop until they regained the cover of Seminary Ridge. By quick subtraction, four of Pettigrew's regiments, nearly one fourth of the total in his division, thus were removed from his calculations as effectively as if they had stepped into bottomless quicksand. Osborn's gunners, observing the flight of the brigade which up to now had been their sole concern, cheered lustily and swung their muzzles without delay along a short arc to the left. Their first shell burst in the midst of Davis's brigade, killing five men in one of his Mississippi regiments.

Nothing quite like this abrupt defection had ever happened before, at least not in Lee's army, though the sight had been fairly common in the ranks of its opponents over the past two years, beginning at First Manassas and continuing through Second Winchester. Most Confederate witnesses reacted first with unbelief and then with consternation; but not Longstreet, who had steeled himself at the outset by expecting the very worst. Still seated on the snake rail fence at the far end of the field, he moved at once to counteract what he had seen through the shellbursts to the north, sending word for Anderson to commit his three remaining brigades — Wright's and Posey's and Mahone's; Lang and Wilcox had already been instructed to furnish such help for Pickett if it was needed — in support of the line thus weakened. No one could know whether the sudden collapse of this one brigade was indicative of what the others would do when the pressure intensified, but there was always the danger, even in quite sound units, that when a flank started to crumble, as this one had done, the reaction would continue all down the line. And in fact it did continue in one regiment under Davis, some of whose green troops took off rearward in the wake of the Virginians, but the other three held steady, taking in turn the end-on pounding from the batteries on the height as they kept up their steady progress across the valley. By now the interior flanks of Pettigrew and Pickett had come together on the near side of the fence-lined Emmitsburg Road, beyond which the blue skirmishers fired a volley or two before hurrying back to their own line, some four hundred yards up the slope behind them. The resultant crowding of Fry's and Garnett's brigades, which occurred before the latter received the order that brought its marchers off the oblique, presented a close-packed target the Union gunners did not neglect from point-blank range on the ridge ahead. "Don't crowd, boys!" a rebel captain shouted, his voice as lackadaisical amid the bursting shells as that of a dancing master. There was in fact a certain amount of formal politeness as the two brigades came together, Tennesseans on the one hand and Virginians on the other, under circumstances designed to favor havoc. Southern courtesy had never been more severely tried, yet such protest as was heard was mild in tone. It was here that the classic Confederate line was spoken: "Move on, cousins. You are drawing the fire our way."

Armistead was hard on Garnett's heels by now, and Kemper's men had drifted left, not only in an attempt to keep in touch with the latter's contracting line, but also in obedience to a natural inclination to flinch from the increasingly effective fire directed at their exposed flank from Little Round Top as well as from the south end of the Federal ridge, where McGilvery's seven batteries were massed. From close in rear of his advancing troops, Pickett saw his and Pettigrew's lead brigades, crowded into a blunted wedge perhaps five hundred yards in width, surge across the road and its two fences, taking severe losses from the opening blasts of canister loosed by guns that had been silent until now, and begin their climb up the slope toward the low stone wall behind which the blue infantry was crouched. He saw that his men were going to make it, a good part of them anyhow; but he saw, too — so heavy had their casualties been on the way across the valley, and so heavy were they going to be in storming the wall itself, which extended the length of the front and beyond — that unless the survivors were stoutly reinforced, and soon, they would not be able to hold what they were about to gain. Accordingly, he sent a courier to inform Longstreet of this close-up estimate of the situation. The courier, a staff captain, galloped fast to find Old Peter, but even so he took time to draw rein in an attempt to rally some stragglers he found trotting toward the rear. "What are you running for?" he demanded, glaring down at them.

One of the men looked up at him as if to say the question was a foolish waste of breath, though what he actually said was: "Why, good gracious, Captain, aint you running yourself?" Too flustered to attempt an answer, the courier gave his horse the spur and continued on his mission, feeling rather baffled by the encounter.

He found Old Peter still perched atop the snake rail fence, observing through his binoculars the action on the ridge. The general listened attentively to Pickett's message, but before he could reply a distinguished British visitor rode up: Lieutenant Colonel Arthur Fremantle, of Her Majesty's Coldstream Guards. Despite his high rank in a famous regiment, this was his first experience of battle. "General Longstreet," he said, breathless with excitement, "General Lee sent me here, and said you would place me in a position to see this magnificent charge." Then, observing for himself the struggle in progress on the ridge across the way, he exclaimed: "I wouldn't have missed this for anything!" Old Peter laughed, an incongruous sound against that backdrop of death and destruction. "The devil you wouldn't!" he said; "I would like to have missed it very much. We've attacked and been repulsed. Look there." All the colonel could see, amid swirls of smoke on the slope at which the general was pointing, half a mile in the distance, was that men were fighting desperately; but Longstreet spoke as if the issue was no longer in doubt. "The charge is over," he said flatly. And then, having attended in his fashion to the amenities due a guest, he turned to the courier and added: "Captain Bright, ride to General Pickett and tell him what you have heard me say to Colonel Fremantle." The courier started off, but the general called after him: "Captain Bright!" Drawing rein, Bright looked back and saw Old Peter pointing northward. "Tell General Pickett that Wilcox's brigade is in that orchard, and he can order him to his assistance."

The courier galloped off at last, and the burly Georgian returned to watching the final stages of the action, pausing only to countermand his recent order for Anderson's three reserve brigades to be committed. Wilcox and Lang could go forward, in accordance with Lee's original arrangements — Longstreet's final instructions, shouted after the courier when he first started back to Pickett, were more in the nature of a reminder than a command — but if what was happening on the ridge was only the prelude to a repulse, as he believed, then Anderson's three and Pender's two uncommitted brigades would be needed to meet the counterattack Meade would be likely to launch in the wake of the Confederates as they fell back down the slope and recrossed the valley. Fremantle marveled at his companion's self-possession under strain, remarking afterwards that "difficulties seem[ed] to make no other impression on him than to make him a little more savage." In point of fact, though Old Peter kept his binoculars trained on the flame-stabbed turmoil halfway up the enemy ridge, he watched the fighting not so much in suspense as to the outcome — for that had been settled already, at least to his own disgruntled satisfaction — as to study the manner in which it came about. Convinced that the attack had failed, even before the first signs of retreat were evident, he was mainly interested in seeing how many of his soldiers would survive it.

But they themselves had no such detached view of the holocaust in which they were involved. Massed as they were on a narrow front, flailed by canister from both flanks and dead ahead, the men of the five lead brigades were mingled inextricably; few of them had any knowledge of anything except in their immediate vicinity, and very little of that. "Everything was a wild kaleidoscopic whirl," a colonel would recall. Fry, for one, thought victory was certain. "Go on; it will not last five minutes longer!" he shouted as he fell, shot through the thigh while urging his brigade to hurry up the slope. Nearby a lieutenant waved his sword and exulted as if he saw the end of the war at hand. "Home, boys, home!" he cried. "Remember, home is over beyond those hills!" Sheets of flame leaped out at the charging graybacks as the blue infantry opened fire along the wall, but they held their own fire until Garnett passed the word, which was taken up by officers all up and down the front: "Make ready. Take good aim. Fire low. *Fire!*" Uphill sheets of flame flashed in response and blue-capped heads dropped from sight beyond the wall. "Fire! Fire!" they could hear the Federal officers shouting through the smoke and muzzle-flashes. Still wrapped in his old army overcoat, Garnett rocked back in the saddle and fell heavily to the ground, dead, the Kernstown stain removed at last. Kemper meanwhile had turned and called to Armistead, who was close in his rear: "Armistead, hurry up! I am going to charge those heights and carry them, and I want you to support me!" His friend called back, "I'll do it!" and added proudly: "Look at my line. It never looked better on dress parade." But Kemper by then was in no condition to observe it; he had fallen, shot in the groin as he ordered the final assault. Pickett thus was down to a single brigade commander, and Pettigrew was in the same condition on the left, where only Davis remained, Marshall having been killed at about the same time Fry went down. Unhorsed by a shell on his way across the valley, Pettigrew had crossed the Emmitsburg

Road on foot and then had been wounded painfully in the hand as he began to climb the ridge. He remained in command, though his troops were mingled beyond the possibility of over-all control, even if he could have managed to make himself heard above the tremendous clatter of firing and the high screams of the wounded. Nevertheless, like Pickett's leaderless two on the right, his three brigades continued their uphill surge, eager to come to grips with their tormentors beyond the wall, and for the first time on this field today the rebel yell rang out.

On the Union right, near Ziegler's Grove, Hancock watched with admiration as Hays, whose northern flank considerably overlapped the enemy left, swung his end regiment forward, gatelike, to make contact with the Ohioans who had halted after routing Mayo and had taken up a position facing southwest with their left on the Emmitsburg Road. As a result of this pivoting maneuver, which was accompanied by two brass Napoleons firing double-shotted canister, some 450 men who otherwise would have had no share in the fighting after the rebels actually struck the blue defenses, well down the line and beyond their angle of sight, were placed where they could and did pump heavy volleys into the mangled flank of the attackers, adding greatly to the confusion and the carnage. Hancock shouted approval of this happy improvisation and took off southward at a gallop, intending to see whether the same could not be done at the opposite end of the position, which likewise extended well beyond the huddled mass of graybacks driving hard against his center. He rode fast, but even so he had cause to fear he would be too late. The stone wall along which his five brigades were deployed ran due south for a couple of hundred yards from Ziegler's Grove, then turned sharply west for eighty yards, thus avoiding the clump of umbrella-shaped trees, before it made as sharp a turn again to resume its former direction. The jog in the wall — described thereafter as The Angle — had caused Gibbon's men to be posted eighty yards in advance of Hays's, which meant that they would be struck first: as indeed they were. Galloping southward along the ridge, Hancock was hailed by Colonel Arthur Devereux, who commanded one of two regiments Gibbon had placed in reserve, well up the slope behind his center. "See, General!" Devereux cried, pointing. "They have broken through; the colors are coming over the stone wall. Let me go in there!" Reining his horse in so abruptly that he brought the animal back on its haunches, Hancock looked and saw that the report was all too true. Less than two hundred yards away, due west and northwest of the clump of trees, which partly obscured his view, he saw a host of butternut soldiers, led by a gray-haired officer who brandished a sword with a black hat balanced on its point, boiling over the wall in hot pursuit of a blue regiment that had bolted. Some two hundred undefended feet of the south leg of the angle had been overrun. "Go in there pretty God-damned quick!" the general shouted, and spurred on southward to order Doubleday to repeat the flanking maneuver that was working so well at the far end of the line. That way, the breakthrough might at least be limited in width, and if Devereux got there in time it might even be contained.

Arriving, Hancock found that Doubleday, or anyhow the commander of the one I Corps brigade attached for defense of the Union center, had anticipated the order; Brigadier General G. J. Stannard, a former Vermont dry-goods merchant and militia officer, had already begun the pivot maneuver and was wheeling two of his three regiments into an advance position from which to tear the flank of the attackers pressing forward to exploit their narrow penetration of the south leg of the angle, directly in front of the clump of trees and less than two hundred yards north of the point where Stannard's gatelike swing was hinged. Vermonters all, the 900 men of these two outsized regiments were nine-month volunteers; "nine monthlings hatched from $200 bounty eggs," scornful veterans had dubbed them on their recent arrival from the soft life of the Washington defenses. They had seen their first action yesterday and their army time was almost up, but they were determined to give a good account of themselves before returning home. Now the opportunity was at hand. Company by company, they opened fire as they wheeled into line, blasting the rebel flank, and as they delivered their murderous volleys they continued to move northward, closing the range until their officers were able to add the fire of their revolvers to the weight of metal thrown into the writhing mass of graybacks. "Glory to God! Glory to God!" Doubleday shouted, swinging his hat in approval as he watched from up the slope. "See the Vermonters go it!"

Hancock too was delighted, but while he was congratulating Stannard on the success with which his green troops had executed the difficult maneuver, a bullet passed through the pommel of his saddle and buried itself in the tender flesh of his inner thigh, along with several jagged bits of wood and a bent nail. Two officers caught him as he slumped, and when they had lowered him to the ground Stannard improvised a tourniquet — a knotted handkerchief wound tight with a pistol barrel — to stanch the flow of blood from the ugly wound. Hancock himself extracted the saddle nail unaided, though he mistook its source. "They must be hard up for ammunition when they throw such shot as that," he said wryly. Stretcherbearers came on the run, but he refused to be carried off the field just yet. He insisted on staying to watch the action, which now was mounting swiftly toward a climax.

The gray-haired Confederate officer he had glimpsed through the screen of trees as he rode southward in rear of the center was his old friend Armistead, whom he had seen last in California and did not recognize now because of the distance and the smoke. Working his way forward to assume command of the frantic press of troops after Garnett and Kemper had fallen, Armistead found himself at the stone wall, midway of the 200-foot stretch from which a regiment of Pennsylvanians had bolted to avoid contact with the charging rebels. There the gray advance had stopped, or anyhow paused, while those in front knelt behind its welcome cover and poured a heavy fire into the secondary blue line up the slope. He saw, however, that it would not do to lose momentum or allow the Federals time to bring up reinforcements. "Come on, boys! Give them the cold steel!" he cried, and holding his saber high, still with the black hat balanced on its tip for a guidon, he stepped over the wall, yelling as he did so: "Follow me!" Young Cushing's two guns were just ahead, unserved and silent because Cushing himself was dead by now, shot through the mouth as he called for a faster rate of fire, and Gibbon had been taken rearward, a bullet in his shoulder. Then Armistead fell too, killed as he reached with his free hand for the muzzle of one of the guns, and the clot of perhaps 300 men who had followed him over the wall was struck from the right front by the two regiments Devereux had brought down "pretty God-damned quick" from the up-hill slope beyond the clump of trees. The fight was hand to hand along the fringes, while others among the defenders stood back, left and front and right, and fired into the close-packed, heaving mass of rebel troops and colors. "Every man fought on his own hook," a bluecoat would recall, with little regard for rank or assignment, high or low. Even Hunt was there, on horseback, emptying his revolver into the crush. "See 'em! See 'em!" he cried as he pulled trigger. Then his horse went down, hoofs flailing, with the general underneath. Men on both sides were hollering as they milled about and fired, some cursing, others praying, and this, combined with the screams of the wounded and the moans of the dying, produced an effect which one who heard it called "strange and terrible, a sound that came from thousands of human throats, yet was not a commingling of shouts and yells but rather like a vast mournful roar."

Neither on the left nor on the right of the shallow penetration of the center, assailed as they were from north and south by the double envelopment Hays and Stannard had improvised, could the Confederates make real headway. Pettigrew's troops, advancing up their additional eighty yards of slope, which one of them noted incongruously was "covered with clover as soft as a Turkish carpet," were in fact outnumbered by the defenders of the two hundred yards of wall above the angle. Fry's brigade and part of Marshall's having gone in with the Virginians to the south, all that remained were Davis's brigade and Marshall's remnant, and though they kept coming on, torn by rifle fire and canister from the flank and dead ahead, they had not the slightest chance of scoring a breakthrough and they knew it. The most they could hope to accomplish was to keep the enemy units in their front from being shifted to meet the threat below the angle, and this they did, though at a cruel cost. A Mississippi regiment — including the University Greys, a company made up exclusively of students from the state university, which suffered a precisely tabulated loss of 100% of its members killed or wounded in the charge — managed to plant its colors within arm's length of the Union line before it was blasted out of existence, and a sergeant from a North Carolina outfit, accompanied by one man bearing the regimental colors, got all the way up to the wall itself, but only because the admiring defenders held their fire as they drew near. "Come over to this side of the Lord!" a bluecoat shouted: whereupon the two surrendered and crossed over with their flag. Some others availed themselves of the same mercy at various points along the line, but these were all. Except as captives, or as corpses tumbling headlong under pressure from the rear, not an attacker got over the wall north of the angle.

Blood dripping from his wounded hand, Pettigrew sent word for Trimble to bring his two supporting brigades forward and add their weight to the attack. Trimble did so, ordering Lowrance to the right, against the angle, and Lane to reinforce the battered left. Mounted, he watched with pride as they swung past him. "Charley, I believe those fine fellows are going into the enemy's line," he told an aide. But he was wrong. Moreover, as he watched them waver and recoil under the impact of the heavy fire the Federals brought to bear, he was hit a bone-splintering blow in the leg he had nearly lost at Manassas, just over ten months back, from a wound that had kept him all those fretful months out of combat. He passed the command to Lane, whom he had succeeded only four hours ago, but stayed to watch the outcome of the action. Discouraged by what he saw, the sixty-one-year-old Marylander, whose reputation for hard-handed aggressiveness was unsurpassed by any man in either army, went rapidly into shock from pain and loss of blood, and declined to permit his aide to attempt to rally the troops for a renewal of the assault, which he now perceived could not succeed. "No," he said slowly, sadly, in response to the aide's request. "The best thing the men can do is get out of this. Let them go."

They did go, here and on the right and in the center — at any rate, those who had not surrendered and were still in any condition, either physical or mental, to undertake the long walk back across the shell-torn valley. This was harder for those within the angle, not only because they had to run the longest gauntlet between the two converging wings under Hays and Stannard, but also because they were the last to realize that the assault had failed. For them, the let-down was abrupt and sickening. "I looked to the right and left," a Virginia lieutenant would recall, "and felt we were disgraced. . . . We had, for the first time, failed to do our duty." It was only after he started back and saw for himself that the friends he missed were casualties, not skulkers, that he began to comprehend the nature of the failure, and "felt that after all we were not disgraced." He made it back across, as did June Kimble, the

Tennessee sergeant who had resolved to do his duty and had done it, but who now admitted frankly: "For about a hundred yards I broke the lightning speed record." Once more, however, his conscience intervened. With a horror of being shot in the back, he turned to face the bluecoats firing downhill at him and walked backwards until he was out of musket range, then turned again and plodded uphill amid shellbursts that plowed the farther reaches of what a Federal observer called "a square mile of Tophet." Fortunately, the final stages of the withdrawal were favored somewhat by the advance of Wilcox and Lang, who came forward in response to calls from Pickett. Although Wilcox later reported that by the time he emerged from cover "not a man of the division that I was ordered to support could I see," his limited advance had at least the effect of causing Stannard, who was wounded too by now, to order his Vermonters back into line to meet this new menace to their flank, thus easing the pressure on those Confederates who were last to leave the angle and the more stubbornly defended portions of wall above and below it.

Even so, barely more than half of the 11,000 men in the nine-brigade assault force — including Mayo's defectors, whose losses had been comparatively light, and those disabled stalwarts who managed to hobble or crawl the westward distance across the valley — returned to the ridge they had left with such high hopes an hour ago. The rest, some 5000 in all, were either killed or captured. Further allowance for the wounded among the survivors, as well as for those who were killed or injured during the preliminary bombardment and in the belated advance of Lang and Wilcox, raised the total to about 7500 casualties, which amounted to sixty percent of the 12,500 Confederates engaged from first to last. In the five leading brigades under Pickett and Pettigrew the ratio of losses was considerably higher, no less indeed than seventy percent; so that it was no wonder that the former, writing five days later to his fiancée, spoke of "my spirit-crushed, wearied, cut-up people," especially if he had reference to his subordinate commanders. Not only had he lost all three of his brigadiers, but of his thirteen colonels eight were killed and all the rest were wounded. In fact, of his thirty-five officers above the rank of captain only one came back unhit, a one-armed major, and Pettigrew's losses were almost as grievous in that regard. In Fry's brigade two field officers escaped, in Marshall's only one, and in Davis's all were killed or wounded. Moreover, the Union infantry force, with half as many troops as came against them, suffered no more than 1500 casualties, barely one fifth of the number they inflicted while maintaining the integrity of their position. "We gained nothing but glory," a Virginia captain wrote home before the week was out; "and lost our bravest men."

The gloom that settled over the western ridge was more than

matched, at least in intensity, by the elation of the victors on the one across the way. On Cemetery Hill, watching as the rebel lines began to come unhinged, a captain shouted: "By God, boys, we've got 'em now. They've broke all to hell!" And down on the blood-splotched ridge below, when it became apparent that such was indeed the case, a wild celebration got under way before the gunfire stopped. Hays, who had had two horses shot from under him and had lost all but six of his twenty orderlies, was so exuberant that he grabbed and kissed young David Shields, a lieutenant on his staff. "Boys, give me a flag!" he cried. "Get a flag, Corts, get a flag, Dave, and come on!" There was no shortage of such trophies; for of the 38 regimental flags that had been brought within musket range of the wall, here on the right and on the left, no less than 30 had been captured. Hays and the two staff officers he had invited to join him in a horseback victory dance rode up and down the division line, each trailing a stand of rebel colors in the dust behind his mount, cheered by those of their grinning soldiers who were not still busy taking pot shots at the butternut figures retreating in disorder across the valley. Recalling his excitement, Shields wrote later: "My horse seemed to be off the ground traveling through the air." His impression was that if he could survive what he had just been through, he could survive almost anything, in or out of the catalogue of war. He was going to live forever. "I felt though a shot as large as a barrel should hit me in the back, it would be with no more effect than shooting through a fog bank."

Meanwhile the nearly 4000 rebel prisoners, wounded and unwounded, were being rounded up and sent to the rear. "Smart, healthy-looking men," one Federal called them, adding: "They move very quick, walk like horses." It was strange to see them thus, close up and de-fanged, without their guns and yells. They had a simple dignity about them which their ragged clothes served more to emphasize than lessen. Nor were all of them in rags. "Many of their officers were well dressed, fine, proud gentlemen," another observer wrote soon afterwards, "such men as it would be a pleasure to meet, when the war is over. I had no desire to exult over them, and pity and sympathy were the general feelings of us all upon the occasion." This last was not entirely true. At least one Union officer was alarmed by the thought that the prisoners — who, after all, numbered only a few hundred less than the surviving defenders of the ridge — might take it into their heads to renew the fight with the discarded weapons thickly strewn about the ground at their feet. There was, as it turned out, no danger of this; but the commander of a reserve battery, galloping forward in response to belated orders to reinforce the badly pounded guns along the center, received a different kind of shock. As he came up the reverse slope of the ridge he saw a mass of gray-clad men come over the crest ahead, and his first thought was that the position had been overrun. He signaled a halt and was about to give the order to fall back, when he saw that the Confederates bore no arms and were under guard.

Meade had much the same original reaction. Arriving at last from Powers Hill, he too mistook the drove of prisoners for evidence of a breakthrough. Then, as he realized his mistake and rode on past them toward the crest, he encountered a lieutenant from Gibbon's staff. "How is it going here?" he asked eagerly, and received the reply: "I believe, General, the enemy's attack is repulsed." Meade could scarcely credit the information, welcome though it was. "What!" he exclaimed. "Is the assault already repulsed?" By that time he had reached the crest, however, and the lieutenant's assurance, "It is, sir," was confirmed by what he saw with his own eyes: more captives being herded into clusters along the left and right and center, his own troops cavorting with abandoned rebel flags, and the fugitives withdrawing amid shellbursts on the far side of the valley, all unmistakable evidence of a victory achieved. "Thank God," he said fervently. The lieutenant observed that Meade's right hand jerked involuntarily upward, as if to snatch off his slouch hat and wave it in exultation, but then his concern for dignity prevailed. Instead he merely waved his hand, albeit rather self-consciously, and cried, just once: "Hurrah!" This done, he gave the staffer instructions for the posting of reinforcements expected shortly, "as the enemy might be mad enough to attack again." Adding: "If the enemy does attack, charge him in the flank and sweep him from the field," he rode on down the ridge, where he was greeted with cheers of recognition and tossed caps. A band had come up by now from somewhere, and when it broke into the strains of "Hail to the Chief" a correspondent remarked, not altogether jokingly: "Ah, General Meade, you're in very great danger of being President of the United States."

Despite the evidence spread before him that the Confederates were in a state of acute distress, and therefore probably vulnerable to attack, the northern commander's words had made it clear that he had no intention of going over to the offensive. No one on the other side of the valley had heard those words, however. If they had, their surprise and relief would have been at least as great as his had been on learning that their attempt to pierce his center had been foiled. This was especially true of Longstreet. A counter-puncher himself, he expected Meade to attack without delay, and he moved at once to meet the threat as best he could, sending word for Wright, whom he had halted when he saw the charge must fail, to collect and rally the fugitives streaming back toward the center, while he himself attended to that same function on the right. Now that the painful thing he had opposed was over, he recovered his bluff and hearty manner. He rode among the returning troops and spoke reassuringly to them, meantime sending word for Mc-

Laws and Law to pull back to the line they had taken off from yesterday and thus place their divisions in position to assist in the defense of
the weakened center. When one commander protested that his men
could not be rallied, Old Peter mocked at his despair. "Very well; never
mind then, General," he told him. "Just let them remain where they are.
The enemy's going to advance, and will spare you the trouble." Fremantle thought the Georgian's conduct "admirable," and when he
paused at one point to ask if the colonel had anything to drink, the
Britisher not only gave him a swig of rum from a silver flask but also
insisted that he keep the rest, together with its container, as a token of
his esteem. Longstreet thanked him, put the flask in his pocket for future reference, and continued to move among the fugitives with words
of cheer and encouragement, preparing to meet the counterattack which
he believed Meade would be delivering at any moment now.

But most of the survivors came streaming back the shortest way,
straight across the valley toward the command post midway of its western rim, like hurt children in instinctive search of solace from a parent:
meaning Lee. There the southern commander had remained throughout
their advance and their brief, furious struggle on the distant ridge, until
he saw them falter and begin their slow recoil; whereupon he rode forward to meet them coming back, to rally them with words of reassurance, and to share with them the ordeal of the counterattack he believed
would soon be launched. Nor did he disappoint them in their expectations of solace and sustainment. "All this will come right in the end,"
he told them. "We'll talk it over afterwards. But in the meantime all
good men must rally. We want all good and true men just now." He
made it clear to all he met that he considered the failure of the charge
not their fault, but his, for having asked of them more than men could
give. To Fremantle, who had ridden over from the right, he said: "This
has been a sad day for us, Colonel. A sad day. But we can't always expect
to win victories." After advising the visitor to find a safer point for observation, he continued to move among his soldiers in an attempt to
brace them for the storm he thought was coming. "Very few failed to
answer his appeal," Fremantle noted, "and I saw many badly wounded
men take off their hats and cheer him."

One among the fugitives most in need of encouragement was
Pickett, who came riding back with an expression of dejection and bewilderment on his face. Leading his division into battle for the first time,
he had seen two thirds of it destroyed. Not only had his great hour come
to nothing; tactically speaking, it added up to considerably less than
nothing. Lee met him with instructions designed to bring him back to
the problem now at hand. "General Pickett, place your division in
rear of this hill," he told him, "and be ready to repel the advance of the
enemy should they follow up their advantage." At least one bystander

observed that in his extremity Lee employed the words "the enemy" rather than his usual "those people." But Pickett was in no state to observe anything outside his personal loss and mortification.

"General Lee, I have no division now," he said tearfully; "Armistead is down, Garnett is down, and Kemper is mortally wounded —"

"Come, General Pickett," Lee broke in. "This has been my fight, and upon my shoulders rests the blame. The men and officers of your command have written the name of Virginia as high today as it has ever been written before. . . . Your men have done all that men can do," he added after a pause for emphasis. "The fault is entirely my own."

He repeated this as he rode from point to point about the field: "It's all my fault," "The blame is mine," and "You must help me." To Wilcox, who was about as unstrung as Pickett in reporting that he was not sure his troops would stand if the Federals attacked, Lee was particularly solicitous and tender. "Never mind, General," he told him, taking his hand as he spoke. "All this has been my fault. It is I who have lost this fight, and you must help me out of it the best way you can." Fremantle, who had not followed his advice to find a place of safety, thought it "impossible to look at him or listen to him without feeling the strongest admiration," and when he rode forward to the line of guns, the Britisher found the cannoneers ready to challenge any blue attack on the disrupted center. They had much the same reaction as his own to Lee's appeal. "We've not lost confidence in the old man," they assured him, speaking defiantly, almost angrily, as if someone had suggested otherwise. "This day's work will do him no harm. Uncle Robert will get us into Washington yet. You bet he will."

By no means all responded in that fashion, however — especially among the troops who had been all the way to the enemy ridge and back, as the artillerists had not — and even concerning those who did there was considerable doubt as to whether they would stand their ground, this soon after their delivery from chaos, if they were exposed to more than the possibility of further danger. In point of fact, there was strong evidence that they would not. When some officers managed to form a line along the forward slope of Seminary Ridge, still in plain view of the Union batteries, the rallied fugitives broke badly under the long-range fire their concentration drew. "Then commenced a rout, that increased to a stampede," an indignant witness later wrote. Fleeing rearward over the crest, the mass of several hundred fear-crazed men was funneled into a ravine along the western slope, and there, without regard for orders or appeals from their officers, who were swept along in the crush, they "pushed, poured, and rushed in a continuous stream, throwing away guns, blankets, and haversacks," until at last a straggler line, composed of the more stalwart few among them, was thrown across their path and "dammed [them] up."

Lee did not reproach them even then, knowing as he did that time alone could heal the wounds their morale had suffered in the hour just past. What was more, his ready acceptance of total blame for the failure of the assault was not merely a temporary burden he assumed for the sake of encouraging his troops to resist the counterattack he believed Meade was about to launch at them; he continued to say the same things in the future, after the immediate need for them was past and the quite different but altogether human need for self-justification might have been expected to set in. "It's all my fault. I thought my men were invincible," he told Longstreet the next day, perhaps by way of making specific admission that he had been wrong in overruling his chief lieutenant's objection that the charge was bound to fail. And in his official report to the President, forwarded on the last day of the month, he repeated for the record his assertion that such fault as might be found could not properly be applied to the men who had bled and died to sustain his pride in them. "The conduct of the troops was all that I could desire or expect," he wrote, "and they deserved success so far as it can be deserved by heroic valor and fortitude. More may have been required of them than they were able to perform, but my admiration of their noble qualities and confidence in their ability to cope successfully with the enemy has suffered no abatement from the issue of this protracted and sanguinary conflict."

✕ 5 ✕

Protracted the conflict had certainly been, and sanguinary too, three days of fighting having produced a combined total of about 50,000 casualties North and South. Nor was it quite over yet. Although Lee could not and Meade would not renew the infantry action, two indecisive and as it were extraneous cavalry engagements — one three miles east of Gettysburg, deep in the Federal right rear, and the other just west of Round Top, on the Confederate right flank — were, respectively, still to be ended and begun. The former, which reached a climax at about the time Pickett and Pettigrew surged up Cemetery Ridge, was the result of Jeb Stuart's attempt to carry out his instructions for placing his troopers in a position from which to harry the expected, or at any rate hoped-for, blue retreat; whereas the latter, fought about an hour after the gray attackers fell back across the valley, was the result of Judson Kilpatrick's attempt, in the absence of instructions, to strike while the tactical iron was hot and thus not only throw the rebels into retreat but also provoke a panic that would prevent them from achieving a getaway. Neither Stuart nor Kilpatrick, quite different in makeup and ability, but altogether similar in their thirst for action and applause, succeeded in accomplishing what he set out to do. In fact, as the two things turned out, both generals would have done better to remain within their respective lines, together with all their men: especially Kilpatrick.

At midday Stuart rode eastward out the York Pike with the brigades of Chambliss and Jenkins, the latter now under Colonel M. J. Ferguson since its regular commander had been wounded the day before; Hampton and Fitz Lee followed at a distance, bringing the total to just over 6000 sabers. One night's rest could scarcely have restored either the men or their mounts after a week on the go, but Jeb was eager for a fight. On Evelington Heights a year ago this morning, by way of providing the just-concluded drama of the Seven Days with an upbeat epilogue, he had opened fire with a single howitzer on McClellan's blue host encamped at Harrison's Landing, and though he had been criticized for flushing the game in this fashion, he would have liked nothing better today than another such opportunity, especially after the chilling reception his chief had given him yesterday when he rejoined the army that had been groping blindfold in his absence. For more than two miles, however, he did not sight a single enemy soldier. The Pennsylvania countryside looked altogether peaceful, its rolling farmlands untouched by war, despite the thunder of the great cannonade behind him, south of Gettysburg, which began soon after 1 o'clock and continued to rumble without diminution as he turned south about 2.30 along Cress Ridge, which extended down to the Hanover Road and the Baltimore Pike beyond. Presently he spotted horsemen a mile to the east on the Low Dutch Road, a lane that paralleled the ridge, and promptly decided to defeat or drive them off, thus clearing his path to the Union rear. Accordingly, after posting Chambliss behind a screen of woods, he dismounted Ferguson's men and sent them forward to take position around a large barn on the farm of a family named Rummel. They would serve as bait to draw the Federals, whose strength was so far undisclosed, after which Stuart planned to attack with Chambliss, then sweep the field with Hampton and Lee, whom he warned by courier to remain under cover of the ridge as they came up, thereby adding the shock of surprise to the weight of their horseback assault on the unsuspecting bluecoats whose attention would be fixed on the dismounted and presumably vulnerable band of graybacks in the Rummel barnyard.

It did not work out quite that way, for several reasons. For one, the blue riders were in much greater numbers than he knew. Two brigades of David Gregg's division, reinforced by one brigade from Kilpatrick's, were at hand, 5000 strong, armed with repeating carbines, and apparently as eager for a clash as Stuart was. This by itself would have been all right — the Confederates still had the numerical advantage — but it presently developed that Ferguson's men, through a misinterpretation of instructions, had drawn only ten rounds of ammunition each, with the result that they ran out of bullets almost as soon as the fight got started. Stuart had to send in Chambliss prematurely, in order to keep the bait from being gobbled before he was set to spring the trap. Even this was not too bad, or anyhow it need not have been, if Hampton and Lee had come up as planned; but they did not. Disclosing their presence while still too far away to achieve surprise, they gave the Federals time to fall back from the melee around the barn and form their ranks to receive the charge. In fact, a good many of the bluecoats did a great deal more than that. They moved to meet it. The brigade attached from Kilpatrick included four Michigan regiments commanded by a recently promoted brigadier named George A. Custer, bottom man in the West Point class of '61, which had lost its top man yesterday on Little Round Top. Custer, whose love of combat was only exceeded by his ache for glory, saw the rebel column approaching and moved fast. "Come on, you Wolverines!" he shouted, four lengths in front of the lead regiment, his long yellow ringlets streaming in the wind. A Federal witness described what followed. "As the two columns approached each other, the pace of each increased, when suddenly a crash, like the falling of timber, betokened the crisis. So sudden and violent was the collision that many of the horses were turned end over end and crushed their riders beneath them. The clashing of sabers, the firing of pistols, the demands for surrender and cries of the combatants now filled the air."

Gregg dealt ably with the situation that developed, sending in other units to strike the flanks of the gray column which Custer had brought to a standstill by meeting it head-on, and while the saber-to-saber conflict was in progress, cannoneers on both sides threw in shell and canister whenever they could do so without too great risk of hitting their own men. Hampton went down with a deep gash in his head, but was brought off the field in time to prevent his capture. Stuart, perhaps reasoning that it was not after all his mission to stage a cavalry fight at this stage of the battle — which he had no way of knowing was now at its climax, back on Cemetery Ridge, with Armistead crying "Follow me!" as he stepped over the low stone wall along Meade's center — withdrew his troopers to the ridge from which they had charged, and Gregg, who had cause to be well satisfied, was content to let them go. The artillery exchange continued till past sundown, at which time the Confederates retired northward and went unmolested into bivouac alongside the York Pike, near the point where they had left it six hours back. Gregg reported 254 casualties, most of them Custer's, whose Michiganders would suffer, before the war was over, a larger number of killed and wounded than any other cavalry brigade in the Union army. Stuart listed 181, but since this was exclusive of Ferguson's brigade and the artillery, the losses probably were about equal on both sides. Jeb made the most of the affair in his report, praising the conduct of some of his regiments by saying that "the enemy's masses vanished before them like grain before the scythe." Yet the fact remained that, for once, he had failed to drive an outnumbered foe from a fair field of fight. "Defeated at every point, the enemy withdrew," Gregg declared, and while Stuart objected strenuously to the claim — he had withdrawn when he got good and ready, he maintained — there could be no denying that he had failed in his purpose of reaching the Union rear, even though it later developed that there was no retreat for him to harry and therefore no real work for him to do if he had been there.

Four miles southwest of the Rummel farm, the other cavalry action was over too by now. Beginning some two hours later, it ended some two hours earlier, and if, despite this brevity, its potential fruits were greater — the intention had been to throw Lee's right into confusion, hard on the heels of the Pickett-Pettigrew repulse, and thus set him up for a crumpling assault to be launched by the blue infantry from the western slopes of the Round Tops — so too was the failure, which amounted to nothing more or less than a fiasco. Kilpatrick's remaining brigade, commanded by twenty-six-year-old Brigadier General Elon J. Farnsworth, was in position on the rebel flank, opposed by a skirmish line of Texans from Law's division, which extended from the base of Round Top west to the Emmitsburg Road. A year older than Farnsworth, and four years older than Custer, who had been a West Point classmate, Kilpatrick rode back and forth among his troopers, expressing what one of them called "great impatience and eagerness for orders." There was nothing unusual in this, for that was his accustomed manner, all the way back to his boyhood in New Jersey. "A wiry, restless, undersized man with black eyes [and] a lantern jaw," as a fellow officer described him, he had stringy blond side whiskers, bandy legs that gave him a rolling gait, and a burning ambition which he attempted to assuage and advance with constant aggressiveness and bluster. The result was not uncomical, at least to some observers; Sherman, for one, was to call him "a hell of a damned fool," and a member of Meade's staff remarked that "it was hard to look at Kilpatrick without laughing." But this last was not always the case for those who served under him — "Kill Cavalry," they had dubbed him, somewhat ruefully — and it was especially not the case today, so far as Farnsworth was concerned; for Kilpatrick kept insisting that he make horseback probes at the rebel skirmish line, despite the boulder-strewn terrain, which was highly unsuitable for cavalry operations, and the renowned marksmanship of the Texans, who had emptied a good many saddles by now and were backed up, moreover, by Law's old brigade of Alabamians, whose skill was scarcely less in that respect. However, the worst was still to come for Farnsworth and his men.

It came shortly before 5 o'clock, when an orderly arrived on a lathered horse from Cemetery Ridge, shouting as he drew near: "We turned the charge! Nine acres of prisoners!" That was enough for Kil-

patrick. Though he had no instructions to go over to the offensive, he
assumed that Meade was on the lookout for a chance to strike at the
rebel line, especially if some part of it could be thrown into confusion
beforehand, and he quickly determined to provide such an opportunity
for the forces gazing down from the slopes of Round Top. Turning to
Farnsworth, he told him to commit a West Virginia regiment at once,
with orders to hack a gap in the butternut skirmish line, then go for the
Confederate main body, deployed along the base of the height beyond
Plum Run, opposing the blue infantry above. The West Virginians tried
it and were repulsed, losing heavily when the Texans rose from behind a
rail fence and slammed massed volleys at them. They tried it again —
and again, by way of demonstration that the terrain was unsuited to
horseback maneuver, were driven back. But Kilpatrick was not satisfied.
Having often maintained that cavalry could "fight anywhere except at
sea," he was out to prove it here today. He told Farnsworth to send in a
second regiment, this time one of Vermonters who had suffered cruelly
in the earlier skirmishing. Farnsworth had shown his mettle in some forty
engagements since the first days of the war, and only four days ago he
had been promoted from captain to brigadier in recognition of his bravery under fire. There could scarcely be any question of his courage, but
after what they had both just seen he could not believe he had heard
his chief aright. "General, do you mean it?" he asked. "Shall I throw my
handful of men over rough ground, through timber, against a brigade
of infantry? The 1st Vermont has already been fought half to pieces.
These are too good men to kill." But Kilpatrick not only meant it; he
wanted it done without question or delay. "Do you refuse to obey my
orders?" he snapped. "If you are afraid to lead this charge, I will lead it."
Farnsworth rose in his stirrups, flushed with anger. "Take that back!" he
cried, and an observer thought the tall young man "looked magnificent
in his passion." Kilpatrick bristled back at him for a moment, but then
repented and apologized. "I didn't mean it. Forget it," he said. Farnsworth's anger subsided as quickly as it had risen. "General, if you order the charge, I will lead it," he replied; "but you must take the responsibility." Kilpatrick nodded. "I take the responsibility," he said.

The Texans were even readier now than they had been before.
Posted within earshot, they had overheard the hot exchange between the
two young brigadiers: with the result that they not only had time to
brace themselves for what was coming, but also time to pass the word
along to Law that his rear would be threatened if the troopers managed
to punch a hole in the widespread skirmish line. The Vermonters were
prepared to do just that, though one of them later wrote: "Each man felt,
as he tightened his saber belt, that he was summoned to a ride to death."
Farnsworth having massed them in depth, they broke through on a narrow front about midway of the line, taking losses along both flanks as
they made their penetration, then swung hard east to strike the rear of

the rebel infantry on the far side of Plum Run, which was bone dry at this season. They crossed, still at a gallop, but it would have been far better for them if they had not. As they approached what they thought was the Confederate rear, their drawn sabers flashing sunlight, it was as if the head of the column struck a trip wire. Oates, forewarned, had faced his Alabamians about, ignoring the enemy infantry uphill, and presented a solid front to the blue riders. The survivors turned sharply north again, in an attempt to avoid a second volley; but that too was a mistake, since it carried them directly along the line of marksmen who did not neglect the rare opportunity for point-blank firing at cavalry in profile. For some, indeed, it was like a return to happier days. A company commander, seeing a horse collapse in midstride with a bullet through the brain, heard a private alongside him shout: "Captain, I shot that black!" Asked why he had not aimed for the rider instead of the horse, the Alabamian grinned. "Oh, we'll get him anyhow," he said. "But I'm a hunter, and for two years I haven't looked at a deer's eye. I couldn't stand it."

By that time Law had reinforced the skirmishers with another regiment; so that when the blue survivors turned back west and south, they found the entry gap resealed. What had been intended as a havoc-spreading charge now degenerated into a sort of circus, Roman style, with the penned-in horsemen riding frantically in large circles, ricocheting from cluster to cluster of whooping rebels as they tried to find a way out of the fire-laced coliseum. Farnsworth had his mount shot from under him, took another from a trooper who was glad to go afoot, and in final desperation — perhaps with Kilpatrick's taunt still ringing in his ears — made a suicidal one-man charge, saber raised, against a solid mass of Confederates who brought him down with five mortal wounds. Some 65 of his men had fallen with him by the time the remnant found an exit and regained the safety of the Union lines. No earthly good had been accomplished, except by way of providing a show for the spectators, blue and gray, who had watched as in an amphitheater. Still, Kilpatrick did not regret having ordered the attempt; he only regretted that the infantry onlookers, high on the slopes of Round Top, had failed to seize the advantage offered them by the Vermonters on the plain below; in which case, he reported, "a total rout would have ensued." As for Farnsworth: "For the honor of his young brigade and the glory of his corps, he gave his life. . . . We can say of him, in the language of another, 'Good soldier, faithful friend, great heart, hail and farewell.' " Thus Kilpatrick, who had sent him to his death with words of doubt as to his courage.

The infantry had not come down to join the mix-up in the valley for the sufficient reason that it had received no instructions to do so, although there were those who urged this course on Meade in no uncertain terms. One such was Pleasonton, who was quite as cocky as his lieutenants. "I will give you half an hour to show yourself a great general," he told his chief, soon after the latter's arrival on Cemetery Ridge. "Order the army to advance, while I take the cavalry and get in Lee's rear, and we will finish the campaign in a week." But Meade was having no part of such advice. Six days in command, he had spent the last three locked in mortal combat, all of it defensive on his side, and he had no intention of shifting to the offensive on short notice, even if that had been possible, simply because another in the sequence of all-out rebel assaults on his fishhook line had been repulsed. Besides, he was by no means convinced that this was the last of them. "How do you know Lee will not attack me again?" he replied. "We have done well enough." Pleasonton continued to press the point, maintaining that the Confederates, low on supplies by now and far from base, would be obliged to surrender if nailed down; to which Meade's only response was an invitation for the cavalryman to accompany him on the triumphal ride along the ridge to Little Round Top. It seemed to Pleasanton that the cheers of the troops "plainly showed they expected the advance," but the army commander did not swerve from the opinion he had just expressed: "We have done well enough."

Hancock made a similar appeal, with similar results. Lifted into an ambulance after the charge had been repulsed, he ordered the vehicle halted as soon as it reached the Taneytown Road, where shells from long-range Whitworths north of Gettysburg were still landing, and began to dictate a message to be delivered at once to Meade. After explaining that he had been "severely but I trust not seriously wounded," he made it clear that he had not left his troops "so long as a rebel was to be seen upright." Interrupted by the attending surgeon, who protested against the delay, especially under enfilading fire from the rebels, the wounded general replied testily: "We've enfiladed *them*, God damn 'em," and went on with his dictation. He urged his chief to hurl Sedgwick and Sykes at Seminary Ridge without delay — if, indeed, this had not been done already. "If the VI and V corps have pressed up, the enemy will be destroyed," he predicted, and he added, by way of reinforcing his claim that Lee was in no condition to withstand a determined attack: "The enemy must be short of ammunition, as I was shot with a tenpenny nail." However, all he heard from Meade was a verbal message that avoided the central issue altogether. "Say to General Hancock," his fellow Pennsylvanian replied, "that I regret exceedingly that he is wounded, and that I thank him for the country and for myself for the service he has rendered today."

By this time McLaws had begun the withdrawal Longstreet ordered, and when the Federal skirmishers followed the graybacks out to the Emmitsburg Road, reclaiming the salient lost the day before, they were met by heavy volleys from guns and rifles; which tended to confirm the wisdom of Meade's decision, as he afterwards explained, not to advance on Seminary Ridge "in consequence of the bad example [Lee] had set for me, in ruining himself attacking a strong position." Nor was the northern commander alone in this belief. Henry Hunt, who had been pulled from under his toppled horse at the climax of the rebel assault and suffered only minor aches and pains from the injuries received, sided absolutely with his chief. "A prompt counter-charge after combat between two small bodies of men is one thing," the artillerist later wrote; "the change from the defensive to the offensive of an army, after an engagement at a single point, is quite another. To have made such a change to the offensive, on the assumption that Lee had made no provision against a reverse, would have been rash in the extreme." Warren thought so, too. It was generally felt, he subsequently declared, "that we had saved the country for the time and that we had done enough; that we might jeopardize all that we had done by trying to do too much." Such were the opinions of the two surviving members of the quartet of generals — the dead Reynolds and the wounded Hancock were the other pair — who were commonly given credit, then and later, for having done most to prevent another defeat from being added to the Union record: a defeat, moreover, which, given the time and place, some would maintain the Union could not have survived.

   In point of fact, the greatest deterrent was the mute but staggering testimony of the casualty lists. Including Reynolds, Sickles, and Hancock, the three most aggressive of its corps commanders, a solid fourth of the Federal army had been killed or wounded or captured, and well over half again as many skulkers and stragglers had simply wandered off or been knocked loose from their units. A head count next morning would show 51,414 present of all ranks. Of the more than 38,000 men who thus were absent, the actual casualties numbered 23,049 — precisely tabulated a few days later at 3155 killed, 14,529 wounded, 5365 captured — which left some 15,000 not accounted for, just now at least, and encouraged the belief that the losses had been even greater than they were in fact. Moreover, they were quite unevenly distributed. Of Meade's seven infantry corps, the four led into action by Reynolds, Hancock, Sickles, and Howard had suffered almost ninety percent of the casualties, and if this had its brighter aspect — Sedgwick's corps, the largest in the army, had scarcely been engaged at all, and might therefore be considered available for delivery of the counterstroke urged by Pleasonton and Hancock — it also cast a corresponding gloom over those who had done the bleeding. All in all, when they became available, these figures did much to support the judgment of the responsible commander that, notwithstanding the tactical desirability of launching an immediate mass assault, which was as clear to him as it was to any man on the field, the troops were in no condition to sustain it.

   On the other hand there was testimony from Lee's own ranks that the Confederates were in no condition to resist an assault if one had

been made against them. "Our ammunition was so low," Alexander confessed, "and our diminished forces at the moment so widely dispersed
along the unwisely extended line, that an advance by a single fresh corps,
[Sedgwick's] for instance, could have cut us in two." Few on that same
side of the line agreed with this, however. After all, it was not Lee's army
that had been shattered in the desperate charge that afternoon, but only
eight of his thirty-seven brigades, five of which — Anderson's other
three and Pender's two: the same number that had stood fast for Meade
across the way — were on hand to defend his center. Moreover, all his
cavalry was up by now, including Imboden's 2000 troopers who had arrived at midday, and not one piece of artillery had been lost. Far from
being depressed by the repulse, many along the rebel line had been angered by what they had seen and were eager for revenge; they asked for
nothing better than a chance to serve the blucoats in the same manner,
if they could be persuaded to attack. "We'll fight them, sir, till hell freezes
over," one grayback told an observer, "and then, sir, we will fight them
on the ice." Indeed, adversity seemed to knit them closer together as a
family, which was what they had become in the past year under Lee,
and brought out the high qualities that would stand them in good stead
during the downhill months ahead. Longstreet, for example, riding out
after dark to inspect his skirmish line, found a battery still in position
near the Peach Orchard, though he had ordered all his artillery withdrawn to the cover of the western ridge some time before. "Whose are
these guns?" he demanded; whereupon a tall man with a pipe in his
mouth stepped out of the shadows. "I am the captain," he said quietly,
and when the general asked why he had stayed out there in front of the
infantry, the artilleryman replied: "I am out here to have a little skirmishing on my own account, if the Yanks come out of their holes."
Amused by the prospect of a skirmish with 12-pounder howitzers, and
heartened by such evidence of staunchness in a time of strain, Old Peter
threw back his head and let his laugh ring out once more across that
somber field.

Incongruous as his laughter had seemed that afternoon, just before the 11,000-man assault wave broke and began to ebb, it sounded
even stranger now in the darkness, under cover of which the extent of
the army's losses could begin to be assessed. From the top down, they
were unremittingly grievous. Of the 52 Confederate generals who had
crossed the Potomac in the past three weeks, no less than 17 — barely
under one third — had become casualties in the past three days. Five
were killed outright or mortally wounded: Semmes and Barksdale,
Pender, Armistead and Garnett. Two were captured: Archer, who had
been taken on the first day, and Trimble, who had not been able to
make it back across the valley today with a shattered leg: and this figure
would be increased to three when the army began its withdrawal, since
Kemper was too badly injured to be moved. Nine more were wounded:

some lightly, such as Heth and Pettigrew, others gravely, such as Hood, whose arm might have to be taken off, and Hampton, who had received not one but two head cuts and also had some shrapnel in his body. When the list was lengthened by 18 colonels killed or captured, many of them officers of high promise, slated for early promotion, it was obvious that the Army of Northern Virginia had suffered a loss in leadership from which it might never recover. A British observer was of this opinion. He lauded the offensive prowess of Lee's soldiers, who had marched out as proudly as if on parade in their eagerness to come to grips with their opponents on the ridge across the way; "But they will never do it again," he predicted. And he told why. He had been with the army since Fredericksburg, ticking off the illustrious dead from Stonewall Jackson down, and now on the heels of Gettysburg he asked a rhetorical question of his Confederate friends: "Don't you see your system feeds upon itself? You cannot fill the places of these men. Your troops do wonders, but every time at a cost you cannot afford."

That might well be. Certainly there was no comfort in a comparison of the representation on the list of those of less exalted rank. Here, too, no less than a third had fallen — and possibly more, for the count was incomplete. Lee recorded his losses as 2592 killed, 12,709 wounded, and 5150 captured or missing, a total of 20,451: which was surely low, for a variety of reasons. For one, a few units that had fought made no report, and for another he had directed in mid-May that troops so lightly wounded that they could remain with their regiments were not to be listed as casualties, although such men were included in the Federal tabulations. Moreover, his figure for the number captured or missing could not be reconciled with the prisoner-of-war records in the Adjutant General's office at Washington, which bore the names of 12,227 Confederates captured July 1-5. The true total of Lee's losses in Pennsylvania could hardly have been less than 25,000 and quite possibly was far heavier; 28,063 was the figure computed by one meticulous student of such grisly matters, in which case the butcher's bill for Gettysburg, blue and gray together, exceeded 50,000 men. This was more than Shiloh and Sharpsburg combined, with Ball's Bluff and Belmont thrown in for good measure. And while there was considerably less disparity of bloodshed among the several corps of the attackers — Hill had suffered most and Ewell least, but both were within a thousand of Longstreet, who had lost perhaps 8500 — this was by no means true of smaller units within the corps. Gordon's exultation, "The Almighty has covered my men with his shield and buckler," could scarcely have been echoed by any commander of the eight brigades that went up Cemetery Ridge, and even within these there was a diversity of misfortune. Most regiments came back across the valley with at least a skeleton cadre to which future recruits or conscripts could be attached; but not all. The 14th Tennessee, for example, had left Clarksville in 1861 with 960 men on its muster roll, and in the past two years, most of which time their homeland had been under Union occupation, they had fought on all the major battlefields of Virginia. When Archer took them across Willoughby Run on the opening day of Gettysburg they counted 365 bayonets; by sunset they were down to barely 60. These five dozen survivors, led by a captain on the third day, went forward with Fry against Cemetery Ridge, and there — where the low stone wall jogged west, then south, to form what was known thereafter as the angle — all but three of the remaining 60 fell. This was only one among the forty-odd regiments in the charge; there were others that suffered about as cruelly; but to those wives and sweethearts, parents and sisters and younger brothers who had remained at its point of origin, fifty miles down the Cumberland from Nashville, the news came hard. "Thus the band that once was the pride of Clarksville has fallen," a citizen lamented, and he went on to explain something of what he and those around him felt. "A gloom rests over the city; the hopes and affections of the people were wrapped in the regiment.... Ah! what a terrible responsibility rests upon those who inaugurated this unholy war."

No one felt the responsibility harder than Lee, though, far from inaugurating, he had opposed the war at the outset, when some who now were loudest in their lamentations had called for secession or coercion, whatever the consequences, and had allowed themselves to be persuaded that all the blood that would be shed could be mopped up with a congressman's pocket handkerchief; whereas it now turned out that, at the modest rate of a gallon for every dead man and a pint for each of the wounded, perhaps not all the handkerchiefs in the nation, or both nations, would suffice to soak up the blood that had been spilled at Gettysburg alone. Such macabre calculations might be of particular interest down the years — a fit subject, perhaps, for a master's thesis when centennial time came round — but Lee's tonight were of a different nature. From the moment he saw the shattered brigades of Pickett and Pettigrew begin their stumble back across the valley, it was obvious that what was left of his army, low on food and with only enough ammunition on hand for one more day of large-scale action, would have to retreat. After riding forward to help rally the fugitives and thus present as bold a front as possible to discourage a counterattack, he went to his tent and there, by candlelight, resumed his study of the maps over which he had pored throughout the hectic week preceding the blindfold commitment to battle. If his problems now were no less difficult, they were at least much simpler, having been reduced to the logistics of withdrawing his survivors, together with his wounded, his supply train, and his prisoners, from the immediate front of a victorious opponent deep in hostile territory. He chose his routes, decided on the order of march, and then, despite the lateness of the hour and his bone-deep weariness after three days of failure and frustration, went in person to make certain that his plans were understood by the responsible commanders. By dawn, Ewell and Longstreet were to have their troops disposed along Seminary Ridge, north and south of Hill's present position in the center. All day tomorrow, whether Meade attacked or not, they were to hold their ground and thus afford a head start for the wounded, as well as for the supply train and the captives; after which they were to take up the march themselves, under cover of darkness, with Hill in the lead, followed by Longstreet, and Ewell bringing up the rear. Pickett's remnant — a scant 800 of his badly shaken men would be on hand at daylight — was assigned to guard the 5000-odd Federal prisoners on the return, and Imboden's troopers would escort the miles-long column of ambulances and forage wagons loaded with such of the wounded as the surgeons judged could survive the long ride home. By this arrangement, the last infantry division to reach the field, as well as the last cavalry brigade, would be the first to depart. Before leaving his tent, Lee sent word for Imboden to report to headquarters and wait for his return, intending to give him detailed instructions for the conduct of the march. Then he went out into the night.

Unlike the vague and discretionary orders he had issued throughout the week leading up to battle and even during the past three days of fighting, in the course of which his messages had been verbal and for the most part tentative, his instructions now were written and precise, allowing no discretion whatsoever to anyone at all. In Hill's case, moreover, since his was the corps that would mark the route and set the pace, Lee took the added precaution of conferring with him in person, tracing for him the line of march on the map and making certain there was no possibility of a misunderstanding. This might have waited for morning; the infantry movement would not begin until the following evening at the earliest; but evidently Lee felt that he should not, or could not, sleep until the matter had been disposed of to his satisfaction. Delegation of authority, under orders that not only permitted but encouraged a wide degree of latitude in their execution by subordinates, had been the basis for his greatest triumphs, particularly during the ten months he had had Jackson to rely on; Second Manassas and Chancellorsville were instances in point. But at Gettysburg, with Stonewall just seven weeks in his grave, the system had failed him, and his actions tonight were an acknowledgment of the fact. Though he would return to the system in time, out of necessity as well as from choice, on this last night of his greatest and worst-fought battle he abandoned it entirely. He relied on no one but himself.

It was late, well after midnight, by the time he left Hill and rode back through the quiet moonlit camps along Seminary Ridge to his headquarters beside the Chambersburg Pike. Imboden was waiting for him there, as instructed, though no one else was stirring; his staff had gone to sleep so tired that not even a sentry had been posted. Lee drew rein and sat motionless for a time, apparently too weary to dismount, but as the cavalryman stepped forward, intending to assist him, he swung down and leaned for another long moment against Traveller, head bowed and one arm thrown across the saddle for more rest. Imboden watched him, awed by the tableau — "The moon shone full upon his massive features and revealed an expression of sadness that I had never before seen upon his face" — then, hoping, as he said later, "to change the silent current of his thoughts," ventured to speak of his obvious fatigue: "General, this has been a hard day on you." Lee raised his head, and his fellow Virginian saw grief as well as weariness in his eyes. "Yes, this has been a sad, sad day to us," he replied, emphasizing the word he had used that afternoon in speaking to Fremantle. Again he fell silent, but presently he "straightened up to his full height" and spoke "with more animation and excitement" than Imboden had ever seen him display: "I never saw troops behave more magnificently than Pickett's division of Virginians did today in that grand charge upon the enemy. And if they had been supported as they were to have been — but, for some reason not yet fully explained to me, were not — we would have held the position and the day would have been ours." This last was a strange thing for him to say, for he himself had denied Hill permission to throw his whole corps into the assault. However, there was no mistaking the extent of his regret. "Too bad; too bad," he groaned; "Oh, too bad!"

Suppressing his emotion, he invited Imboden into his tent for a study of the map and the long road home, which he was about to take. "We must now return to Virginia," he said.

CHAPTER

✗ **3** ✗

Unvexed to the Sea

★ ✗ ☆

ALL NEXT MORNING, HAVING COMPLETED THE
perilous nighttime disengagement of both wings in order to form a
continuous line of defense along Seminary Ridge, from Oak Hill on the
north to the confronting loom of Round Top on the south, the Confederates awaited the answer to the question that was uppermost in their
minds: Would the Federals attack? Apparently they would not. "What
o'clock is it?" Longstreet finally asked an artillerist standing beside him.
"11.55," the officer replied, and ventured a prediction: "General, this is
the 'Glorious Fourth.' We should have a salute from the other side at
noon." Noon came and went but not a gun was fired. Old Peter believed
he knew why. "Their artillery was too much crippled yesterday to think
of salutes," he said with satisfaction. "Meade is not in good spirits this
morning."

Presently there was evidence that he was wrong. Across the way,
in the vicinity of the Peach Orchard, a Union brigade was seen deploying
for battle. Nothing came of this, however; for just at that time — about
1 o'clock — rain began to fall, first a drizzle, then a steady downpour;
the bluecoats jammed their fixed bayonets into the ground to keep the
water from running down their rifle barrels, then squatted uncom-
fortably beside them, shoulders hunched against the rain. Obviously they
had abandoned all notion of attack, if indeed they had had any such real
intention in the first place. On their separate ridges, an average mile apart,
the men of both armies peered at one another through the transparent
curtain of rain as it sluiced the bloodstains from the grass and rocks
where they had fought so savagely the past three days, but would not
fight today.

Lee appeared calm and confident as he watched the departure of
the long column of wounded at the height of the afternoon rainstorm
and continued his preparations for the withdrawal of the infantry and
artillery that night. Beneath the surface, however, he was testy: as was

shown by his response to a well-meant pleasantry from one of Ewell's young staff officers who came to headquarters with a report from his chief. "General," he said encouragingly, "I hope the other two corps are in as good condition for work as ours is this morning." Lee looked at him hard and said coldly, "What reason have you, young man, to suppose they are not?" Even before it became evident that the Federals were not going to attack he proposed, by means of a flag of truce, a man-for-man exchange of prisoners, thus risking a disclosure of his intentions in hope of lightening his burden on the march. Nothing came of this; Meade prudently declined, on grounds that he had no authority in such matters, and Lee continued his preparations for the withdrawal, prisoners and all. Imboden and the wounded were to return by way of Cashtown and Chambersburg, Greencastle and Hagerstown, for a Potomac cross-ing near Williamsport, a distance of forty-odd miles, while the infantry would follow a route some dozen miles shorter, southwest through Fair-field to Hagerstown for a crossing at the same point, its left flank pro-tected by units of Stuart's cavalry on the road to Emmitsburg. Though he felt confident that his opponent would be restricted in maneuver by the continuing obligation to cover Baltimore and Washington, Lee rec-ognized the impending retrograde movement as probably the most haz-ardous of his career. His troops did not seem greatly dispirited by the failure of the campaign, but their weariness was apparent to even a casual eye and a good third of those who had headed north with such high hopes a month ago would not be returning. Including the walking wounded who remained with their commands, he had fewer than 50,000 effectives of all arms. Moreover, Meade by now must have received heavy reinforcements from the surrounding northern states, as well as from his nearby capital: whereas Lee could expect no such transfusions of strength until he crossed the Potomac, if at all.

Leaving his campfires burning on the ridge, Hill began the with-drawal soon after nightfall. Longstreet followed, still in a driving rain that served to muffle the sound of the army's departure from its oppo-nent across the valley. There were delays, however, and it was 2 o'clock in the morning before Ewell began his march. By now the roads were troughs of mud, which made for heavy going: so heavy, indeed, that it was 4 o'clock in the afternoon by the time the lead elements of the Second Corps plodded into Fairfield, only nine miles from the now de-serted ridge just west of Gettysburg. Part of the delay was caused by free-swinging Union troopers, who got among the trains and captured a number of wagons, together with their guards and drivers. Old Bald Head was so outraged by this development that he was for facing about and fighting, then and there. But Lee would not agree. "No, no, General Ewell," he said; "we must let those people alone for the present. We will try them again some other time." Hill and Longstreet, well beyond Fair-field before sundown, had no such difficulties. The latter, in fact, was in high good spirits when he called a halt that evening, conveniently near a roadside tavern where his staff had arranged for dinner to be served. Apparently the troops outside were getting theirs, too, for in the course of the meal there was a sound of scuffling in the adjoining chamber, followed by the appearance of a hard-faced farmwife who pushed her way into the dining room, exclaiming as she advanced: "Which is the General? Where is the great officer? Good heavens, they are killing our fat hogs! Our milk cows now are going!" On the march northward, such a complaint would have brought sudden and heavy reprisal on the offenders, but not now. "Yes, Madam," Old Peter told her, shaking his head in disapproval, "it's very sad; very sad. And this sort of thing has been going on in Virginia for more than two years. Very sad."

He took over the lead from Hill next day, July 6, and though the rain continued to fall and the mud to deepen, the men stepped out smartly once they were clear of Monterey Pass and beyond South Mountain. "Let him who will say it to the contrary," a Texan wrote home, "we made Manassas time from Pennsylvania." At 5 p.m. Longstreet entered Hagerstown, and Lee, who rode with him as usual, was relieved to learn that the train of wounded had passed through earlier that day and should have reached the Potomac by now, half a dozen miles away. Imboden had made good speed with his 17-mile-long column, though at the cost of much suffering by the wounded, whose piteous cries to be left by the road to die were ignored by the drivers in obedience to orders that there were to be no halts for any reason whatever, by day or night. Many of the injured men had been without food for thirty-six hours, he later wrote, and "their torn and bloody clothing, matted and hardened, was rasping the tender, inflamed, and still oozing wounds. Very few of the wagons had even a layer of straw in them, and all were without springs.... From nearly every wagon as the teams trotted on, urged by whip and shout, came such cries and shrieks as these: 'Oh, God! Why can't I die?' 'My God, will no one have mercy and kill me?' 'Stop! Oh, for God's sake, stop just for one minute; take me out and let me die on the roadside!' 'I am dying, I am dying!' ... During this one night," the cavalryman added, "I realized more of the horrors of war than I had in all the two preceding years." Bypassing Chambersburg in the darkness, the lead escort regiment rode through Greencastle at dawn, and when the troopers were a mile beyond the town, which had offered no resistance at all in the course of the march north the week before, some thirty or forty citizens rushed out of their houses and "attacked the train with axes, cutting the spokes out of ten or a dozen wheels and dropping the wagons in the streets." Imboden sent a detachment of troopers back, and this put an end to the trouble there. Beyond Hagerstown, however, the Union cavalry appeared in strength from Frederick and began to harass the column. At Williamsport, finding the pontoon bridge destroyed by raiders from downstream on the opposite bank, Imboden called a halt and deployed his men and vehicles in the style employed by wagon trains when attacked by Indians on the plains. Arming his drivers with spare rifles and placing his 23 guns at regular intervals along the half-circle of wagons, he faced northeast, the river at his back, and managed to hold off the attackers until Fitz Lee arrived and drove them away.

The army commander got there the following morning, still riding with Longstreet at the head of the infantry column, and though he was pleased to learn that Imboden and his nephew Fitz had staved off the immediate threat by the blue horsemen, who had greatly outnumbered the defenders until now, he could see for himself that his predicament, here on the north bank of the river he had marched so hard to reach, was worse by far than the one in which he had found himself three days ago at Gettysburg, after the failure of his final attempt to break the Union fishhook. Not only was the pontoon bridge destroyed, but the recent torrential rains had swollen the Potomac well past fording. Low on food, as well as ammunition for its guns, the army was cut off from Virginia, together with its prisoners and its wounded. Lee's first thought was for these last; he directed that all the ferryboats in the region were to be collected and used in transporting the injured men to the south bank; the wagons, like the infantry and the artillery, would have to wait until the river subsided or the bridge could be rebuilt. Meanwhile, if Meade attacked, the Confederates, with small chance to maneuver and none at all to retreat, would have to give him battle under conditions whereby victory would yield but little profit and defeat would mean annihilation.

Accordingly, the engineers began their task of laying out a system of defense that extended some three miles in each direction, upstream and down from Williamsport, where in normal times a man could wade across. Both of its extremities well covered, the six-mile curve of line was anchored north on Conococheague Creek and south on the Potomac below Falling Waters, the site of the wrecked bridge. As at Gettysburg, Hill took the center and Ewell and Longstreet the left and right — they had by now about 35,000 effectives between them, including the cannoneers whose limber chests were nearly empty — while Stuart's troopers reinforced the flanks and patrolled the front. By next day, July 8, the dispositions were complete, though the men continued to improve them with their shovels, and Lee received the welcome news that ammunition for his guns was on the way from Winchester; it would arrive tomorrow and could be brought across by the ferries already hard at work transporting the wounded to the Virginia bank. Foam-flecked and swollen, the river was still on the boom, however, farther than ever past fording and with no decrease predicted. So far, Meade's infantry had not appeared, but Lee did not believe it would be long in coming — and in strength much greater than his own. He kept up a show of calmness, despite a precarious shortage of food and the personal strain of having been informed that his son Rooney, taken to Hanover County to recover from his Brandy Station wound, had been captured by raiders and hauled off to Fort Monroe, where he was being held as a hostage to insure the safety of some Federal prisoners charged with various crimes against the people of the Old Dominion. Despite the fret of such distractions, Lee wrote that night to the President, proposing once more that Beauregard's "army in effigy" march at once for the Rappahannock and thus create a diversion in his favor through this anxious time of waiting for the Potomac to subside.

"I hope Your Excellency will understand that I am not in the least discouraged," he added, somewhat apologetic over this second appeal for help from outside his department, "or that my faith in the protection of an all-merciful Providence, or in the fortitude of this army, is at all shaken. But, though conscious that the enemy has been much shattered in the recent battle, I am aware that he can be easily reinforced, while no addition can be made to our numbers. The measure, therefore, that I have recommended is altogether one of a prudential nature."

Learning from scouts the following evening that the Federal main body was on the march from Frederick, he was convinced that his army would soon have to fight for its survival, which in turn meant the survival of the Confederacy itself. In this extremity he occupied himself with the inspection and improvement of his defenses, the distribution of the newly arrived ammunition for his batteries, and the nerving of his troops for the shock he believed was coming. Though the river continued to rise in his rear and food and forage were getting scarcer by the hour — the men were now on half rations and the horses were getting nothing to eat but grass and standing grain — he kept up a show of confidence and good cheer. Only those who knew him best detected his extreme concern: Alexander, for example, who later testified that he had never seen his chief so deeply anxious as he appeared on July 10, one week after the guns of Gettysburg stopped roaring. This did not show, however, in a dispatch the general sent Davis that night from his still bridgeless six-mile bridgehead on the north bank of the still unfordable Potomac. "With the blessing of Heaven," he told the President, "I trust that the courage and fortitude of the army will be found sufficient to relieve us from the embarrassment caused by the unlooked-for natural difficulties of our situation, if not to secure more valuable and substantial results. Very respectfully, your obedient servant, R. E. LEE."

In all this time, Sunday through Saturday, no two opposing infantrymen had looked at one another along the barrels of their rifles, and the source of this week-long lethargy on the part of those who should have been pursuers lay in the make-up of the man who led them. His caution, which had given the blue army its first undeniable large-scale victory to balance against the five major defeats it had suffered under as many different leaders in the past two years, was more enlarged than reduced by the discovery, on the morning of July 5, that the Confederates were no longer in position on the ridge across the way; so that while the first half of Lee's prediction — "General Meade will commit no blunder on my front" — had been fulfilled, the second half — "If I make one, he will make haste to take advantage of it" — had not. Not that there was no occasion for this increase of caution. The defenders had suffered heavily in the three-day conflict, particularly in the loss of men of rank. Schimmelfennig, who emerged from his woodshed hiding place when Gettysburg was reoccupied on the 4th, was meager compensation for the sixteen brigade and division commanders killed or wounded in the battle, let alone for the three corps commanders who had fallen. Besides, avoidance of risk having gained him so much so far, Meade had no intention of abandoning that policy simply because the winds of chance appeared to have shifted in his favor for the moment.

Whether they had in fact shifted, or had merely been made to seem to, was by no means certain. Lee was foxy, as Meade well knew from old acquaintance. He was known to be most dangerous when he appeared least so: particularly in retreat, as McClellan had discovered while pursuing him under similar circumstances, back in September, after presuming to have taken his measure at South Mountain. Moreover, he was not above tampering with the weather vane, and there was evidence that such was the case at present. Francis Barlow, who had been wounded and captured on the opening day of battle while commanding one of Howard's overrun divisions north of town, was left behind in Gettysburg when the rebels withdrew to their ridge on the night of July 3. He got word to headquarters next morning that Lee's plan, as he had overheard it from his sick-bed, was to feign retreat, then waylay his pursuers. Meade took the warning much to heart and contented himself that afternoon, at the height of the sudden rainstorm, with issuing a congratulatory order to the troops "for the glorious result of the recent operations." That those operations had not ended was evident to all, for the graybacks were still on Seminary Ridge, less than a mile across the rain-swept valley. "Our task is not yet accomplished," the order acknowledged, "and the commanding general looks to the army for greater efforts to drive from our soil every vestige of the presence of the invader."

It was read to all regiments that evening. In one, when the reading was over, the colonel waved his hat and called for three cheers for Meade. But the men were strangely silent. This was not because they had no use for their new chief, one of them afterwards observed; it was simply because they did not feel like cheering, either for him or for anyone else, rain or no rain. Many of them had been engaged all day in burying the dead and bringing in the wounded of both armies, and this was scarcely the kind of work that put them in the frame of mind for tossing caps and shouting hurrahs. Mostly though, as the man explained, the veterans, "with their lights and experiences, could not see the wisdom or the occasion for any such manifestation of enthusiasm." They had done a great deal of cheering over the past two years, for Hooker and Burnside and Pope and McDowell, as well as for Little Mac, and in the course of time they had matured; or as this witness put it, their "business sense increased with age." Someday, perhaps, there would be a reason for tossing their caps completely away and cheering themselves hoarse, but this did not seem to them to be quite it. So they remained silent, watching the colonel swing his hat for a while, then glumly put it back on his head and dismiss them.

That evening the corps commanders voted five to two to hold their present ground until it was certain that Lee was retreating. Next morning — Sunday: Meade had been just one week in command — they found that he was indeed gone, but there was doubt as to whether he was retreating or maneuvering for a better position from which to renew the contest. Sedgwick moved out in the afternoon, only to bog down in the mud, and fog was so heavy the following morning that he could determine nothing except that the Confederates had reached Monterey Pass, southwest of Fairfield. "As soon as possible," Meade wired Halleck, "I will cross South Mountain and proceed in search of the enemy." On second thought, however, and always bearing in mind his instructions to "maneuver and fight in such a manner as to cover the capital and Baltimore," he decided that his best course would be to avoid a direct pursuit, which might necessitate a costly storming of the pass, and instead march south into Maryland, then westward in an attempt to come up with Lee before he effected a crossing near Williamsburg, where French's raiders had wrecked the pontoon bridge the day before. In Frederick by noon of July 7, fifty-odd hours after finding that his opponent had stolen away from his front under cover of darkness, the northern commander indulged himself in the luxury of a hot bath in a hotel and put on fresh clothes for the first time in ten days. This afforded him considerable relief, but it also provided a chance for him to discover how profoundly tired he was. "From the time I took command till to-day," he wrote his wife, "I . . . have not had a regular night's rest, and many nights not a wink of sleep, and for several days did not even wash my face and hands, no regular food, and all the time in a state of mental anxiety. Indeed, I think I have lived as much in this time as in the last thirty years."

The men, of course, were in far worse shape from their exertions. Four of the seven corps had been shot almost to pieces, and some of the survivors had trouble recognizing their outfits, so unequal had been the losses in the various commands, including more than 300 field and company grade officers lost by the quick subtractive action of shells and bullets and clubbed muskets. III Corps veterans, who were among the hardest hit in this respect, sardonically referred to themselves as "the III Corps as we understand it." Their uniforms were in tatters and their long marches through dust and mud, to and from the three-day uproar, had quite literally worn the shoes off their feet. Meade's regular army soul was pained to see them, though the pain was salved considerably by a wire received that afternoon from Halleck: "It gives me pleasure to inform you that you have been appointed a brigadier general in the Regular Army, to rank from July 3, the date of your brilliant victory." This welcome message was followed however by two more from Old Brains that were not so welcome, suggesting as they did a lack of confidence in his aggressive qualities. "Push forward and fight Lee before he can cross the Potomac," one directed, while the other was more specific: "You have given the enemy a stunning blow at Gettysburg. Follow it up, and give him another before he can reach the Potomac. . . . There is strong evidence that he is short of artillery ammunition, and if vigorously pressed he must suffer." Meade wanted it understood that the suffering was unlikely to be as one-sided as his superior implied. He too was having his troubles and he wanted them known to those above him, who presumed to hand down judgments from a distance. "My army is assembling slowly," he replied, still in Frederick on July 8. "The rains of yesterday and last night have made all roads but pikes almost impassable. Artillery and wagons are stalled; it will take time to collect them together. A large portion of the men are barefooted. . . . I expect to find the enemy in a strong position, well covered with artillery, and I do not desire to imitate his example at Gettysburg and assault a position where the chances were so greatly against success. I wish in advance to moderate the expectations of those who, in ignorance of the difficulties to be encountered, may expect too much. All that I can do under the circumstances I pledge this army to do."

Apparently Halleck did not like the sound of this, for he replied within the hour: "There is reliable information that the enemy is crossing at Williamsport. The opportunity to attack his divided forces should not be lost. The President is urgent and anxious that your army should move against him by forced marches." Meade had not heard a word from Lincoln, either of thanks for his recent victory or of encouragement in his present exertions, and now there was this indirect expression of a lack of confidence. Forced marches! The Pennsylvanian bristled. "My army is and has been making forced marches, short of rations and barefooted," he wired back, pointing out in passing that the information as to a rebel crossing differed from his own, and added: "I take occasion to repeat that I will use my utmost efforts to push forward this army." Old Brains protested that he had been misconceived. "Do not understand me as expressing any dissatisfaction," he replied; "on the contrary, your army has done most nobly. I only wish to give you opinions formed from information received here." But having entered this disclaimer he returned to his former tone, ignoring Meade's denial that any appreciable part of the rebel force had crossed the Potomac, either at Williamsport or elsewhere. "If Lee's army is so divided by the river," he persisted, "the importance of attacking the part on this side is incalculable. Such an opportunity may never occur again.... You will have forces sufficient to render your victory certain. My only fear now is that the enemy may escape."

At Middletown on July 9, having replaced Butterfield with Humphreys as chief of staff and thus got rid of the last reminder of Hooker's luckless tenure, Meade was pleased that no rain had fallen since early the day before. Though the Potomac remained some five feet above its normal level and therefore well past fording, the roads were drying fast and permitted better marching. Moreover, Halleck was keeping his word as to reinforcements. The army had 85,000 men present for duty and 10,000 more on the way, which meant that its Gettysburg losses had been made good, although a number of short-term militia and grass-green conscripts were included. "This army is moving in three columns," Meade informed Halleck before midday, "the right column hav-

ing in it three corps.... I think the decisive battle of the war will be fought in a few days. In view of the momentous consequences, I desire to adopt such measures as in my judgment will tend to insure success, even though these may be deemed tardy." Delighted to hear that Meade was in motion again, however tardy, the general-in-chief was careful to say nothing that might cause him to stop and resume the telegraphic argument. "Do not be influenced by any dispatch from here against your own judgment," he told him. "Regard them as suggestions only. Our information here is not always correct." In point of fact, now that contact seemed imminent, it was Old Brains who was urging caution. More troops were on the way, he wired next day, and he advised waiting for them. "I think it will be best for you to postpone a general battle till you can concentrate all your forces and get up your reserves and reinforcements.... Beware of partial combats. Bring up and hurl upon the enemy all your forces, good and bad."

Meade agreed. He spent the next two days, which continued fair, examining the curved shield of Lee's defenses and jockeying for a position from which to "hurl" his army upon them. By early afternoon of

July 12 — Sunday again: he now had been two full weeks in command — he was ready, though the skies again were threatening rain. Selected divisions from the II, V, and VI Corps confronted a rebel-held wheat field, pickets out, awaiting the signal to go forward, when a Pennsylvania chaplain rode up to the command post and protested the violation of the Sabbath. Couldn't the battle be fought as well tomorrow? he demanded. For once Meade kept his temper, challenged thus by a home-state man of the cloth, and explained somewhat elaborately that he was like a carpenter with a contract to construct a box, four sides and the bottom of which had been completed; now the lid was ready to be put on. The chaplain was unimpressed. "As God's agent and disciple I solemnly protest," he declared fervently. "I will show you that the Almighty will not permit you to desecrate his sacred day.... Look at the heavens; see the threatening storm approaching!" Whereupon there were sudden peals of thunder and zigzags of lightning, as in a passage from the Old Testament, and rain began to pour down on the wheat field and the troops who were about to move against it. Meade canceled the probing action, returned to his quarters, and got off a wire to Halleck. "It is my intention to attack them tomorrow," he wrote; but then — perhaps with the chaplain's demonstration in mind — he added, "unless something intervenes to prevent it."

So he said. But a council of war he called that evening showed that his chief subordinates were opposed to launching any attack without a further examination of Lee's position. Only Wadsworth, commanding the I Corps in the absence of Newton, who was sick, agreed with Meade wholeheartedly in favoring an assault, although Howard, anxious as always to retrieve a damaged reputation, expressed a willingness to go along with the plan. Despite reports that the Potomac was falling rapidly after four days of fair weather, Meade deferred to the judgment of five of his seven corps commanders, postponed the scheduled advance, and spent the next day conducting a further study of the rebel dispositions. Informing Halleck of the outcome of the council of war, he told him: "I shall continue these reconnaissances with the expectation of finding some weak point upon which, if I succeed, I shall hazard an attack." Old Brains was prompt to reply that he disapproved of such flinching now that the two armies were once more face to face. "You are strong enough to attack and defeat the enemy before he can effect a crossing," he wired. "Act upon your own judgment and make your generals execute your orders. Call no council of war. It is proverbial that councils of war never fight. Reinforcements are pushed on as rapidly as possible. Do not let the enemy escape."

It was plain that the advice as to councils of war amounted to an attempt to lock the stable after the pony had been stolen. And so too did the rest of it, as the thing turned out. When Meade at last went forward next morning, July 14, he found the rebel trenches empty and all but a rear-guard handful of graybacks already on the far bank of the Potomac. Aside from a number of stragglers picked up in the rush, together with two mud-stalled guns — the only ones Lee lost in the whole campaign — attacks on the remnant merely served to hasten the final stages of the crossing, after which the delivered Confederates cut their rebuilt pontoon bridge loose from the Maryland shore and looked mockingly back across the swirling waters, which were once more on the rise as a result of the two-day rainstorm the chaplain had invoked.

Meade was not greatly disappointed, or at any rate he did not seem so in a dispatch informing Halleck of Lee's escape before it had even been completed. The closing sentence was downright bland: "Your instructions as to further movements, in case the enemy are entirely across the river, are desired."

For Lee, threatened in front by twice his number and menaced within the perimeter by starvation, the past three days had been touch and go, all the time with the receding but still swollen Potomac mocking his efforts to escape. In the end it was Jackson's old quartermaster, Major John Harman, who managed the army's extraction and landed it safe on the soil of Virginia, having improvised pontoons by tearing down abandoned houses for their timbers and floating the finished products down to Falling Waters, where they were linked and floored; "a good bridge," Lee called the result, and though a more critical staff officer termed it a "crazy affair," it served its purpose. Its planks overlaid with lopped branches to deaden the sound of wheels and boots, it not only permitted the secret withdrawal of the guns and wagons in the darkness; it also made possible the dry-shod crossing of the two corps under Longstreet and Hill, while Ewell managed to use the ford at Williamsport, his tallest men standing in midstream, armpit deep, to pass the shorter waders along. By dawn the Second Corps was over, but the First and Third were still waiting for the trains to clear the bridge. At last they did, and Longstreet crossed without interference, followed by Hill's lead division: at which point guns began to roar.

"There!" Lee exclaimed, turning his head sharply in the direction of the sound. "I was expecting it — the beginning of the attack."

He soon learned, however, that Heth, who had recovered from his head injury and returned to the command of his division, had faced his men about and was holding off the attackers while Hill's center division completed the crossing; whereupon Heth turned and followed, fighting as he went. It was smartly done. Despite an official boast by Kilpatrick that he captured a 1500-man Confederate brigade, only about 300 stragglers failed to make it over the river before the bridge was cut loose from the northern bank, and the loss of the two stalled guns, while regrettable, was more than made up for by the seven that had been taken in Pennsylvania and brought back. Another loss was more grievous.

On Heth's return to duty, Johnston Pettigrew had resumed command
of what was left of his brigade, which served this morning as rear guard.
He had his men in line, awaiting his turn at the bridge, when suddenly
they were charged by a group of about forty Union cavalrymen who
were thought at first to be Confederates brandishing a captured flag, so
foolhardy was their attack. Pettigrew, one of whose arms was still weak
from his Seven Pines wound, while the other was in a sling because of
the hand that had been hit at Gettysburg, was tossed from his startled
horse. He picked himself up and calmly directed the firing at the blue
troopers, who were dashing about and banging away with their carbines. Eventually all of them were killed — which made it difficult to
substantiate or disprove the claim that they were drunk — but meantime
one took a position on the flank and fired so effectively that the general
himself drew his revolver and went after him in person. Determined to
get so close he could not miss, Pettigrew was shot in the stomach before
he came within easy pistol range. He made it over the bridge, refusing
to be left behind as a prisoner, and lived for three days of intense suffering before he died at Bunker Hill, Virginia, the tenth general permanently lost to the army in the course of the invasion. The whole South
mourned him, especially his native North Carolina, and Lee referred to
him in his report as "an officer of great merit and promise."

Saddened by this last-minute sacrifice of a gallant fighter, but
grateful for its delivery from immediate peril, the army continued its
march that day and the next to Bunker Hill, twenty miles from the Potomac, and there it went into camp, as Lee reported, for rest and recruit-
ment. "The men are in good health and spirits," he informed Richmond,
"but want shoes and clothing badly. . . . As soon as these necessary arti-
cles are obtained we shall be prepared to resume operations." That he
was still feeling aggressive, despite the setback he had suffered, was
shown by his reaction on July 16 to information that the enemy was
preparing to cross the river at Harpers Ferry. "Should he follow us in
this direction," Lee wrote Davis, "I shall lead him up the Valley and endeavor to attack him as far from his base as possible."

Meade's exchanges with his government, following his laconic
report of a rebel getaway, were of a different nature. Halleck was
plainly miffed. "I need hardly say to you," he wired, "that the escape of
Lee's army without another battle has created great dissatisfaction in
the mind of the President, and it will require an active and energetic
pursuit on your part to remove the impression that it has not been
sufficiently active before." This was altogether more than Meade could
take, particularly from Lincoln, who still had sent him no word of appreciation or encouragement, by way of reward for the first great victory in the East, but only second-hand expressions of doubt and disappointment. The Pennsylvanian stood on his dignity and made the
strongest protest within his means. "Having performed my duty con-

scientiously and to the best of my ability," he declared, "the censure of the President conveyed in your dispatch . . . is, in my judgment, so undeserved that I feel compelled most respectfully to ask to be immediately relieved from the command of this army." There Halleck had it, and Lincoln too. They could either refrain from such goadings or let the victorious general depart. Moreover, Meade strengthened his case with a follow-up wire, sent half an hour later, in which he passed along Kilpatrick's exuberant if erroneous report of capturing a whole rebel brigade on the near bank of the Potomac. Old Brains promptly backtracked, as he always seemed to do when confronted with vigorous opposition from anyone, blue or gray, except Joe Hooker. "My telegram, stating the disappointment of the President at the escape of Lee's army, was not intended as a censure," he replied, "but as a stimulus to an active pursuit. It is not deemed a sufficient cause for your application to be relieved."

In the end Meade withdrew his resignation, or at any rate did not insist that it be accepted, and on July 17, 18, and 19 — the last date was a Sunday: he now had been three weeks in command — he crossed the Potomac at Harpers Ferry and Berlin, half a dozen miles downstream, complying with his instructions to conduct "an active and energetic pursuit," although he was convinced that such a course was overrisky. "The proper policy for the government would have been to be contented with driving Lee out of Maryland," he wrote his wife, "and not to have advanced till this army was largely reinforced and reorganized and put on such a footing that its advance was sure to be successful." In point of fact, however, he had already been "largely reinforced." His aggregate present on July 20 was 105,623 men, including some 13,500 troopers, while Lee on that same date, exclusive of about 9000 cavalry, had a total of 50,178, or barely more than half as many infantry and cannoneers as were moving against him. Confronted with the danger of being cut off from Richmond, he abandoned his plan for drawing the enemy up the valley and instead moved eastward through Chester Gap. On July 21 — the second anniversary of First Manassas, whose twice-fought-over field lay only some thirty miles beyond the crest of the Blue Ridge — Federal lookouts reported dust clouds rising; the rebels were on the march. Lee reached Culpeper two days later, and Meade, conforming, shifted to Warrenton, from which point he sent a cavalry and infantry column across the Rappahannock on the last night of the month. Gray horsemen opposed the advance, but Lee, aware of the odds against him and unwilling to take the further risk of remaining within the V of the two rivers, decided to fall back beyond the Rapidan. This was accomplished by August 4, ending the sixty days of marching and fighting which comprised the Gettysburg campaign. Both armies were back at their approximate starting points, and Meade did not pursue.

He had at last received from Washington the accolade that had been withheld so long, though the gesture still was not from Lincoln. "Take it altogether," Halleck wrote, "your short campaign has proved your superior generalship, and you merit, as you will receive, the confidence of the government and the gratitude of your country." But Meade had already disclaimed such praise from other sources. "The papers are making a great deal too much fuss about me," he wrote home. "I claim no extraordinary merit for this last battle, and would prefer waiting a little while to see what my career is to be before making any pretensions.... I never claimed a victory," he explained, "though I stated that Lee was defeated in his efforts to destroy my army." Thin-skinned and testy as he was, he found it hard to abide the pricks he received from his superiors. He doubted, indeed, whether he was "sufficiently phlegmatic" for the leadership of an army which he now perceived was commanded from Washington, and he confided to his wife that he would esteem it the best of favors if Lincoln would replace him with someone else. Who that someone might be he did not say, but he could scarcely have recommended any of his present subordinates, whose lack of energy he deplored. Most of all, he missed his fellow Pennsylvanians, the dead Reynolds and the convalescing Hancock. "Their places are not to be supplied," he said.

With nine of his best generals gone for good, and eight more out with wounds of various depth and gravity, Lee had even greater cause for sadness. Just now, though, his energies were mainly confined to refitting his army, preparing it for a continuation of the struggle he had sought to end with one hard blow, and incidentally in putting down a spirit of contention among his hot-tempered subordinates as to where the blame for the recent defeat should go. Few were as frank as Ewell, who presently told a friend that "it took a dozen blunders to lose Gettysburg and [I] committed a good many of them," or as selfless as Longstreet, who wrote to a kinsman shortly after the battle: "As General Lee is our commander, he should have the support and influence we can give him. If the blame, if there is any, can be shifted from him to me, I shall help him and our cause by taking it. I desire, therefore, that all the responsibility that can be put upon me shall go there, and shall remain there." Later he would vigorously decline the very chance he said he hoped for, but that was in the after years, where there was no longer any question of sustaining either the army commander or the cause. Others not only declined it now but were quick to point out just where they thought the blame should rest: Pickett, for instance, whose report was highly critical of the other units involved in the charge tradition would give his name to. Lee returned the document to him with the suggestion that it be destroyed, together with all copies. "You and your men have covered yourselves with glory," he told him, "but we have the enemy to fight and must carefully, at this critical moment, guard against dissensions which the reflections in your report would create. . . . I hope all will yet be well."

His own critique of the battle, from the Confederate point of view, was given five years later to a man who was contemplating a school history. Referring the writer to the official accounts, Lee avoided personalities entirely. "Its loss was occasioned by a combination of circumstances," he declared. "It was commenced in the absence of correct intelligence. It was continued in the effort to overcome the difficulties by which we were surrounded, and [a success] would have been gained could one determined and united blow have been delivered by our whole line. As it was, victory trembled in the balance for three days, and the battle resulted in the infliction of as great an amount of injury as was received and in frustrating the Federal campaign for the season." Reticent by nature in such matters, he was content to let it go at that, except for once when he was out riding with a friend. Then he did speak of personalities, or anyhow one personality. "If I had had Stonewall Jackson with me," he said, looking out over the peaceful fields, "so far as man can see, I should have won the battle of Gettysburg."

That was still in the future, however. For the present he reserved his praise for the men who had been there. "The army did all it could," he told one of his numerous cousins in late July. "I fear I required of it impossibilities. But it responded to the call nobly and cheerfully, and though it did not win a victory it conquered a success. We must now prepare for harder blows and harder work."

❊　2　❊

Having failed in his effort to "conquer a peace" by defeating the principal Union army north of its capital, Lee had failed as well in his secondary purpose, which had been to frighten the Washington authorities into withdrawing Grant and Banks from their strangle-hold positions around Vicksburg and Port Hudson, thereby delivering from danger not only those two critical locations but also the great river that ran between them, the loss of which would cut the South in two. But Lee's was not the only attempt to forestall that disaster. In addition to Joe Johnston, whose primary assignment it was, Kirby Smith too had plans for the relief of Pemberton and Gardner, on whose survival depended his hope of remaining an integral part of the Confederacy. Though these included nothing so ambitious as an intention to end the war with a single long-odds stab at the enemy's vitals, they were at least still in the course of execution when Pickett's and Pettigrew's men came stumbling back from Cemetery Ridge, leaving the bodies of their comrades to indicate the high-water mark of Lee's campaign, which now was on the

ebb. Nor were these Transmississippi plans without the element of boldness. Encouraged by Magruder's success in clearing Texas of all trace
of the invader, Smith hoped his other two major generals, Holmes in
Arkansas and Taylor in West Louisiana, might accomplish as much in
their departments. If so, he might attain the aforementioned secondary
purpose of causing the Federal high command to detach troops from
Grant and Banks, in an attempt to recover what had been lost across the
river from their respective positions, and thus lighten the pressure on
Vicksburg and Port Hudson. At any rate Smith thought it worth a
try, and in mid-June, being frantically urged by Richmond to adopt
some such course of action — Davis and Seddon by then had begun losing
confidence that anything was going to come of their increasingly stri-
dent appeals to Johnston along those lines — he instructed Taylor and
Holmes to make the effort.

Taylor, who had just returned disgruntled to Alexandria after
his strike at Milliken's Bend — a tactical success, at least until Porter's
gunboats hove onto the scene, but a strategic failure, since the objective
turned out to be little more than a training camp for the Negro recruits
Grant had enlisted off the plantations roundabout — was pleased to be
ordered back onto what he considered the right track, which led down
to New Orleans. His plan, as he had outlined it before the fruitless excursion opposite Vicksburg, was to descend the Teche and the Atchafalaya, recapture Berwick Bay and overrun the Bayou Lafourche region,
which lay between Grand Lake and the Mississippi, deep in Banks's rear,
interrupting that general's communications with New Orleans and threatening the city itself; whereupon Banks would be obliged to raise his
siege of Port Hudson in order to save New Orleans, whose 200,000 citizens he knew to be hostile to his occupation, and Gardner then could
march out to join Johnston for an attack on Grant's rear and the quick
delivery of beleaguered Vicksburg. Such at least were Taylor's calculations — or more properly speaking, his hopes; for his resources were
admittedly slim for so ambitious a project. He had at Alexandria three
small cavalry regiments just arrived from Texas under Colonel J. P.
Major, a twenty-seven-year-old Missouri-born West Pointer whose
peacetime army career had included service in Albert Sidney Johnston's
2d Cavalry, which already had provided the South with eight and
the North with two of their leading generals. Awaiting instructions on
the upper Teche, to which they had returned in the wake of Banks's
withdrawal in mid-May, were five more such mounted regiments under
Thomas Green, the Valverde hero who had been promoted to brigadier
for his share in the New Year's triumph at Galveston, along with three
regiments of Louisiana infantry under Brigadier General Alfred Mouton, thirty-four years old and a West Pointer, a Shiloh veteran and native of nearby Vermilionville, son of the former governor and brother-
in-law to Frank Gardner, whose rescue was the object of the campaign.

The combined strength of the three commands was about 4000 effectives, barely one tenth of the force available to Banks, but Taylor intended to make up in boldness for what he lacked in numbers.

The advance was made in two widely divided columns. While Mouton and Green swung down the west bank of the Teche, marching unopposed through Opelousas and New Iberia, Taylor rode with Major across the Atchafalaya, then down Bayou Fordoche to within earshot of the guns of Port Hudson. At that point he left him, on June 18, with orders to move rapidly to the rear of Brashear City, the objective upon which the two forces were to converge for a simultaneous attack five days later. The distance was one hundred miles, entirely through occupied territory, but Major made it on schedule. Skirmishing briefly that afternoon with the bluecoats on guard at Plaquemine, a west-bank landing below Baton Rouge, he bypassed fortified Donaldsonville after nightfall and set off next morning down Bayou Lafourche, which left the Mississippi just above the town. Some thirty miles below on the 20th, he rode into Thibodaux, whose garrison had fled at the news of his approach, and next day he struck the railroad at Terrebonne, thirty miles east of Brashear, then turned due west to complete his share of the convergence Taylor had designed. Moving crosscountry with relays of quick-stepping mules hitched to his ambulance, that general had joined Mouton and Green on their unopposed march through Franklin to Fort Bisland. By nightfall of June 22 they were at Berwick and were poised for an amphibious attack, having brought with them a weird collection of "small boats, skiffs, flats, even sugar-coolers," which they had gathered for this purpose during their descent of the Teche. Batteries were laid under cover of darkness for a surprise bombardment in support of the scheduled dawn assault on the Brashear fortifications, just eastward across the narrow bay. Taylor's old commander in the Shenandoah Valley doubtless would have been proud to see how well his pupil, whose preparatory work had been done not at West Point but at Yale, had learned the value of well-laid plans when the object was the capture or destruction of an enemy force in occupation of a fixed position.

Old Jack's pride would have swelled even more next morning, when the Louisianian gathered the fruits of his boldness and careful planning. While some 300 dismounted Texans manned the 53 boats of his improvised flotilla — it was fortunate that there was no wind, Taylor said later, for the slightest disturbance would have swamped them — Green's cannoneers stood to their pieces. At first light they opened fire, and as they did so the sea-going troopers swarmed ashore, encouraged by the echoing boom of Major's guns from the east. Flustered by the sudden bombardment, which seemed to erupt out of nowhere, and by the unexpected assault from both directions, front and rear, the blue defenders milled about briefly, then surrendered. The take was great, for here at the western terminus of the railroad Banks had cached the ordnance and quartermaster supplies he intended to use in his planned return up the Teche and the Red. In addition to 1700 prisoners, a dozen heavy-caliber guns and 5000 new-style Burnside repeaters and Enfield rifles were captured, together with two locomotives and their cars, which were unable to get away eastward because Major had wrecked the bridge at Lafourche Crossing, and commissary and medical stores in such abundance that they brought to more than $2,000,000 the estimated profit from Taylor's well-engineered strike. The general's pleasure was as great as that of his men, who wasted no time before sitting down to gorge themselves on the spoils. Their main concern was food, but his was the acquisition of the implements with which to continue his resistance to the invasion of his homeland. "For the first time since I reached western Louisiana," he exulted afterwards, "I had supplies."

All in all, it was the largest haul any body of Confederates had made since Stonewall followed up his raid on Manassas Junction with the capture of Harpers Ferry, back in September. Like his mentor, however, Taylor did not allow his exultation to delay his plans for the further discomfiture of his adversary. Next morning, leaving one regiment to sort the booty and remove it to Alexandria for safekeeping, he pressed on north and east, once more in two columns. While Green and Major marched for Donaldsonville, near which they were to establish batteries for the purpose of disrupting traffic on the Mississippi and thus sever the main line of supply and communications available to the besiegers of Port Hudson, Mouton's infantry went by rail to Thibodaux, from which point he sent pickets down the line to Bayou des Allemands, within twenty-five miles of New Orleans. It was during the early morning hours of June 28 that Taylor encountered his first setback, though not in person. Approaching Donaldsonville the night before, Green had meant to bypass it, as Major had done on his way south, but the existence of an earthwork at the junction of the Lafourche and the Mississippi proved irresistible, perhaps in part because the Yankees had given it a hated name: Fort Butler. He disposed 800 dismounted troopers for attack and sent them forward two hours before dawn. The result was a bloody repulse, administered by the 225 defenders and three gunboats that arrived in time to support them. Green, who had suffered 261 casualties and inflicted only 24, pulled back, chagrined, and went about his proper business of establishing his three batteries on the west bank of the river, some ten miles below the town. He opened fire on July 7 and for three days not only kept the Mississippi closed to transports and unarmored supply boats, but also sent out mounted patrols as far downstream as Kenner, barely a dozen miles from the heart of New Orleans, which was already in a turmoil of expectancy as a result of Mouton's continued presence at Thibodaux and nearby Bayou des Allemands.

Secessionists were joyously predicting the imminent entry of the graybacks who were knocking at the gates, and William Emory, with fewer than 1000 men to oppose a rebel host he reckoned at 13,000, was altogether in agreement that the place was the Confederacy's for the taking. What was more, as we have seen already, he had said as much to Banks. "It is a choice between Port Hudson and New Orleans," he informed him on July 4, adding: "You can only save this city by sending me reinforcements immediately and at any cost." Dick Taylor thus had accomplished the preliminary objective of his campaign; that is, he had brought the pressure he intended upon Banks, who now would be obliged to withdraw from Port Hudson, permitting Gardner to join Johnston for the delivery of Pemberton by means of an attack on Grant's intrenchments from the rear. So much Taylor had planned or anyhow hoped for. But Banks, as we have also seen, refused to cooperate in the completion of the grand design. If New Orleans fell, he told Halleck, he would retake it once the business at hand was completed and his army was free to be used for that purpose; but meantime he would hang on at Port Hudson till it surrendered, no matter what disasters threatened his rear. Observing this perverse reaction, Taylor was obliged to admit that once again, as at Milliken's Bend a month ago, though his tactics had been successful his strategy had failed. He had gained much in his brief campaign — particularly at Brashear City, whose spoils would greatly strengthen his future ability to resist the blue invaders — but he had not accomplished the recapture of New Orleans, which he saw as a cul-de-sac to be avoided, or the raising of the siege at Port Hudson.

Theophilus Holmes, though neither as energetic nor as inventive as Zachary Taylor's son and Stonewall Jackson's pupil, was also under compunction to do something toward relieving their hemmed-in friends across the way. Since the turn of the year, when Marmaduke made his successful raid into Missouri, burning the Springfield supply base and bringing a hornetlike swarm of guerillas out of the brush and canebrakes, all the elderly North Carolinian had attempted in this regard was a repeat performance by that same general in late April, this time with twice as many men and instructions to put the torch to the well-stocked military depots along the west bank of the Mississippi north of Cairo, particularly Cape Girardeau, from which Grant was drawing much of his subsistence for the campaign far downriver. Little came of this, however. Marmaduke and his 5000 troopers — the largest body of horsemen ever assembled in the Transmississippi — struck and routed an inferior blue force at Fayetteville on April 18, then crossed the line into his native state and rode eastward across it in two columns, one through Fredericktown and the other through Bloomfield, driving Yankee outpost garrisons before him as he advanced. Secessionists, many of whom had kinsmen riding with him, greeted their favorite with cheers. His father had been governor before the war and he himself would be governor after it, a bachelor just past thirty now, tall and slender, quick-tempered and aristocratic in manner, with a full beard, delicate hands and feet, and fine hair brushed smooth on top and worn long in back so that it flared in a splendid ruff behind his head. His eyes were kindly and intelligent, though they had a disconcerting squint that came from his being at once near-sighted and unwilling to disfigure himself with glasses. He had studied both at Harvard and Yale before his graduation from West Point six years ago, but neither this formal preparation nor his success on the similar mission back in January stood him in much stead on April 25, when he completed his investment of Cape Girardeau with a demand for an immediate surrender; to which Brigadier General John McNeil, a fifty-year-old former Boston hatter and St Louis insurance agent, who had increased the strength of the garrison to 1700 by bringing in his brigade the day before, replied with an immediate refusal. Marmaduke attacked and found the resistance stiff, all the approaches being covered by well-served artillery. Not only was he repulsed, but scouts reported steamers unloading reinforcements from St Louis at the Cape Girardeau dock. So he withdrew next morning, after launching one more attack designed to discourage pursuit. It failed in its purpose, however, and the retreat southward across the St Francis bottomlands of the Missouri boot heel required all his skill to avoid being intercepted by the now superior forces of the enemy. By May Day he was back in Arkansas, having suffered 161 casualties, and though he claimed that Federal losses "must have been five times as great as mine in killed and wounded" — McNeil and the others who had opposed him admitted a scant 120, combined — all he had to show for his pains, aside from some 150 recruits picked up in the course of the 400-mile-long ride, was "a great improvement in the number and quality of horses" in his command.

Grant was over the river by then, hard on the march for Jackson, but Holmes attempted nothing more in the way of interference until he received in mid-June an excerpt from a letter the Secretary of War had written Johnston in late May, after Pemberton was besieged, suggesting that he urge the Transmississippi commanders to "make diversions for you, or, in case of the fall of Vicksburg, secure a great future advantage to the Confederacy by the attack on, and seizure of, Helena, while all the available forces of the enemy are being pushed to Grant's aid." Seddon added that, though he was cut off from those commanders and therefore had no means of ordering the adoption of his suggestion, its tactical soundness was "so apparent that it is hoped it will be voluntarily embraced and executed." He was right, so far at least as concerned its being "embraced," for Holmes had already conferred with Sterling Price on the same notion, and Price, who had taken command in early June of two brigades of infantry, not only declared that his men were "fully rested and in excellent spirits," but also expressed confidence that if Holmes would bring up two more brigades, together they could "crush the foe" at Helena. He had, moreover, an up-to-the-minute report from "an intelligent lady" just arrived from the west-bank Arkansas town, in which she described the enemy garrison as "exceedingly alarmed," much reduced by downriver calls for reinforcements, "and apprehensive that you will attack them daily." Seddon's suggestion reached Holmes at Little Rock on June 14, together with a covering letter from Kirby Smith, who left its adoption or rejection up to him. Holmes was eager, for once, being greatly encouraged by Price's coincidental approval of the project. "I believe we can take Helena. Please let me attack it," he replied next day, and Smith consented promptly. "Most certainly do it," he told him. That was on June 16. Two days later Holmes issued orders for a concentration of his forces, preparatory to launching the attack.

He had available for the effort just under 5000 infantry in Price's two brigades and a third under Brigadier General James Fagan, a thirty-five-year-old Kentucky-born Arkansan who was a veteran of the Mexican War as well as of Shiloh and Prairie Grove, and just over 2500 cavalry in the two brigades remaining with Marmaduke — two others had been detached since his repulse at Cape Girardeau — and a third under Brigadier General Lucius Walker, who was thirty-three, a nephew of Tennessee's James K. Polk and a West Point graduate, though he had abandoned army life to enter the mercantile business in Memphis until Sumter put him back in uniform. Holmes's instructions called for a cavalry screen to be thrown around Helena as soon as possible, in order to conceal from its blue defenders the infantry concentration scheduled for June 26 across the St Francis River at Cotton Plant and Clarendon, within fifty miles of the objective. Walker and Marmaduke moved out promptly, followed by Price and Fagan. Anxious to get back onto the victory trail that had led to Wilson's Creek and Lexington, up in his home state, before he was sidetracked into defeat at Pea Ridge and more recently at Iuka and Corinth, Price had announced to his troops that they would "not only drive the enemy from our borders, but pursue him into his own accursed land." The men, who idolized him and affectionately called him Pap, cheered at the news that these words were about to be translated into action, and Fagan likewise reported that his brigade was "ready and in high condition and spirit" as the march got under way. Those spirits were soon dampened, however, by torrents of rain that turned the roads to quagmires and flooded the unbridged streams past fording. As a result, it was June 30 before the infantry reached the areas designated. Holmes remained calm, despite the strain of a four-day wait, and engaged in no useless criminations. "My dear general," he wrote Price while the former Missouri governor was still on the march through calf-deep mud, "I deeply regret your misfortune." Revising his schedule accordingly, he moved

out from Clarendon and Cotton Plant on July 1, arrived within five
miles of Helena on the evening of July 3, and issued detailed instructions
for an attack at dawn next morning. Much depended on concert of action, for the Union position featured mutually supporting earthworks
and intrenchments, but Holmes counted also on his assumed superiority
in numbers. His strength was 7646 effectives, and he reckoned that of
the enemy at "4000 or 5000" at the most.

It was in fact much closer to the lower than to the higher figure;
4129 bluecoats were awaiting him in the Helena defenses. But what he
did not know was that they had been warned of his coming and had
made special preparations to receive him, including arrangements for
the support of the gunboat *Tyler*, whose 8-inch guns had helped to save
the day at Shiloh under similar circumstances. The post commander,
Benjamin M. Prentiss, had done even stouter service on that bloody field
by holding the Hornets Nest until he and his division were overrun and
captured. Exchanged in October, the Virginia-born Illinois lawyer had
won promotion to major general and assignment to command of the
District of East Arkansas — meaning Helena, since this was the only
Union-occupied point in the region below Memphis. For the past four
days, disturbed by the rebel cavalry thrashing about in the brush outside
his works, Prentiss had had the garrison up and under arms by 2.30
each morning, and just yesterday he had issued an order forbidding a
Fourth of July celebration his officers had planned for tomorrow. However, the most effective preparation of all had begun in late December,
when Fred Steele went downriver with Sherman and three fourths of
his corps, leaving the remnant exposed to a sudden thrust such as Holmes
was launching now. At that time, six months ago, the total defense consisted of a single bastioned earthwork, called Fort Curtis for the then
commander of the department, whose guns could sweep the gently
rising ground of the hills that cradled the low-lying town beside the
river, but since then Prentiss had constructed breastworks and dug rifle
pits along the brow of the ridge, an average half mile beyond the fort,
overlooking the timber-choked terrain of its more precipitous eastern
slopes, and on the three dominant heights, Rightor Hill on the right,
Graveyard Hill in the center, and Hindman Hill on the left, he had in-
stalled batteries which he designated, north to south, as A, B, C, D.
Stoutly emplaced and mutually supporting, so that if one fell those adjoining could turn their fire on it, those four batteries and their protec-
tive intrenchments, which linked them into an iron chain of defense,
covered the six roads that passed over the semicircular ridge and converged on Fort Curtis like so many spokes on the hub of half a
wheel, and the cannoneers who manned them could feel secure — especially after a look back over their shoulders at the *Tyler* riding at anchor beyond the town — in the knowledge that Prentiss and his engineers had made the most of what nature had placed at their disposal,

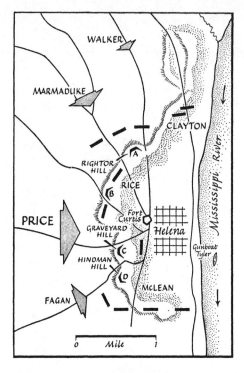

Brigadier General Frederick Salomon commanded the division Steele had left behind. One of four immigrant brothers who served the Union through this crisis — three of them as colonels and brigadiers and the fourth as wartime governor of Wisconsin, to which they had fled from their native Prussia to avoid the consequences of having fought on the losing side in the Revolution of 1848 — he had three small brigades, each led by a colonel: two of infantry, under William McLean and Samuel Rice, and one of cavalry under Powell Clayton. Like Salomon, these three officers were all in their middle or early thirties, nonprofessionals who had risen strictly on merit if not in action, and their troops were Westerners to a man, mostly farm boys out of Missouri, Iowa, and Wisconsin. Except for a single regiment of Hoosiers who had served with Pope in the taking of New Madrid and Island Ten, some fifteen months ago, the total field experience of the garrison had been the recent Yazoo Pass fiasco, in which they had been matched primarily against gnats and mosquitoes while the navy tried in vain to reduce Fort Pemberton. Still irked by the memory of that unhappy experience, and in accordance with Prentiss's standing instructions, they turned out of their bunks and took their posts at 2.30, an hour before dawn and a good two hours before sunrise of this Independence Day. Clayton's troopers were on the far right, guarding the river road north of town; McLean's and Rice's cannoneers and riflemen were disposed along the hilltop chain of batteries and intrenchments. Half an hour after they were in position, Holmes's attack opened against the left center. At first it was rather tentative, driving the Federal outpost pickets back up the rugged western slopes of Hindman and Graveyard hills, but presently it exploded in full fury as the butternut pursuers came yelling after them, massed shoulder to shoulder in a solid drive for possession of the two high-sited batteries Prentiss had labeled C and D.

Their repulse was not as sudden as their eruption, but it was equally emphatic. In part this was because they had found the last five miles of road, which they covered after dark, in even worse shape than the hundred-odd they had traversed so painfully during the past week:

with the result that they had been unable to bring their guns along and therefore had to attack without artillery support, of which the Federals had plenty. Fagan's brigade struck first, storming Hindman Hill — so called because it was here that the former Confederate commander had built the fine brick house Curtis had taken for his headquarters soon after occupying the town the year before. Three successive lines of half-bastions were rapidly penetrated and seized, but not the hilltop battery itself, which met the attackers with volleys of grape that shattered their formation, sent them scrambling for cover, and pinned them down so effectively that they could not even retreat. Price's two brigades did better, at least at first. Battery C was taken in a rush, the graybacks swarming over Graveyard Hill and whooping among the captured guns. The weaponless rebel artillerymen came up, prepared to turn the pieces on their late owners, only to find that the retreating cannoneers had carried off all the friction primers, which left the guns about as useless to their captors as so much scrap iron. Moreover, they came under enfilade fire from the two adjoining batteries and took a pounding as well from Fort Curtis, dead ahead at the foot of the gradual eastern slope. Nor was that all. Receiving word that Hindman Hill was under assault, Prentiss had signaled Lieutenant Commander J. M. Prichett of the *Tyler:* "Open fire in that direction." Now Prichett did, and with a vengeance, the fuzes of his 8-inch shells cut at ten and fifteen seconds. So demoralized were the attackers by the sudden deluge of heavy-caliber projectiles that, according to one blue officer, two groups of about 250 men each responded "by hoisting a white flag, their own sharpshooters upon the ridge in their rear firing from cover upon and cursing them as they marched out prisoners of war."

Holmes did what he could to expand the lodgment, sending one of Price's brigades to co-operate with Fagan in the stalled drive on Battery D. But to no avail; McLean and Rice held steady, backed up stoutly by Fort Curtis and the *Tyler*, whose bow and stern guns were firing north and south, respectively, while her ponderous broadside armament tore gaps in the rebel center. The early morning coolness soon gave way to parching heat; men risked their lives for sips of water from the canteens of the dead. Around to the north, Marmaduke had even less success against the defenders of Rightor Hill, and though he later complained vociferously that Walker had not supported him on his vulnerable left flank, the fact was he had already found Batteries A and B too hot to handle. He and Walker together lost a total of 66 men, only a dozen of whom were killed. As usual, it was the infantry that suffered, and in this case most of the sufferers wore gray. Including prisoners, the three brigades under Price and Fagan lost better than 1500 men between them. Holmes was not only distressed by the disproportionate losses, which demonstrated the unwisdom of his unsupported assault on a fortified opponent; he also saw that the attack would have been a mistake even if it had been successful, since the force in occupation would have been at the mercy of the *Tyler* and other units of the Federal fleet, which would make the low-lying river town untenable in short order. By 10.30, after six hours of fighting, all this was unmistakably clear; Holmes called for a withdrawal. By noon it had been accomplished, except for some minor rear-guard skirmishing, although better than one out of every five men who had attacked was a casualty. His losses totaled 1590, nearly half of them captives pinned down by the murderous fire and unable to retreat.

Prentiss lost 239: less than six percent of his force, as compared to better than twenty percent of the attackers. However, even with the odds reduced by this considerable extent, he still had too few men to risk pursuit. Reinforcements arrived next day from Memphis, together with another welcome gunboat, but he was content to break up a rebel cavalry demonstration which he correctly judged to be nothing more than a feint designed to cover a general retirement. By dawn of July 6 the only live Confederates around Helena were captives, many of them too gravely wounded to be moved. In praising his troops for their stand against nearly twice their number, Prentiss did not neglect his obligation to the *Tyler*, whose skipper in time received as well a letter of commendation from the Secretary of the Navy. "Accept the Department's congratulations for yourself and the officers and men under your command," the Secretary wrote, "for your glorious achievement, which adds another to the list of brilliant successes of our Navy and Army on the anniversary of our nation's independence."

❌ 3 ❌

It was indeed a Glorious Fourth, from the northern point of view; Gideon Welles did not exaggerate in speaking wholesale of a "list of brilliant successes" scored by the Union, afloat and ashore, on this eighty-seventh anniversary of the nation's birth. For the South, however, the day was one not of glory, but rather of disappointment, of bitter irony, of gloom made deeper by contrast with the hopes of yesterday, when Lee was massing for his all-or-nothing attack on Cemetery Ridge and Johnston was preparing at last to cross the Big Black River, when Taylor was threatening to retake New Orleans and Holmes was moving into position for his assault on Helena. All four had failed, which was reason enough for disappointment; the irony lay in the fact that not one of the four, Lee or Johnston, Taylor or Holmes, was aware that on this Independence Eve, so far at least as his aspirations for the relief of Vicksburg or Port Hudson were concerned, he was too late. At 10 o'clock that morning, July 3, white flags had broken out along a portion of Pemberton's works and two high-ranking officers, one a colonel, the other a major general, had come riding out of their lines and into those of the besiegers, who obligingly held their fire. The senior bore a letter from his commander, addressed to Grant. "General," it began: "I have the honor to propose to you an armistice for several hours, with a view to arranging terms for the capitulation of Vicksburg."

Pemberton's decision to ask for terms had been reached the day before, when he received from his four division commanders, Stevenson, Forney, Smith, and Bowen, replies to a confidential note requesting their opinions as to the ability of their soldiers "to make the marches and undergo the fatigues necessary to accomplish a successful evacuation." After forty-six days and forty-five nights in the trenches, most of the time on half- and quarter-rations, not one of the four believed his troops were in any shape for the exertion required to break the ring of steel that bound them and then to outmarch or outfight the well-fed host of bluecoats who outnumbered them better than four to one in effectives. Forney, for example, though he expressed himself as "satisfied they will cheerfully continue to bear the fatigue and privation of the siege," answered that it was "the unanimous opinion of the brigade and regimental commanders that the physical condition and health of our men are not sufficiently good to enable them to accomplish successfully the evacuation." There Pemberton had it, and the other three agreed. "With the knowledge I then possessed that no adequate relief was to be expected," the Pennsylvania Confederate later wrote, "I felt that I ought not longer to place in jeopardy the brave men whose lives had been intrusted to my care." He would ask for terms. The apparent futility of submitting such a request to a man whose popular fame was based on his having replied to a similar query with the words, "No terms except an unconditional and immediate surrender can be accepted," was offset — at least to some extent, as Pemberton saw it — by two factors. One was that the Confederates had broken the Federal wigwag code, which permitted them to eavesdrop on Grant's and Porter's ship-to-shore and shore-to-ship exchanges, and from these they had learned that the navy wanted to avoid the troublesome, time-consuming task of transporting thousands of grayback captives far northward up the river. This encouraged the southern commander to hope that his opponent, despite his Unconditional Surrender reputation, might be willing to parole instead of imprison the Vicksburg garrison if that was made a condition of avoiding at least one more costly assault on intrenchments that had proved themselves so stout two times before. The other mitigating factor, at any rate to Pemberton's way of thinking, was that the calendar showed the proposed surrender would occur on Independence Day. Some among the defenders considered a capitulation on that date unthinkable, since it would give the Yankees all the more reason for crowing, but while Pemberton was aware of this, and even agreed that it would involve a measure of humiliation, he also counted it an advantage. "I am a northern

man," he told the objectors on his staff. "I know my people. I know
their peculiar weaknesses and their national vanity; I know we can get
better terms from them on the Fourth of July than on any other day of
the year. We must sacrifice our pride to these considerations."

One other possible advantage he had, though admittedly it had
not been of much use to Buckner at Donelson the year before. John
Bowen had known and befriended Grant during his fellow West Pointer's hard-scrabble farming days in Missouri, and it was hoped that this
might have some effect when the two got down to negotiations. Although Bowen was sick, his health undermined by dysentery contracted
during the siege — he would in fact be dead within ten days, three
months short of his thirty-third birthday — he accepted the assignment,
and that was how it came about that he was the major general who
rode into the Union lines this morning, accompanied by a colonel from
Pemberton's staff. However, it soon developed that the past seventeen
months had done little to mellow Grant in his attitude toward old
friends who had chosen to do their fighting under the Stars and Bars. He
not only declined to see or talk with Bowen, but his reply to the southern
commander's note, which was delivered to him by one of his own officers, also showed that he was, if anything, even harsher in tone than he
had been in the days when Buckner charged him with being "ungen-
erous and unchivalrous." Pemberton had written: "I make this proposition to save the further effusion of blood, which must otherwise be shed
to a frightful extent." Now Grant replied: "The useless effusion of
blood you propose stopping by this course can be ended at any time you
may choose, by an unconditional surrender of the city and garrison. . . .
I do not favor the proposition of appointing commissioners to arrange
terms of capitulation, because I have no terms other than those indicated above."

There were those words again: Unconditional Surrender. But
their force was diminished here at Vicksburg, as they had not been at
Donelson, by an accompanying verbal message in which Grant said
that he would be willing to meet and talk with Pemberton between the
lines that afternoon. Worn by strain and illness, Bowen delivered the
note and repeated the off-the-record message, both of which were dis-
cussed at an impromptu council of war, and presently — by then it was
close to 3 o'clock, the hour Grant had set for the meeting — he and the
colonel retraced in part the route they had followed that morning, accompanied now by Pemberton, who spoke half to himself and half to
his two companions as he rode past the white flags on the ramparts. "I
feel a confidence that I shall stand justified to my government, if not to
the southern people," they heard him say, as if he saw already the scapegoat role in which he as an outlander would be cast by strangers and
former friends for whose sake he had alienated his own people, including two brothers who fought on the other side. First, however, there

came a ruder shock. Despite the flat refusal expressed in writing, he had interpreted Grant's spoken words, relayed to him through Bowen, as an invitation to parley about terms. But he soon was disabused of this impression. The three Confederates came upon a group of about a dozen Union officers awaiting them on a hillside only a couple of hundred yards beyond the outer walls of the beleaguered city. Ord, McPherson, Logan, and A. J. Smith were there, together with several members of Grant's staff and Grant himself, whom Pemberton had no trouble recognizing, not only because his picture had been distributed widely throughout the past year and a half, but also because he had known him in Mexico, where they had served as staff lieutenants in the same division. Once the introductions were over, there was an awkward pause as each waited for the other to open the conversation and thereby place himself in somewhat the attitude of a suppliant. When Pemberton broke the silence at last by remarking that he understood Grant had "expressed a wish to have a personal interview with me," Grant replied that he had done no such thing; he had merely agreed to such a suggestion made at second hand by Bowen.

Finding that this had indeed been the case, though he had not known it before, Pemberton took a different approach. "In your letter this morning," he observed, "you state that you have no other terms than an unconditional surrender." Grant's answer was as prompt as before. "I have no other," he said. Whereupon the Pennsylvanian — "rather snappishly," Grant would recall — replied: "Then, sir, it is unnecessary that you and I should hold any further conversation. We will go to fighting again at once." He turned, as if to withdraw, but fired a parting salvo as he did so. "I can assure you, sir, you will bury many more of your men before you will enter Vicksburg." Grant said nothing to this, nor did he change his position or expression. The contest was like poker, and he played it straight-faced while his opponent continued to sputter, remarking, as he later paraphrased his words, that if Grant "supposed that I was suffering for provisions he was mistaken, that I had enough to last me for an indefinite period, and that Port Hudson was even better supplied than Vicksburg." Grant did not believe there was much truth in this, but he saw clearly enough from Pemberton's manner that his unconditional-surrender formula was not going to obtain without a good deal more time or bloodshed. So he unbent, at least to the extent of suggesting that he and Pemberton step aside while their subordinates talked things over. The Confederate was altogether willing — after all, it was what he had proposed at the outset, only to be rebuffed — and the two retired to the shelter of a stunted oak nearby. In full view of the soldiers on both sides along this portion of the front, while Bowen and the colonel talked with the other four Union generals, the blue and gray commanders stood together in the meager shade of the oak tree, which, as Grant wrote afterwards, "was made historical by the event. It was but a short time before the last vestige of its body, root and limb had disappeared, the fragments taken as trophies. Since then the same tree has furnished as many cords of wood, in the shape of trophies, as 'The True Cross.' "

But that was later, after the souvenir hunters had the run of the field. For the present, the oak remained as intact as almost seven weeks of bullets and shells from both sides had allowed, and Grant and Pemberton continued their pokerlike contest of wills beneath its twisted branches. If the Confederate played a different style of game, that did not necessarily mean that he was any less skillful. In point of fact — at any rate in the limited sense of getting what he came for — he won; for in the end it was the quiet man who gave way and the sputterer who stood firm. In the adjoining group, Bowen proposed that the garrison "be permitted to march out with the honors of war, carrying with them their arms, colors, and field batteries," which was promptly denied, as he no doubt had expected; whereupon Pemberton, after pointing out that his suggestion for the designation of commissioners had been rejected, observed that it was now Grant's turn to make a counteroffer as to terms. Grant agreed; Pemberton would hear from him by 10 o'clock that evening, he said; and with that the meeting broke up, though it was made clear that neither opponent was to consider himself "pledged." Both returned to their own lines and assembled councils of war to discuss what had developed. Pemberton found that all his division commanders and all but two of his brigade commanders favored capitulation, provided it could be done on a basis of parole without imprisonment. Grant found his officers of a mind to offer what was acceptable, although he himself did not concur; "My own feelings are against this," he declared. But presently, being shielded in part from the possible wrath of his Washington superiors by the overwhelming vote of his advisers, he "reluctantly gave way," and put his terms on paper for delivery to Pemberton at the designated hour. Vicksburg was to be surrendered, together with all public stores, and its garrison paroled; a single Union division would move in and take possession of the place next morning. "As soon as rolls can be made out, and paroles signed by officers and men," he stipulated, "you will be allowed to march out of our lines, the officers taking with them their side-arms and clothing, and the field, staff, and cavalry officers one horse each. The rank and file will be allowed all their clothing, but no other property." Remembering Pemberton's claim that he had plenty of provisions on hand, Grant added a touch that combined generosity and sarcasm: "If these conditions are accepted, any amount of rations you may deem necessary can be taken from the stores you now have, and also the necessary cooking utensils for them. . . . I am, general, very respectfully, your obedient servant, U. S. GRANT, Major General."

Now that he had committed his terms to paper, he found them

much more satisfactory than he had done before. "I was very glad to give the garrison of Vicksburg the terms I did," he afterwards wrote. To have shipped the graybacks north to Illinois and Ohio, he explained, "would have used all the transportation we had for a month." Moreover, "the men had behaved so well that I did not want to humiliate them. I believed that consideration for their feelings would make them less dangerous foes during the continuance of hostilities, and better citizens after the war was over." So he said, years later, making a virtue of necessity and leaving out of account the fact that he had begun with a demand for unconditional surrender. For the present, indeed, he was so admiring of the arrangement, from the Union point of view, that he did what he could to make certain Pemberton could not reject it — as both had reserved the right to do — without risking a mutiny by the beleaguered garrison. He had Rawlins send the following note to his corps commanders: "Permit some discreet men on picket tonight to communicate to the enemy's pickets the fact that General Grant has offered, in case Pemberton surrenders, to parole all the officers and men and to permit them to go home from here."

He could have spared himself the precaution and his courier the ride. "By this time," a Confederate declared, "the atmosphere was electric with expectancy, and the wildest rumors raced through camp and city. Everyone had the air of knowing something vital." What was more, a good deal of back-and-forth visiting had begun on both sides of the line. "Several brothers met," a Federal remarked, "and any quantity of cousins. It was a strange scene." Whatever the blue pickets might say, on whatever valid authority, was only going to add to the seethe of speculation within and without the hilltop fortress which was now about to fall, just under fourteen months after its mayor replied to the first demand for surrender, back in May of the year before: "Mississippians don't know, and refuse to learn, how to surrender to an enemy. If Commodore Farragut and Brigadier General Butler can teach them, let them come and try." The upshot was that Grant had come and tried, being so invited, and now Pemberton had been taught, although it galled him. Assembling his generals for a reading of the 10 o'clock offer, he remarked — much as his opponent had done, an hour or two ago, across the way — that his "inclination was to reject these terms." However, he did not really mean it, any more than Grant had meant it, and after he had taken the all but unanimous vote for capitulation, he said gravely: "Gentlemen, I have done what I could," then turned to dictate his reply. "In the main, your terms are accepted," he told Grant, "but in justice both to the honor and spirit of my troops, manifested in the defense of Vicksburg, I have to submit the following amendments, which, if acceded to by you, will perfect the agreement between us. . . ." The added conditions, of which there were two, were modest enough in appearance. He proposed to march his soldiers out of the works, stack arms, and then move off before the Federals took possession, thus avoiding a confrontation of the two armies. That was the first. The second was that officers be allowed "to retain their . . . personal property, and [that] the rights and property of citizens . . . be respected." But Grant declined to allow him either, and for good cause. As for the first, he replied, it would be necessary for the troops to remain under proper guard until due process of parole had been formally completed, and as for the second, while he was willing to give all citizens assurance that they would be spared "undue annoyance or loss," he would make no specific guarantees regarding "personal property," which he privately suspected was intended to include a large number of slaves, freed six months ago by Lincoln's Proclamation. "I cannot consent to leave myself under any restraint by stipulations," he said flatly. Denial of the proposed amendments was contained in a dispatch sent before sunrise, July 4. Pemberton had until 9 a.m. to accept the original terms set forth in last night's message; otherwise, Grant added, "I shall regard them as having been rejected, and shall act accordingly."

Now it was Pemberton's turn to bend in the face of stiffness, and this he did the more willingly since the morning report — such had been the ravages of malnutrition and unrelieved exposure — showed fewer than half his troops available for duty as effectives. "General," he answered curtly about sunrise: "I have the honor to acknowledge the receipt of your communication of this day, and in reply to say that the terms proposed are accepted." The rest was up to Grant, and it went smoothly. At 10 o'clock, in response to the white flags that now fluttered along the full length of the Confederate line, John Logan marched his division into the works. Soon afterwards the Stars and Stripes were flying over the Vicksburg courthouse for the first time in two and a half years. If the victors were somewhat disappointed professionally that seven weeks of intensive shelling by 220 army cannon, backed up by about as many heavier pieces aboard the gunboats and the mortar rafts, had done surprisingly little substantial damage to the town, it was at least observed that the superficial damage was extensive. Not a single pane of glass remained unbroken in any of the houses, a journalist noted. It was also observed that, despite the southern commander's claim that he had ample provisions, the gauntness of the disarmed graybacks showed only too clearly, not only that such was not the case, but also that it apparently had not been so for some time. One Federal quartermaster, bringing in a train of supplies for the troops in occupation, was so affected by the hungry looks on the faces of the men of a rebel brigade that he called a halt and began distributing hardtack, coffee, and sugar all around. Rewarded by "the heartfelt thanks" of the butternut scarecrows, he said afterwards that when his own men complained that night about the slimness of their rations, "I swore by all the saints in the calendar that the wagons had broken down and the Johnny Rebs had stolen all the grub." Not only was there little "crowing," which some Confederates had feared would be encouraged and enlarged by a Fourth of July surrender, but according to Grant "the men of the two armies fraternized as if they had been fighting for the same cause." Though that was perhaps an overstatement of the case, there was in fact a great deal of mingling by victors and vanquished alike — "swapping yarns over the incidents of the long siege," as one gray participant put it — and even some good-natured ribbing back and forth. "See here, Mister; you man on the little white horse!" a bluecoat called out to Major Lockett, whose engineering duties had kept him on the move during lulls in the fighting. "Danged if you aint the hardest feller to hit I ever saw. I've shot at you more'n a hundred times." Lockett took it in good part, and afterwards praised his late adversaries for their generosity toward the defeated garrison. "General Grant says there was no cheering by the Federal troops," he wrote. "My recollection is that on our right a hearty cheer was given by one Federal division 'for the gallant defenders of Vicksburg!' "

Pemberton did not share in the fraternization, not only because of his present sadness, his sense of failure, and his intimation of what the reaction of his adoptive countrymen would be when they got the news of what had happened here today, but also because of his nature, which was invariably distant and often forbidding. For him, congeniality had been limited mainly to the family circle he had broken and been barred from when he threw in with the South. Even toward his own officers he had always been stiffly formal, and now toward Grant, who came through the lines that morning on his way to confer with Porter at the wharf, he was downright icy; indeed, rude. Perhaps it was the northern commander's show of magnanimity, when he knew that such concessions as had been granted — parole of the garrison, for example, instead of a long boat ride to prison camps in Ohio and Illinois — had been the result of hard bargaining and a refusal to yield to his original demand for unconditional surrender. In any event, one of his staff found Pemberton's manner "unhandsome and disagreeable in the extreme." No one offered Grant a seat when he called on Pemberton in a house on the Jackson road, this officer protested, and when he remarked that he would like a drink of water, he was told that he could go where it was and help himself. He did not seem perturbed by this lack of graciousness, however; he went his way, taking no apparent umbrage, content with the spoils of this Independence Day, which were by far the greatest of the war, at any rate in men and materiel. Confederate casualties during the siege had been 2872 killed, wounded, and missing, while those of the Federals totaled 4910; but now the final tally of captives was being made. It included 2166 officers, 27,230 enlisted men, and 115 civilian employees, all paroled except one officer and 708 men, who preferred to go north as prisoners rather than risk being exchanged and required to fight again. In ordnance, too, the harvest was a rich one, yielding 172 cannon, surprisingly large amounts of ammunition of all kinds, and nearly 60,000 muskets and rifles, many of such superior quality that some Union regiments exchanged their own weapons for the ones they found stacked when they marched in.

One additional prize there was, richer by far than all the rest combined and to which they had served as no more than prologue. The Mississippi would return to its old allegiance as soon as one remaining obstruction had been removed, and that allegiance would be secure as soon as one continuing threat had been abolished. The obstruction — Port Hudson — was not really Grant's concern except for the dispatching of reinforcements, which he could now quite easily afford, to help Banks get on with the job. He kept his attention fixed on Joe Johnston — the threat — who continued to hover, off to the east, beyond the Big Black River. Conferring with Porter, Grant requested his co-operation in flushing out the rebels up the Yazoo, re-established there by Johnston while the Federals were concentrating on the reduction of Vicksburg. As usual, the admiral was altogether willing; he assigned an ironclad and two tinclads the task of escorting 5000 infantry upstream to retake Yazoo City, which the Confederates had refortified since their flight from the approaching gunboats back in May. But the northern army commander's main concern was Johnston himself and the force he was assembling west of Jackson. Yesterday, while surrender negotiations were under way, Grant had notified Sherman, whose troops were already faced in that direction, that he was to strike eastward as soon as Vicksburg fell. "I want Johnston broken up as effectually as possible, and roads destroyed," he wired. This message was followed shortly by another, in which he was more specific as to just what breakage was expected. "When we go in," he told his red-haired lieutenant, "I want you to drive Johnston from the Mississippi Central Railroad, destroy bridges as far as Grenada with your cavalry, and do the enemy all the harm possible. You can make your own arrangements and have all the troops of my command, except one corps — McPherson's, say. I must have some troops to send to Banks, to use against Port Hudson."

As it turned out, there was no need for more troops at Port Hudson. All that was required was valid evidence that its companion bluff 240 miles upriver was in Union hands, and this arrived before the reinforcements: specifically, during the early hours of July 7. That evening Gardner received from one of his three brigade commanders — Miles, whose position on the far right afforded him a view of the river, as well as of the extreme left of the Federal intrenchments — a report of strange doings by the enemy, ashore and afloat: "This morning all his land batteries fired a salute, and followed it immediately [by another] with shotted guns, accompanied by vociferous yelling. Later in the day the fleet fired a salute also. What is meant we do not know. Some of them hallooed over, saying that Vicksburg had fallen on the 4th instant. My own impression is that some fictitious good news has been given to his troops in order to raise their spirits; perhaps with a view of stimulating them to a charge in the morning. We will be prepared for them should they do so."

The colonel's men shared his skepticism as well as his resolution, even when confronted with documentary evidence in the form of a "flimsy" tossed into their lines, bearing the signature of the Federal adjutant-general and announcing Pemberton's surrender three days ago. "That's another damned Yankee lie!" a butternut defender shouted back. But Gardner himself was not so sure. He had fought well, inflicting 4363 casualties at a cost of only 623 of his own, and though by now the trenches were less than twenty feet apart in places and the enemy was obviously about to launch another massive assault, which was likely to succeed at such close range, he was prepared to fight still longer if need be. On the other hand, it was no part of his duty to sacrifice the garrison for no purpose — and obviously Port Hudson's purpose, or anyhow its hope of survival, was tied to that of Vicksburg. If the Mississippi bastion had fallen, so must the Louisiana one, exposed as it would be to the possible combination of both Union armies. So Gardner adopted the logical if somewhat irregular course of inquiring of his opponent, by means of a flag of truce next morning, as to whether the report of Vicksburg's fall was true. And when Banks supplied confirming evidence, in the form of a dispatch Grant had sent on the surrender date, Gardner decided that the time for his own capitulation was at hand. Final details were not worked out until the following day, July 9, when the besiegers marched in and took possession, but a train of wagons had already entered Port Hudson the previous afternoon, loaded with U.S. Army rations for the half-starved garrison. Banks combined firmness and generosity. Though his terms had been unconditional, he paroled his 5935 enlisted captives and sent only their 405 officers to New Orleans to await exchange or shipment north. Moreover, having acquired some 7500 excellent rifles and 51 light and heavy guns, he closed the formal surrender ceremony with "a worthy act, well merited." Thus his adjutant characterized the gesture in describing it years later. "By General Banks's order, General Gardner's sword was returned to him in the presence of his men, in recognition of the heroic defense."

If there was haste in the northern commander's method, including parole of all his enlisted prisoners, there was also method in his haste. Albeit they were the sweeter, being his first, Banks was no more inclined than Grant to sit down and enjoy the fruits of his victory; for just as the latter took out after Joe Johnston as soon as Vicksburg fell, so did the former concern himself with Dick Taylor as soon as Port Hudson followed suit. Faced as he was with the departure of the nine-month volunteers who made up a considerable portion of his army, Banks had to choose between using the remainder as guards for the captured garrison or as a mobile force for driving out the reported 13,000 Confederates who had moved into his rear and were threatening New Orleans from Bayou Lafourche and Berwick Bay. Quite aside from the pleasure he derived from being generous to a defeated foe, that was why he paroled nearly 6000 of his 6340 prisoners: to get them off his hands and thus be free to deal with Taylor. Having decided, he wasted no time. While the surrender ceremony was in progress he put Weitzel's and Grover's divisions aboard transports and sent them at once to Donaldsonville, where they would begin their descent of the Lafourche, disposing of infiltrated rebels as they went. The debarkation was completed on July 11; next afternoon the two blue divisions began their advance down opposite banks of the bayou. Early the following morning, however — July 13 at Koch's Plantation, six miles from Donaldsonville — Weitzel's two west-bank brigades, and indirectly Banks himself, were given a cruel demonstration of the fact that haste sometimes made waste, even in pursuit.

Tom Green, with his own and Major's brigade of mounted Texans, had been having a fine time disrupting traffic on the Mississippi with the guns he had established on its right bank, ten miles below the town. Though they could do no real damage to the *Essex*, which came down to challenge them, they did succeed in driving the ironclad off and puncturing the steam-drums of several less heavily armored vessels. A battery commander referred to the 12-foot levee as "the best of earthworks," and Green was prepared to stay there indefinitely, finding balm in his present success for the sting of the recent setback at Fort Butler. After three days of such fun, however, he learned of the arrival of ten transports at Donaldsonville and the debarkation of two blue divisions with better than five times his number of men. Determined not to leave without a fight, whatever the odds, he pulled back from the river, crossed the Lafourche, and lay in wait for what was coming. What was coming was Weitzel, supported by Grover across the way. Green struck hard, soon after sunrise of July 13, caught the bluecoats off guard, and threw them into such hasty retreat that they abandoned three of their guns to their pursuers. They lost 50 killed, 223 wounded, and 186 captured or missing, while Green lost 9 killed and 24 wounded. He withdrew westward, unmolested, and rejoined Taylor at Vermilionville, that general having retired with all his spoils from Brashear City when he learned of Gardner's surrender and the intended return downriver of the besieging army. By no means strong enough for a full-scale battle with the greatly superior forces of the Federals near their base, he was content to wait for them to attempt a second ascent of the Teche. They would find him better equipped for resistance than he had been before his recent brief but profitable drive to the outskirts of New Orleans.

Banks accepted the Koch's Plantation check with his usual easy grace, even setting aside a court-martial's findings that one of Weitzel's brigade commanders had been guilty of drunkenness on duty and misconduct in the presence of the enemy. The former Speaker was looking for no scapegoat; he would take whatever blame there was, along with the praise, as designer and director of the campaign from start to finish. And of praise there was much. It was Banks, after all, who had removed the final obstruction to Union control of the Mississippi, following Grant's extraction of "the nail that held the South's two halves together." On July 16, one week after the fall of Port Hudson, the unarmed packet *Imperial* tied up at New Orleans and began unloading cargo she had brought unescorted from St Louis. For the first time in thirty months, the Father of Waters was open to commerce from Minnesota to the Gulf.

Meanwhile Porter and Sherman had gone about their assignments, though for both there had been irksome delays followed by mishaps for which irksome was all too mild a word; Porter's, in fact, had occurred on the same day as Weitzel's, and while it had been considerably less bloody it was also a good deal more expensive. Originally intended as reinforcements for Banks, since they had spent less than a month in the Vicksburg trenches, 5000 men of Herron's division were shifted to lighter-draft transports on July 11, when news of the fall of Port Hudson arrived, and set out up the Yazoo next morning, escorted by two 6-gun tinclads and the 14-gun ironclad *Baron de Kalb*, formerly the *St Louis* but rechristened when it developed that the navy already had a warship by that name. One of the original seven built by James Eads in the fall of '61 and a veteran of all the major engagements on the Tennessee, the Cumberland, and the Mississippi north of Vicksburg, she had carried the flag eight weeks ago on a similar expedition to Yazoo City and beyond, which had resulted in much damage to the enemy at no cost to the fleet. This last was not to be the case this time, however. Isaac Brown, who had sunk the *De Kalb*'s sister ship *Cairo* with a demijohn of powder up this same winding river in December, was back again with forty survivors of the crew from his lost ram *Arkansas*, and he had plans for a repeat performance. His navy artillerists managed to drive the ironclad back around the bend when she appeared below the town at noon of July 13, but a Tarheel regiment assigned to the place by Johnston withdrew on learning that Herron had landed three of his own with instructions to bag the defenders. Obliged to pull back for lack of support, Brown and his sailors left something behind them in addition to their guns: as Porter and Herron presently discovered. The two were on the bridge of the flagship, steaming slowly upstream toward the undefended town, when — just after sunset, abreast of the yards where, about this time a year ago, the *Arkansas* had acquired her rusty armor — one of Brown's improvised torpedoes exploded directly under her bow.

As she began to settle, another went off under her stern, which hastened her destruction. Within fifteen minutes, though all aboard managed to escape with nothing worse than bruises, she was on the muddy bottom, providing a multichambered home for gars and catfish. Herron, having survived this violent introduction to one of the dangers involved in combined operations, went ashore to complete his share of the mission, afterwards reporting the destruction of the Yazoo City fortifications and five of the nine rebel steamboats found lurking in the vicinity, together with the capture of some 300 prisoners, six guns, and about 250 small-arms, as well as 2000 bales of cotton and 800 horses and mules which he commandeered from the planters roundabout. He was enthusiastic; no less than 50,000 more bales were awaiting discovery and seizure in the region, he declared. Porter, on the other hand, summed up the operation somewhat ruefully. "But for the blowing up of the *Baron de Kalb*, it would have been a good move," he informed his superiors, and he added, by way of extenuating this loss of his fourth ironclad since December: "While a rebel flag floats anywhere the gunboats must follow up. The officers and men risk their lives fearlessly on these occasions, and I hope the Department will not take too seriously the accidents which happen to the vessels when it is impossible to avoid them."

Sherman made no such apology, though his particular mishap had occurred the day before and had been preceded by a week of hot and profitless activity. Grant's instructions for him to "do the enemy all the harm possible," accompanied as they were by the prospect of having close to 50,000 troops with which to carry them out, had put the red-haired Ohioan in what he liked to call "high feather," and when they were followed next day — July 4 — by the news that Vicksburg had fallen, his excitement reached fever pitch. "I can hardly restrain myself," he replied. Nor did he: adding, "This is a day of jubilee, a day of rejoicing to the faithful. . . . Already are my orders out to give one big huzza and sling the knapsack for new fields." Those new fields lay on the far side of the Big Black, however, which was now past fording because of a sudden four-foot rise resulting from heavy rains upstate. Sherman spent two days throwing bridges at Birdsong's Ferry and Messinger's Ford and due east of Bovina, thus providing a crossing for each of his three corps, and on July 6 the "Army of Observation," so called from the days of the siege, passed over the river in pursuit of Johnston, who had retired toward Jackson the day before, on learning of Pemberton's surrender. As the rebels withdrew eastward along roads that were ankle-deep in dust — no matter how many inches of rain had fallen upstate, not a drop had fallen here in weeks — they made things difficult for their pursuers by leading animals into such few ponds as had not dried in the heat, then killing them and leaving their carcasses to pollute the water. It was Johnston's intention not only to delay his opponent by such devices, but also to goad him into attempting a reckless, thirst-crazed assault on the

Jackson intrenchments, which the Confederates had repaired and improved since Grant's departure and in which they had taken refuge by the time the superior Federal force completed its crossing of the Big Black, twenty-five miles away.

The crafty Virginian's attempt to discourage and torment his pursuers with thirst was unsuccessful, however, for several reasons. For one, the siege-toughened bluecoats simply dragged the festering carcasses from the ponds, gave the water a few minutes to settle, then brushed the scum aside and drank their fill, apparently with no ill effects at all. For another, the rain soon moved down from the north, sudden thunderous showers under which the marchers unrolled their rubber ponchos and held them so that the water trickled into their mouths as they slogged along. Lifted so recently by the greatest victory of the war, their spirits were irrepressible, whether the problem was too little moisture or too much. "The dirt road would soon be worked into a loblolly of sticky yellow mud," one veteran was to recall. "Thereupon we would take off our shoes and socks, tie them to the barrel of our muskets, poise the piece on the hammer on either shoulder, stock uppermost, and roll up our breeches. Splashing, the men would swing along, singing 'John Brown's Body,' or whatever else came handy." They gloried in their toughness and took pride in the fact that they never cheered their generals, not even "Uncle Billy" Sherman. A surgeon wrote home that they were "the noisiest crowd of profane-swearing, dram-drinking, card-playing, song-singing, reckless, impudent daredevils in the world." They would have accepted all this as a compliment, second only to one Joe Johnston had paid them in warning his Richmond superiors not to underrate Grant's Westerners, who in his opinion were "worth double the number of northeastern troops." They thought so, too, and were ready to prove it on July 10 when their three columns converged on the rebel intrenchments outside Jackson and took up positions before them, Ord's four divisions to the south, Steele's three in the center, and Parke's two on the north.

Within the semicircular works — which, as usual, he considered "miserably located" — Johnston had four divisions of infantry confronting the Union nine, plus a small division of cavalry which he used to patrol the flanks along Pearl River, above and below the town. He made several brief sorties in an attempt to provoke the bluecoats into attacking, but Sherman, though he enjoyed a better than two-to-one numerical advantage, had had too much experience with earthworks these past eight weeks to be tempted into rashness. Instead, he spent two days completing his investment, meantime sending raiders north and south to break the Mississippi Central and thus cut Jackson off from any possible rail connection with the outside world, the bridge in its rear not having been rebuilt since its destruction back in May. Then on July 12, despite his admonitions as to caution, the mishap came. On Ord's front, Lauman was advancing his division through an area obscured by trees and brush, when the lead brigade of 880 veterans suddenly found itself exposed to a withering crossfire from guns and rifles, losing 465 men and three stands of colors, as well as most of the cannoneers and horses of a section of artillery, before the remnant could recover from the shock and back-pedal. "I am cut all to pieces," Lauman lamented; Ord relieved him of command. Sherman approved the brigadier's removal, but refused to be disconcerted by the affair, which had at least confirmed his assumption that Joe Johnston was a dangerous man when cornered: so much so, in fact, that the Ohioan began to wish the Virginian gone. "I think we are doing well out here," he informed Grant two days later, "but won't brag till Johnston clears out and stops shooting his big rifle guns at us. If he moves across Pearl River and makes good speed, I will let him go."

That was just what Johnston had in mind, now that Sherman had the capital invested on three sides. "It would be madness to attack him," he wired Richmond that same day. "In the beginning it might have been done, but I thought then that want of water would compel him to attack us." By next morning, July 16, he was convinced that his only hope for survival lay in retreat. "The enemy being strongly reinforced, and able when he pleases to cut us off," he notified Davis, "I shall abandon this place, which it is impossible for us to hold." Accordingly, after nightfall, he proceeded to carry out the most skillful of his with-drawals so far in the war. Previously — at Manassas and Yorktown, as well as here at Jackson two months ago yesterday, on the day after his arrival from Tennessee — it had been his practice to leave guns and heavy equipment in position lest their removal, which was likely to be noisy, warn the enemy of his intention; but not now. Silently the guns were withdrawn by hand from their forward emplacements while the sick and wounded were being sent eastward across the river, followed by brigade after brigade of soldiers who had been kept busy with picks and shovels till after midnight, drowning out the sounds of the evacua-tion. Breckinridge's Orphans, who had accomplished Lauman's discomfi-ture four days ago, went last. The lines of the aborted siege, which had cost the Federals 1122 casualties and the Confederates 604, yawned empty in the darkness and remained so until daylight brought a blue advance and the discovery that Johnston had escaped across the Pearl, much as Lee had done across the Potomac three nights earlier with some-what less success.

He took with him everything movable but he could not take the railroad or the town. Undefended, Jackson was reoccupied — and re-burned. That task was assigned to Sherman's old corps, primarily to Blair's division, which was fast becoming proficient in such work, while Ord moved south with instructions to break up the Mississippi Central "absolutely and effectually" for a distance of ten miles, and Parke did the same in the opposite direction. Steele's men did a thorough job on the capital, sparing little except the State House and the Governor's Mansion. Pettus had departed, but the victorious generals held a banquet in his mansion on the second night of the occupation, and when one brigadier was missing next morning he was found asleep beneath the table, so freely had the wine flowed. "You can return slowly to Black River," Grant replied to news that the town had fallen, but Sherman stayed on for a week, supervising the extensive demolition his chief had prescribed at the outset. Added to what had been done in May, this new damage converted the Mississippi capital into what he referred to as "one mass of charred ruins." (Blair's exuberant veterans had a briefer, more colorful description of the place; "Chimneyville," they called it.) Though he found the stripping of the countryside by his foragers for fifteen miles around "terrible to contemplate," Sherman thought it proper to add that such was "the scourge of war, to which ambitious men have appealed rather than [to] the judgment of the learned and pure tribunals which our forefathers have provided for supposed wrongs and injuries." Characteristically, however, before his departure he distributed supplies to civilian hospitals and turned over to a responsible committee enough hard bread, flour, and bacon to sustain five hundred people for thirty days, his only condition being that none of this food was to be converted "to the use of the troops of the so-called Confederate states." Despite the damage to their pride, the committeemen were glad to accept the offer, whatever the condition. "The inhabitants are subjugated. They cry aloud for mercy," Sherman informed his commander back at Vicksburg.

How lasting the damage would be, either to their pride or to their property, was open to some question. Up to now, particularly in regions where the occupation had been less than constant, the rebels had shown remarkable powers of recovery from blows about as heavy. On the march eastward from the Big Black, for example, one of the Federal columns had crossed a portion of the field that took its name from Champion Hill, which the shock of battle had left all torn and trampled, scorched and scored by shells and strewn with wreckage. That was how the marchers remembered the scene from their passage this way a little less than two months back; but now, to their considerable surprise, they found that much of the field had been plowed and planted and corn stood four feet tall in neat, lush rows, not only as if the battle had never been fought, but also as if, except for the reappearance of the soldiers, there had never been a war at all, either here or anywhere else. It was in a way discouraging. This time, though, as Johnston faded back before them without fighting, they were less distracted and could give their full attention to the destruction which had been more or less incidental on the western march. They blazed a trail of devastation; gins, barns, farmhouses, almost everything burnable went up in flames and smoke; rearward the horizon was one long smudge. Looting took on new dimensions, sometimes of absurdity. One officer, watching a cavalryman stagger along with a grandfather's clock in his arms, asked what on earth he planned to do with it, and the trooper explained that he was going to take it apart "and get a pair of the little wheels out of it for spur rowels." There was time, too, for bitterness. A colonel viewing a porticoed mansion set back from the road in a grove of trees, neatly fenced and with a well-kept lawn and outbuildings, including slave quarters, burst out hotly: "People who have been as conspicuous as these in bringing this thing about *ought* to have things burned! I would like to see those chimneys standing there without any house." That his troops had taken his words to heart was evident on the return from Jackson, when the regiment passed that way again. His wish had been fulfilled. All that remained of the plantation house was its blackened chimneys. "Sherman monuments," they were called; or, perhaps more aptly, "Sherman tombstones."

Some among the Confederates in and out of uniform, but most particularly Richmond friends of Davis and Seddon, put the blame for much of this on Johnston, whose policy it had ever been to sacrifice mere territory, the land and all it nourished, rather than risk avoidable bleeding by any soldier in his charge. Always, everywhere in this war except at Seven Pines — which battle, poorly fought as it was, had done more to sustain than refute his theory: especially from the personal point of view, since it had cost him two wounds and command of the South's first army — he had backed up after a minimum of fighting, leaving the civilians of the evacuated region to absorb the shocks he evaded. So some said, angered by his apparent lack of concern for the fate of Vicksburg, which he had been sent to save. Others not only disagreed; they even pointed to the recent campaign as an example of his superior generalship. Unlike Pemberton, who had lost his army by accepting risks Johnston had advised him to avoid, the Virginian had saved his men to fight another day, and in the process had inflicted nearly twice as many casualties as he suffered. Mainly such defenders were members of his army, who not only had good cause to feel thankful for his caution, but also had come under the sway of his attractive personality. A genial companion, as invariably considerate of subordinates as he was critical of superiors, he won the affection of associates by his charm. There were, however, a few who were immune, and one among them was Pemberton, though this was only recently the case. At the outbreak of the war they had been friends; Johnston in fact had chosen the Pennsylvanian as his adjutant before the northern-born officer's transfer to South Carolina. But that was far in the past, in the days before the siege one friend had waited in vain for the other to raise.

Soon afterwards, in mid-July and in accordance with Grant's instructions for the paroled lieutenant general to report to his immediate superior, Pemberton found the Virginian "sitting on a cleared knoll on a moonlight night surrounded by members of his staff." Thus a witness described the scene, adding that when Johnston recognized the "tall, handsome, dignified figure" coming toward him up the slope, he sprang from his seat and advanced to meet him, hand outstretched.

"Well, Jack old boy," he cried. "I'm certainly glad to see you!"

Pemberton halted, stood at attention, and saluted.

"General Johnston, according to the terms of parole prescribed by General Grant, I was directed to report to you."

The two men stood for a moment in silence as Johnston lowered his unclasped hand. Then Pemberton saluted once more, punctiliously formal, and turned away.

They never met again.

✗ 4 ✗

News that Meade had stopped Lee at Gettysburg sent Lincoln's expectations soaring; he foresaw the end of the war, here and now, if only the victory could be pressed to its logical conclusion with "the literal or substantial destruction" of the rebel host before it recrossed the Potomac. Then came the letdown, first in the form of the northern commander's Fourth of July congratulatory order to his troops, calling for still "greater efforts to drive from our soil every vestige of the presence of the invader." Lincoln's spirits took a sudden drop. "My God, is that all?" he exclaimed, and presently he added: "This is a dreadful reminiscence of McClellan. . . . Will our generals never get that idea out of their heads? The whole country is our soil." His fears were enlarged the following day by word that Lee had stolen away in the night, and no dispatch from Meade, that day or the next, gave any assurance of a vigorous pursuit. Lincoln fretted as much *after* as he had done before or during the three-day battle, so high were his hopes and so great was his apprehension that they would be unfulfilled. At a cabinet meeting on July 7 his expression was one of "sadness and despondency," according to Welles, "that Meade still lingered at Gettysburg, when he should have been at Hagerstown or near the Potomac, in an effort to cut off the retreating army of Lee." That afternoon he was conferring with Chase and a few others in his office, pointing out Grant's progress to date on a map of Mississippi, when Welles came running into the room with a broad smile on his face and a telegram from Porter in his hand. The admiral had sent a fast boat up to Cairo, the Memphis wirehead having broken down, and beat the army in getting the news to Washington: "I have the honor to inform you that Vicksburg has surrendered to the U.S. forces on this 4th day of July."

Lincoln rose at once. "I myself will telegraph this news to General Meade," he said, then took his hat as if to go, but paused and turned to Welles, throwing one arm across the shoulders of the bearer of good tidings. "What can we do for the Secretary of the Navy for this glorious intelligence? He is always giving us good news. I cannot in words tell you my joy over this result. It is great, Mr Welles; it is great!" The Secretary beamed as he walked to the telegraph office with his chief, who could not contain his pleasure at the outcome of Grant's campaign. "This will relieve Banks. It will inspire me," he said as he strode along. He thought it might also inspire Meade, and he had Halleck pass the word to him that Vicksburg had surrendered; "Now if General Meade can complete his work so gloriously prosecuted thus far . . . the rebellion will be over."

A wire also went to Grant: "It gives me great pleasure to inform you that you have been appointed a major general in the Regular Army, to rank from July 4, the date of your capture of Vicksburg." Moreover, on Grant's recommendation, Sherman and McPherson soon were made permanent brigadiers, the reward that had gone to Meade at Frederick that same day. The following day, however, when Grant's own announcement of Pemberton's capitulation came limping in behind Porter's — which had said nothing about terms — there was cause to think that his victory was by no means as complete as had been supposed before details of the surrender were disclosed. Surprise and doubt were the reaction to the news that practically all of the nearly 30,000-man garrison had been paroled. Halleck, for instance, protested by return wire that such terms might "be construed into an absolute release, and that the men will immediately be placed in the ranks of the enemy." Grant had already noted that the arrangement left his and Porter's "troops and transports ready for immediate service" against Johnston and Gardner, which otherwise would not have been the case, and when he explained that the parolees had been turned over to an authorized Confederate commissioner for the exchange of prisoners, which made the contract strictly legal, Old Brains was mollified. So was Lincoln, who was a lawyer himself and knew the dangers that lurked in informalities, though what appealed to him most was Grant's further contention that the surrendered troops were "tired of the war and would get home just as soon as they could." There, he believed, they would be likely to create more problems for the Confederacy than if they had been lodged in northern prison camps, a headache for the Union, which would be obliged to feed and guard them while awaiting their exchange.

Others not only disagreed, but some among them formed a delegation to call on Lincoln with a protest against Grant's dereliction and a demand for his dismissal from command. What rebel could be trusted? they asked, and predicted that within the month Pemberton's men would violate their parole and be back in the field, once again doing their worst to tear the fabric of the Union. Referring to his callers as "crossroads wiseacres," though they must have included some influential dignitaries, Lincoln afterwards described to a friend his handling of the situation. "I thought the best way to get rid of them was to tell the story of Sykes's dog. Have you ever heard about Sykes's yellow dog? Well, I must tell you about him. Sykes had a yellow dog he set great store by —" And he went on to explain that this affection was not shared by a group of boys who disliked the beast intensely and spent much of their time "meditating how they could get the best of him." At last they hit upon the notion of wrapping an explosive cartridge in a piece of meat, attaching a long fuze to it, and whistling for the dog. When he came out and bolted the meat, cartridge and all, they touched off the fuze, with spectacular results. Sykes came running out of the house to investigate the explosion. "What's up? Anything busted?" he cried. And then he saw the dog, or what was left of him. He picked up the biggest piece he could find, "a portion of the back with part of the tail still hanging to it," and said mournfully: "Well, I guess he'll never be much account again — as a dog." Lincoln paused, then made his point. "I guess Pemberton's forces will never be much account again as an army." He smiled, recalling the reaction of his callers. "The delegation began looking around for their hats before I had got quite to the end of the story," he told his friend, "and I was never bothered any more after that about superseding the commander of the Army of the Tennessee."

Now as always he shielded Grant from the critics who were so quick to come crying of butchery, whiskey, or incompetence. "I can't spare this man. He fights," he had said after Shiloh, and more than a month before the surrender of Vicksburg he had called the campaign leading up to the siege "one of the most brilliant in the world." In a sense, this latest and greatest achievement was a vindication not only of Grant but also of the Commander in Chief who had sustained him. Perhaps Lincoln saw it so. At any rate, though previously he had corresponded with him only through Halleck, even in the conferring of praise and promotions, this curious hands-off formality, which had no counterpart in his relations with any of the rest of his army commanders, past or present, ended on July 13, when he wrote him the following letter:

My dear General
I do not remember that you and I ever met personally. I write this now as a grateful acknowledgment for the almost inestimable service you have done the country. I wish to say a word further. When you first reached the vicinity of Vicksburg, I thought you should do what you finally did — march the troops across the neck, run the batteries with the transports, and thus go below; and I never had any faith, except a general hope that you knew better than I, that the Yazoo Pass expedition and the like could succeed. When you got below and took Port Gibson, Grand Gulf, and vicinity, I thought you should go down the river and join General Banks; and when you turned north-

ward, east of the Big Black, I feared it was a mistake. I now wish to make the personal acknowledgment that you were right and I was wrong.

Yours very truly
A. LINCOLN

Though in time, when news of the fall of Port Hudson arrived, a congratulatory dispatch also went to Banks, expressing Lincoln's "thanks for your very successful and very valuable military operations this year" — "The final stroke in opening the Mississippi never should, and I think never will, be forgotten," he wrote — no such letter went to Meade, nor did Lincoln mention him by name in responding to a White House serenade on the evening of July 7, tendered in celebration of the double victory. "These are trying occasions," he said, adding a somber note to the tone of jubilation, "not only in success, but also for want of success." He withheld personal praise of Meade because he was waiting for a larger occasion that did not come, though he kept hoping against hope. Finally, his hopes dwindling, he turned cynical. On July 12, when the general wired that he would attack the flood-stalled Confederates next day "unless something intervenes to prevent it," Lincoln ventured a prediction: "They will be ready to fight a magnificent battle when there is no enemy there to fight." Nevertheless, the news two days later that Lee had made a getaway came as an awful shock to him. "We had them in our grasp," he groaned. "We had only to stretch forth our hands and they were ours. And nothing I could say or do could make the army move." He told his son Robert, home from Harvard: "If I had gone up there, I could have whipped them myself." So great was his distress, he adjourned a cabinet meeting on grounds that he was in no frame of mind for fit deliberation. Nor was he. In his extremity — having passed in rapid succession from cynicism, through puzzlement and exasperation, to the edge of paranoia — he questioned not only the nerve and competence of Meade and his subordinates, but also their motives. "And that, my God, is the last of this Army of the Potomac!" he cried as he walked out with the Secretary of the Navy. "There is bad faith somewhere. Meade has been pressed and urged, but only one of his generals was for an immediate attack, was ready to pounce on Lee; the rest held back. What does it mean, Mr. Welles? Great God, what does it mean?"

Halleck did not exaggerate in wiring Meade of Lincoln's "great dissatisfaction" on that day; Welles recorded in his diary that "on only one or two occasions have I ever seen the President so troubled, so dejected and discouraged." Meade's request to be relieved of command, submitted promptly in response to Halleck's wire, shocked Lincoln into recovering his balance. For this was more than a military matter; it was a downright political threat, with sobering implications. The Administration simply could not afford to be placed in the position of having forced the resignation of the man who, in three hard days of fighting, had just turned back the supreme Confederate effort to conquer a peace: an effort, moreover, launched hard on the heels of Union defeats at Fredericksburg and Chancellorsville, which had been fought under leaders now recognized as hand-picked incompetents, both of whom had been kept in command for more than a month after their fiascos. No matter what opinion the citizenry might have as to whether or not the rebels had been "invaders," politically it would not do to make a martyr of the hero who had driven them from what he called "our soil." After instructing Old Brains to decline the general's request to be relieved, Lincoln sat down and wrote Meade a letter designed to assuage the burning in his breast. So great was his own distress, however, that the words came out somewhat differently from what he had intended. In the end it was Lincoln's burning that was assuaged, at least in part. For example, yesterday's letter to Grant had begun: "My dear General," whereas today's bore no salutation at all, merely the heading: "Major General Meade." He opened by saying, "I am very — *very* — grateful to you for the magnificent success you gave the cause of the country at Gettysburg, and I am sorry now to [have been] the author of the slightest pain to you. But I was in such deep distress myself that I could not restrain some expression of it." Whereupon he proceeded to extend that expression of dissatisfaction in a review of the events of the past ten days. Meade had "fought and beat the enemy," with losses equally severe on both sides; then Lee's retreat had been halted by the swollen Potomac, and though Meade had been substantially reinforced and Lee had not, "yet you stood and let the flood run down, bridges be built, and the enemy move away at his leisure, without attacking him." The words were cutting, but those that followed were sharper still. "Again, my dear general, I do not believe you appreciate the magnitude of the misfortune involved in Lee's escape. He was within your easy grasp, and to have closed upon him would, in connection with our other late successes, have ended the war. As it is, the war will be prolonged indefinitely.... It would be unreasonable to expect, and I do not expect you can now effect much. Your golden opportunity is gone, and I am distressed immeasurably because of it."

He ended with a further attempt at reassurance: "I beg you will not consider this a prosecution or persecution of yourself. As you had learned that I was dissatisfied, I have thought it best to kindly tell you why." But on reading the letter over he could see that it was perhaps not so "kindly" after all; that, in fact, rather than serve the purpose of soothing the general's injured feelings, it was more likely to provoke him into resubmitting his request to be relieved of his command. So Lincoln put the sheets in an envelope labeled "To General Meade, never sent or signed," filed it away in his desk, and having thus relieved his spleen contented himself with issuing next day a "Proclamation of Thanksgiving," expressing his gratitude, not to Grant or Meade or Banks or Prentiss, but to Almighty God for "victories on land and on the sea so signal and so effective as to furnish reasonable grounds for augmented confidence that the Union of these States will be maintained, their Constitution preserved, and their peace and prosperity permanently restored." He further besought the public to "render the homage due to the Divine Majesty, for the wonderful things He has done in the nation's behalf, and invoke the influence of His Holy Spirit to subdue the anger which has produced and so long sustained a needless and cruel rebellion, to change the hearts of the insurgents, to guide the counsels of the Government with wisdom adequate to so great a national emergency, and to visit with tender care and consolation throughout the length and breadth of our land all those who, through vicissitudes of marches, voyages, battles, and sieges, have been brought to suffer in mind, body, or estate, and finally to lead the whole nation, through the paths of repentance and submission to the Divine Will, back to the perfect enjoyment of Union and fraternal peace. In witness whereof," the Proclamation ended, "I have hereunto set my hand and caused the seal of the United States to be affixed."

Though it was in large part a reaction to the knowledge that the suffering and bloodshed of the past two years would continue indefinitely past the point at which he believed they could have been stopped, Lincoln's extreme concern over the fact that one of his two great victories had been blunted was also based on fear that if he did not win the war in the field, and soon, he might lose it on the home front. There appeared to be excellent grounds for such apprehension. Ever since the fall elections, which had gone heavily against him in certain vital regions of the country, the loyal and disloyal opposition had been growing, not only in size but also in boldness, until now, in what might have been his hour of triumph, he was faced with the necessity for dealing with riots and other domestic troubles, the worst of which reached a climax in the nation's largest city on the day he issued his Proclamation of Thanksgiving. Though he could assign a measure of the blame to Meade, whose timidity had cost him the chance, as Lincoln saw it, of ending the war with a single stroke, he knew well enough that the discontent had been cumulative, the product of an almost unbroken seven-month sequence of military reverses, a good many of which he had engineered himself, and that the failure might be defined more reasonably as one of leadership at the top. Indeed, many did so define it, both in speeches and in print. During the past two years, while healing the split in his cabinet and winning the respect of those who were closest to him, he had grown in the estimation of the great mass of people who judged him solely from a distance, by his formal actions and utterances and by the gathering aura of his honesty and goodness. There were, however, senators and congressmen, together with other federal and state officials of varying importance, who saw him only occasionally and were offended by what they saw.

"The lack of respect for the President in all parties is unconcealed," Richard Dana, a U.S. district attorney from Massachusetts, had written home from the national capital at the beginning of a visit in late February. Author of *Two Years Before the Mast*, a founder of the Free Soil party and now a solid Republican, Dana spent two weeks looking and listening, then delivered himself of a still harsher judgment based on what he had seen and heard: "As to the politics of Washington, the most striking thing is the absence of personal loyalty to the President. It does not exist. He has no admirers, no enthusiastic supporters, none to bet on his head. If a Republican convention were to be held tomorrow, he would not get the vote of a State. He does not act, or talk, or feel like the ruler of a great empire in a great crisis. This is felt by all, and has got down through all the layers of society. It has a disastrous effect on all departments and classes of officials, as well as on the public. He seems to me to be fonder of details than of principles, of tithing the mint, anise, and cummin of patronage, and personal questions, than of the weightier matters of empire. He likes rather to talk and tell stories with all sorts of persons who come to him for all sorts of purposes than to give his mind to the noble and manly duties of his great post. It is not difficult to detect that this is the feeling of his cabinet. He has a kind of shrewdness and common sense, mother wit, and slipshod, low-leveled honesty, that made him a good Western jury lawyer. But he is an unutterable calamity to us where he is. Only the army can save us."

If there was some perception here, there was also much distortion, and in any event the judgment was merely personal. More serious were the signs of organized obstruction. "Party spirit has resumed its sway over the people," Seward had lamented in the wake of the fall elections, and Sumner had written a friend soon after the turn of the year: "The President tells me that he now fears 'the fire in the rear' — meaning the Democracy, especially at the Northwest — more than our military chances." When the Bay State senator spoke of "the Democracy" he meant the Democrats, particularly that wing of the party which opposed the more fervent innovations of his own: Emancipation, for example, and the draft. At any rate Lincoln's anxiety seemed well founded. "I am advised," Governor Oliver P. Morton of Indiana had wired the Secretary of War, "that it is contemplated when the Legislature meets in this State to pass a joint resolution acknowledging the Southern Confederacy and urging the States of the Northwest to dissolve all constitutional relations with the New England States. The same thing is on foot in Illinois." The same thing, or something resembling it, was indeed on foot in the President's home state, where the legislature had likewise gone Democratic in the fall. However, though the Illinois house passed resolutions praying for an armistice and recommending a convention of all the

states North and South to agree upon some adjustment of their differences, the senate defeated by a few votes the proposal to discuss the matter; Governor Richard Yates was not obliged to exercise the veto. On
the other hand, Morton did not allow matters to progress even that far
in Indiana. He had spies in the opposition ranks, and when he saw what
he believed was coming he dissolved the legislature by the simple expedient of advising the Republican minority to withdraw, which left the
body without a quorum. The trouble with this was that it also left the
Hoosier governor without funds for running the state for the next two
years. But he solved the dilemma by strenuous and unconstitutional efforts. After obtaining loans from private sources and the counties,
amounting to $135,000 in all, he appealed to Lincoln for the necessary
balance. Lincoln referred him to Stanton, who advanced him $250,000
from a special War Department fund. Morton had what he needed to keep
Indiana loyal and going, though it bothered him some that the law had
been severely bent if not broken in the process. "If the cause fails, you
and I will be covered with prosecutions, imprisoned, driven from the
country," he told Stanton, who replied: "If the cause fails I do not wish
to live."

Stanton believed in rigorous methods, especially when it came
to dealing with whatever seemed to him to smack or hint of treason, and
he had been given considerable sway in that regard. Perceiving at the
outset that the septuagenarian Bates was unequal to the task, Lincoln had
put Seward in charge of maintaining internal security, which included
the power to arrest all persons suspected of disloyalty in those regions
where habeas corpus had been suspended despite the protest of the
courts, including the Supreme Court itself. The genial New Yorker did
an effective job, particularly in Maryland and Kentucky during their
periods of attempted neutrality; judges and legislators, among others
who seemed to the government or the government's friends to favor the
government's enemies, were haled from their benches and chambers,
sometimes from their beds, and clapped into prisons, more often than not
without being told of the charges or who had preferred them. When
protests reached Lincoln he turned them aside with a medical analogy,
pointing out that a limb must sometimes he amputated to save a life but
that a life must never be given to save a limb; he felt, he said, "that
measures, however unconstitutional, might become lawful by becoming indispensable to the preservation of the Constitution, through the
preservation of the nation." After Seward came Stanton, who assumed
the security duties soon after he entered the cabinet in early '62. In addition to the fierce delight he took in crushing all advocates of disunion, he
enjoyed the exercise of power for its own sake. "If I tap that little bell,"
he told a visitor, obviously relishing the notion, "I can send you to a
place where you will never hear the dogs bark." Apparently the little
bell rang often; a postwar search of the records disclosed the names of

13,535 citizens arrested and confined in various military prisons during Stanton's tenure of office under Lincoln, while another survey (not concerned with names, and therefore much less valid) put the total at 38,000 for the whole period of the war. How many, if indeed any, of these unfortunates had been fairly accused — and, if so, what their various offenses had been — could never be known, either then or later, since not one of all those thousands was ever brought into a civil court for a hearing, although a few were sentenced by military tribunals.

One of these last was Ohio's Vallandigham, who had continued to fulminate against the abuses of the minority by the majority, including the gerrymandering of his district by the addition of a Republican county, which had resulted in his defeat in the fall election. "I learned my judgment from Chatham: 'My lords, you cannot conquer America.' And you have not conquered the South. You never will. . . . The war for the Union is, in your hands, a most bloody and costly failure," he told his fellow congressmen during the following lame duck session. His main targets were the Emancipation Proclamation and the Conscription Act. With the former, he declared, "war for the Union was abandoned, war for the Negro openly begun, and with stronger battalions than before. With what success? Let the dead at Fredericksburg and Vicksburg answer. . . . Will men enlist now at any price? Ah, sir, it is easier to die at home. I beg pardon, but I trust I am not 'discouraging enlistments.' If I am, then first arrest Lincoln, Stanton, and Halleck and some of your other generals, and I will retract; yes, I will recant. But can you draft again? Ask New England, New York; ask Massachusetts; [but] ask not Ohio, the Northwest. She thought you were in earnest, and gave you all, all — more than you demanded. Sir, in blood she has atoned for her credulity, and now there is mourning in every house and distress and sadness in every heart. Shall she give you any more? Ought this war to continue? I answer, no; not a day, not an hour. What then? Shall we separate? Again I answer, no no, no! What then? . . . Stop fighting, Make an armistice."

So he counseled, and though a Republican member wrote in his diary that this was "a full exhibition of treason" and downright "submission to the rebels," Vallandigham and others like him considered themselves dedicated rather to opposing men like Thaddeus Stevens, whose avowed intent it was to "drive the present rebels as exiles from this country" and to "treat those states now outside of the Union as conquered provinces and settle them with new men." Democrats knew only too well who these "new men" would be: Republicans. To ask them to support this redefined conflict was asking them to complete the stripping of their minority of its former greatest strength, the coalition with conservatives of the South, and thus assure continuing domination by the radical majority down the years. Faced with this threat of political extinction, and having seen their friends arrested by thousands in defiance of their rights, diehard anti-Republicans banded together in secret organizations, especially in Ohio, Indiana, and Illinois, where a prewar society known as "Knights of the Golden Circle," so called because it had been founded to promote the advancement of national interests around the sun-drenched rim of the Caribbean, was revived and enlarged; "Order of American Knights," its new members called it, and later changed the name again to "Sons of Liberty." Their purpose was to promote the success of the Democratic party — first in the North, while the war was on, and then in the South when it was over, which they hoped would be soon — and to preserve, as they said, "the Constitution as it is, the Union as it was." By way of identification to one another, in addition to such intricate handclasps and unpronounceable passwords as were common in secret fraternities, they wore on their lapels the head of Liberty cut from an old-style penny; "Copperheads," their enemies called them, in scornful reference to the poisonous reptile by that name.

Vallandigham was their champion, and when Congress adjourned in March he came home and addressed them from the stump, along the same lines he had followed in addressing his former colleagues. A tall man in his early forties, handsome and gifted as a speaker, with clear gray eyes, a mobile mouth, and a dark fringe of beard along his lower jaw and chin, he found his words greeted with more enthusiasm here than they had received in Washington, where one or another of his opponents had threatened from time to time to cut his throat. On May Day, with Hooker stalled in the Wilderness and Grant on the march across the Mississippi, the Ohioan addressed a crowd of thousands assembled in his home state for a mass Democratic meeting at Mount Vernon. He made a rousing speech, asserting that the war could be concluded by negotiation but that the Republicans were prolonging the bloodshed for political purposes. The Union had gone by the board as a cause, he added; what was being fought for now, he said, was liberation of the blacks at the cost of enslaving the whites. This brought him more than the cheers of the crowd, which included a large number of men wearing copper Liberty heads in their buttonholes. It also resulted, four days later — or rather three nights later, for the hour was 2.30 a.m. May 5 — in his arrest by a full company of soldiers at his home in Dayton, by order of Major General Ambrose Burnside, commander of the Department of the Ohio.

Still smarting from the whips and scorns that followed Fredericksburg and the Mud March, the ruff-whiskered general had established headquarters in Cincinnati in late March and, outraged by Copperhead activities in the region, issued on April 13 a general order prescribing the death penalty for certain overt acts designed to aid or comfort the Confederacy. Moreover, he added, "the habit of declaring sympathy for the enemy will not be allowed. . . . It must be distinctly understood that treason, expressed or implied, will not be tolerated in this department."

Then on May Day had come Vallandigham's speech at Mount Vernon, reported to Burnside by two staff captains he had sent there in civilian clothes to take notes. Clearly this was a violation of the general order, and on May 4, without consulting his superiors or subordinates or even an attorney, he instructed an aide-de-camp to proceed at once to Dayton and arrest the offender. The aide boarded a special train, taking a company of soldiers along, and by 2.30 next morning was banging on Vallandigham's door. Refused admittance, the soldiers broke it down, seized the former congressman in his bedroom, and carried him forthwith to prison in Cincinnati. Brought before a military commission eight days later — though he declined to plead, on grounds that the tribunal had no jurisdiction over a civilian — he was given a two-day trial, at the close of which he was found guilty of violating the general order and was sentenced to close confinement for the duration of the war. Burnside approved the findings and the sentence that same day, May 16, and designated Fort Warren in Boston Harbor as the place of incarceration.

From the outset, though he promptly assured the general of his "firm support," Lincoln had doubted the wisdom of the arrest. Now his doubts were abundantly confirmed. Vallandigham had declined to plead his case before the tribunal, but he did not hesitate to plead it before the public in statements issued from his cell in Cincinnati. Denouncing Burnside as the agent of a despot, he asserted: "I am here in a military bastille for no other offense than my political opinions." Newspapers of various shades of opinion were quick to champion his basic right to freedom of speech, war or no war. As a result, he progressed overnight from regional to national prominence, his cause having been taken up by friends and sympathizers who sponsored rallies for him all across the land. Vallandigham in jail was a far more effective critic of the Administration than he had been at large; Lincoln was inclined to turn him loose, despite his previous assurance of "firm support" for Burnside and his subsequent reply to a set of resolutions adopted at a protest meeting in Albany, New York: "Must I shoot a simple-minded soldier boy who deserts, while I must not touch a hair of a wily agitator who induces him to desert? ... I think that in such a case to silence the agitator and save the boy is not only constitutional but withal a great mercy." However, this was leaving out of account the fact that the soldier and the agitator came under different codes of law, and the last thing Lincoln wanted just now was for the legality of Burnside's general order to be tested in the civil courts. He cast about, and as usual he came up with a solution. Burnside had warned that offenders might be sent "beyond our lines and into the lines of their friends." Early the previous year, moreover, Jefferson Davis had done just that to Parson Brownlow, arrested under suspicion of treasonous activities in East Tennessee. Wherever the notion came from, Lincoln found in it the solution to his problem of what to do with Vallandigham, and on May 26 commuted his sentence to banishment,

thereby creating the prototype for "The Man Without a Country."
Soon afterwards, south of Murfreesboro, the Ohioan was delivered by a
detachment of Federal cavalry, under a flag of truce, to a Confederate
outpost north of Tullahoma. Informed that he could not remain in the
South if he considered himself a loyal citizen of the Union, he made his
way to Wilmington, where he boarded a blockade-runner bound for the
West Indies. On July 5, two months after his arrest, he turned up in Nova
Scotia. Ten days later — having been nominated unanimously for governor by the state Democratic convention, which had been held at
Columbus in mid-June — he opened his campaign for election to that
high office with an address to the people of Ohio, delivered from the
Canadian side of the border at Niagara Falls. Under the British flag, he
said, he enjoyed the rights denied him by "usurpers" at home, and he
added that he intended to "return with my opinions and convictions . . .
not only unchanged, but confirmed and strengthened."

In time he did return, wearing false hair on his face and a large
pillow strapped beneath his waistcoat. Presently he threw off these Fal-
staffian trappings and campaigned openly, despite the warning that the
original sentence would be imposed if he broke the terms of his com-
mutation. Lincoln did not molest him this time, however, nor would he
allow the military to do so, having learned from the experience in May.
Moreover, he had acted by then to prevent further unnecessary roiling
of the citizenry by Burnside. In early June, encouraged by his apparent
success in suppressing freedom of speech in his department, the general
moved against the press in a similar heavy-handed manner. At 3 o'clock
in the morning, June 3, cavalry vedettes rode up to the offices of the
Chicago *Times*, which he had charged with "repeated expression of disloyalty and incendiary statements." Reinforced an hour later by two
companies of infantry from Camp Douglas, they stopped the presses,
destroyed the papers already printed, and announced that the *Times* was
out of business. The reaction was immediate and uproarious. A noon
meeting of prominent Chicagoans, presided over by the mayor, voted
unanimously to request the President to revoke the suppression, and in
Court House Square that evening a crowd of "20,000 loyal citizens," including many Republicans, gathered to hear speeches against such ar-
bitrary seizures of power by the military and to cheer the news that in
Springfield that afternoon the legislature had denounced the general for
his action. Confronted with such outbursts of indignation, which seemed
likely to spread rapidly beyond his home-state borders, much as the
Vallandigham affair had spread beyond the borders of Ohio, Lincoln
rescinded Burnside's order the following morning. What was more, he
followed this up by having Stanton direct his over-zealous subordinate to
arrest no more civilians and suppress no more newspapers without first
securing the approval of the War Department.

In all conscience, he had troubles enough on his hands without the help or hindrance of the fantastically whiskered general in Cincinnati, whose brief foray against the Illinois paper was by no means an isolated example of all-out censorship. From start to finish, despite Lincoln's instructions for department commanders to exercise "great caution, calmness, and forbearance" in the matter, no less than 300 newspapers large and small, including such influential publications as the New York *World,* the Louisville *Courier,* the New Orleans *Crescent,* the Baltimore *Gazette,* and the Philadelphia *Evening Journal* — Democratic all — were suppressed or suspended for a variety of offenses, ranging from the usual "extension of aid or comfort to the enemy" to the release of a bogus proclamation which had the President calling for "400,000 more." In thus increasing the public's apprehension of an extension of the draft, he was treading on dangerous ground — dangerous to the government, that is — for nothing so inflamed resentment as did the Conscription Act which Congress had passed in early March and which had begun to be placed in operation by early summer. This resentment was directed less against the draft itself, which was plainly necessary, than it was against the way the act was written and administered. Actually, though it provoked a good deal of volunteering by men who sought to avoid the stigma of being drafted and the discomfort of not being able to choose their branch of service, it was far from effective in accomplishing its avowed purpose, as postwar records would show; 86,724 individuals escaped by paying the $300 commutation fee, while of the 168,649 actually drafted, 117,986 were hired substitutes, leaving a total of 50,663 men personally conscripted, and of these only 46,347 went into the ranks. Though barely enough to make up the losses of two Gettysburgs, draftees and substitutes combined amounted to less than ten percent of the force the Union had under arms in the course of the war; in fact, they fell far short of compensating for the 201,397 deserters, many of whom had been drafted in the first place. However, the popular furor against conscription was provoked not by its end results, which of course were unknown at the time, but rather by the vexations involved in its enforcement, which brought the naked power of military government into play on the home front and went very much against the national grain. While provost marshals conducted house-to-house searches, often without the formality of warrants, boards of officers sentenced drafted boys as deserters for failing to report for induction, and troops were used without restraint to break up formal protest meetings as well as rowdy demonstrations. In retaliation, conscription officials were roughed up on occasion, a few being shot from ambush as they went about their duties, and others had their property destroyed by angry mobs, all in the good old American way dating back to the Revolution. So-called "insurrections," staged at scattered points throughout the North, invariably met with harshness at the hands of soldiers who did not always bother to discriminate between foreign and domestic "rebels," especially when brought back from the front to deal with this new home-grown variety. In mid-June, for example, an uprising in Holmes County, Ohio, was quelled so rigorously by the troops called in for that purpose that their colonel felt obliged to account for their enthusiasm when he made his report of the affair. "The irregularities committed by some of the men," he wrote, "were owing more to their having campaigned in the South than to any intention on their part of violating my express orders to respect private property."

This rash of draft disturbances, which broke out during the long hot summer leading up to and continuing beyond the two great early-July victories, was by no means limited to the Old Northwest or the Ohio Valley, where secret societies were most active in opposition to the Administration and its measures. Boston and Newark had their clamorous mobs, as did Albany and Troy, New York, and Columbia and Bucks counties, Pennsylvania. There were uprisings in Kentucky and New Hampshire, and the governor of Wisconsin had to call out the state militia to deal with demonstrations in Milwaukee and Ozaukee County, where immigrants from Belgium, Holland, and Germany, especially vigorous in resisting what they had left Europe to escape, attacked the draft headquarters with guns and clubs and stones. By far the greatest of all the riots, however, was the one that exploded in New York City, hard on the heels of Vicksburg and Gettysburg, while Lincoln was writing his sent and unsent letters to Grant and Meade. Partly the trouble was political; protests had been made by party orators that Democratic districts were being required to furnish more than their fair share of conscripts and that ballot boxes were being stuffed with imported Republican soldier votes. Partly, too, it was racial; charges were also made that Negro suffrage was a device for overthrowing the white majority, including Tammany Hall, and that Negroes were being shipped in from the South to throw the Tammany-loyal workers, mostly Irish, out of work. Whatever began it, the three-day riot soon degenerated into violence for its own sake. On Monday, July 13, a mob wrecked the draft office where the drawing of names had begun two days before, then moved on to the Second Avenue armory, which was seized and looted, along with jewelry stores and liquor shops. By nightfall, with the police force overpowered, much of the upper East Side had been overrun. Segments of the mob were reported to be "chasing isolated Negroes as hounds would chase a fox," and the chase generally ended beneath a lamppost, which served conveniently as a gibbet. All next day this kind of thing continued, and nearly all of the next. A colored orphanage was set afire and the rioters cheered the leaping flames, seeing the Negroes not only as rivals for their jobs but also as the prime cause of the war. According to one witness of their fury, "three objects — the badge of a defender of the law, the uniform of the Union army, the skin of a helpless and outraged race — acted upon these madmen as water acts upon a rabid dog." By morning of the third day, however, representatives of all three of these hated categories were rare. The mob had undisputed control of the city.

In Washington, Lincoln and Stanton reacted to news of the violence by detaching troops from Meade to deal with the situation. They arrived on Wednesday evening and got to work at once. "We saw the grim batteries and weatherstained and dusty soldiers tramping into our leading streets as if into a town just taken by siege," another witness recorded in his diary. According to him, the action was brief and bloody. "There was some terrific fighting between the regulars and the insurgents; streets were swept again and again by grape, houses were stormed at the point of the bayonet, rioters were picked off by sharpshooters as they fired on the troops from housetops; men were hurled, dying or dead, into the streets by the thoroughly enraged soldiery; until at last, sullen and cowed and thoroughly whipped and beaten, the miserable wretches gave way at every point and confessed the power of the law." Estimates of the casualties ranged from less than 300 to more than 1000, though some Democrats later protested that the figures had been enlarged by Republican propagandists and that there was "no evidence that any more than 74 possible victims of the violence of the three days died anywhere but in the columns of partisan newspapers." Whether the dead were few or many, one thing was clear: Lincoln was determined to enforce the draft. "The government will be able to stand the test," Stanton had replied by wire to Mayor George Opdyke's request for troops at the height of the trouble, "even if there should be a riot and mob in every ward of every city."

Conscription resumed on schedule, August 19, and though there was grumbling, there was no further violence in the nation's largest city; the Secretary had seen to the fulfillment of his prediction by sending in more troops, with orders to crack down hard if there was any semblance of resistance. Lincoln stood squarely behind him, having denied Governor Horatio Seymour's plea for a suspension of the draft. "Time is too important," he told the Democratic leader, and while he agreed to look into the claim that the state's quota was unfair, he made it clear that there would be no delay for that or any other purpose. "We are contending with an enemy who, as I understand, drives every able-bodied man he can reach into his ranks, very much as a butcher drives bullocks into a slaughter pen. No time is wasted, no argument is used. This produces an army ... with a rapidity not to be matched on our side if we first waste time to re-experiment with the volunteer system." His intention, he said in closing, was to be "just and constitutional, and yet practical, in performing the important duty with which I am charged, of maintaining the unity and free principles of our common country." And so it was. Under Lincoln there was Stanton, and under Stanton there was Provost Marshal General James B. Fry, who headed a newly created bureau of the War Department. Under Fry, in charge of enrollment districts corresponding roughly to congressional districts all across the land, were the provost marshals, who were responsible not only for the functioning of the conscription process but also for the maintenance of internal security within their individual districts. Each could call on his neighboring marshals for help in case of trouble, as well as on Fry in Washington, and Fry in turn could call on Stanton, who was prepared to lend the help of the army if it was needed and the Commander in Chief approved. Lincoln's long arm now reached into every home in the North, as well as into every home in the South that lay in the wake of his advancing armies, east and west.

Now that he had had time to absorb the shock Lee's getaway had given him, he felt better about the outcome of the battle in Pennsylvania and the capacity of the general who had won it. Though he was still regretful — "We had gone through all the labor of tilling and planting an enormous crop," he complained, "and when it was ripe we did not harvest it" — he was also grateful. That was the word he used: saying, "I am very grateful to Meade for the service he did at Gettysburg," and asking: "Why should we censure a man who has done so much for his country because he did not do a little more?" All the same, he could scarcely help contrasting the eastern victory with the western one, which had left him not even "a little more" to wish for. Nor could he avoid comparing the two commanders. More and more, he was coming to see Grant as the answer to his military problem: not only because of his obvious talent, demonstrated in the capture of two rebel armies intact, but also because of his attitude toward his work. For example, when Lorenzo Thomas was sent to Mississippi to direct the recruiting of Negro troops, Grant had been instructed to assist him, and though he said quite frankly, "I never was an abolitionist, not even what could be called anti-slavery," he had replied forthrightly: "You may rely upon it I will give him all the aid in my power. I would do this whether the arming the negro seemed to me a wise policy or not, because it is an order that I am bound to obey and I do not feel that in my position I have a right to question any policy of the government."

Lincoln liked the tone of that. In contrast to the petulance he had encountered in his dealings with five of the six commanders of the eastern army (McDowell, the exception, had also turned sour in the end, after two months of service under Pope) Grant had the sound of a man he could enjoy working closely with, and apparently he had the notion of bringing him East, although Halleck and Charles Dana, who had returned to Washington shortly after the fall of Vicksburg, were certain that the general would prefer to continue his service in the West. Presently there was first-hand evidence that such was indeed the case; for

Dana wrote to Grant in late July, telling him what was afoot, and got a reply in early August. "General Halleck and yourself were both very right in supposing that it would cause me more sadness than satisfaction to be ordered to the command of the Army of the Potomac. Here I know the officers and men and what each general is capable of as a separate commander. There I would have all to learn. Here I know the geography of the country and its resources. There it would be a new study. Besides, more or less dissatisfaction would necessarily be produced by importing a general to command an army already well supplied with those who have grown up, and been promoted, with it. . . . While I would disobey no order, I should beg very hard to be excused before accepting that command." This too was forthright; the President, if he saw the letter, was left in no doubt as to Grant's own preference in the matter. At any rate Lincoln decided to stick with Meade for the time being, much as he had done with Burnside and Hooker after telling a friend that "he was not disposed to throw away a gun because it missed fire once; that he would pick the lock and try it again." Grant would keep, Grant would be there in case he was needed; Grant was his ace in the hole.

Meanwhile there was the war to get on with, on the political front as well as on the firing line. In mid-June out in Illinois, at the height of the Vallandigham controversy and two weeks after Burnside's suppression of the Chicago *Times*, a monster protest rally had been staged in Lincoln's own home town; Copperhead orators had whipped the assembly into frenzies of applause, and the meeting had closed with the adoption of peace resolutions. Now, with the fall elections drawing near, Republicans were calling for loyal Democrats to join them, under the banner of a "National Union" party, in campaigning for support of the Administration's war aims. They planned a record-breaking turn-out at Springfield in early September, to offset whatever effect the previous gathering might have had on voters of the region, and the arrangements committee invited Lincoln to come out and speak. He considered going — after all, except for military conferences, he had not left Washington once in the thirty months he had been there — but found the press of business far too great. Instead, he decided in late August to write a letter to the chairman of the committee, James Conkling, to be read to the assembly and passed on to the rest of the country by the newspapers, giving his views on the conflict at its present stage. He began by expressing his gratitude to those "whom no partizan malice, or partizan hope, can make false to the nation's life," then passed at once, since peace seemed uppermost in men's minds nowadays, to a discussion of "three conceivable ways" in which it could be brought about. First, by suppressing the rebellion; "This I am trying to do. Are you for it? If you are, so far we are agreed." Second, by giving up the Union; "I am against this. Are you for it? If you are, you should say so plainly." Third, by negotiating some sort of armistice based on compromise with the Confederates; but "I do not believe any compromise, embracing the maintenance of the Union, is now possible. All I learn leads to a directly opposite belief."

After disposing thus, to his apparent satisfaction, of the possibility of achieving peace except by force of arms, he moved on to another matter which his opponents had lately been harping on as a source of dissatisfaction: Emancipation. "You say you will not fight to free negroes. Some of them seem willing to fight for you; but no matter. Fight you, then, exclusively to save the Union. I issued the Proclamation on purpose to aid you in saving the Union. Whenever you shall have conquered all resistance to the Union, if I shall urge you to continue fighting, it will be an apt time then for you to declare you will not fight to free negroes. I thought that in your struggle for the Union, to whatever extent the negroes should cease helping the enemy, to that extent it weakened the enemy in his resistance to you. Do you think differently? I thought that whatever negroes can be got to do, as soldiers, leaves just so much less for white soldiers to do in saving the Union. Does it appear otherwise to you? But negroes, like other people, act upon motives. Why should they do anything for us if we will do nothing for them? If they stake their lives for us, they must be prompted by the strongest motive — even the promise of freedom. And the promise, being made, must be kept."

And having progressed so far in what an associate called a "stump speech" delivered by proxy, Lincoln passed to the peroration. Here he broke into a sort of verbal buck-and-wing:

> The signs look better. The Father of Waters again goes unvexed to the sea. Thanks to the great Northwest for it. Nor yet wholly to them. Three hundred miles up, they met New England, Empire, Keystone, and Jersey, hewing their way right and left. The Sunny South, too, in more colors than one, also lent a hand. On the spot, their part of the history was jotted down in black and white. The job was a great national one, and let none be banned who bore an honorable part in it. And while those who have cleared the great river may well be proud, even that is not all. It is hard to say that anything has been more bravely and well done than at Antietam, Murfreesboro, Gettysburg, and on many fields of lesser note. Nor must Uncle Sam's web-feet be forgotten. At all the watery margins they have been present. Not only on the deep sea, the broad bay, and the rapid river, but also up the narrow muddy bayou, and wherever the ground was a little damp, they have been and made their tracks. Thanks to all. For the great republic, for the principle it lives by and keeps alive, for man's vast future — thanks to all.
>
> Peace does not appear so distant as it did. I hope it will come soon, and come to stay, and so come as to be worth the keeping in all future time. It will then have been proved that among free men there

can be no successful appeal from the ballot to the bullet, and that they who take such appeal are sure to lose their case and pay the cost. And then there will be some black men who can remember that, with silent tongue and clenched teeth and steady eye and well-poised bayonet, they have helped mankind on to this great consummation, while I fear there will be some white ones unable to forget that, with malignant heart and deceitful speech, they have strove to hinder it.

Still, let us not be over-sanguine of a speedy final triumph. Let us be quite sober. Let us diligently apply the means, never doubting that a just God, in his own good time, will give us the rightful result.

✗ 5 ✗

In their first reports of Gettysburg, southern newspapers hailed the battle as a climactic triumph. "A brilliant and crushing victory has been achieved," the Charleston *Mercury* exulted on July 8, and two days later the Richmond *Examiner* informed its readers that the Army of Northern Virginia, with upwards of 30,000 prisoners in tow, was on the march for Baltimore. Presently, when it was learned that the graybacks had withdrawn instead to the Potomac, these and other southern journals assured the public that there was "nothing bad in this news beyond a disappointment"; Lee, whose "retrograde movement" had been "dictated by strategy and prudence," was "perfectly master of the situation." Though the victory "had not been decisive" because of "the semblance of a retreat," the outcome of the Pennsylvania conflict remained "favorable to the South." Not until the last week of the month did the *Examiner* refer to the "repulse at Gettysburg." By that time, however, the *Mercury*'s editor had also come full circle and like his Richmond colleague had recovered, through hindsight, his accustomed position as an acid critic of the Administration's conduct of the war. "It is impossible for an invasion to have been more foolish and disastrous," he pronounced.

For the most part, Lee's weary soldiers were content to leave such public judgments to the home-front critics, but privately there were some who agreed with the angry Carolinian. They had been mishandled and they knew it. "The campaign is a failure," a Virginia captain wrote home on his return to native soil, "and the worst failure the South has ever made. Gettysburg sets off Fredericksburg. Lee seems to have become as weak as Burnside. And no blow since the fall of New Orleans had been so telling against us." News of the loss of Vicksburg, which the strike across the Potomac had been designed in part to prevent, served to deepen the gloom, especially for those whose lofty posts afforded them a long-range view of the probable consequences. Longstreet, for example, wrote years later, looking back: "This surrender, taken in connection with the Gettysburg defeat, was, of course, very discouraging to our superior officers, though I do not know that it was felt as keenly by the rank and file. For myself, I felt that our last hope was gone, and that it was now only a question of time with us." Officials in Richmond also were staggered by the double blow, and of these perhaps the hardest hit was Seddon, who had put his faith in Johnston. Nowadays, according to a War Department clerk, the Secretary resembled "a galvanized corpse which has been buried two months. The circles around his eyes are absolutely black." Others about the office were as grim, particularly after reading the preliminary reports of the commanders in the field. "Gettysburg has shaken my faith in Lee as a general," R. G. H. Kean, chief of the Bureau of War, recorded in his diary on July 26. "To fight an enemy superior in numbers at such terrible disadvantage of position in the heart of his own territory, when the freedom of movement gave him the advantage of selecting his own time and place for accepting battle, seems to have been a great military blunder. [Moreover] the battle was worse in execution than in plan. . . . God help this unhappy country!" Two days later another high-placed diarist, Chief of Ordnance Josiah Gorgas, who had worked brilliantly and hard to provide the enormous amounts of matériel lost or expended, west and east, confessed an even darker view of the situation. "It seems incredible that human power could effect such a change in so brief a space," he lamented. "Yesterday we rode on the pinnacle of success; today absolute ruin seems to be our portion. The Confederacy totters to its destruction."

The one exception was Davis, who neither contributed to nor shared in the prevailing atmosphere of gloom that settled over the capital as a result of the triphammer blows struck by the Federals east and west. It was not that he failed to appreciate the gravity of the situation, the extent and intensity of the danger in both directions. He did. "We are now in the darkest hour of our political existence," he admitted in mid-July. Rather, it was as if defeat, even disaster, whatever else it brought, also brought release from dread and a curious inverse lift of the spirit after a time of strain which had begun with Grant's crossing of the Mississippi River and the death of Stonewall Jackson. Visitors to the White House in mid-May found him "thin and frail and gaunt with grief," and the tension increased tremendously when Vicksburg was besieged and Lee started north on June 3, the President's fifty-fifth birthday. Mrs Davis said afterwards that throughout this time her husband was "a prey to the acutest anxiety": so much so, indeed, that he found it nearly intolerable to have to wait deskbound in Richmond while his and the nation's fate was perhaps being decided in Pennsylvania and far-off Mississippi. He yearned for the field, a return to his first profession, and like Lincoln — who would declare somewhat later, under a similar press of anxiety: "If I had gone up there I could have whipped them myself" — he considered personal intervention. At any rate he expressed such a hope aloud, if only to his wife. "If I could take one wing and Lee the other," she heard him say one hot June night, "I think we could between us wrest a victory from those people." But that was not to be, either for him or his opponent, though presently there was disquieting news from Bragg and Buckner that Rosecrans and Burnside were on the march in Middle and East Tennessee, and hard on the heels of this came the first vague reports of Lee's retreat and Pemberton's surrender. Moreover, on July 10, when Vicksburg's fall was officially confirmed and Lee reported his army marooned on the hostile northern bank of the Potomac, bad news arrived from still another quarter. Beauregard wired that the enemy had effected a sudden lodgment on Morris Island; Fort Wagner had not been taken, the Creole declared, but the build-up and the pressure were unrelenting. Three days later, however, with Bragg in full retreat and the possible loss of Charleston increasing the strain on the President's frayed nerves, word came from Lee that his army was over the swollen river at last and back on the soil of Virginia, unpursued. Davis seized upon this one gleam of brightness in the gloom, and the clerk who had noted the black circles around Seddon's eyes recorded in his diary: "The President is quite amiable now. The newspaper editors can find easy access and he welcomes them with a smile."

There was more to this than a grasping at straws, though of course there was that as well; nor was his smile altogether forced, though of course it was in part. Davis saw in every loss of mere territory a corresponding gain, if only in the sense that what had been lost no longer required defending. Just as the early fall of Nashville and New Orleans had permitted a tighter concentration of the Confederacy's limited military resources and had given its field commanders more freedom of action by reducing the number of fixed positions they were obliged to defend, so might the loss of the Mississippi make the defense of what remained at once more compact and more fluid. What remained after all was the heartland. Contracted though its borders were, from the Richmond apex south through the Carolinas to Savannah on the Atlantic and southwest through East Tennessee and Alabama to Mobile on the Gulf, the nation's productive center remained untouched. There the mills continued to grind out powder, forge guns, weave cloth; there were grown the crops and cattle that would feed the armies; there on the two seaboards were the ports into which the blockade-runners steamed. In the final analysis, as Davis saw it, everything else was extra — even his home state, which now was reduced to serving as a buffer. Besides, merely because the far western portion of the country had been severed from the rest, it did not follow that the severed portion would die or even, necessarily, stop fighting. In point of fact, some of the advantages he saw accruing to the East as a result of the amputation might also obtain in the Transmississippi, if only the leaders there were as determined as he himself was. Accordingly, after making himself accessible to the Rich-

mond editors so that they might spread these newest views among the
defenders of the heartland, he took as his first task next day, July 14, the
writing of a series of letters designed to encourage resolution among the
leaders and people whose duties and homes lay beyond the great river
just fallen to the Union.

Of these several letters the first went to Kirby Smith, commander of that vast region which in time would be known as Kirby-
Smithdom. "You now have not merely a military, but also a political
problem involved in your command," Davis told him, and went on to
suggest that necessity be made a virtue and a source of strength. Cut off
as it was, except by sea, the Transmississippi "must needs be to a great
extent self-sustaining," he wrote, urging the development of new plants
in the interior to manufacture gun carriages and wagons, tan leather
for shoes and harness, and weave cloth for uniforms and blankets, as
well as the establishment of a rolling mill for the production of ironclad
vessels, "which will enable you in some contingencies to assume the offensive" on the Arkansas and the Red. In any case, he added, "the endurance of our people is to be sorely tested, and nothing will serve more
to encourage and sustain them than a zealous application of their industry to the task of producing within themselves whatever is necessary for
their comfortable existence. And in proportion as the country exhibits a
power to sustain itself, so will the men able to bear arms be inspired with
a determination to repel invasion. . . . May God guide and preserve
you," the long letter ended, "and grant to us a future in which we may
congratulate each other on the achievement of the independence and
peace of our country." This was followed by almost as long a letter to
Theophilus Holmes, the only one of Smith's three chief subordinates
who had suffered a defeat. Far from indulging in criminations for the
botched assault on Helena, the details of which were not yet known in
Richmond, Davis chose rather "to renew to you the assurance of my full
confidence and most friendly regards. . . . The clouds are truly dark over
us," he admitted, but "the storm may yet be averted if the increase of
danger shall arouse the people to such a vigorous action as our situation
clearly indicates." Nor were the military leaders the only ones to whom
the President wrote in this "darkest hour." He also addressed himself,
in a similar vein of encouragement, to Governors Harris Flanagin of
Arkansas, Francis R. Lubbock of Texas, and Thomas C. Reynolds of
Missouri. And having received from Senator R. W. Johnston a gloomy
report of dissatisfaction in Arkansas, including some talk of seceding
from the sundered Confederacy, he replied on this same July 14:
"Though it was well for me to know the worst, it pained me to observe
how far your confidence was shaken and your criticism severe on men
who I think deserve to be trusted. In proportion as our difficulties increase, so must we all cling together, judge charitably of each other, and
strive to bear and forbear, however great may be the sacrifice and bitter

the trial. . . . The sacrifices of our people have been very heavy both of blood and of treasure; many like myself have been robbed of all which the toil of many years had gathered; but the prize for which we strive — freedom, and independence — is worth whatever it may cost. With union and energy, the rallying of every man able to bear arms to the defense of his country, we shall succeed, and if we leave our children poor we shall leave them a better heritage than wealth."

In urging these Westerners to "judge charitably of each other, and strive to bear and forbear," he was preaching what he practiced in the East in regard to Lee and Pemberton. Both had come under a storm of criticism: especially the latter, who not only had suffered a sounder defeat, but also had no earlier triumphs to offset it. So bitter was the feeling against him in the region through which he marched his Vicksburg parolees on their way to Demopolis, Alabama — a scarecrow force, severely reduced by desertions which increased with every mile it covered — that the President was obliged in mid-July to detach Hardee from Bragg, despite the touch-and-go situation in Tennessee, and send him to Demopolis to gather up the stragglers and assume the task of remolding them into a fighting unit. This left Pemberton without a command, though he had been exchanged and was available for duty. In early August, Davis wrote him a sympathetic letter: "To some men it is given to be commended for what they are expected to do, and to be sheltered, when they fail, by a transfer of the blame which may attach. To others it is decreed that their success shall be denied or treated as a necessary result, and their failures imputed to incapacity or crime. . . . General Lee and yourself have seemed to me to be examples of the second class, and my confidence has not been diminished because 'letter writers' have not sent forth your praise on the wings of the press. I am no stranger to the misrepresentation of which malignity is capable, nor to the generation of such feeling by the conscientious discharge of duty." However, it was no easy thing to find employment for a discredited lieutenant general. Bragg at first expressed a willingness to take him, but presently, having conferred with his officers, reported somewhat cryptically that it "would not be advisable." Pemberton returned to Richmond, and after waiting eight months for an assignment, appealed to the Commander in Chief to release him for service "in any capacity in which you think I may be useful." Davis replied that his confidence in him was unimpaired — "I thought and still think that you did right to risk an army for the purpose of keeping command of even a section of the Mississippi River. Had you succeeded none would have blamed; had you not made the attempt, few if any would have defended your course" — but ended, two months later, by accepting the Pennsylvanian's resignation as a lieutenant general, at which rank he was unemployable, and by presenting him with a commission as a lieutenant colonel of artillery, the rank he had held in that same branch when he first crossed over and threw in with the South. In this capacity Pemberton served out the war, often in the thick of battle, thereby demonstrating a greater devotion to the cause he had adopted than did many who had inherited it as a birthright.

To Lee, too, went sustaining letters expressive of the President's confidence after the late reverse in Pennsylvania. "I have felt more than ever before the want of your advice during the recent period of disaster," Davis wrote in late July, closing "with prayers for your health, safety and happiness," and in early August, after assuring the general that he could "rely upon our earnest exertions to meet your wants," he offered the opinion that the Virginian might do well to withdraw his army closer to Richmond and thus encourage the enemy to attack him in a position that could be reinforced more readily; but he made it clear that now as always he was leaving the final decision to the commander in the field, who might prefer to defend the line of the Rappahannock, as he had done so successfully twice before. In closing, Davis spoke again of how sorely Lee had been missed throughout the fourteen months since he had left his post as presidential adviser: "I will not disturb your mind by reciting my troubles about distant operations. You were required in the field and I deprived myself of the support you gave me here. I need your counsel, but must strive to meet the requirements of the hour without distracting your attention at a time when it should be concentrated on the field before you. . . . As ever, truly your friend, Jeffn Davis."

No such letter went to Joe Johnston, though the correspondence between the Chief Executive and this other top-ranking Virginian was a good deal more voluminous. When a friend remarked, one day amid these troubles, that Vicksburg had fallen "apparently from want of provisions," Davis replied scathingly: "Yes, from want of provisions inside, and a general outside who wouldn't fight." First his anger and then his scorn had been aroused by efforts on the part of Johnston and his friends to free the general of all responsibility for the loss not only of Vicksburg and Port Hudson, but even of Jackson, their claim being based on a renewal of the complaint that he had not been allowed enough authority to permit decisive action. Davis replied on July 15 with a fifteen-page letter in which he reviewed the entire case, order by order, dispatch by dispatch, showing that Johnston had been given unlimited authority to act as he thought best, and he concluded in summation: "In no manner, by no act, by no language, either of myself or of the Secretary of War, has your authority . . . been withdrawn, restricted, or modified." Johnston's response was a request that he be relieved of all responsibility for the disaster that seemed to be shaping up for Bragg, and Davis was prompt to comply. On July 22 the Department of Tennessee was removed from the Virginian's control. However, the apparent effect of this was to afford the general and his staff more time for self-justification.

There now began to appear, in various anti-Administration journals throughout the South, excerpts from a 5000-word "letter" written by Dr D. W. Yandell, Johnston's medical director, ostensibly to a fellow physician in Alabama. Secret dispatches and official orders were quoted, certain evidence that the writer had had access to the general's private files, and Johnston was praised extravagantly at the expense of Pemberton and the Commander in Chief, who were charged with indecision and lack of foresight. On August 1 Davis sent a copy of this "article-letter," which was being passed around in Richmond, directly to Johnston with a covering note that combined irony and contempt: "It is needless to say that you are not considered capable of giving countenance to such efforts at laudation of yourself and detraction of others, and the paper is sent to you with the confidence that you will take the proper action in the premises." The effect, of course, was to widen the rift between the two leaders, whose rupture was soon complete. An acquaintance observed that from this time forward Johnston's "hatred of Jeff Davis became a religion with him." Davis, on the other hand, was content to restrict himself to slighting references such as those he had made while the latest of the Virginian's "retrograde adjustments" was still in progress. "General Johnston is retreating on the east side of Pearl River," he informed Lee on the second anniversary of Manassas, "and I can only learn from him of such vague purposes as were unfolded when he held his army before Richmond." A week later the veil lifted a bit, but only to descend again. "General Johnston, after evacuating Jackson, retreated to the east, to the pine woods of Mississippi," Davis wrote Lee on July 28, "and if he has any other plan than that of watching the enemy, it has not been communicated."

Meanwhile Johnston, having advised the War Department of his intention "to hold as much of the country as I can and to retire farther only when compelled to do so," was enjoying a brief vacation in Mobile with his wife, who told a friend in early August that she had found her husband looking well and in "tolerable spirits, as cheerful as if Jeff was throwing rose leaves at him, instead of nettles and thorns."

"Misfortune often develops secret foes," Davis had said in a letter written earlier that week to Lee, "and oftener still makes men complain. It is comfortable to hold someone responsible for one's discomfort." Lee could testify to the truth of this, having seen it demonstrated first on his return from western Virginia, back in the rainy fall of '61, and now again on his return from Pennsylvania, when some of the same irate critics took him to task for blunders in the field. But the President had something else to say, of which Lee, concerned almost exclusively with army matters throughout the past year, was perhaps much less aware. Convinced that "this war can only be successfully prosecuted while we have the cordial support of the people," Davis had been pained to observe what he set down next: "In various quarters there are mut-terings of discontent, and threats of alienation are said to exist, with preparation for organized opposition.... If a victim would secure the success of our cause," he added in closing, "I would freely offer my-self."

This last was scarcely necessary, however, since a good many in-fluential men had already singled him out for that distinction. In Charleston, for instance, the Robert Barnwell Rhetts, Senior and Junior, stepped up their attacks against him in the columns of their *Mercury*, and the father was in Columbia even now, suggesting as a member of the South Carolina convention, still in session, that Davis be impeached. There was considerable disagreement as to whether his sins were mainly ones of omission or commission, but his critics agreed that, whichever they were, he had them to a ruinous extent. Old Edmund Ruffin, Vir-ginia's secession leader who had gone down to Sumter to fire the first shot of the war, referred contemptuously nowadays to "our tender conscienced and imbecile President," while James L. Alcorn, a fellow Mississippian of doubtful loyalty to the Confederacy, pulled out all the stops in calling him a "miserable, stupid, one-eyed, dyspeptic, arrogant tyrant." Two of his more vehement opponents, W. L. Yancey and seventy-year-old Sam Houston, were removed from the political scene by death before the end of July — the former as a result of a kidney ail-ment, though some editors hostile to Davis claimed the Alabamian died of a broken heart and acute regret at having presented "the man and the hour" to the inaugural crowd thirty months ago in Montgomery — but plenty of others remained: Robert Toombs, for example, whose wounded pride continued to fester down in Georgia. "Toombs is ready for another revolution," a diarist observed, "and curses freely every-thing Confederate from the President down to a horse boy." North Carolina's Governor Zebulon Vance, who had fought against secession as a Unionist and then against the Yankees as an officer of the line, was equally ready to take on the Richmond government as a champion of States Rights. "I can see but little good, but a vast tide of inflowing evil from these inordinate stretches of military powers which are fast dis-gracing us equally with our northern enemies," he told his constituents, and he was so zealous in his concern for their comfort and welfare that he was said to have in his warehouses, on the chance they might be needed some day, more uniforms than were on the backs of the ragged soldiers in Lee's army, to which he himself had belonged until he resigned and came home to campaign for the election he had won last fall.

How a nation which at the outset had been practically without industrial facilities for warfare, which had lost more than half its harbors and had the remaining few blockaded, which was penetrated from the landward side by large and well-organized columns of invasion, and which was outnumbered worse than five to one in available manpower for its armies, could hope to survive unless its people were united in die-hard resistance Vance did not say. His concern at that particular time had been the suspension of habeas corpus during a crisis, and apparently his concern stopped there, whatever concomitant problems loomed alongside it or lurked in the background. Other leaders had other concerns as exclusive. Georgia's Joe E. Brown — "Joseph the Governor of all the Georgias," a home-state editor dubbed him; another said that he suffered from delusions in which he was "alternately the State of Georgia and the President of the Confederate States" — saw conscription as the great evil to be feared and fought. "The people of Georgia will refuse to yield their sovereignty to usurpation," he had notified Davis in October, and since then he had done much to prove he meant it, beginning with an executive order forbidding the taking or shipment of firearms from the state. Under his guidance the legislature elected Herschel V. Johnson, Stephen Douglas's 1860 running mate, to the Confederate senate on a program of opposition to the central government. Its members cheered wildly an address Johnson delivered before his departure, protesting the concentration of power in Richmond, and were joined in their applause by a fellow Georgian in whose hands a good part of that power had supposedly been placed: Vice President Alexander Stephens. There was nothing unusual in his presence at Milledgeville on this occasion, for he had early become disenchanted with the republic he had helped to establish and now he spent more time at home in nearby Crawfordville than he did at his duties in the national capital. Nor was there anything unusual, by now, in his indorsement of a speech against the Administration of which he was nominally a part. Like his friend Toombs, he was "ready for another revolution" whose cause would be the same as the First and Second, staged respectively in 1776 and 1861: both of which, as Stephens saw it, had since been betrayed. What he feared most, whether it was dressed in red or blue or gray, was what he later termed "the Demon of Centralism, Absolutism, Despotism!" That was the true enemy, and with it there could be no compromise whatever. "Away with the idea of getting independence first, and looking after liberty afterward," he declared. "Our liberties, once lost, may be lost forever."

Such opinions, voiced by such leaders — "impossiblists," they would be called one day — made waverers of many among their listeners who had been steadfast up to then, and defeatists of those who were wavering already. Moreover, their influence ranged well beyond the halls and stumps from which they spoke, for their words were broadcast far and wide by newspapers whose editors shared their views. The Rhetts and Edward Pollard of the *Examiner*, who referred to Davis as "a literary dyspeptic [with] more ink than blood in his veins, an intriguer busy with private enmities," were only three among the many, including the editors and owners of the Lynchburg *Virginian*, the Atlanta *Southern Confederacy*, the Macon *Telegraph* and *Intelligencer*, the Columbus *Sun*, and the Savannah *Republican*. Georgians were thus predominant, but the most blatant in his approach to downright treason was William Holden of the Raleigh *Standard*. Unsuppressed (for the Confederate government never censored so much as a line in a single paper throughout the war) Holden continued to rail against the Administration and all it stood for, uninterrupted except for one day in September when a brigade from Lee's army, passing through the North Carolina capital, indignantly wrecked the office of the *Standard*. Holden resumed publication without delay; but meanwhile, the soldiers having departed, a crowd of his admirers marched in retaliation on the plant of the rival *State Journal*, a Davis-loyal paper just up the street, and destroyed its type, presses, and machinery. Despite a presidential warning that those who sowed "the seeds of discontent and distrust" were preparing a "harvest of slaughter and defeat," hostile editors not only continued their attacks on the government, but also carried in their news columns the identification of military units in their areas, plans of yet unfought battles and campaigns, the arrival and departure times of blockade-runners, descriptions and locations of vital factories and munition works, all in such detail, a diarist remarked, that the North had no need for spies; "Our newspapers tell every word there is to be told, by friend or foe." Helpful though all this was to the enemy, the worst effect on the nation's chances for survival lay in the undermining of the public's confidence in eventual victory. Profoundly shaken by the double defeat of Gettysburg and Vicksburg, the people looked to their leaders for reassurance. From some they got it, while from others all they got was "I told you so" — as indeed they had, with a stridency that increased with every setback. All too often, as a result, enthusiasm was replaced by apathy. "They got us into it; let them get us out," men were saying nowadays, and by "them" they meant the authorities in Richmond.

In point of fact, if the public's faith in its government's paper money was a fair reflection of its attitude in general, the decline of confidence had begun much earlier. For the first two years of the war — that is, through April of the present year — the dollar had fallen gradually, if steadily, to a ratio of about four to one in gold. This was not too bad; the Federal greenback had fallen to about three to one in the same period. However, in the next four months, while Union money not only held steady but even rose a bit, Confederate notes declined nearly twice as much in value as they had done in the course of the past two years. In May, despite the splendid victory at Chancellorsville, the dollar fell from 4.15 to 5.50, the worst monthly drop to date. In June, moreover, with Lee on the march in Pennsylvania to offset Grant's progress in Mississippi, it took an even greater drop, from 5.50 to 7. In July, with Vicksburg lost and Lee in retreat, it tumbled to 9, and by the end of August, with the full impact of the two defeats being felt by all the people, one gold dollar was worth an even dozen paper dollars. To some extent, though the figures themselves could not be argued with, their effect could be discounted; men — some men; particularly money men — were known to be more touchy about their pocketbooks than they were about their lives, withholding the former while risking the latter for a cause. Davis, for one, could maintain that the shrinking of the dollar, even though the damage was to a large extent self-inflicted, was only one more among the hardships to be endured if independence was to be achieved. "Our people have proven their gallantry and patriotic zeal," he had written Lee; "their fortitude is now to be tested. May God endow them with all the virtue which is needed to save a suffering country and maintain a just cause."

Beyond the northern lines, as we have seen, there were many who agreed with Davis that his cause was just; who at any rate were willing to have the Confederates depart in peace. Similarly, or conversely, there were many behind the southern lines who disagreed with him; who were also for peace, but only on Union terms. Some had lost heart as a result of the recent reverses, while others had had no heart for the war in the first place. The latter formed a hard core of resistance around which the former gathered in numbers that increased with every Federal success. It was these men Davis had in mind when, after referring to "mutterings of discontent," he spoke of downright "threats of alienation" and "preparation for organized opposition." Such preparations had begun more than a year ago, but only on a small scale, as when some fifty men in western North Carolina raised a white flag and marched slowly around it praying for peace. Since then, the movement had grown considerably, until now the South too had its secret disloyal societies: Heroes of America, they called themselves, or Sons of America, or sometimes merely "Red Strings," from the identifying symbol they wore pinned to their lapels. While neither as numerous nor as active as their counterparts in the North, they too had their passwords, their signs and grips and their sworn objectives, which were to discourage enlistment, oppose conscription, encourage desertion, and agitate for an early return to the Union. Mostly the members were natives of a mountainous peninsula more than a hundred miles in width and six hundred miles in length, extending from the Pennsylvania border, southwest through western Virginia and eastern Tennessee, down into northern Georgia and Alabama. Owning few or no slaves, and indeed not much of anything else in the way of worldly goods, a good portion of these people wanted no part of what they called "a rich man's war and a poor man's fight." War or fight, its goals were those of the Piedmont and Tidewater regions, not their own, and they contributed substantially to the total of 103,400 Confederate desertions computed to have occurred in the course of the war. So far, they had amounted more to a potential than to an actual danger; Streight's raid across North Alabama, for example, had been planned with their support in mind, but they had not been of much use to him with Forrest close in his rear. However, the coming months would show that Davis had been quite right to give them his attention in late July, when they made their first significant gains outside the fastness of the Appalachian chain.

Reverses in the field, increasingly forthright opposition to the central government by regional States Rights leaders, the formation and expansion of societies dedicated to sabotage of the entire Confederate effort, all combined to increase the discouragement natural to the hour. If not convictions of defeat, then anyhow widespread doubts of ultimate victory took root for the first time. In the present "gloom of almost despondency," a Richmond editor wrote in mid-August, "many faint-hearted regard all as lost." This was Pollard, who tended to exaggerate along these lines for reasons of his own; but even so staunch a supporter of the Administration as Congressman Dargan of Alabama — who had proved his mettle, if not his effectiveness, by making an unsuccessful bowie knife attack on his opprobrious colleague Henry Foote — fell into a midsummer state of desperation. "We are without doubt gone up; no help can be had," he wrote Seddon from Mobile in late July. "The failure of the Government to reinforce Vicksburg, but allowing the strength and flower of the Army to go north when there could be but one fate attending them, has so broken down the hopes of our people that even the little strength yet remaining can only be exerted in despair." He pinned his own hopes, such as they were, on foreign intervention, and since he believed that what stood in the way of this was slavery, he favored some form of Confederate emancipation. "So would the country," he declared, if the people were given the choice between abolition and defeat — especially in light of the fact that defeat would mean abolition anyhow. At any rate, he told his friend the Secretary of War, "If anything can be done on any terms in Europe, delay not the effort. If nothing can, God only knows what is left for us."

Dargan would perhaps have done better to write to the Secretary whose proper business was diplomacy. But it was as well he did not; Benjamin's department was having the least success of all this summer, both at home and abroad. In June, for example, Davis had had a letter from the Vice President down in Georgia, suggesting that he be sent on a mission to Washington, ostensibly to alleviate the sufferings of prisoners and humanize the conduct of the war, but actually, once negotiation on these matters was under way, to treat for peace on a basis of "the recognition of the sovereignty of the States and the right of each in its sovereign capacity to determine its own destiny." Just what he meant by this was not clear, and anyhow his disapproval of the government was too well known to permit his use as a spokesman, particularly at a conference on peace with the government's enemies. But Davis too was distressed by the growth of what he considered barbarism in the conflict, and he wired for Stephens to come to Richmond at once. Though he had no intention of allowing the Georgian any large authority — "Your mission is one of humanity, and has no political aspects," he informed him — he thought it might be advantageous to have an emissary on northern soil, whatever his basic persuasion, when Lee delivered the knockout blow he planned as a climax to the invasion about to be launched. Armed with two identical letters, one from Commander in Chief Davis to Commander in Chief Lincoln, the other from President Davis to President Lincoln — his instructions were to deliver whichever was acceptable — Stephens set off down the James, July 3, on the flag-of-truce steamer *Torpedo*. His hopes were high, despite the imposed restrictions, for he and Lincoln had been fellow congressmen and friends before the war. Off Newport News next morning, however, he submitted to the Union commander a request that he be allowed to proceed to Washington, only to be kept sweltering for two days aboard the motionless *Torpedo* while waiting for an answer. At last it came, in the form of a wire from Stanton on July 6: "The request is inadmissible. The customary agents and channels are adequate for all needful military communications and conference between the United States forces and the insurgents." Back at Richmond next day, the frail and sickly Georgian, who was barely under average height but weighed less than one hundred pounds with his boots on, learned that Gettysburg had been fought and lost — which explained, as a later observer remarked, why "Lincoln could afford to be rude" — and that evening the first reports of the fall of Vicksburg arrived. Discomfited and disgruntled, Stephens remained in Richmond for a couple of months, then returned to Crawfordville before Congress reconvened. A guidebook to the capital, listing the office and home addresses of government officials, contained the note: "The Vice President resides in Georgia."

Events abroad had taken a turn no more propitious than those on the near side of the Atlantic, although this too came hard on the heels of revived expectations. Despite the North's flat rejection of Mercier's offer to mediate a truce in February, friends of the Confederacy had been encouraged since then by what seemed to them an increasing conviction in Europe that the South could never be conquered. Chancellorsville had served to confirm this impression, even in the minds of men unwilling to admit it, and the London *Times* on May 2, unaware that the Wilderness battle was in mid-career, had noted that the Union was "irreparably divided." Looking back on the earlier Revolution, the editor said of the former Colonies: "We have all come to the conclusion that they had a right to be independent, and it was best they should be. Nor can we escape from the inference that the Federals will one day come to the same conclusion with regard to the Southern States." James Mason drew much solace from such remarks. Observing the hard times the cotton shortage had brought to the British spinning industry, he found himself emerging from the gloom into which more than a year of diplomatic unsuccess had plunged him. "Events are maturing which must lead to some change in the attitude of England," he informed Benjamin. Across the way in Paris, John Slidell was even more hopeful. "I feel very sanguine," he wrote, "that not many months, perhaps not many weeks, will elapse without some decided action on Napoleon's part." Grant's slam-bang May campaign in Mississippi offset considerably the brilliance of Lee's triumph over Hooker, but when it was followed by the determined resistance of Vicksburg under siege, with Johnston supposedly closing on Grant's rear, the Confederate flame of independence burned its brightest. Moreover, it was at this point that Lee set out on his second invasion of the North. The first, launched just under ten months ago, had come closer to securing foreign intervention than anyone outside the British cabinet knew; now if ever, with the second invasion in progress, was the time for an all-out bid for intervention. To ease the way, Benjamin assured a distinguished English visitor — Arthur Fremantle, who passed through Richmond in mid-June on his way to join Lee in Pennsylvania — that the South's demands were modest. To draw up a treaty of peace acceptable to the Confederacy, he said, it would only be necessary to write the word "self-government" on a blank sheet of paper. "Let the Yankees accord that," he told the colonel, "and they might fill up the paper in any manner they choose. . . . All we are struggling for is to be let alone."

There were those in the British Parliament who not only saw the opportunity as clearly as did anyone in the Confederate State Department, but also were willing to act. Two such were William S. Lindsay and John A. Roebuck, opposition stalwarts who, perceiving their chance for action after months of forced delay, crossed the Channel for an interview with Napoleon on June 20. Informed of his views that the time was ripe for joint intervention in the war across the sea, they hastened back to present them in a motion Roebuck brought before the house on June 30, requesting the Queen to enter into negotiations with foreign powers for the purpose of welcoming the Confederacy into the family of nations. They hoped thereby to place the government in a dilemma between recognition and resignation; however, they had neglected in their enthusiasm to make sure of their forces. When the ministry replied that no such proposal had been received from France, Napoleon failed to confirm their account of the interview, and thus exposed their veracity to question. John Bright and W. E. Forster, long-time Liberal proponents of the Union, both made powerful speeches against the motion, laced with sarcastic remarks on Roebuck's efforts to represent the Emperor on the floor of Parliament. What was more, as the debate wore on it developed that other pro-Confederate members did not approve of such overzealous methods, and Benjamin Disraeli, the Conservative leader, declined to commit the party to what amounted in the popular mind to a defense of slavery. Finally, on July 13, after waiting two weeks in vain for word of a victory won by Lee on northern soil, Roebuck — a diminutive individualist of somewhat ridiculous aspect; "Don Roebucco," *Punch* had dubbed him, "the smallest man 'in the House'" — admitted defeat by moving the discharge of his motion. Three days later the first reports of Gettysburg reached London, followed within the week by news of the fall of Vicksburg; after which there was no hope of a revival of the motion, either by Roebuck or anyone else. In fact, the ill-managed debate had done a good deal more to lower than to raise the Confederacy's chances of securing foreign recognition, particularly in England, where some of the ineptness and downright absurdity of its champions was connected, as a general impression, with the cause they had sought to further.

Benjamin perceived in this another instance of the attitude he had complained of earlier: "When successful fortune smiles on our arms, the British cabinet is averse to recognition because 'it would be unfair to the South by the action of Great Britain to exasperate the North to renewed efforts.' When reverses occur . . . 'it would be unfair to the North in a moment of success to deprive it of a reasonable opportunity of accomplishing a reunion of the States.'" Davis agreed with this bleak assessment of the situation. "'Put not your trust in princes,'" he had told his people before New Year's, "and rest not your hopes on foreign nations. This war is ours; we must fight it out ourselves." All the same, he had kept Mason in London all this time, suffering under snubs, on the off-chance that something would occur, either on this or that side of the water, to provoke a rupture between the Unionists and the British, who in that case would be glad to find an ally in the South. But this latest development, with its tarnishing absurdities, was altogether too much for him to bear. The game was no longer worth the candle, and he had Benjamin notify Mason of his decision. On August 4 the Secretary wrote as follows to the Virginian in England: "Perusal of the recent debates in the British Parliament satisfies the President that the government of Her Majesty has determined to decline the overtures made through you for establishing, by treaty, friendly relations between the two governments, and entertains no intention of receiving you as the accredited minister of this government near the British court. Under these circumstances, your continued residence in London is neither conducive to the interests nor consistent with the dignity of this government, and the President therefore requests that you consider your mission at an end, and that you withdraw, with your secretary, from London."

A private letter accompanied the dispatch, authorizing the envoy to delay his departure "in the event of any marked or decisive change in the policy of the British cabinet." But Mason too had had all he could

bear in the way of snubs by now. Before the end of the following month
he gave up his fashionable West End residence, removed the diplomatic
archives, and took his leave of England, sped on his way by a hec-
toring editorial in the *Times* on the South's folly in demanding recognition before it had earned it. Despite the high hopes raised at the start of
his mission by the *Trent* Affair, all he had to show for twenty months
of pains was a note in which the foreign minister, Lord John Russell,
after explaining that his reasons for declining the Virginian's overtures
were "still in force, and it is not necessary to repeat them," expressed
"regret that circumstances have prevented my cultivating your personal
acquaintance, which, in a different state of affairs, I should have done
with much pleasure and satisfaction." Joining Slidell in Paris, only a day
away from London by train and packet, Mason kept himself and his
staff in readiness for a return to England on short notice. Moreover, he
believed he knew what form, if any, this notice was likely to take.
Translating his diplomatic problems into British political terms, he pinned
his remaining hopes on a Tory overthrow of Palmerston's coalition
government, whose continuance in power he felt depended on the
survival of the elderly Premier, and his correspondence with friends
he had left behind, across the Channel, was peppered from this time forward with anxious inquiries as to the octogenarian's health. But Lord
Palmerston — who, in point of fact, had been friendlier to the South than
Mason knew — had a good two years of life left in him, and those two,
as it turned out, were six months more than quite enough.

The shock felt by Davis at this all but final evidence that the Confederacy would have to "fight it out," as he had said, without the hope
of foreign intervention — for it was generally understood that France
could not act without England, and Russia had been pro-Union from the
start — was lessened somewhat, or at any rate displaced, by an even
greater shock which he received on reading a letter the South's first
soldier had written him four days after Benjamin wrote Mason. From
Orange Courthouse, his new headquarters south of the Rapidan, Lee sent
the President on August 8 what seemed at first to be some random mus-
ings on the outcome of the Gettysburg campaign. His tone was one of
acceptance and resolution, of confidence in what he called "the virtue of
the whole people. . . . Nothing is wanting," he declared, "but that their
fortitude should equal their bravery to insure the success of our cause.
We must expect reverses, even defeats. They are sent to teach us wisdom
and prudence, to call forth greater energies, and to prevent our falling
into greater disasters. Our people have only to be true and united, to
bear manfully the misfortunes incident to war, and all will come right in
the end." Davis agreed. In fact he had spent the past month saying much
the same thing, not only to the public at large, but also, more specifically, to the heads of the nation's armies, including Lee. Nor did he
disagree with what came next, having heard it before from his dead

friend and hero Albert Sidney Johnston, who had been the subject of far more violent attacks by the press in another time of crisis. "I know how prone we are to censure," Lee continued, "and how ready [we are] to blame others for the non-fulfillment of our expectations. This is unbecoming in a generous people, and I grieve to see its expression. The general remedy for want of success in a military commander is his removal. This is natural, and in many instances proper. For no matter what may be the ability of the officer, if he loses the confidence of his troops disaster must sooner or later ensue." For all his basic agreement with the principle here expressed, Davis was by no means prepared for the application Lee made in the sentence that followed: "I have been prompted by these reflections more than once since my return from Pennsylvania to propose to Your Excellency the propriety of selecting another commander for this army."

There was where the shock came in. Davis read on with mounting apprehension as Lee explained what had brought him to make this request. Moreover, the care with which he had chosen his words indicated plainly that the letter had not been written as a mere gesture, but rather with publication in mind, as the closing document of a career that had ended in failure and sadness, but not in bitterness or despair:

> I have seen and heard of expression of discontent in the public journals at the result of the expedition. I do not know how far this feeling extends in the army. My brother officers have been too kind to report it, and so far the troops have been too generous to exhibit it. It is fair, however, to suppose that it does exist, and success is so necessary to us that nothing should be risked to secure it. I therefore, in all sincerity, request Your Excellency to take measures to supply my place. I do this with the more earnestness because no one is more aware than myself of my inability for the duties of my position. I cannot even accomplish what I myself desire. How can I fulfill the expectations of others? In addition I sensibly feel the growing failure of my bodily strength. I have not yet recovered from the attack I experienced the past spring. I am becoming more and more incapable of exertion, and am thus prevented from making the personal examinations and giving the personal supervision to the operations in the field which I feel to be necessary. I am so dull that in making use of the eyes of others I am frequently misled. Everything, therefore, points to the advantages to be derived from a new commander, and I the more anxiously urge the matter upon Your Excellency from my belief that a younger and abler man than myself can readily be obtained. . . .
>
> I have no complaints to make of anyone but myself. I have received nothing but kindness from those above me, and the most considerate attention from my comrades and companions at arms. To Your Excellency I am specially indebted for uniform kindness and consideration. You have done everything in your power to aid me in

the work committed to my charge, without omitting anything to
promote the general welfare. I pray that your efforts may at length
be crowned with success, and that you may long live to enjoy the
thanks of a grateful people.

With sentiments of great esteem,

I am very respectfully and truly yours,
R. E. LEE, General

Davis was dismayed. He had by now become reconciled to the
permanent loss of some 15,000 of the South's best fighting men at Gettysburg, but if that defeat was also going to cost him Lee, who had held
the North's main army at bay for more than a year and had provoked the
removal of four of its commanders in the process, the loss might well
be insupportable. Moreover, recent adversity East and West had drawn
the two men even closer to one another, in their service to an imperiled
cause, than they had been fifteen months ago in Richmond during a
similar time of strain. Whether the nation could survive without Lee at
the head of its first-line army Davis did not know, but he doubted that
he himself could. "I need your counsel," he had written him earlier that
week. Besides, for Davis, loyalty rendered was invariably returned, and
Lee was not only personally loyal, he was also modest, magnanimous,
and unselfish. Contrasting these qualities with those lately encountered in
that other Virginian, that other Johnston — Joe — Davis could tell his
ranking field commander: "Were you capable of stooping to it, you
could easily surround yourself with those who would fill the press with
your laudations, and seek to exalt you for what you had not done
rather than detract from the achievements which will make you and
your army the subject of history and object of the world's admiration
for generations to come." Such words might serve to ease the sting of
the lashings the journalists had been handing out. As for the general's
failing health, this too could be set aside as no valid reason for resigning,
Davis believed, even without the example of his own debilitation, which
included loss of sight in one eye and searing pain that sometimes made
the other almost useless. "I am truly sorry to know that you still feel the
effects of the illness you suffered last spring, and can readily understand
the embarrassment you experience in using the eyes of others, having
been so much accustomed to make your own reconnaissances. Practice
will however do much to relieve that embarrassment, and the minute
knowledge of the country which you have acquired will render you less
dependent for topographical information."

These things he could and did say, along with much else, in an
attempt to dissuade Lee from resigning and thus spare the nation the
calamitous loss of his service in the field. Fully conscious of the importance of choosing the proper tone and phrasing, he spent two days study-
ing the general's letter and composing his own thoughts by way of re-

buttal. Then on August 11, incorporating the sentences quoted above, he wrote his answer:

General R. E. Lee,
Commanding Army of Northern Virginia:

Yours of the 8th instant has been received. I am glad to find that you concur so entirely with me as to the want of our country in this trying hour, and am happy to add that after the first depression consequent upon our disasters in the West, indications have appeared that our people will exhibit that fortitude which we agree in believing is alone needful to secure ultimate success.

It well became Sidney Johnston, when overwhelmed by a senseless clamor, to admit the rule that success is the test of merit, and yet there has been nothing which I have found to require a greater effort of patience than to bear the criticisms of the ignorant, who pronounce everything a failure which does not equal their expectations or desires, and can see no good result which is not in the line of their own imaginings. I admit the propriety of your conclusions, that an officer who loses the confidence of his troops should have his position changed, whatever may be his ability; but when I read the sentence I was not at all prepared for the application you were about to make. Expressions of discontent in the public journals furnish but little evidence of the sentiment of an army. . . .

But suppose, my dear friend, that I were to admit, with all their implications, the points which you present, where am I to find that new commander who is to possess the greater ability which you believe to be required? I do not doubt the readiness with which you would give way to one who could accomplish all that you have wished, and you will do me the justice to believe that if Providence should kindly offer such a person for our use, I would not hesitate to avail of his services.

My sight is not sufficiently penetrating to discover such hidden merit, if it exists, and I have but used to you the language of sober earnestness when I have impressed upon you the propriety of avoiding all unnecessary exposure to danger, because I felt our country could not bear to lose you. To ask me to substitute you by someone in my judgment more fit to command, or who would possess more of the confidence of the army or of the reflecting men in the country, is to demand of me an impossibility.

It only remains for me to hope that you will take all possible care of yourself, that your health and strength may be entirely restored, and that the Lord will preserve you for the important duties devolved upon you in the struggle of our suffering country for the independence which we have engaged in war to maintain.

As ever, very respectfully and truly yours,
JEFFERSON DAVIS

After this, there was no more talk of Lee resigning. As long as the Army of Northern Virginia existed he would remain at its head.

LIST OF MAPS

Maps drawn by George Annand, of Darien, Connecticut, from originals by the author. All are oriented north.

BIBLIOGRAPHICAL NOTE

The following bibliographical note was included with the full text of
THE CIVIL WAR: A Narrative—Fredericksburg to Meridian.

In the course of this second of three intended five-year stints, the third
of which will bring me to defeat and victory at Appomattox, my debt
has grown heavier on both sides of the line where the original material
leaves off, but most particularly on the near side of the line. Although
the *Official Records,* supplemented by various other utterances by the
participants, remain the primary source on which this narrative is based,
the hundredth anniversary has enriched the store of comment on that
contemporary evidence with biographies, studies of the conflict as a
whole, examinations of individual campaigns, and general broodings on
the minutiae—all of them, or anyhow nearly all of them, useful to the
now dwindling number of writers and readers who, surviving exposure
to the glut, continue to make that war their main historical concern. So
that, while I agree in essence with Edmund Wilson's observation that "a
day of mourning would be more appropriate," the celebration of the
Centennial has at least been of considerable use to those engaged, as I
am, in the process Robert Penn Warren has referred to as "picking the
scab of our fate."

   Not that my previous obligations have not continued. They have
indeed, and they have been enlarged in the process. Kenneth P. Williams,
Douglas Southall Freeman, J. G. Randall, Lloyd Lewis, Stanley F. Horn,
Carl Sandburg, Bell I. Wiley, Bruce Catton, T. Harry Williams, Allan
Nevins, Robert S. Henry, Jay Monaghan, E. Merton Coulter, Clifford
Dowdey, Burton J. Hendrick, Margaret Leech are but a handful among
the many to whom I am indebted as guides through the labyrinth. With-
out them I not only would have missed a great many wonders along the

way, I would surely have been lost amid the intricate turnings and the uproar. Moreover, the debt continued to mount as the exploration proceeded: to Hudson Strode, for instance, for the extension of his *Jefferson Davis* at a time when the need was sore, and to Mark Mayo Boatner for his labor-saving *Civil War Dictionary*. Specific accounts of individual campaigns, lately published to expand or replace the more or less classical versions by Bigelow and others, have been of particular help through this relentless stretch of fighting. Edward J. Stackpole's *Chancellorsville*, for example, was used in conjunction with two recent biographies of the hero of that battle, Frank E. Vandiver's *Mighty Stonewall* and Lenoir Chambers' *Stonewall Jackson*. Similarly, for the Vicksburg campaign, there were Earl Schenck Miers's *The Web of Victory* and Peter F. Walker's *Vicksburg, a People at War*, plus biographies of the two commanders, *Pemberton, Defender of Vicksburg* and *Grant Moves South*, by John C. Pemberton and Bruce Catton. For Gettysburg, there were Clifford Dowdey's *Death of a Nation*, Glenn Tucker's *High Tide at Gettysburg*, and George R. Stewart's *Pickett's Charge*. For the battles around Chattanooga, there were Glenn Tucker's *Chickamauga* and Fairfax Downey's *Storming of the Gateway*. James M. Merrill's *The Rebel Shore*, Fletcher Pratt's *Civil War on Western Waters*, and Clarence E. Macartney's *Mr. Lincoln's Admirals* contributed to the naval actions, as Benjamin P. Thomas' and Harold M. Hyman's *Stanton* did to events in Washington. These too were only a few of the most recent among the many, old and new, which I hope to acknowledge in a complete bibliography at the end of the third volume, *Red River to Appomattox*. Other obligations, of a more personal nature, were carried over from the outset: to the John Simon Guggenheim Memorial Foundation, which extended my fellowship beyond the norm: to the National Park Service, whose guides helped me (as they will you) to get to know so many confusing fields: to the William Alexander Percy Memorial Library, in my home town Greenville, Mississippi, which continued its loan of the *Official Records* and other reference works: to Robert D. Loomis of Random House, who managed to keep both his temper and his enthusiasm beyond unmet deadlines: to Memphis friends, who gave me food and whiskey without demanding payment in the form of talk about the war. To all these I am grateful: and to my wife Gwyn Rainer Foote, who bore with me.

Other, less specific obligations were as heavy. The photographs of Mathew Brady, affording as they do a gritty sense of participation—of being in the presence of the uniformed and frock-coated men who fought the battles and did the thinking, such as it was—gave me as much to go on, for example, as anything mentioned above. Further afield, but no less applicable, Richmond Lattimore's translation of the *Iliad* put a Greekless author in close touch with his model. Indeed, to be complete, the list of my debts would have to be practically endless. Proust I believe has taught me more about the organization of material than even Gibbon has done, and Gibbon taught me much; Mark Twain and Faulkner would also have to be included, for they left their sign on all they touched, and in the course of this exploration of the American scene I often found that they had been there before me. In a quite different sense, I am obligated also to the governors of my native state and the adjoining states of Arkansas and Alabama for helping to lessen my sectional bias by reproducing, in their actions during several of the years that went into the writing of this volume, much that was least admirable in the position my forebears occupied when they stood up to Lincoln. I suppose, or in any case fervently hope, it is true that history never repeats itself, but I know from watching these three gentlemen that it can be terrifying in its approximations, even when the reproduction—deriving, as it does, its scale from the performers—is in miniature.

As for method, it may explain much for me to state that my favorite historian is Tacitus, who dealt mainly with high-placed scoundrels, but that the finest compliment I ever heard paid a historian was tendered by Thomas Hobbes in the foreword to his translation of *The Peloponnesian War,* in which he referred to Thucydides as "one who, though he never digress to read a Lecture, Moral or Political, upon his own Text, nor enter into men's hearts, further than the Actions themselves evidently guide him . . . filleth his Narrations with that choice of matter, and ordereth them with that Judgement, and with such perspicuity and efficacy expresseth himself that (as Plutarch saith) he maketh his Auditor a Spectator. For he setteth his Reader in the Assemblies of the People, and in their Senates, at their debating; in the Streets, at their Seditions; and in the Field, at their Battels." There indeed is something worth aiming at, however far short of attainment we fall.

—S.F.

INDEX

ABOUT THE AUTHOR

Shelby Foote was born in Greenville, Mississippi, and attended school there until he entered the University of North Carolina. During World War II he served in the European theater as a captain of field artillery. In the period after the war he wrote five novels: *Tournament, Follow Me Down, Love in a Dry Season, Shiloh,* and *Jordan County.* He was twice awarded a Guggenheim fellowship. A longtime resident of Memphis, Tennessee, he died in 2005 at the age of 88.

The
VICKSBURG
Campaign

All Corps
McClernand
Sherman
McPherson

Miles
0   5

Jackson
14 May

Clinton

Brownsville
JOHNSTON HOVERED
IN THIS REGION
THROUGHOUT JUNE

Bolton

Raymond
12 May

Champion Hill 16 May

Fourteen Mile Creek
Dillon

Auburn

Utica

Burtonton

Bayou Pierre

Bridgeport
Birdsong's Ferry
Big Black River

Oak Ridge

Haines Bluff

Yazoo River

Deer Creek

Steele Bayou

Old River

Old Canal

Young's Point

New Duckport
New Canal

Milliken's Bend

Tallulah

Richmond

Willow Lake

Roundaway Bayou

Bayou Vidal

New Carthage

Smith's

Perkins Plantation

Lake St. Joseph

Bruin's Lake

Bayou

SHERMAN REPULSED
DEC '62

WALNUT HILLS

Vicksburg
(ASSAULTS: 19, 22 MAY.
SIEGE: 18 MAY-4 JULY.)

Big Bayou

Warrenton

LINE OF BLUFFS

Hall's Ferry

Baldwin's Ferry

Big Black River

Rocky Springs

Cayuga

Willow Springs

Grindstone Ford

Hankinson's Ferry

Hard Times

De Shroon's

Grand Gulf
(evacuated 2 May)
(Gunboat repulse, 29 April)

Port Gibson
1 May

Brunsburg

Pearl River

Terry

Livingston

Tugaloo

Bovina

Edwards
17 May

Baker's Cr.